WITHDRAWN

	DATE DUE	
NOV 2 0 1995 S		

The Politics of
Food in Mexico

Food Systems and Agrarian Change

Edited by Frederick H. Buttel, Billie R. DeWalt,
and Per Pinstrup-Andersen

A complete list of titles in the series appears at the end of this book.

THE POLITICS OF FOOD IN MEXICO

State Power and Social Mobilization

Jonathan Fox

Cornell University Press

ITHACA AND LONDON

International Standard Book Number 0-8014-2716-9
Library of Congress Catalog Card Number 92-25948
Printed in the United States of America
Librarians: Library of Congress cataloging information
appears on the last page of the book.

To my parents

Contents

Tables and Figures

Tables

Figures

Acknowledgments

When I began the field research for this book, I thought I knew what I would find. But the most interesting facts turned out not to fit the conventional frameworks, challenging me to revise my assumptions. I very much appreciate the encouragement offered by friends and colleagues along the way. I first thank Peter Smith, now of the University of California, San Diego, and James Austin of the Harvard Business School for their advice and support as I prepared the first version of this work. Peter Smith's urging to keep the "big picture" in focus was especially helpful, and James Austin taught me a great deal about how policies become actions.

The field research and initial writing were supported by generous and timely grants from the Inter-American Foundation during 1984–85 and the Center for U.S.-Mexican Studies at the University of California, San Diego during 1985–86. Follow-up research in 1986 was supported in part by the Institute for the Study of World Politics.

I was fortunate to find many generous teachers in the countryside, especially the hundreds of campesinos and rural development workers who shared their experiences with me. I also thank David Barkin, Gustavo Esteva, and Fernando Rello, who helped orient me when I first began working in Mexico in 1982. Many present and former government officials at all levels (most of whom will remain anonymous) were very helpful and trusted my pledge of confidentiality. Cassio Luiselli and Jesús Rubiell were especially insightful.

Numerous collaborative research projects with Mexican colleagues began at an early stage. Three working friendships were especially important. Meeting Gustavo Gordillo in 1984 was a turning point for my understanding of the subtleties and contradictions embedded in the relationship between reformist policymakers and peasant movements. One of my greatest pleasures was attending peasant movement assemblies and working in villages with Manuel Fernández; his sensitivity to grassroots politics helped me bridge the cultural gaps one must never underestimate. Luis Hernández's intellectual generosity, creative insights, and way with words never cease to amaze me.

Many other friends and colleagues provided invaluable comments on the work in progress. I have especially appreciated theoretical discussions over the years with José Antonio Aldrete Haas, Viviane Brachet de Márquez, Richard Cloward, Joshua Cohen, María Lorena Cook, Gary Herrigel, Sylvia Maxfield, Gerardo Munck, Frances Fox Piven, Jeffrey Rubin, Margaret Sherraden, and Lynn Stephen. I am grateful for insights and support from Betsy Aron, Marta Guidi, Raúl Hinojosa, Julio Moguel, Susan Pezzullo, Charlie Roberts, and Mauricio Sánchez. Jennie Purnell, Lydia Fraile, and Stephen Van Evera, as well as Cornell's reviewers and editors, provided excellent editorial suggestions. Figures 1 and 2 were designed with invaluable technical assistance from Michael Fox of Rebus Technologies (on both) and Gerardo Munck (on Figure 2). Eva Nagy's and Peter Kubaska's able assistance helped greatly in the editing, and Helen Shapiro's support made revision much less daunting.

This book is based primarily on extensive interviews with more than fifty key participants at all levels of the food policy process, supported by a systematic survey of published materials and access to several collections of unpublished documents from both policy-makers and peasant leaders. Most of those interviewed are still involved in complex and sometimes dangerous political conflicts and therefore requested anonymity. Translations are my own unless otherwise indicated.

Some sections have been published before. Chapter 4 is based in part on an article I originally wrote with James Austin, "State-Owned Enterprises: Food Policy Implementers," in *Food Policy in Mexico*, ed. James Austin and Gustavo Esteva (Ithaca: Cornell University Press, 1987). A much shorter version of Chapter 6 appeared as "Popular Participation and Access to Food: Mexico's Community Food Councils," in *Harvest of Want, Struggles for Food Security in Central America and Mexico*, ed. Scott Whiteford and Ann Ferguson (Boulder, Colo.: Westview, 1991). Those interested in a Spanish version can consult "La dinámica del cambio en el Sistema Alimentario Mexicano, 1980–82," in *Historia de la cuestión agraria mexicana: Los tiempos de la crisis, 1970–1982*, ed. Julio Moguel, part 1, vol. 9 (Mexico City: Siglo XXI CEHAM, 1990), which summarizes Chapters 4–6.

JONATHAN FOX

Cambridge, Massachusetts

The Politics of
Food in Mexico

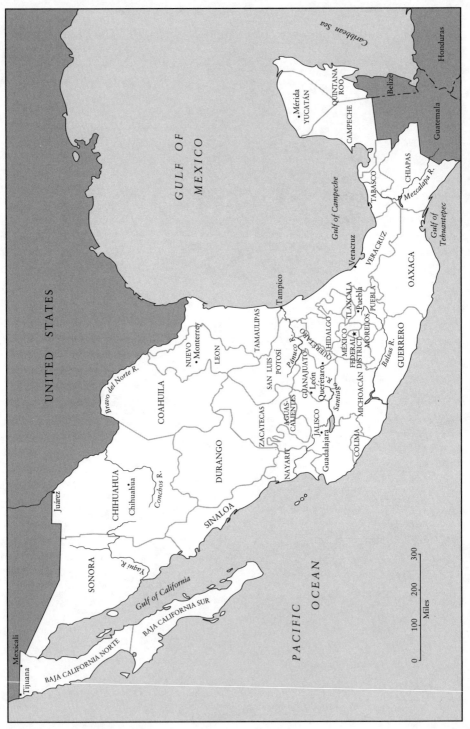

Adapted with permission of the Center for U.S.-Mexican Studies at the University of California, San Diego.

I

Introduction

This is a book about an unexpected outcome. From 1980 through 1982, the Mexican government pursued a top-down reform strategy to confront the twin crises of low food production and widespread hunger. Since most past rural antipoverty programs had failed to overcome entrenched elite interests, one would expect this new round of reforms to have led only to "more of the same." Indeed, much of the effort to undo the long-standing policy bias against the poor was effectively blunted or co-opted. One of the reforms, however, made a surprising difference; the rural food distribution program contradicted the dominant pattern. This social safety net program reached large numbers of Mexico's poorest people not because resources "trickled down" through the market, but because state reformists developed a political strategy for targeting the rural poor directly. For the first time in Mexico, an antipoverty program made it possible for its ostensible beneficiaries to hold the bureaucrats accountable. This time, reformists actively encouraged the empowerment of the rural poor.

This was an exception to the usual authoritarian patterns of Mexican politics. Mutually reinforcing, constructive interaction between state reformists and poor citizens is quite uncommon in most political regimes, yet it tends to change those systems when it does happen, thereby raising more general questions about our understanding of why states do what they do. Explanations of distributive reforms in other countries focus on the role of competitive electoral politics and the action of mass political parties that represent the poor to some degree.[1] But electoral politics were not competitive in Mexico, and the ruling party was more prone to "divide and conquer" through clientelism than to challenge the authoritarian regional elites that kept the rural poor from representing themselves. Why, then, would Mexico's extremely stable, centralized, single-party regime, whose rulers chose their own successors rather than being directly accountable to the will of the electorate, encourage the inherently open-ended mobilization of the disfranchised? This book explains who got what, why, and how the reciprocal interaction between state reformists and social movements changed the boundaries of the politically possible.

The search for explanations leads us in two directions. First, it takes us "inside" a state that turns out to be much less monolithic than it seems. The Mexican political system revolves around extremely centralized executive authority, but behind the state's imposing pyramid one finds complex networks of competing institutions and political currents that cut across formal lines of authority.

Second, if we must "unpack" the state to understand how reformists manage to create openings from above, we must also look to society to see how interests, identities, and institutions shape social actors' capacity to take advantage of such political opportunities. This book suggests that relatively autonomous reformists—those concerned with long-term political stability—may be able to initiate distributive reforms, but that their capacity to benefit poor people in practice depends on the mobilization of poor people themselves.

Rural Politics and Regime Stability

Mexico's dominant political institutions and culture still show the impact of a revolution that led to the death of one citizen in ten. Beginning in 1910, the turbulence took almost thirty years to end, but since then many outside observers have tended to see Mexican politics as predominantly static, occasionally punctuated by easily contained outbursts of discontent. It is certainly remarkable that Mexico has had the most stable regime in Latin America, with uninterrupted civilian transfers of power since 1929. But political stability has not been based simply on the legacy of the past. Rather, it has been the result of the periodic renewal of a process of bargaining with the key forces in civil society.

---

1. Kohli (1987) makes this argument convincingly for the Indian experience in his comparison of varying state antipoverty efforts.

The Mexican government has long presided over extremes of poverty and inequality that might well have led to revolutions elsewhere in Latin America. Electoral fraud and the selective repression of dissent have played an integral part in maintaining stable single-party rule, but the political management of conflict has been even more important. The state's origins in an agrarian revolution combined with later cycles of social unrest to produce periodic waves of concern for renewing political legitimacy at the highest levels of policy-making.

The relative social peace since the 1930s was based on the dynamic interaction between state actors promoting reforms from above and mobilization from below. Apparent political legitimacy in both city and countryside rested on the widespread belief that life could be improved by working within the system. The lack of viable alternative channels of political expression for most people, most of the time, along with periodic partial reforms, has served to renew the basis for this belief.

The future of this system is now in doubt; the path of Mexico's political transition is uncertain. International attention has focused on waves of urban political dissent since the mid-1980s, but Mexico's political future will also depend on reformists' capacity to renew the state's relationship with the rural citizenry. Mexico's population has been predominantly urban for more than two decades, but the ascendency of the city does not mean that the countryside is no longer of national political importance. The number of rural inhabitants continues to grow in absolute terms; in the past forty years it has more than doubled, to over twenty-seven million.

Since the early 1980s, the official political party has relied on overwhelming rural majorities for its national electoral victories. According to the hotly contested official 1988 returns, President Salinas's slim majority depended largely on rural votes.[2] Most of the question-

2. In "very urban" areas, he reportedly won only 34 percent, but in "very rural" areas, he received 77 percent of the votes counted. While the rural and semirural districts accounted for 43 percent of the electorate, they produced 57 percent of Salinas's official vote (López et al. 1989:31–33). For a more critical analysis of the 1988 election statistics, see Barberán et al. 1988. After the 1991 mid-term congressional elections, the ruling party claimed to have recovered its urban base. In the context of its search for a more "modern" identity, its electoral dependence on rural votes had come to seem embarrassingly "backward." It seems clear that the party did recover urban support, but continued controversy over the validity of the general turnout figures makes it difficult to evaluate the urban/rural breakdown (officially, turnout was significantly higher than in the much more important 1988 race). Moreover, the congressional race was much less seriously contested than were the 1991 governor's races, where the ruling party's continued reliance on overwhelming victories in rural districts was quite evident (especially in the states of Guanajuato and San

able ballots were cast in rural precincts, where citizen oversight was especially difficult and dangerous.[3] The opposition's restricted access to the broadcast media also had a disproportionately greater impact in rural areas. The same abuses of basic political freedoms that promote widespread rural election fraud also reinforce a lack of accountability in the implementation of public policy.[4]

Broader Lessons from Mexican Food Policy

Mexico's blend of revolutionary politics and a mixed economy offers useful lessons about how freely states can maneuver without undergoing fundamental economic and political change. This book explores the limits and possibilities of reform by analyzing one of the most reformist initiatives of one of the capitalist world's most reformist states. The Mexican state's willingness and capacity to exercise power over society have varied greatly over time, and in this book I compare the full range of food policies pursued during one of its most autonomous moments, the 1978–82 oil-debt boom. An analysis of the Mexican state's shifting capacity for reform is also essential to an understanding of its future evolution, following the unprecedented strain of economic and political crisis since the early 1980s.

Food politics provides a useful lens for viewing the prospects for reform in Mexico. The official ideology acknowledges that an adequate diet is a basic right of all citizens, yet the regime has increasingly fallen short of meeting that commitment. Widespread malnutrition therefore undermines the legitimacy of what is officially called the "institutionalized revolution." National dependence on imported food, moreover, is widely considered to compromise national sovereignty. Since the class issue of hunger intersects with the nationalist question of self-sufficiency, the politics of food reflects and refracts the most basic tensions within the Mexican state and society.

Luis Potosí). The voting process in most of these rural districts was not systematically scrutinized by either independent observers or the national and international media.

3. According to Juan Molinar's comprehensive overview of party politics (1991:9), "electoral fraud is a generalized practice in the Mexican electoral system, but it is not universal or homogeneous. It is more common and intense in rural and remote areas. . . . This is not only because the PRI gets better results using cacique-style clientelistic mechanisms of electoral mobilization rather than modern campaign techniques; it also has to do with the opposition, which, with a few exceptions, only goes as far as the paved road."

4. On the rural human rights situation, see Amnesty International 1986 and Americas Watch 1990.

The Mexican Food System (Sistema Alimentario Mexicano [SAM]) reform experience is an important case of state initiative because it raises fundamental questions about the limits and possibilities of state-initiated social change in Mexico. The 1980 SAM decision attempted to shift from a long-standing policy bias favoring large private farmers and ranchers with privileged access to subsidized inputs to a "pro-peasant" approach that attempted to recover national self-sufficiency by revitalizing smallholder grain production while increasing consumption subsidies.

Because earlier policy had been so biased against peasant producers, the SAM decision caught most analysts of the Mexican countryside completely by surprise. Some reacted by contending that no meaningful change had taken place, while others developed expectations that far outstripped the state's capacity for change. The SAM became a major presidential priority because of its promise to revitalize both food production and long-run rural political stability, but antipeasant interests entrenched in the state apparatus were too powerful to be offset by pressure only from above.

Explanatory approaches that exclusively stressed the state's power over society were unable to account for the limits of reform: the strength of the forces that blocked the implementation of most pro-peasant policies. But approaches that stressed the veto power of private capital and the effects of inexorable internationalization could not account for those food policy reforms that actively encouraged democratic community participation in carrying out policy.

Structural explanations can account for some aspects of the decision, such as the allocation of oil revenue to encourage food production for urban consumption. At a time of great nationalism and rising oil prices, it was not surprising that the budget for grain production increased. It was by no means "structurally necessary," however, for state actors to promote grass-roots peasant mobilization outside the domininant political party and the traditional corporatist control mechanisms. An alliance between moderate and radical reformists within the state gained access to significant political and economic resources, which they used to encourage the creation of autonomous peasant organizations to offset the entrenched power of regional elites. The result was a significant democratizing of subsidized food distribution in many of the poorest regions of rural Mexico.

Chapter 2 begins with a theoretical overview of state-society relations, laying out some of the key theoretical assumptions about the dynamics of distributive reform in Mexico that frame the comparative case analyses that follow. The Mexican state is clearly one of the most powerful and interventionist in Latin America. Yet it is by no means all-powerful, and state initiatives have often failed. Most analyses of Mexican politics have difficulty capturing both the limits and the possibilities of such initiatives. Some focus exclusively on the all-powerful figure of the president. Others see all state action as driven by pressures imposed from the outside, as responses forced by external actors such as labor unions, peasant groups, business organizations, the United States or transnational capital.

More generally, most explanations of distributive reform tend to emphasize one-way causation, relying on static distributions of power, and they rarely capture the dynamic interaction between state and society. The way Mexico's food policy reforms combined continuity with change challenges both state- and society-centered explanations of state action. Society-driven explanations have difficulty explaining state initiatives that recast the organization of important social groups, while societal responses to such initiatives which in turn leave their imprint on the state, do not fit easily within state-centered frameworks.

The underlying theoretical question is: how do changes in the balance of forces within the state affect the changing balance of forces within society, and vice versa? Chapter 2 shows how an interactive approach can transcend single-actor views of the state, distinguishing between the autonomy and capacity of competing policy currents within it. Conflicting embedded orientations and policy currents within state institutions create opportunities for different social actors to influence state action. These opportunities create "access routes" that influence the process of social mobilization in a reciprocal process of state-society interaction. This conceptual framework shows how reformist state actors can increase their capacity by opening political space for pressure from below, changing the distribution of power within both state and society. Shifts in the correlation of forces within the state interact recursively with changes in the balance of power within society.

Chapter 3 examines the revolutionary roots of reform in Mexico. Analyzing the mix of expected and unexpected outcomes of Mexican reform dynamics requires us to take several steps back in history, to understand how the state was constructed through shifting and contradictory alliances among different social forces. The historical account of the subsequent ebb and flow of rural reform efforts leads to an analysis of the changes in the national political environment that made it possible for food policy reform to become a major presidential priority in 1980. The economic boom lifted the usual constraints on distributive policy so that policy currents long concerned with renewing the state's mass political legitimacy could gain influence.

Chapter 4 shows that in practice most food programs during the SAM period delivered more resources to traditionally favored elites inside and outside the state than to peasants. More money was spent on agriculture, and grain production rose dramatically, but few programs effectively targeted previously excluded peasants. Smaller producers with the potential to produce a surplus did gain greater access to subsidies, but only as long as the oil-debt boom made the politics of resource allocation a positive-sum game.

The fifth and sixth chapters explain why not all food policy of the SAM period led to more of the same. Two national programs tried to change the balance of power between peasants and rural elites. By regulating two different stages of grain marketing, both of them attempted to improve peasants' bargaining power with oligopolistic intermediaries. The first, the Rural Marketing Support program, offered transportation subsidies for producers without irrigation who sold their corn surplus to the state, while the second, the Peasant Store program, provided subsidized basic foods to thousands of the lowest-income villages in Mexico. The crucial difference between these two programs was that one focused on the individual grain producer while the other deliberately relied on the democratic collective action of peasant communities. The first led to no lasting change, but the second created its own constituency and significantly democratized an important area of government activity in the countryside. The rural food distribution program created thousands of community-managed stores to deliver subsidized grain to Mexico's lowest-income rural population. Success depended on coordinated pressure on the bureaucracy both from strategically located reformists and from democratic social movements.

Chapter 6 goes to the core of the argument by showing how the rural food program permitted autonomous peasant organization at the *regional* level for the first time in many of Mexico's poorest rural areas. Access to food as a material incentive was not sufficient to explain collective action—food could have been delivered through traditional clientelistic channels, dividing people rather than creating new horizontal linkages within and between communities. Instead, by producing new sets of external enemies and allies, the program promoted a shared regional identity as a basis for social mobilization.

This new motivation for action, combined with more freedom of assembly than ever before, greatly encouraged collective action and undermined the power of regional elites in many remote regions.

Chapter 7 summarizes how a small political opening from above became significant when it was occupied from below, creating further space for collective action and the emergence of representative peasant organizations. The conclusions explore how this "sandwich strategy," involving an objective alliance between entrepreneurial reformists and autonomous social movements, can offset the power of entrenched authoritarian elites and may well account for rural reform dynamics across a wide range of political systems.

In a brief comparison with Mexico's new generation of targeted antipoverty policies of the 1990s, the conclusions highlight the uncertain relationship between pluralism in the social and political arenas. Under the rubric of *concertación social* (social bargaining), some reformists continued the spirit of pluralism initiated with the rural food distribution program of the early 1980s. Mexico's most recent antipoverty umbrella program, the National Solidarity Program, was sometimes willing to treat autonomous social organizations as citizens rather than clients. But in contrast to its precursor, the National Solidarity Program took shape in a period marked by closely contested elections, and the Mexican electoral system's partial openings still failed to convince much of the population that their votes would be respected. The relationship between more pluralistic distributive reforms and guaranteed respect for the ballot remains uncertain. Is the liberalization of social policy instead of, or in spite of the lack of, more comprehensive democratization? The Mexican political system has been in a fitful process of evolution at least since 1968, but its direction remains unclear; contradictory tendencies point toward brittle rigidity in some areas and marked flexibility in others. The lessons gleaned from past openings to civil society are extremely important for understanding the future prospects for the democratization of the Mexican state.

2

State-Society Interaction and Distributive Reform in Mexico

Why do some reforms lead to more of the same while others make a difference? If a state decides to pour more money through an undemocratic distributive apparatus, we would expect at most limited material gains—certainly not the mass empowerment of poor people. Most states, most of the time, wield their power to favor their own interests and those of private elites, but this book focuses on a revealing exception to the dominant pattern: an innovative social policy that permitted previously excluded poor people to gain a small but significant degree of power relative to both the state and rural elites.

Mexico's food policy reform of the early 1980s poses an apparent contradiction for general analyses of state power. Some suggest that the effective exercise of state power requires the unity and autonomy associated with insulation from external influence. This situation often holds for state bargaining in the international context, where decision making is highly centralized, but implementing distributive reforms usually requires highly decentralized actions. When policies need both coordination and extreme decentralization, as do many antipoverty efforts, state capacity depends in large measure on society's response.[1]

In Mexico, effective application of distributive reforms necessitated

1. Much of political analysis is concerned with what states can and cannot do, yet not all analyses of state capacity clearly specify power over *what* (Baldwin 1979). In the policy literature, Thomas and Grindle 1990 and Grindle and Thomas 1989 analyze how state capacity varies in terms of different types of reforms. More theoretically, Mann 1988 offers a provocative distinction between dimensions of state power.

a shift in the rural balance of power *away* from the state and in favor of relatively autonomous organizations of poor people. Such a shift rarely happened in practice, and most official policy reform led to continued antipeasant bias. By themselves, even high-level reformists were unable to overcome the resistance of elite interests entrenched both inside and outside the state. In the case of one important food program, however, reformists provoked social conflict by ceding power to peasants; this conflict was then "internalized" within the state, and meaningful reform took place. The government's capacity to carry out distributive reforms depended on the beneficiaries' autonomous mobilization in defense of their interests against antireform elements within the state itself. To explain this *interdependence* between the power of reformist state actors and the power of social organizations to hold the bureaucratic apparatus accountable, we must develop a more dynamic alternative to conventional explanations of public policy outcomes.

Distributive reforms are qualitative changes in the way states allocate public resources to large social groups. I am concerned here specifically with distributive reforms that benefit the poor. *Redistributive* reforms are a special case of distributive policies: they change the relative shares between groups.[2] This distinction is important for two principal reasons. First, many apparently redistributive reforms are not, and to call them so implicitly begins with what should be the ultimate outcome of analysis: determining what a social reform actually does, and why.[3] Second, redistribution implies zero-sum action, whereas social programs often are carried out precisely because they avoid clearly taking from one group to give to another. In a context of economic growth, moreover, antipoverty spending may well rise in absolute terms without changing its relative share of the government budget. The label "redistribution" builds in an assumption about where the resources come from, whereas the notion of distribution limits the focus to who gets what.[4]

2. Lowi's (1964, 1972) distinction between distribution, regulation, and redistribution highlights the ways different types of policies structure political conflict. The boundaries between these categories, however, are difficult to draw. See Wilson's critique (1973:327).

3. Most Latin American land reforms are cases of such deceptive appearances (de Janvry 1981). Not coincidentally, most were preemptive state initiatives rather than responses to the political power of the landless.

4. For example, even when governments raise some of their revenue from nominally progressive income taxes, the actual direction of redistribution is a highly complex empirical question that depends on how all taxes are levied, how public debts are paid, and how budgets are really spent (Fitzgerald 1978; Page 1983).

Explanations of distributive reforms require general analytical frameworks for understanding the state. Since the nineteenth century, political and sociological theories have tended to emphasize either how values, actors, and structures outside the state condition its behavior or how the state leadership and bureaucracy pursue their own distinct interests. These contending theoretical explanations of state actions have been framed largely in terms of dichotomous, one-way views of state-society relations.

Society-centered approaches tend to stress the constraints on state action, while state-centered frameworks emphasize autonomous room for maneuver. Each explains part of the policy process, but neither is complete. In this chapter, I argue that neither state-centered nor society-centered explanations fully capture both the limits and possibilities of reform dynamics. To understand how a state can be strong in some ways and weak in others, we need a third approach. The framework developed below highlights general patterns of reciprocal interaction between actors inside and outside the state.

This chapter starts with a brief overview of theories of the state, discussing how one-way explanations of public policy outcomes fail to distinguish adequately between state capacity and state autonomy.[5] I then propose an interactive framework for "unpacking" state-society interaction, with illustrations drawn primarily from the Mexican experience. The key units of analysis are the social and state actors whose interplay shapes policy outcomes, particularly in distributive reforms that favor the poor.

Specifying State Power: Autonomy versus Capacity

The state comprises the ensemble of political, social, economic, and coercive institutions that exercise "public" authority in a given terri-

5. For especially useful overviews of state theory, see, among others, Alford and Friedland 1985, Carnoy 1984, and Jessop 1983. See Canak 1984 for a comprehensive review of the literature on the state in Latin America. The most important contributions to the study of the Latin American state have been more concerned with state-capital relations and the dynamics of national regime change than with theoretical analysis of state power to carry out distributive reform (e.g., Cardoso and Falleto 1979; Collier 1979; Evans 1979). Stepan's (1978) analysis of the Peruvian state is remarkably balanced in this regard, since he deals with its relationships with a wide range of societal actors. In spite of the institutional, historical, and structural factors that are specific to Latin American states, it is difficult to define a "theory" that is specific to them. Moreover, few theoretical discussions of the Latin American state have fully engaged the Mexican experience. Hamilton (1982) is one of the most systematic (see discussion in Chapter 3).

tory. To analyze why states act in particular ways, we need to distinguish between two distinct dimensions of their power: the autonomy and the capacity of state actors. State *autonomy* is defined here in terms of state leaders' "independent goal formation" (Skocpol 1985: 9). State *capacity* is related but distinct: "the ability of state leaders to use the agencies of the state to get people in the society to do what they want them to" (Migdal 1988:xi). Distinguishing autonomy from capacity helps us understand how state actors decide to exercise their power. This distinction is especially important for explaining why reform decisions get implemented to the degree that they do.

The widely used dichotomy between state strength and weakness implicitly treats the state as a single actor and inherently conflates autonomy and capacity. In Nordlinger's definition, for example, "A state is autonomous to the extent that it translates its own preferences into authoritative actions" (1987:361). One might look at a state's frustrated attempts to carry out certain reforms and then conclude that it failed because it was too weak or because the constraints were too powerful, but there are two principal problems with this approach. First, how does one distinguish between committed reform efforts that failed because of lack of capacity and reforms that were never seriously tried and therefore did not test the state's capacity or the immutability of structural constraints? State actors may have autonomy, the independence from societal interests needed to set their own goals, but lack the capacity to carry them out. Conversely, state actors may possess the potential institutional capacity to act but lack the autonomy required to wield it against the dominant interests in society.[6] Second, reform possibilities are not determined by a static prior distribution of power alone; strategic interaction can make a difference, especially if it manages both to strengthen allies and to weaken adversaries.[7] In short, intent and capacity are distinct, but political strategy can change capacity in certain circumstances.

6. Przeworski points out that "the notion of 'strong state' continues to be a source of confusion when it juxtaposes the 'weakest state . . . that is completely permeated by pressure groups' to 'one that is able to remake the society and culture in which it exists'" (cited in Krasner 1984:56). A state completely permeated by pressure groups may be highly effective in changing economic institutions, values, and patterns of interaction; indeed, the "strongest" state, if this word has any meaning, is probably one that uses organized violence on behalf of economically dominant interests and not a state that ventures against them" (Przeworski 1990).

7. Ascher's comparison (1984) of distributive reforms in Argentina, Peru, and Chile argues that power can be created through strategic interaction that weakens, or at least does not provoke, powerful potential enemies. This approach is so voluntaristic, however, that reform possibilities appear unbounded.

One-Way Approaches to State-Society Relations

Different frameworks for explaining state action flow from their fundamental assumptions and units of analysis.[8] Whereas some begin with society to explain the outcomes of state action, others look first at the state with its structures and actors. Society-centered approaches explain state action based on the interests, relations, and structures of civil society. Some stress the influence social forces exert directly on the state while others highlight the external constraints they impose (Offe 1974). State-centered approaches, in contrast, begin with the interests and actions of the state as an organization, emphasizing institutional goals, personnel, and structures.[9]

Both approaches deal with state capacity in similar ways; however, states that are relatively insulated from interest group pressures, and therefore presumably unified and coherent, are considered strong; those that are penetrated by social forces, and hence fragmented and conflictual, are seen as weak. Such coherence may account for many strong-sounding policy decisions, but it does not necessarily explain which groups benefit from the actual application of those policies, especially reforms that reach the poor.

8. Alford and Friedland (1985) refer to three core perspectives' "home domains," showing how each approach, and its corresponding strengths and weaknesses, is conditioned by its primary level of analysis: "For the pluralist perspective, power is situational and is measured by influence over the outcomes of conflictual participation. For the managerial perspective, power is structural and is observed in the capacity of politically biased state and corporate organizations to dominate each other. For the class perspective, power is systemic and is inferred from the reproduction of exploitative power relations." They argue that political conflict "always involves all three levels of power, and cannot be fully understood without a synthetic analysis incorporating all three. Their relative importance . . . depends on specific historical and political conditions" (1985:7–8).

9. There are two corresponding approaches in the particular case of the literature on state intervention in Latin American agriculture. Some see economic forces as determining state action, specifically the internationalization of capital. De Janvry's study (1981:259) is the most comprehensive in this tradition, defining rural reform as "the policy expression of class relations." Grindle in her major overview of Latin American agrarian policy (1986:3–4) argues, in contrast, that the state "does not merely reflect and reproduce class relationships in the society, assuming relative autonomy only when economic and legitimacy crises threaten the basis of capital accumulation. . . . [S]tate elites have a variable capacity for autonomous decision-making and often have specific interests in national development that cause the state to become active in shaping economic and social relationships with dominant-class interests in a society." Grindle's empirical analysis stresses that the state's autonomous initiatives in support of capitalist agriculture end up constraining the state, but this key "interactive" finding is not integrated into her theoretical approach. Grindle and Thomas (1989) move in this direction, however.

Society-Centered Approaches

Influence theories explain state action as the result of direct intervention from outside the state apparatus. The state has little or no autonomy vis-à-vis social forces, and politico-administrative actors and institutions have little part in shaping the outcome of state action. Diverse theoretical traditions overlap here, including pluralism and instrumentalist Marxism.

In the pluralist approach, the state is a neutral arena for conflicting groups in society: "Bureaucratic organizations are assumed to be ultimately responsive to a clientele, controlling agency or democratic political process" (Alford 1975:147).[10] In its early version, pluralism also contended that social and political groups competed on a level playing field. The modified neopluralist approach also casts the state as essentially neutral but holds that capital is privileged over other interest groups, notably labor, in competition for influence over policy (Lindblom 1977:176). Similarly, instrumentalist Marxism analyzes the state as a direct instrument of capitalist rule, converging with the "power elite" sociological approach. As Ralph Miliband (1969) and William Domhoff (1979) stress, capitalists' domination of commanding positions both inside and outside the state is crucial, as is their influence over the socialization of state actors.

Influence theories' emphasis on class actors' intervention in the policy process is both a strength and a weakness, for indeed such intervention does often shape state action.[11] Yet as innumerable critiques have pointed out, by no means can all significant state action be clearly attributed to external intervention alone. State actors have their own economic and political interests, as individuals and as a group. They also have their own views on how to respond to chal-

10. Strictly speaking, the pluralist view is not a contender for explaining Mexican state action, since it assumes a competitive electoral system as well as unrestrained freedom of expression and organization. Bennett and Sharpe (1985:39), however, see Purcell and Purcell's (1980) analysis of bureaucratic and group conflict within the Mexican state as inspired by the pluralist approach. For a comprehensive pluralist approach to Latin American politics more generally, see Anderson (1965), who emphasizes competing "power contenders" with differing "power resources."

11. Influence theories have produced some masterpieces of empirical investigation of external manipulation of the state, but some more functionalist Marxists skip this step and simply infer the political character of the state from the economic distribution of the benefits of its actions. If state actions benefit capitalists, then the state must be their monolithic instrument. Much of the "new political economy," which applies neoclassical economic assumptions to politics, shares a similar tendency to derive political process from the a posteriori distribution of economic benefits of state action. See Grindle's useful discussion of this approach (1991).

lenges from both inside and outside the state, and their control over state organizations often gives them the capacity to put these ideas into practice.

Constraint theory, in contrast, emphasizes the broader external limits within which the state operates, regardless of how it is actually "run." In the structural Marxist view, the limits on state action are determined not by the direct influence of class actors, but by the constraints imposed by the capitalist system. Within these limits, a degree of state autonomy from social forces not only is possible, it is necessary if the state is to act independently of particular interests to defend the dominant social order as a whole.

Within this tradition, James O'Connor's work drew attention to a crucial constraint on state capacity to carry out reforms. The "fiscal crisis of the state" argument stresses that "the capitalistic state must try to fulfill two basic and often mutually contradictory functions—*accumulation* and *legitimation*" (1973:3). Because it depends on the stable functioning of the economy for its revenues, the state must attempt to maintain or create the conditions for profitable capital accumulation. At the same time, however, it must try to maintain or create the conditions for social peace and political stability. States try, often contradictorily, to maintain both accumulation and legitimation. Although O'Connor does not fully explain how state actors make choices to balance these competing pressures, he nevertheless shows how social conflict can affect economic structures by pushing the state to carry out reforms.[12]

Nicos Poulantzas, the principal structuralist Marxist analyst of the state, began with a highly functionalist framework but later developed an approach that recognized that subordinated classes can influence the state even while it remains capitalist (1974, 1980). The state's degree of autonomy depends on class struggle and on historically contingent factors. In cases of stalemate, the state is called upon in some way to transcend the fray and find a path leading toward the long-range stability of the capitalist system.[13] Why do some states manage this task of rising above classes to the degree that they do,

12. Fitzgerald (1978) has gone the furthest in analyzing the history of the fiscal crisis of the state in Latin America. (See also Fishlow 1990.)

13. This approach has roots in Marx's discussion of the Bonapartist state and Gramsci's analysis of Caesarism. The problem of specifying the limits to state autonomy while remaining within the Marxist framework is not new, as is indicated by Marx's own analysis of the Bonapartist state (Tucker 1978:606), which "enmeshes, controls, regulates, superintends and tutors civil society."

when they do, given that many do not? Social and political conflict helps explain why states can gain autonomy, but without an analysis of the interests and initiatives of state actors, it is difficult to explain *how* states exercise their autonomy—even if it is "relative" and constrained by structural pressures. Given a certain degree of autonomy, why do states choose one response over another? The answer may require dealing with the interests and ideas of the state actors themselves, posing a dilemma for a framework where civil society must determine the outcome of state action "in the final analysis" (Poulantzas 1980:67). Constraint theory is torn between deriving the limits of state autonomy from the ascribed long-run objective interests of the capitalist system and deriving them from the historical clash of classes that it posits as the driving force of change.[14]

In summary, both influence and constraint theories offer partial explanations of state action.[15] For both, societal interests are the "inputs" that determine the scope for state action. Neither variant fully recognizes that state actors might have the willingness and the capacity to initiate and pursue their own interests amid contending social forces. This analytical limitation is especially pronounced when dealing with distributive reforms. When states show the capacity to carry out reforms that benefit poor people, society-centered approaches

14. Hamilton's (1982) highly nuanced study of the Mexican state's most autonomous and reformist phase deals with this challenge by distinguishing "instrumental" from "structural" autonomy. The first refers to freedom from direct pressure by dominant class interests. Structural state autonomy, involving frontal action against dominant class interests, is possible when state actors ally themselves with subordinate groups to confront weakened private elites. These instrumental and structural variants can also be understood as state autonomy with and without the capacity (and willingness) to exercise it. In this view, state capacity for structural reform depends on the strength of the often unstable alliance between autonomous state actors and subordinate groups (Hamilton 1982:12).

15. As Offe (1974:2–3) put it, "whereas the Influence Theories stress the strict *instrumentalization* of the State apparatus in the service of accumulation interest, the Constraint Theories are based on the assumption that the institutions of the political system cannot effectively become the instrument of *any non-capitalist interest* whatsoever. . . . Both, however, imply the assumption of the neutrality of the State apparatus as an instrument" (emphasis added). These approaches are therefore not necessarily contradictory. The differences between, for example, neopluralism and instrumentalist Marxism are more ideological and empirical than analytical. Moreover, instrumentalist and structural Marxist approaches share a concern for specifying the autonomy of the political sphere, in sharp contrast to more functionalist orthodox approaches such as the "capital logic" school. Also known as the "derivationists," these theorists view politics as essentially a reflection of economics (Holloway and Piccioto 1978:4). See Carnoy's review (1984:128). A common weakness of the orthodox Marxist literature is its inability to explain social or political reform. Either the change is ascribed to the functional requirements of the system or it is defined as trivial. The orthodox literature on the Mexican state tends toward the inherently contradictory assertions that its reforms both are trivial and help to strengthen the system (e.g., Cockcoft 1983:219).

tend to explain them exclusively as responses to pressures from below, concessions required to save the system. But pressure from below
often leads to repression or inaction rather than to reform. Because
both society-centered theories focus exclusively on external factors,
they have difficulty explaining, first, why states respond with reform
at all; second, why they respond with one kind of reform rather than
another; and third, why some state actors occasionally initiate reform
without direct pressure from below.

State-Centered Approaches

The state-centered literature offers an alternative explanation for
state action.[16] Its focus on state actors' goals and institutional capacities stresses possibilities rather than limits for policy change. Like the
instrumental Marxists and the neopluralists, such authors are concerned with the ways the state's institutional structures promote or
inhibit penetration by groups in society, but they are distinguished by
their emphasis on the attitudes and organizations that shape the goals
and capacities of state actors themselves.

The state-centered approach represents the convergence of two distinct theoretical currents, beginning with a Weberian emphasis on the
state's organizational power and interests. The state is seen as the
dominant organization of society in a world made up of competing
organizations.[17] The principal strand in this tradition emphasizes international geopolitical and economic conflict as a determinant of
state interests. The state-centered approach differs from the bureaucratic politics framework, however, which focuses narrowly on interagency competition, rather than state interests in general.

The state-centered approach also emerged from the neo-Marxist
analysts whose study of the state led them to emphasize institutional
actors and structures. Claus Offe analyzes the role of state apparatuses as "processors" of inputs from social forces. He stresses the role
of the politico-administrative system's "structurally selective" mecha-

16. Susan Kaufman Purcell (1975:3) put her state-centered view of Mexico succinctly:
"The model of an authoritarian regime is premised on the assumption that the government
or (more accurately) the executive is the independent variable and the complex of interest
groups is the dependent variable." Mexico seems to be a paradigm case, since the state that
emerged from the ashes of the first twentieth-century revolution largely reconstructed the
social fabric. Bizberg (1990) develops a sophisticated synthesis of the Mexican state-centered approach.
17. Alford and Friedland (1985:161) call this the "managerial perspective," to emphasize the elite's organizational base in control of the state and its strategic orientation.

nisms for systematically "filtering" certain inputs into the policy process and not others. This bias is seen to result from the way the state itself is structured, not from the orientation of particular state actors or necessarily from the "capture" of a particular agency by a given social force. Instead, he argues, it is *"the institutional self-interest of the actors in the state apparatus which determines policy outputs and outcomes"* (Offe 1974:6; cited in Carnoy 1984:135).[18] Offe also stresses the state's role in consciously shaping interest organization as a way of dealing with the threat of "demand overload." Corporatist organizations serve the state by limiting social demands that political parties and formal state apparatuses may be incapable of managing (Offe 1981).[19]

The state-centered approach is especially attentive to the distinction between the state's process of goal formation, which may well be autonomous, and its shifting capacity to carry out its goals (Skocpol 1985:15–16). The relation between the state and its component structures is not always well specified, however. In the "bureaucratic politics" approach, the state is understood as the sum of its compartmentalized parts. In contrast, the state-centered approach sees the whole as greater than the sum of its parts—that is, there is a broader institutional "state interest" and therefore an overarching logic of state action. From positing an overall shared state interest, the approach often slides into suggesting an implicitly unified "institution and social actor" (Evans, Rueschemeyer, and Skocpol 1985:347).

The state-centered approach has yet to develop a coherent distinction between the state as actor and the state as an ensemble of actors. Theda Skocpol does refer to the state, at times, as "a set of organizations" (1985:20). Secondarily, Peter Evans and his colleagues do acknowledge that "interactions among parts of the state apparatus itself

18. This argument is largely consistent with the "mobilization of bias" approach, which emerged in the early 1960s in political science as an alternative to the dominant pluralist-power elite debate. As Schattschneider (1960:71) put it, "All forms of political organization have a bias in favor of the exploitation of some kinds of conflict and the suppression of others because *organization is the mobilization of bias*. Some issues are organized into politics while others are organized out" (emphasis in original; cited in Bachrach and Baratz 1962:949).

19. In Latin America, military and technocratic state elites responded to increased "perception of threat" from "demand overload" combined with economic crisis by taking the initiative to overthrow elected governments and replace them with "bureaucratic-authoritarian" regimes. For an overview of bureaucratic-authoritarianism, see Collier 1979. In spite of differing political contexts, Offe's (1981) analysis of corporatism's class bias echoes O'Donnell's (1977a) penetrating discussion of the simultaneous "bifrontal" ("statizing" some groups while privatizing others) and "segmentary" (increasing control over some classes rather than others) nature of corporatist political forms in Latin America.

may provide the key to changing state capacities and degrees of autonomy," and they encourage research into the "systematic fault lines within state structures" (Evans, Rueschemeyer, and Skocpol 1985: 355, 360). This should lead them to encourage comparative research into public policies across particular states, since one can thereby hold most variables constant and contrast the behavior of different institutions. The single-actor view of the state seems to prevail, however, when they equate studies of individual nation-states with "mere case descriptions," defining comparative research as necessarily cross-national (1985:348). This assumption downplays the importance of systematic variation in the autonomy and capacity of actors and agencies *within* states.[20] As Arend Lijphart has argued, this kind of "whole-nation bias" excludes much of what it is interesting and useful to compare (1975:166–167).

Critics have also noted a tendency toward "state-centrism," deemphasizing the systematic interaction between state and society (e.g., Colburn 1988). Along similar lines, Fred Block distinguishes between a "soft" and a "hard" version of Skocpol's work. On the most general level, he agrees that "states act in the context of social struggles," but he contends that much of Skocpol's case analysis goes further, claiming "that state-centered variables are more important than society-centered variables in explaining particular historical outcomes" (Block 1987:20).[21]

A full explanation of state action requires determining not only its proximate cause in the context of intrastate conflict, but also how the external environment may have made it possible for some state actors to exercise more power than others and how the responses of nonstate actors shape their eventual impact.[22] The argument here is that

20. Evans's (1979) own comparative study of Brazilian state interaction with private capital across sectors was a fundamental contribution along these lines, as was Stepan's (1978, 1989) seminal work on Peru and the politics of military institutions in the course of transitions to civilian rule. Finegold and Skocpol (1984) also find an "island of state strength in an ocean of weakness" in their study of the U.S. Department of Agriculture.

21. Przeworski's criticism is more forceful (1990:47): "State-centric theories assert that states create, organize and regulate societies. . . . thus the problem of the autonomy of the state with regard to society has no sense within this perspective. It should not even appear. The concept of 'autonomy' is a useful instrument of analysis only if the domination by the state over society is a contingent situation." Stepan's (1978, 1985) contribution to the state-centered literature, in contrast, is quite relational, positing a number of scenarios in which the power of states and civil societies can rise or fall together or can move in opposite directions. For a provocative critique of both Skocpol and Stepan, see Cammack (1989).

22. This dilemma of where to look for the explanation of state action was posed by Gramsci's "Analysis of Situations, Relations of Forces," which pointed out analysts' com-

only a fully interactive approach that analyzes conflicts, constraints, interests, and identities in state *and* society can capture both the limits and the possibilities of state action, particularly distributive reforms that reach the poor. In the chapters that follow I apply such an approach to explain a contradictory combination of distributive reforms in Mexico.

Distributive reforms usually require deep state intervention in society, regulating rights, privileges, and access to resources that would otherwise be determined through the market, culture, and coercion. Policy-making is essentially a conflict between state and social actors over who makes the rules that regulate social behavior (Migdal 1988). As Dietrich Rueschemeyer and Peter Evans observe (1985:69), the more deeply the state penetrates society, the more the contradictions of society become embedded in the state. The state-centered approach suggests that this internalization of conflict tends to weaken the state, which helps explain revolutionary situations: intraelite conflicts certainly undermine old regimes (Skocpol 1979). In contrast, the interactive approach developed in the rest of this chapter contends that in nonrevolutionary situations—that is, most of the time—internal divisions within the state may *increase* its capacity to carry out reforms that favor the poor. If distributive reforms depended on unified, insulated states, they would be even rarer than they have been historically. The combination of competing claims on public resources, the frequent penetration of states by private elites, the anti-redistributive biases of most state agencies, and the inherently decentralized nature of most social reforms makes it quite difficult to find states that pursue such reforms in a unified way (Grindle 1980; Migdal 1988).

Even in very insulated authoritarian regimes, where political openings often result primarily from internal factional conflicts, such divisions create possibilities for "resurrecting" civil society, which in turn shifts the balance of forces within the state and increases reformists' room for maneuver (O'Donnell and Schmitter 1986).[23] Similarly, dis-

---

mon errors in finding "the correct relation between what is organic and what is conjunctural. This leads to presenting causes as immediately operative which in fact operate only indirectly, or to asserting that the immediate causes are the only effective ones. In the first case there is an excess of 'economism,' . . . in the second, an excess of 'ideologism.' In the first case there is an overestimation of mechanical causes, in the second an exaggeration of the voluntaristic and individual element" (Gramsci 1971:178).

23. Much of the literature on this dialectical process of regime change emerged in reference to Brazil (Alves 1985; Stepan 1988, 1989).

tributive policy outcomes are often made possible precisely because reformists inside and outside the state are able to weaken entrenched conservatives, dividing the state and increasing the leverage of popular movements. Equitable implementation of distributive policies frequently requires especially great state capacity because of their highly decentralized nature.[24] Within the realm of distributive reforms, some are clearly less vulnerable to elite monopolization of benefits than others, especially those involving public goods (Tendler 1982). Goods and services that are divisible (nonpublic) are less likely to reach the poor because fending off interested elites often requires unattainable levels of state capacity.[25]

The state-centered literature highlights organizational coherence and insulation from social actors as prerequisites for effective state capacity to make distributive reform *decisions,* but an interactive approach stresses that intrastate conflict and responsiveness to social demands are often necessary for their effective *implementation,* whether or not reform was initiated in direct response to pressures from below. Whether increased social mobilization is primarily a cause or an effect of reform policies varies empirically, and analysis requires a dynamic perspective that can account for both.[26]

Toward an Interactive Approach

State power, like power more generally, is often treated as an implicitly one-way capacity, but it is more usefully understood in terms of relationships (Lukes 1974:31). The rest of this chapter elaborates an interactive approach to state-society relations which builds on the

24. In this sense Lowi's (1964) "policies determine politics" is a useful reminder of how the task structures the range of issues, interests, and actors involved. For example, it may be far easier for states to regulate foreign capital than to change the economic activity of large numbers of dispersed individuals. As Migdal observed (1987:53), "The same Mexican government that had considerable success in regulating the share of equity and the operations of foreign-owned firms repeatedly failed to execute a fair-price-for-the-poor policy in rural areas." Contrast Bennett and Sharpe 1985 and Gereffi 1983, on the former, with Grindle 1977 and this book on the latter.

25. Among rural development programs, for example, subsidized credit or irrigation programs are inherently divisible and therefore more attractive and vulnerable to diversion by elites than, say, public schools, roads, or health services. See Leonard 1982 and Tendler 1982.

26. For a classic comparative study of the interaction between autonomous social mobilization and divided political elites, see Piven and Cloward 1977. For a useful related debate between state- and society-centered explanations of reform in the case of New Deal labor legislation in the United States, see Finegold and Skocpol 1984 and Goldfield 1989.

strengths of both state- and society-centered approaches while attempting to compensate for their limitations. I argue that state action is the result of a reciprocal cause and effect relationship between changes in the balance of power within the state and shifts in the balance of power within society. Through conflict, each is transformed.[27]

The framework developed below begins with the units of analysis—the key actors—and then begins to "map" the state and its constituent structures. This discussion emphasizes the opportunities and constraints faced by different state actors allied or in conflict with other state actors as well as with social forces.

The key actors in an interactive approach are defined in part by their relations with one another. To explain why one political actor wins out over another requires understanding how they manage to organize allies or to disorganize opponents in society. Most states actively structure and regulate the organization and representation of many of the interests and identities apparently "outside" the state, requiring one to define actors in terms that span state and society.[28] This process of interaction is recursive (Migdal 1990:2), meaning that the rules of engagement with the state apparatus are shaped by past struggles with social forces but in turn define the terrain on which new rounds of social conflict over state action take place.

An interactive approach needs to account for how different actors' capacities to pursue their goals change through conflict and convergence.[29] Mobilizations provoke countermobilizations among both

27. See Bright and Harding (1985). Joel Migdal (1990:1) calls this the "state-in-society" approach. "Historical institutionalism" emerges from a different tradition but points in a similar direction, developing an "analytic bridge" between state- and society-centered analyses (Thelen and Steinmo 1992). "As a corrective to interest group theories, the institutionalist perspective illuminates how institutions structure and channel political battles in ways that affect their outcomes. As an alternative to broad and often abstract Marxist, functionalist and systems theory approaches, institutionalism provides an understanding of politics and public policy sensitive to historical contingency and national-political diversity. . . . Institutions constrain and refract politics but they are never the only 'cause' of outcomes. Institutional analyses do not deny the broad political forces that animate various theories of politics—class struggle in Marxism, group dynamics in pluralism. Instead, they point to the way that institutions structure these battles and, in doing so, influence their outcomes" (Thelen and Steinmo 1992).

28. As Martin points out (1989:189–91), "One reason the [state] autonomy debate has not been definitively resolved is that the real world presents empirical evidence to confirm both sides. . . . The autonomy question as traditionally posed allows for neither mutuality of interests nor reciprocity of influence. Nor can either side explain the blurring of the boundaries between the public and private spheres."

29. As Przeworski put it, "In O'Donnell's (1977b) felicitous phrase, 'the map'—the distribution and density—of the state institutions in each historical case is the map of the

state and social actors, and the ways these processes unfold are not predetermined by a static initial distribution of power resources. Rather, the strength or weakness of pro-reform forces is shaped through their strategic interaction with each other and with their opponents.[30]

Social Actors

Beyond the formal boundaries of the state, "social actors" are groups of people who identify common interests and share ideas about how to pursue them. "Civil society" is a common but too general concept for identifying and analyzing actors outside the state. It is a residual category—"nonstate"—that does not offer analytical tools for understanding its internal dynamics and articulation with the state beyond general notions of strong or weak.

Social actors relate to the analysis of distributive reform in two principal ways. First, some reforms—perhaps most—are responses to direct pressures from society. More indirectly, *preemptive* reforms may appear to be exclusively state initiatives, but they are often responses to perceived potential pressures from society. Second, whatever their origin, the way they are carried out depends on the re-

---

sutures of past social conflicts. These are sutures, not scars: they are produced by *responses* to wounds; not by the wounds" (Przeworski 1990:51–52; emphasis added).

30. Hirschman's (1963) landmark study of "reform mongering" in Latin America stressed the importance of "non-antagonistic reforms" and a concomitant "revolution by stealth" in political systems where reformists lacked power vis-à-vis traditional elites. This approach had two major weaknesses, perhaps a reflection of the optimism of the Alliance for Progress period. First, it seemed to accept the prereform balance of forces as static, without analyzing the potentially dynamic interaction between reformists at the top and ostensible beneficiaries at the bottom. Second, Hirschman did not account for the actual outcome of reform implementation. As Anderson (1965) observed, two out of three of the case studies of reform were blocked or reversed in practice within three years of the book's appearance. He emphasized the importance of beneficiary mobilization to the politics of implementation: "For programs to be effective, they must be applied with consistent effort over time, long after the dramatic incident that led to the 'contriving of reform' has passed. For reforms to be effective 'over the long haul' of implementation may require a constancy of pressure on administrators that the reform monger himself is unable to generate or maintain. It may only come from the *sustained pressure of the actual and potential clientele of government programs*" (emphasis added; Anderson 1965:36). Cleaves (1980:292) further developed this approach, noting that reformist leaders face the challenge of developing policies "with the capability of generating, during the stage of implementation, wide popular participation that can later be directed toward *other* objectives benefitting these classes." (For other important interactive analyses of distributive policy reforms in Latin America, see also Ascher 1984; Cleaves 1974; Cleaves and Scurrah 1980; Grindle 1977, 1980, 1986; Jacobi 1989; McClintock 1981; Malloy 1979; and Spalding 1981, among others.) Much of the rest of the Latin American public policy literature describes "policy output" (e.g., Hughes and Mijelski 1984; Sloan 1984).

sponse from society. Although these societal pressures and responses may be diffuse, they have the greatest impact on the state when they coalesce into group action.

Collective action by social actors requires two minimal conditions: the *perception* of shared interests or identities and the *opportunity* to act as a group. This distinction parallels the difference between state autonomy and capacity. Social actors may be independent of the state but lack the capacity to pursue their goals successfully, or they may be less autonomous but have power, at least to pursue certain interests through certain channels.

The perception of common interests or identities may or may not be "determined" by class relations. Social class offers an explanation for a predisposition to experience power in certain ways, but given the many other cross-cutting and overlapping forms of identification, it cannot by itself explain collective action. Class-based movements or organizations rarely mobilize the clear majority of their class, even in revolutionary situations. Community, ethnicity, race, gender, religion, ideology, sexuality, and language all constitute powerful bases for perceived nonclass interests that can motivate collective action, though they may also provoke serious cleavages.

The pursuit of interests and the formation of collective identities are often posed as mutually exclusive motivations for collective action, but this dichotomy is false. Identities are constituted through the definition and defense of interests, while interests are formed through the identification of rights and claims.[31]

The second precondition for collective action is at least some perceived political opportunity. Members of a social group may well share a common view of the world and the changes they would like to see, but the lack of political opportunity may discourage them from taking action to pursue that vision of change. Opportunities shape when, where, and how social forces act politically (Tarrow 1983, 1989). Many factors make up the political opportunity structure, but access to basic political freedoms is among the most important. Intraelite divisions or the availability of powerful allies may encourage large numbers of subordinated people to run the risks inherent in mass defiance, but passive resistance and hidden nonconformity are much more common. As James Scott (1985) has persuasively shown,

31. On identity, interests, and collective action, see among others Berger 1981; Cohen 1985; Cumings 1981; Durand and Cuellar 1989; Melucci 1988; Munck 1990; Pizzorno 1985; Tilly 1978; and Touraine 1985.

the historical fact that, most of the time, most subordinate people do not engage in overt collective action does not necessarily mean they are content with their situation.[32] When coercion plays a fundamental role in preventing overt political conflict, those few spaces where people can exchange views and learn leadership are crucial determinants of the eventual capacity of the social force to become an actor.[33]

For example, many social groups in Latin America identify shared interests, but public and private sector elites frequently block autonomous collective action with coercion. To take the case of actors especially relevant to the analysis of rural reform in Mexico, many indigenous peoples have preserved an autonomous ethnic/political space at the community level (often too small to be of interest to antagonistic elites), but both internal and external factors create major obstacles to communication and coordination between communities across regions or nationally, which could greatly increase their capacity for self-representation. External allies are especially important for the rural poor more generally to engage in collective action, since they are often especially vulnerable to officially sanctioned terror.[34]

If a social actor begins to develop a common identity and has at least some opportunity to engage in collective action, what are the key determinants of its bargaining power? A social actor's potential capacity to disrupt political or economic stability is fundamental to its relative bargaining power. Disruption is the "withdrawal of a resource on which others depend" (Piven and Cloward 1977:24). The capacity to disrupt is fundamentally class biased: although some groups of skilled workers have significant leverage, such as those in strategic industries, large owners of capital have a fundamentally privileged position in terms of influencing state action through the threat of exit. Capital flight is especially powerful because it requires

32. The literature on "everyday forms of resistance" has made a major contribution to our understanding of political behavior, showing that political values and preferences cannot be deduced from "public" actions or socioeconomic position alone. This new political ethnography has shown that even people on the brink of survival act politically based on strongly held counterhegemonic normative values, though always constrained by their resources as well as by perceived risks and opportunities (see Colburn 1990; Kerkvliet 1990).

33. Evans and Boyte (1986) explain the emergence of mass movements in terms of "free spaces," often based on overlapping class, ethnic, religious, or gender ties that provide opportunities for autonomous interest articulation.

34. For a classic comparative analysis of alliances between peasants and other groups, see Wolf 1969. For further analysis of the external and internal obstacles to collective action facing the rural poor, see Fox 1990a. See also Olson 1986.

little conscious or explicit organization to produce a de facto collective action that disrupts the rest of the society.[35]

State Impact on Social Organizations

Spontaneous forms of popular protest and widespread everyday forms of resistance can have a powerful effect on state action, but it is usually indirect, limited to putting an issue on the agenda. Some form of mass organization is almost always crucial if social actors are to sustain mobilization, to keep issues on the public agenda, and—most important—to affect the design and implementation of the policies that emerge to deal with those issues. In other words, some forms of societal action have more impact on the state at the agenda-setting level (disruption), while other kinds have a greater effect on shaping the state's response (combining mobilization with negotiation and proposition). The contradiction for social organizations is that in the course of their efforts to shape the state, it often manages to shape them.

When social movements regularly interact with the state, whether through defiance or negotiation, they are necessarily affected by that interaction.[36] State responses may or may not alter their identities, but they affect them as actors by making some strategic decisions more costly and others more "effective." The institutional structure of the state, together with its regime governing electoral competition, shapes the political opportunity structure within which movements choose their strategies.[37] Social actors choose between electoral politics, diffuse foot-dragging, mass direct action, and armed struggle when faced with particular regimes at particular points in time, not as the product of material demands or subjective identities alone (Przeworski 1985).

Social actors usually make these strategic decisions through more

35. Capitalist interests certainly divide along sectoral and other lines, especially if the state is adept at manipulating these divisions. For this discussion, however, it is sufficient to point out that collective action is easier for them than for other social classes. (See Block 1987; Hirschman 1981; Offe and Weisenthal 1980; and Przeworski 1985.)

36. This emphasis on the state's structuring of social organizations is compatible with the recognition that many kinds of social identities emerge in complete isolation from the state. If they remain in complete isolation, however, it is difficult for them to affect state action.

37. For example, the nature and scope of social programs, as well as the institutional structure of the delivery system, necessarily frame the context in which reform beneficiaries (actual or potential) shape their identities and formulate their strategies. As Lipsky put it (1980:xiv), "The structure of street-level bureaucracy confronts clients with dilemmas bearing on action."

or less representative leaders. Representative leadership can be a cohesive factor promoting social and political mobilization, as well as holding a group together through the ebbs and flows of mass participation. Representative, coordinated leadership is particularly important for sustaining mass mobilization in societies that lack freedom of communication, assembly, and movement, and therefore where potential allies can be cut off from one another and blocked from strategic decision making.[38] For most people, most of the time, the perceived costs of continuous participation are too great for the constituency as a whole to bear, especially for those who find daily survival a constant challenge. In terms of rational choice, social movement leaders are those who pay the apparently irrational start-up costs of mobilization, long before collective action reaches the critical mass needed to produce clear results for the participants (Oliver, Marwell, and Texeira 1985).[39]

Representation is a matter of degree. Although members' informed, active, and democratic control over leadership selection constitutes one clear pole of representation, it is less clear where the other extreme lies. For example, Mexico's "inclusionary corporatist" heritage leads the state to respond to mobilization with at least the appearance of representation in the political system, as detailed in Chapter 3. Either state actors bargain with "genuine" representatives (*lideres naturales*) in an attempt to channel the mobilization, or they promote alternative leaders in order to compete for the allegiance of the mobilized mass base. The latter route may complement selective repression of genuine leaders if they are unwilling to negotiate on the state's terms. The state will therefore tend to obtain its representatives one way or the other.[40]

38. Representative local leaders who manage to coordinate groups across dispersed communities and regions are crucial to the potential influence of a disfranchised social force, especially when the ballot box is not a viable means of expression. The process through which poor people's organizations gain bargaining power by "scaling up" to form citywide, regional, or national networks is central to the analysis of distributive reform. (See Annis 1988 and Fox 1992a.)

39. For interesting efforts to link the rational choice approach to collective action with the social movement literature, see Hecter 1987; Moe 1980; Marwell and Oliver 1984; and Oliver, Marwell, and Texeira 1985.

40. The Mexican state plays an especially large role in the selection of interest group leaders, although much less in business groups than in others. See Luna, Tirado, and Valdés 1987; Purcell and Purcell 1977; and Story 1986 on Mexican business organizations. For excellent analyses of conflicts over democratic versus authoritarian means of leadership selection in official Mexican unions, see Cook 1990a and Roxborough 1984. On state structuring of organizations of the urban poor, see Cornelius 1975; Eckstein 1977; and Ward 1986.

When corporatist interest groups move back and forth along this continuum, they can give a certain flexibility to an otherwise rigid political system.[41] If they become too inflexible, corporatist interest groups eventually cease to be effective at controlling the social forces they ostensibly represent, which is one reason even leaders appointed by the state may still respond to pressure from below. The state expects such leaders to control their "base," preferably through at least apparent consent (perhaps by dividing and conquering) rather than repression. If the leadership makes no concessions to pressure from below, it will lose its apparent legitimacy and be unable to carry out its state-assigned task. Active competition from alternative organizations is also crucial for giving members leverage over leaders. If corporatist interest groups are to serve the state effectively as organs of control, they must also represent some member interests at least some of the time.[42]

The state's role in regulating formal social and political organizations is particularly important because it structures the nature of societal input into public policy. As Lukes pointed out (1974:24), perhaps the most important expression of power is the capacity to prevent others from articulating and defending their interests autonomously; hence the emphasis here on who organizes whose interests.

States can also gain control over social actors by attaching political conditions to distributive programs. This loss of independence is usually referred to as co-optation. Independence is often understood in absolute, either/or terms. Autonomy, in contrast, is inherently a matter of degree and refers here to the amount of state intervention in the social actor's internal decision making.

In Mexico, independence implies overt opposition to official one-party domination, whereas autonomy is not necessarily measured by a public stance toward the regime. For example, many analysts have shown that militant grass-roots organizations are usually co-opted by the state, meaning that they receive selective and partial benefits in exchange for demobilization and a loss of autonomy. Indeed, this has been the dominant pattern in Mexico. The problem with specifying

41. "Corporatism" is used here to refer to state-structured social organizations. For overviews of the range of corporatist forms of interest articulation in Latin America more generally, see Collier and Collier 1979; Malloy 1977; O'Donnell 1977a; and Stepan 1978.

42. See Sabel 1981. One of the principal weaknesses of the literature on corporatism in Latin America is that it does not take into account the potential for dynamism imposed by competitive alternatives (Purnell 1990). For example, Davis's (1989) survey research shows that Mexican workers' apparent acceptance of their official trade union leadership reflects not consent, but the government's success at blocking alternatives.

co-optation lies in differentiating between a "sellout" and a relatively autonomous decision about the best package of concessions that could be won in the circumstances. An autonomous peasant union may choose, for example, to exert its power by opting out of the ruling Institutional Revolutionary Party (PRI). This decision would be the *result* of a high degree of autonomy rather than the cause. More generally, an interactive approach views state–social actor relations along a continuum of degrees of autonomy rather than in terms of a dichotomy of public political stances.[43]

State Actors

State actors are groups of officials whose actions push or pull in the same political direction.[44] Some state agencies can be treated as actors because they are politically homogeneous, but the overlap is often only partial. In Mexico, as elsewehere, many state agencies appear to lack political coherence; their actions may seem erratic or ineffectual or may be stymied by what is often considered mere bureaucratic infighting (Purcell and Purcell 1980). But the problem may be that the agency is not the appropriate unit of analysis. Many state organizations are composed of a *range* of actors with different interests, who struggle to control the agency, to determine its goals, and to decide how to pursue them.

State- and society-centered approaches tend to have contradictory views about the motivations of state actors. An interactive approach moves beyond the dichotomous assumptions that state actors are motivated either by interests determined externally (no autonomy) or by an a priori commitment to promote an imputed state general interest independent of social forces or structures (complete autonomy). But autonomy is inherently relational. As was true for actors in society, an interactive approach analyzes the autonomy of state actors in

43. For studies of the determinants of social organization's shifting degrees of autonomy from the state over time, see Fox and Hernández 1989 and Fox 1992a. On the emergence of autonomy as a political demand within Mexican social movements, see Foweraker and Craig 1990; Fox and Gordillo 1989; and Fox and Hernández 1992.

44. The concept of "state actor" is not fixed; as a unit of analysis its "level" depends on the particular research agenda (national, state, or local politics, executive versus legislative, etc.). The issue is whether a group of individuals or departments, agencies, and so on, shows sufficient behavioral cohesion to make its designation as an actor a useful tool for analysis (Frey 1985). "State actor" is comparable to Block's (1987) "state manager," although the latter term could be understood to implicitly refer to individuals in a monolithic state with a great deal of control over their environments.

terms of *degrees* of freedom from external interference in decision making about interests and the goals and means of pursuing them.[45]

State actors are motivated by varying combinations of material, institutional, and ideological goals. In the most general sense, all state actors with any power share a common interest in perpetuating state rule because it is a necessary precondition for advancing whatever their particular agendas might be.[46] State power is their primary resource. State actors may gain ideological influence by claiming to act in the "national interest," but their claim to be doing so should be distinguished from the actual existence of such an interest. Neither national interest, privatized rent seeking, nor the straightforward pursuit of power for its own sake exhausts the possibilities for explaining how state actors define their goals.[47] Some change-oriented state actors may even risk their own positions for the sake of broader political ideals, as did the Popular Unity government in Chile. Even if most state actors do pursue risk-averse goals, their preferred means to this end vary widely. How and why different state actors pursue their careers and the preservation of the state more generally is therefore something to be explained rather than assumed.[48]

The broad context for analyzing state actors comes back to the twin foundations of state rule in capitalist societies: the continuation of private capital accumulation and the preservation of some historically conditioned minimum of political legitimacy. As I noted in the discussion of constraint theory, even in a mixed economy with significant state participation, the state is fundamentally dependent on the actions of capitalists because private investment is essential to its functioning.[49] Legitimation refers to the creation and renewal of the

45. The methodological challenge of developing indicators to "measure" changing degrees of autonomy does not make the concept any less important.

46. Shared interests in continuing state rule should be distinguished from stakes in particular governments. State actors often defect during transitions from one set of rulers to find positions with another. Except for unusual cases of social revolution, the basic ensemble of state institutions and personnel usually remains in place regardless of changes in regime (security forces, central bank, judiciary, and even most elected officials). On the continuities of state domination in spite of regime change, see O'Donnell 1988 on the Brazilian experience, as well as Cardoso and Faletto 1979 more generally.

47. See Grindle's useful critique of the rent-seeking literature (1991). For a thoughtful analysis of the relation between bureaucratic careers and broader state interests, see Schneider's (1992) study of Brazilian state enterprises.

48. As Whiting argues (1987:11): "The existence of a general tendency within the state towards self-preservation and of specific state workers who are in favor of preserving their jobs neither explains important decisions—why the state takes on new functions—nor non-decisions—why the state has *not* taken on other functions."

49. "State capitalism" is a widely used but poorly specified term that often refers to the

conditions for social peace—that is, the containment of most conflict within "proper channels." Rather than necessarily implying subjective consent to, or contentment with, the dominant political or economic system, legitimacy refers to a political system's renewable lease on power, which depends on its appearing to function better than plausible alternatives (Przeworski 1985).

Accumulation and legitimation are often contradictory tasks, as discussed above (O'Connor 1973). The ways accumulation and legitimation become official priorities are politically contingent, however, depending both on external demands and on the potentially autonomous, perhaps even preemptive initiatives of state actors. To understand how state actors attempt to balance conflicting demands for accumulation and legitimation, one must specify the nature of their interaction with the contending forces making those demands.

Institutional Access Routes

When state actors decide how to deal with social actors, their preferences are conditioned in part by their institutional environments. Because of their distinct histories and missions, different agencies have varying "embedded orientations," institutional climates that encourage state actors to understand society and to act in particular ways (Bennett and Sharpe 1985:43).

Different agencies "feel" social pressures differently. Their varying administrative or entrepreneurial tasks, institutional ideologies, vulnerability to electoral pressures, recruitment patterns, and bureaucratic structures combine to make one agency especially vulnerable to some social forces and another agency particularly open to other, perhaps competing external pressures. State actors' perceptions of the conflicts and trade-offs between accumulation and legitimation are therefore partly determined by their location within the array of state organizations. Social forces thus face different access routes in pursuing their interests with the state. Access certainly implies vulnerability to pressure, but it does not necessarily require that it be exerted directly.[50] To understand how social conflict is systematically inter-

---

extent rather than to the character of the state's participation in a mixed economy. If it is defined rigorously, in terms of indicators of the state's effective control over the key economic activities in a capitalist society, one finds very few cases (Fitzgerald 1978; Fox 1980).

50. This notion of access routes to the state is similar to Foweraker's (1989) "pressure points" and Alvarez's (1989) "points of access." The principal difference is that the term "access routes" conveys a more recursive, interactive image. Gaining access can be a

nalized in the state, we must map out the range of agency missions and access routes for external actors—foreign as well as domestic. As Migdal has suggested (1990:2–3), "State-society theories must be able to cope with the mutation of state goals as its various parts, operating in dispersed arenas, ally and clash with different social organizations."

Because of this array of agency missions and access routes, state actors value the relative importance of economic growth and social peace differently, within certain historically inherited minima of acceptable economic performance and political legitimacy. Different institutional environments also encourage varying perceptions of the conflicts between accumulation and legitimation. Differing ideological and analytical approaches also lead some state actors to see trade-offs where others do not, understanding the relation between politics and economics differently. Finally, state actors may be within the same institutional environment but still have conflicting policy preferences. Some state actors are more normatively concerned with favoring private capital accumulation, while others care more about political legitimacy. Still others are strictly concerned with individual career advancement or material gain.

The argument that state actors have different understandings of the relations between accumulation and legitimation demands does not mean they are completely free to respond as they wish; they face institutional as well as structural constraints. Most notably, those who actively encourage mass mobilization outside proper channels usually risk confronting other state actors whose institutional mission is to defend the state from perceived subversion. Security forces police the rest of the state apparatus, not just civil society. The capacity of the security forces to purge or restrain other state actors depends on the institutionally conditioned balance of forces within the state as well as on their alliances with like-minded groups in civil society.

What each agency is supposed to do to and for society is central to shaping its orientation toward the trade-offs between accumulation and legitimation, since each agency's job is usually to promote one or the other. Because there is often a relation between how well state actors perform their jobs and their future capacity to pursue their material or political goals, it matters whether their official task obliges them to be concerned primarily with accumulation or with legitimation. Those state organizations whose mission is to promote

---

two-way process that affects both parties rather than the implicitly one-way concept of applying pressure.

both frequently confront contradictory goals, leading to long histories of internal political conflict, often perceived by outside analysts as inefficiency.[51]

Legitimacy concerns are understandable in electoral democracies, but what about authoritarian regimes? The Mexican political class, for example, has traditionally been self-selected rather than chosen by the citizenry, so it is not immediately obvious why it should be especially concerned with political legitimacy. Some agencies and actors continue to focus on legitimacy issues because of the heritage of past cycles of interaction between the state and mobilized social forces, as will be detailed in the next chapter, but here it is enough to say that there is premium on winning the favor of superiors by successfully handling social and political pressures, if possible preempting them before they become articulated demands.[52] Perceived success at conflict management affects the future course both of the agency staff and of the agency itself within the state. As Smith put it (1979:261), the golden rule of Mexican politics is "don't rock the boat. . . . [The] primary task of all Mexican *políticos*, whatever their position, is to contain, control and mediate conflict—so as not to engage the attention or concern of their superiors, especially the President."

How to avoid rocking the boat, however, is institutionally defined. For example, elected officials responsible for territorially defined areas—mayors and governors—are among the most vulnerable because they must maintain peace in a given area in a political system where most basic decisions are made at the federal level. They therefore must bear the political responsibility for many conflicts that they often do not have the resources or the authority to defuse.[53] Among Mexico's federal government agencies, the state food trading enterprise and the Central Bank provide polar examples of how agency goals interact with institutionally structured access routes for social actors.

The primary goal of Mexico's National Basic Foods Company,

51. This is the problem with Purcell and Purcell's (1980) perceived policy incoherence. Actors within each agency often had rather coherent priorities, but they conflicted.

52. See Bizberg's discussion (1990), among others.

53. In their analysis of the structural roots of urban crisis in advanced industrial countries, Friedland, Piven, and Alford (1977:465) argue more generally that "the segregation of accumulation and legitimation functions in different kinds of agencies or different levels of government insulates the state's role in accumulation from political challenge and absorbs popular participation in accessible locations without substantial power. Yet this structural segregation means that the political authority that orchestrates the causes of social problems is insulated from that which manages their political consequences, and is thus without power to deliver a substantive response."

CONASUPO, is to appear to further social justice in the area of food procurement and distribution, and thereby to legitimate the post-revolutionary state. Effective service delivery to peasants is a major official goal, and therefore CONASUPO maintains a vast, high-profile rural presence. The existence of this apparatus does not mean the agency necessarily delivers the services promised, but CONASUPO's widespread rural presence does make the enterprise particularly vulnerable physically and politically to demands for access. When angry peasants take over CONASUPO warehouses, the agency must defuse that pressure, with a premium placed on doing it peacefully. Many warehouse managers are also elected members of their respective communities, constituting an access route for protest. If CONASUPO frequently resorted to coercion to deal with demands from its supposed beneficiaries, it would quickly fail at its task of legitimation.[54] In addition, repression would make grain procurement more difficult, which would interfere with CONASUPO's high-profile task of supplying urban markets with low-cost basic foods and could jeopardize the agency's urban legitimation capacity as well.[55]

CONASUPO's emphasis on the delivery of subsidies makes it a very expensive agency for the federal government, and therefore it is very closely watched by its superiors. As a result, when it fails at its legitimation task both the agency and its leaders pay a political price. The CONASUPO leadership, whether motivated primarily by careerist or ideological goals, faces strong incentives to perform its task well, which institutionally binds it to a preference for noncoercive means of dealing with its ostensible beneficiaries. From the point of view of mobilized peasants, then, the nature of the agency's institutional structure and mission provides access routes to a relatively sensitive state enterprise.

Mexico's Central Bank, in contrast, is responsible for maintaining national financial stability, a key factor in preserving the overall climate for private investment. This task has historically required keeping Mexico internationally creditworthy, in order to attract loans to

---

54. For an analysis of the grain warehouse occupation movements of the 1980s, see Hernández 1992.

55. Since low urban food costs permit industrial employers to keep wages down, this is an accumulation task as well, but the government also imports large amounts of food from the United States—usually cheaper than producing domestically. The state therefore must manage the conflict between urban accumulation and legitimation pressures in favor of cheap imported food, on the one hand, and rural accumulation and legitimation pressures in favor of higher procurement prices on the other. For an economic analysis of this dilemma, see Timmer, Pearson, and Falcon 1983.

compensate for chronic balance-of-payments deficits. This task in turn requires using its influence within the economic policy-making process to favor measures that would please current and potential creditors. If transnational banks are unwilling to lend, then the Central Bank has failed in its task. The Central Bank is therefore institutionally bound to be especially sensitive to the interests of transnational banks, often to the point of acting as their representative within the Mexican political system. From the point of view of private finance capital, the Central Bank as an organization has provided particularly sensitive access routes to influence economic policy-making. The effect of international pressures, broadly defined, depends on how they are internalized within the state and society. As Maxfield's (1990) analysis of transnational "bankers' alliances" clearly shows, apparently external pressures influence Mexican policy largely by strengthening allied national actors in both state and society.

Not all state agencies are selectively vulnerable to particular social forces. Mexico's Planning and Budget Ministry (SPP), for example, has no clear "constituency" beyond perhaps the Mexico City intelligentsia that staff it, and it is characterized by a wide range of policy orientations. Yet even in this case of a state organization that is relatively insulated from direct social pressures, its orientation was biased by its staff's direct bureaucratic (and sometimes ideological) interest in expanding state control over the economy.[56]

Although individual and institutional ideology (if any), determines how state actors define their interests and goals, more contingent political factors are important in accounting for their capacity to realize them. Their capacity is certainly enhanced if their goals fit closely with the priorities of the currently dominant governing leader, party, or coalition. In Mexico an actor's political clout within the state is greatly influenced by its fit with the dominant presidential "political project," which expresses the president's preferred place in history.[57]

56. On the SPP, see Bailey 1980, 1988 and Blair 1981.
57. Within the range of state actors' motivations posited above, from material to ideological, most Mexican presidents pursue ideological goals, but often through pragmatic means. They have virtually no personal material constraints—they can become as wealthy as they want. They have gone as far as they can in terms of power for power's sake; all that remains is to ensure their place in history. "No reelection," a founding principle of the Mexican revolution, has proved much more durable than its original counterpart, "effective suffrage." It is therefore plausible to suppose that no president wants to go down in history as the one who presided over the unraveling of a regime so carefully constructed out of chaos, which brought him to its pinnacle. Yet Mexican presidents interpret threats to stability differently and differ greatly in their strategies for managing of political conflict.

Because the Mexican state combines vertically centralized institutions with a heterodox ideological tradition, the president's explicit, strategic vision of the nation's direction is the political touchstone for all other state actors (Smith 1979). At least superficial consensus is expected, although the prohibition against presidential reelection means that the force of this expectation wanes toward the end of each term.[58]

State actors also draw key political resources from their capacity to win allies and block enemies among contending societal forces, as I noted above. Their bargaining power within the state is closely related to the influence of social forces that are pushing in the same direction, whether or not they consider themselves allies. At one extreme of the policy agenda, state and private security forces often offer mutual support by attacking political contenders considered unduly radical. At the other extreme, radical mass movements may well create pressures that indirectly put reformist policy solutions on the agenda, while modest reforms can also create opportunities for more radical mass movements. When both of these dynamics unfold simultaneously, reform combined with repression can result.[59]

Policy Currents

Different institutional missions and access routes shape the ways state actors can be supported or neutralized by contending state actors or social forces. Societal pressure and the existence of access routes can make the demands felt, but they do not determine the character of the response, since it depends on which state actors control the relevant agencies. If a social force exerts influence on an agency controlled by a state actor whose priorities predispose it to respond with concessions, then one can speak of the *internalization of societal interests within the state.*

58. This "degree of fit" is not by any means the only determinant of the success or failure of each state actor's effort to push its agenda. But in issue areas integral to his project, the president will make the choice among competing alternatives. In areas where a state actor finds no fit with the president's agenda, one can expect that it will be able to push its agenda only semiclandestinely or will choose to work in an area where there is little conflict with other state actors over resources. As shown in the following chapter, both of these factors were important to reformist efforts to encourage the consolidation of representative and autonomous peasant organizations during the latter half of the López Portillo presidency.

59. Mexico experienced this process during the early 1970s, when the state engaged simultaneously in innovative reforms, partial political opening, and extensive violations of human rights in areas of suspected guerrilla activity. The experience of El Salvador after the reformist coup in 1979 was an extreme case. For a thoughtful analysis of how intrastate conflict intensified state terror, see Stanley 1991.

This process is both cause and effect of conflict within state and society over how to deal with the problems of accumulation and legitimation. Contending approaches can be characterized in terms of "policy currents," coalitions between state and social actors that develop strategies to deal with actual or potential challenges to political stability. Linked through institutional access routes, they become political and ideological bridges that span state and society. Policy currents are not bound by national borders, as multiple transnational alliances between public and private sector elites have shown.[60]

Policy currents are forged by shared understandings of the relation between the often competing demands of capital accumulation and political legitimation, as well as the preferred trade-offs between them. Even in times of crisis, some policy currents will advocate the least possible reform. Other policy currents may push to change the rules of the game, perhaps even calling for military intervention when they perceive subversion of the established order. Not all state actors belong to policy currents, but the greater the perceived threat to the system, the greater the range of state actors that will actively participate in the conflict over how to deal with it.[61]

Policy currents also form "objective alliances" with other social and state actors, distinct from explicit coalitions. Objective alliances consist of groups that act on the state in mutually reinforcing ways. The convergence of their actions pushes the state for or against particular kinds of reform, but they do not necessarily consider one another allies. In fact, social movements and state actors may well see each other as opponents, even though they may be "objectively" pushing for the same general policy goals. In the short run, each must pressure the other to give in, but they share a broader interest in each other's gaining strength. A reformist state actor's capacity to make concessions, as well as to gain resources (to compete for resources within the state) may depend on the movement's capacity to challenge the state. At the same time, the movement's growth may well depend on its

60. Joseph 1981 develops the notion of policy currents in his analysis of United States foreign policy, drawing on Schurmann 1974. Katzenstein's "policy networks" are similar (1978:307–8). See also Maxfield 1990 on transnational "banker's alliances", and Martin's (1989) "coalition model" of converging public and private interests in the United States.

61. Not all state actors are always highly politicized in the sense that they all participate in shaping a comprehensive vision of what the state should do in the future (a "political project"). For some, material gain will always be the principal concern. The point is that the state is composed of actors with an overlapping mix of motivations, some more committed to policy currents than others, and that this mix changes over time, across institutions, and under pressure from social forces, depending on the perception of threat.

capacity to extract concessions from reformist state agencies to deliver to its members. If interaction between popular movements and
reformist policymakers is to push distributive change forward, then,
pressure from below must weaken reformists relative to the movement while simultaneously strengthening them in relation to competing policy currents that are less concerned about broad legitimacy.[62]

Whether societal pressure ends up supporting or undermining an
objectively allied state actor depends in part on how such pressure is
applied. If a social actor brings pressure to bear in ways that are seen
to threaten the highest levels of the political system, it risks undermining its allied state actors.[63] For example, when grass-roots movements
carry out direct action in ways the national security apparatus per-
ceives as subversive, they reduce the possibility that reformist policymakers will risk their own careers to support them.[64] Defections of
elite allies are then likely. Calculating populist machine politicians,
for example, would prefer to be able to turn social pressure on and
off like a spigot to bolster their influence within the state. Yet social
movements often need to overflow proper channels in unpredictable
ways if they are to be heard. Relations between objectively allied state
reformists and social movements therefore have an inherent potential
for conflict.

Reformist policy currents' need for some support from social actors, combined with their interest in limiting social actors to "legitimate" channels, builds a contradictory dynamic into the process of
distributive reform. Whether because of their own political agenda or
as a response to eroding legitimacy, policy currents that seek to make
the state more responsive to certain groups face an entrepreneurial
challenge. How willing are they to take political risks? If their posi-

62. O'Donnell and Schmitter (1986) outline a similar interactive logic in their analysis of
"pacted" regime transitions and the important role played by objectively allied military
soft-liners and societal moderates. In this scenario the moderate political party elites gain
power vis-à-vis the military soft-liners when societal mobilization increases, but beyond
some threshold of "perception of threat" the moderates fear that military hard-liners will
gain influence.

63. This applies largely, but not exclusively, to popular movements. For example, when
the Mexican private sector engaged in unrestrained capital flight in 1982, it temporarily
weakened its pro-business allies in the state, paving the way for the abrupt nationalization
of the banks and the imposition of capital controls.

64. Ascher's analysis (1984) highlights this kind of counterproductive strategic interaction, and he is therefore much more concerned with avoiding antagonizing antireform
forces than he is with empowering reform beneficiaries. Ascher contends that they will
never be satisfied anyway, so it is not in the interests of reformist policymakers to empower
beneficiaries, but he does not recognize possible scenarios in which mobilization could "objectively" support reformist policy currents.

tion in the balance of forces within the state depends in part on active or potential pressure that bolsters their priorities, then they need to take the risks inherent in offering support for, concessions to, or at least tolerance of social mobilization they cannot necessarily control. The analysis of Mexico's food policy reform that follows highlights how the contradictory dynamic inherent in the "objective alliance/ subjective conflict" between reformist policymakers and relatively autonomous social movements shapes the contingent boundaries between the limits and possibilities of reform from above.

Conclusions

Reforms from above that change society are difficult to explain with society-centered approaches. Similarly, societal responses to such initiatives that in turn change the state do not fit easily with state-centered frameworks. The challenge is to develop an explanation of state action that can effectively balance both state and societal factors. The most promising approaches focus on the interaction between state and society, the institutions that mediate such interaction, and the factors that account for how those institutions are in turn transformed.

Developing an interactive approach to distributive reform requires recasting conventional notions of state power, carefully distinguishing between the autonomy and the capacity of state actors. The challenge is to develop an approach that can account for how shifts in the balance of power within the state recursively interact with shifts in the correlation of forces in society. Two concepts were introduced to aid such an approach: institutional *access routes* and *policy currents*. Access routes are structurally selective filters in the state apparatus that make some institutions especially vulnerable to the concerns of particular societal actors. Policy currents are objective alliances between state and social actors whose political efforts push the state in similar and mutually reinforcing directions. Sometimes such policy currents are coordinated by explicit coalitions, but at other times those who are pressuring the state in parallel directions are divided. The goal is to "unpack" the state in order to better understand both the limits and the possibilities for distributive reform.

This approach suggests that prospects for distributive reform depend less on the insulation and coherence of a strong state than on internal divisions that favor reformists. Pro-reform policy currents must pursue strategies that strengthen them and their allies while weakening their opponents. Some reforms are initiated from above while others are responses to pressures from below, but in both cases it often takes pressure from below to carry them out—certainly in Mexico. The successful implementation of distributive policies depends on the nature of the political interaction between the pro-reform forces in state and society. If their actions are mutually reinforcing, then the reform effort internalizes social conflict within the state. This reciprocal interaction between state and social actors can lead to unexpected political outcomes.

Mexico's 1980–82 food policy reform was not driven by the usual process of protest and response. Direct pressures from below were not strong enough to require a necessarily reformist response, so the proximate causes of this reform do lie within the state, as the next chapter shows. But an exclusively state-centered analysis is incomplete for two reasons. First, it cannot explain how reformists became an influential policy current within the state in the first place. Here actors outside the state do weigh heavily: past waves of social mobilization embedded a recurrent reformist presence within the state, and the oil boom's positive-sum policy environment gave reformists increased room for maneuver. The second main limitation of the state-centered approach is that while it helps to account for the reform decision, it is insufficient to explain how far reformists were able to get in the process of policy implementation. Although the reform was initiated from above, the varied responses of contending social actors shaped who got what.

The rest of this book shows how Mexico's 1980–82 food policy highlighted both the limits and the possibilities of the dynamic interaction between reformists and social movements. The next chapter explains how Mexico's revolutionary heritage embedded reformist possibilities within the state, although reformists' capacity to overcome powerful opposition in both state and society depended on their efforts to reach out to their counterparts in civil society. As later chapters show, reformists' willingness and capacity to bolster potential peasant movement allies turned out to be limited, but their reform initiative was remarkable in that it went as far as it did. Most important, the encounter between an opening from above and mobilization from below shifted the future boundaries of the politically possible.

3

The Revolutionary Roots of Reform from Above: State Initiative and the Mexican Food System

In 1980 an elite group of reformist policymakers tried to restructure the political economy of Mexico's food system. They convinced the president to attempt a dramatic reversal of a policy that had long favored larger private farmers and ranchers, adopting a more "pro-peasant" approach aimed at promoting basic grain production and recovering national food self-sufficiency.

The new Mexican Food System (Sistema Alimentario Mexicano [SAM]) defined grain as a strategic resource that should be strongly regulated by the state rather than by "comparative advantage" in oligopolistic international markets. Food was politically linked to petroleum—the SAM promised to help stem the "petrolization" of the economy by channeling oil resources productively into the countryside. The SAM also promised to revitalize the state's much eroded political "alliance" with the peasantry, but through production and consumption subsidies rather than through the much more conflictive agrarian reform.

The presidential decision to adopt the SAM strategy was not "required" by increasing peasant movement pressures, but like the Mexican state's preemptive reform initiatives more generally, it had revolutionary roots. To understand the policy process of the 1970s and 1980s, this chapter analyzes how Mexico's revolutionary history built into the state a recurrent concern for rural political legitimacy.

Official ideology legitimated the victors by turning defeated revolutionaries Zapata and Villa into national heroes after they were murdered (O'Malley 1986). Yet the myths have historical foundations.

Mexico's official ideology is so broad and porous that only with great difficulty can it screen out radical social demands as illegitimate; thus it offers a potential arsenal of political weapons for almost all parties to social conflict. The original revolutionary demands for social justice, political democracy, and local autonomy are still widely held to be legitimate, even if far from fulfilled—the popular center-left nationalist electoral challenge to the official party's hegemony in 1988 fell squarely within the ideological tradition of the Mexican revolution.

The relative social peace that has coexisted with wrenching poverty in most of the Mexican countryside was not simply inherited from past reforms. Active state intervention was required to reproduce it. The "politics of promises" provided the state with a "renewable lease on political legitimacy" as long as some promises were occasionally fulfilled (Sanderson 1981:211).

The Mexican government was and still is essentially a coalition made up of distinct policy currents. Some state actors prefer to rely primarily on force to deal with rural unrest. They kill, torture, and imprison uncounted numbers of peasants each year and tolerate the "private" assassination of many more.[1] But some national policy currents are concerned with maintaining at least a minimum of rural social peace and political consent. Sometimes they are willing to pay the political price involved in reining in their violent associates and making concessions to mobilized peasants. The limits and possibilities of reform initiatives from above are shaped by the interaction between policy currents with differing approaches to the legitimacy problem—its importance, its roots, and its possible solutions. A state-centered approach can tell us about the proximate causes of such conflicts over how to deal with rural politics, but it does not fully explain why reformers have been more influential at some moments than at others. The context for intrastate conflict is captured better by an interactive approach that focuses on the recursive relationship between actors in state and in society.

This chapter begins with a brief account of the historical origins of Mexican state actors' capacity to take reform initiatives—in spite of the lack of competitive electoral pressures so central to the process elsewhere (at least until the mid-1980s). The revolution and the state-

---

1. On human rights issues in rural Mexico, see Alcántara 1981; Americas Watch 1990; Amnesty International 1986; Concha 1988; Encinas and Rascón 1983; and López Monjardin 1988.

building process that followed explain why some contemporary policy currents periodically showed both the will and the capacity to attempt to renew rural legitimacy. I then explain why the food crisis rose to the top of the national policy agenda when it did and why the SAM self-sufficiency strategy was chosen as a response.

State-Building and Social Movements: Reform Initiatives in Historical Context

Mexico's state-building process, born of prolonged mass violence, created a terrain of conflict that was wide open to the competing initiatives of entrepreneurial politicians. Several decades of government-led change followed, though a wide range of social actors eventually gained increasing autonomy from the state, limiting its room for maneuver. The official political culture and institutions inherited from the revolution still weighed heavily, however, and the potential range of state-society interaction remained rooted, though less and less firmly, in the original terrain of the revolutionary state-building process.

The Revolutionary Beginnings

The revolution was unleashed in 1910 by a struggle for limited electoral democracy waged by economically influential but politically excluded elites. Francisco Madero, aligned with northern, industrially oriented entrepreneurs, contested the political hegemony of foreign-linked business interests and semifeudal landlords. This conflict created an opening for social mobilization that could not be closed once Madero won the presidency after the 1910 revolt. He disbanded his own military forces and relied on the federal army inherited from the dictatorship to restore order. The new government then turned on those popular forces that continued to press their own political and economic demands, most notably the peasants of Morelos, led by Emiliano Zapata. The Zapatistas' demands had not been addressed: the restoration of their traditional lands, as well as local political freedom and autonomy.[2]

2. They had the capacity to resist because they retained the independent organization of their villages. The revolutionary slogan "Down with the haciendas and long live the pueblos!" was, as Gilly points out (1980:33), a profoundly political demand, "which for

When intraelite conflict erupted again in 1913, it could no longer be resolved within the inherited state apparatus. The destruction of the federal army in June 1914 ended the ancien régime. The turning point was at the battle of Zacatecas, when Francisco Villa led a revolutionary army to victory, against the orders of the new state elite that had originally mobilized it. The mass movement became briefly ascendant, as Villistas from the north united with Zapatistas from the south. The new state builders, embodied by the armies of Venustiano Carranza and Álvaro Obregón, lost control of much of the country. But the more radical revolutionary armies were unable to develop and impose a national political project. They were neither willing nor able to build a new state apparatus, creating a vacuum that permitted the northern entrepreneurial elites to regroup. The revolutionary armies' failure to consolidate politically left them militarily vulnerable to the counterattack by the new state builders.

The new state was founded at the constitutional convention of 1917. Much of the emerging new politico-military apparatus, led by President Carranza, wanted political control without social reform, but the convention followed a different path. Although most participants were upper-class civilians, the military leaders had been exposed to the cutting edge of mass revolutionary sentiment. Even though the revolutionary mass movement had weakened, its course had bolstered the power of those within the emerging new state who defined it in terms of popular legitimacy rather than as simply creating a favorable climate for investment.[3]

The revolutionary mass movements were defeated but not destroyed, embedding in the emerging new state apparatus both the will

---

the peasants' ears spoke not only of the recovery and redistribution of land, but also of the conquest of their capacity to decide, overcoming the *haciendas* as the local incarnation of the omnipotent power of the national state, and delivering to the power to the villages, the peasants instrument of self-government." On Zapatismo, see also Warman 1988a and Womack 1969. On the revolution more generally see, among others, Córdova 1972, 1989; Katz 1981, 1988; Knight 1986; and Tutino 1988.

3. On the constitution, see also Córdova, Unzueta, and Arzate 1984; Smith 1977; and Tannenbaum 1950, among others. Zapata made an especially insightful critique of the emerging new state shortly before his death: "It never crossed your mind that the revolution should be for the benefit of the broad masses, for that immense legion of the oppressed whom you and yours roused up with your speeches. . . . For you to triumph, however, it was necessary to proclaim grand ideals, to affirm principles and to announce reforms. But to keep the popular commotion (a dangerous two-edged sword) from turning against him who used and brandished it, to keep the people, already semifree and feeling strong, from taking justice into their own hands, you devised the creation of a novel 'revolutionary dictatorship'" (open letter from Emiliano Zapata to [President] Venustiano Carranza [March 17, 1919]; cited in Dromundo 1934:178–184).

and the capacity to attempt to restructure Mexico's stark social inequality. In the radical articles 27 and 123, the constitution holds that property is socially defined, not "naturally" private. As guardian of the interests of the collectivity, the state invested itself with the power to regulate property relations.[4] But the constitution's erratic implementation has shown that the state's actions against inequality have been determined more by the dynamic interplay between the state and social forces than by the text of its founding document.[5]

The decade of the 1920s was a turbulent transition period.[6] The new state builders made pacts with both foreign bankers and labor leaders, while some declared the land reform virtually over before it had begun in earnest. Politico-military challenges persisted, both from within the armed forces and from a popular Catholic rebellion.[7] The Mexican state did not begin to consolidate its power fully until national authority was centralized in the presidency. The organizational basis of state power shifted from competing regional politico-military factions to the more centralized National Revolutionary Party (Par-

---

4. In 1983, however, President Miguel de la Madrid amended this basic precept of the Mexican constitution's provisions on property relations. Instead of a system that held the national patrimony superior to the catchall category of all other kinds of ownership, the new amendment redefined property relations in terms of three equal and ostensibly autonomous sectors: state, private, and social. These amendments were perceived in Mexico as major ideological concessions to private capital, as part of the new administration's effort to restore investors' confidence after the abrupt 1982 nationalization of the private banks. The official legitimacy ceded to the "social sector" made the amendment politically feasible within the ruling coalition. The social sector is composed of enterprises owned and managed by trade unions, ejidos, and cooperatives. See Córdova 1983 for a critique of the reforms and Labra 1988 for an optimistic view of the social sector.

5. González Casanova 1970 was among the first to point out the enormous gap between theory and practice in the Mexican political system. Purcell (1975) and Aldrete-Haas (1990) analyze why the state chose to begin implementing constitutional provisions several decades after the document was written, in the cases of corporate profit sharing and workers' housing rights. As Fernando Pérez Correa, former undersecretary of the interior and state manager par excellence, put it (1982:59), "The social project of the 1920s has developed unevenly, sometimes fulfilling itself, sometimes not. We need to see the goals of the Revolution as an essential element in the present interplay of forces. In other words, new social forces are admitted to the political realm to the degree that the Constitution is progressively applied."

6. On the 1920s see, among others, Benjamin and Wasserman 1990; Falcón 1977, 1984; Fowler Salamini 1978; Friedrich 1977; León 1986; Lieuwen 1968; Meyer 1978; Montalvo 1988; Simpson 1937; and Tobler 1988.

7. As Bartra observes (1985:37), "the independent peasant movements of the twenties were weak because they were profoundly divided into two conflicting tendencies: *agrarismo*, framed within the official policy and in a relationship of antagonistic cooperation with the state, and the Cristeros, framed within the politics of the clerical organizations and in a relationship of antagonistic cooperation with the landlord." The Cristero rebellion of the late 1920s was vast, popularly based, and complex, but it is usually left out of analyses of national politics of the period.

tido Nacional Revolucionario [PNR]), founded in 1929 as a response to a crisis in presidential succession and led by former president Plutarco Calles.[8] New national political elites united regional power blocs by agreeing to respect their internal autonomy. At first the new party was dominated by those political actors who considered the revolution over, a rising class of state entrepreneurs who joined forces with finance and industrial capital, building an economic base from their control over government resource allocation. With the deepening impact of the depression, however, the relatively weak left wing of the ruling political coalition deliberately encouraged mobilization of workers and peasants while trying to control the terms of their incorporation into the evolving political system. These political elites both responded to and took advantage of the popular discontent driven by unfulfilled promises and by the economic crisis, gradually shifting the balance of forces within the state in favor of the reformists.

The turning point came in 1933. Conservative forces lost control of the official party convention as external popular pressure bolstered the influence of the Left (largely former military leaders continuing the revolutionary tradition). Conservative forces went along with a reformist platform, perhaps assuming it would not be implemented, but the reformists followed up with a victory whose importance would become apparent only later: the convention nominated General Lázaro Cárdenas as the PNR's 1934 presidential candidate.[9] Cárdenas's campaign and election greatly encouraged popular mobilization; workers and peasants responded to the increased possibilities of making gains, tipping the balance in the mounting power struggle between reformist and conservative policy currents.[10] This "mass poli-

8. As one of the official party's leading ideologues of the 1960s and 1970s summed up its essence in 1963: "Our party was born as an instrument to unify the factions of a victorious revolution. . . . they were more than factions, [they were] currents. The party was born to limit ideological disputes, setting the common denominator of the different currents. . . . This explains why our party is a party of classes and not a class party" (Jesús Reyes Heroles, cited in Gómez Tagle 1982:228).

9. Calles assented to Cárdenas's nomination because he saw it as "a calculated risk which he was forced to assume because of the rising opposition to his behind-the-scenes rule. Coopting someone from the official party's left wing appeared to be the best possible strategy for retaining control without having to make major (and binding) policy concessions" (Cornelius 1973a:438). The pro-Cárdenas coalition was made up of grass-roots peasant leagues, several reformist governors, and a moderate faction of the pro-Calles forces.

10. See, among others, Córdova 1974; Cornelius 1973a; Garrido 1982; González 1981; Hamilton 1982; Hernández 1990b; Meyer 1978; North and Raby 1977; and Tobler 1988. Cárdenas had begun developing a base as governor of his home state and later reinforced his official credentials by successfully demobilizing a more radical governor's peasant militias (Fowler Salamini, 1978).

tics" alliance-building strategy had been pioneered by several reform-ist governors in the 1920s.[11]

The Cardenista alliance between governing reformists and growing popular movements launched a wide range of structural reforms. Landlords and regional bosses were displaced as national political contenders as the "state-peasant alliance" carried out one of Latin America's most far-reaching land reforms. Redistribution extended to hacienda workers for the first time. An estimated one-third of the rural population received land, including some of Mexico's most valuable agroexport estates. Cárdenas backed up his decrees by arming over sixty-thousand peasants to battle the state and private security forces allied with the landlords (Huizer 1972:78–79). He made peace with the church, but thousands of radical teachers brought "socialist education" to the countryside. The foreign-owned oil industry was nationalized, and the railroads were turned over to the unions. The military was brought firmly under civilian control.[12] The ruling party of generals and regional strongmen was expanded and transformed into an "inclusionary corporatist" mass party, the Party of the Mexican Revolution (Partido de la Revolucion Mexicana [PRM]).[13] The result was a layered patchwork—in some areas Cardenista unions and peasant leagues competed with regional elites, while the federal government's balancing act left other regions largely untouched by social reforms or corporatist mass organizations.[14]

11. On these "laboratories of revolution," see especially Benjamin and Wasserman (1990); Martínez Assad 1979; and Paoli and Montalvo 1987.

12. This was a major accomplishment. The transfer of presidential power had been carried out by force in 1916, 1920, 1924, 1928, and 1929, followed by a failed revolt in 1938. The percentage of the military that rebelled was 40 percent in 1923, 20 percent in 1927, 30 percent in 1929, and less than 5 percent in 1938 (Lieuwen 1968, 1984:55).

13. There are two principal interpretations of the limits to Cárdenas's reform project (Collier 1982:71–72). One holds that the mass movement was consciously constrained from above in order to develop the conditions for national capital accumulation, positing the eventual authoritarian corporatist outcome as deliberate and predetermined (e.g., Cockcroft 1983). The principal alternative interpretation acknowledges that Cárdenas certainly limited mass mobilization at times, most notably by blocking an independent worker-peasant alliance, but highlights more fundamental limits to the reformist project. North and Raby (1977) apply Mayer's (1970) analytical approach to right-wing political dynamics and conclude that the limits were set by the decisions and capacities of all the actors involved, not by elite manipulation alone. Michaels 1970, Cornelius 1973a, and Hamilton 1982 are consistent with this more dynamic approach.

14. For further discussion of the difficulties of generalizing from national to regional politics, see Bennett and Rubin 1988; Rubin 1990; and more historically, Knight 1986, 1990.

The Evolution of the Ejido

The *ejido* is a community-based form of land tenure created by the postrevolutionary state, which determines both membership and geographic scope. The ejido is formally protected from the market, since it could not be bought, sold, or rented (until the constitutional reforms of 1991). Under state tutelage, ejidos allocate land-use rights among members, often unequally.[15] Ejido leadership is ostensibly chosen in assemblies through democratic elections. Paternalistic government intervention in ejido decision making is institutionalized, contributing to the internal centralization of power.[16]

Before Cárdenas, the dominant state view of the ejido was as a transitory instrument to contain peasant demands and complement seasonal wage labor. Conservative political adviser Luis Cabrera had pointed out as early as 1912 that partial land concessions would be necessary to pacify the countryside (Esteva 1987:28), leading to President Carranza's weak Agrarian Law of 1915. Cardenista *agrarismo*, in contrast, called upon the ejido to become the central politico-economic actor in the countryside, supplying food and raw materials while broadening the internal market, based on the consumer demand generated by agrarian reform beneficiaries. Simultaneously a state apparatus of political control and an organ of peasant representation, the ejido would also expand the state's mass base, offsetting the power of the clergy and the landlords. Much of the interaction between the postrevolutionary state and the peasantry can be framed in terms of the struggle over which approach to the ejido would dominate (Gordillo 1988b).

The peasant movement of the 1930s came together as an uneven grouping of regional agrarian leagues, varying greatly in their strength and their degree of autonomy from the state. In 1935 the president called for the formation of state level peasant leagues (years after the regime defeated the more autonomous groups of the 1920s). In 1938 Cárdenas created a national pyramidal mass organization along corporatist lines to represent the peasant "sector" in the ruling party.

---

15. For a comprehensive overview of the history and politics of agrarian law, see Ibarra Mendivil 1989. See also Sanderson 1984.

16. Until agrarian legislation was modified in 1983, losing candidates for leadership formed "oversight councils" (*consejos de vigilancia*) in an effort to keep elected leaders accountable and maintain representation of minority positions. "Agrarian communities" (*comunidades agrarias*) are another important form of tenure, limited to land returned to indigenous people based on historical claims. They are institutionally more autonomous from the state than ejidos.

The National Peasant Federation (Confederación Nacional Campesina [CNC]) was formed just as the government's commitment to the reform project peaked, and consolidation began to take priority over further mass mobilization. All agrarian reform beneficiaries were automatically considered members. Although Cárdenas set the terms of the state-peasant alliance, the CNC was formed through the convergence of mobilization from below with state efforts to consolidate its hegemony in the countryside.[17]

The peasant movement's uneven level of prior national organization and its lack of an autonomous political project ruled out reform efforts independent of the Cardenista state—in contrast to the labor movement, with its greater coordination, political autonomy, and disruptive power. Cárdenas blocked union leaders' rural organizing efforts, keeping the peasant movement beholden to the state rather than to the labor movement for its victories. Peasant leaders accepted a degree of state control because they saw an identity of interests with the reformists who had given them arms, land, and credit. Although government control over the peasant movement increased the reformists' leverage in the short run, it would crucially weaken them in later intrastate conflict (as had happened to Cárdenas's predecessors, the reformist governors, in the 1920s). When the balance of forces within the state shifted, the peasant movement was easily demobilized.

The growing weight of the state in the countryside was not limited to the formation of a corporatist political organization. The official agrarian agencies were also vested with a broad range of powers to "guide" the development of ejidos. The formation of collective ejidos in highly developed irrigated zones was also accompanied by the creation of government rural development agencies, most importantly the agricultural bank. In theory these agencies were to support ejidos in an effort to become self-reliant, but their bureaucratic and political priorities led them to emphasize government control over agricultural production and marketing.[18] Government rural institutions evolved a

17. On the CNC in the 1930s, see Bartra 1985; Fowler Salamini 1978; González Navarro 1985; Granados 1983; Hardy 1984; Hernández 1990b; León 1986; Simpson 1937; and Weyl and Weyl 1939.

18. The classic case of the rise and fall of radical reform efforts was in the Laguna region, which had witnessed massive radical strikes of agricultural wage workers, prompting the state to "peasantize" them by creating collective agroindustrial enterprises. The large-scale experiment in self-management that followed was weakened by paternalistic reformist tutelage, followed by deliberate bureaucratic demobilization during the post-Cárdenas counterreform. Research on peasant organizations in the region includes Aguilar Solís and Araujo 1984; Carr 1985; Craig 1990; Gómez Tagle 1974; Hellman 1983:146–63;

division of labor; the CNC managed the channeling of peasant demands, the agrarian agencies handled their regulation and response, and the rural development agencies controlled the economic decisions in the best-endowed part of the reform sector.

The domestic and international reaction to the 1938 oil nationalization led Cárdenas to choose consolidation over radicalization of his project. He named a successor who would begin to reverse many of his more radical initiatives. The wave of reform ended, to be followed by decades of authoritarian counterreforms. But Cardenismo was different from more typical kinds of Latin American populism, which generally served *only* to mobilize popular forces from above to support one state faction against another. Mexican populism was driven not by intraelite competition alone, but by powerful threats as well. The state needed peasant support to offset both military and insurrectionary challenges in the 1920s and 1930s. As Arnaldo Córdova observed (1972:32), "Mexican populism had a counterrevolutionary essence: it was an attempt to prevent the mass movement from turning into a social revolution, and 'they gave the centavo to earn the peso.'"

The two decades of war, revolts, and instability that preceded the institutionalization of the Mexican revolution shaped the sensibilities of generations of state actors. Governance was not seen simply as the task of administering an existing system. Instead, state actors saw stability as the outcome of the continuous management of contending social interests. According to state manager Fernando Pérez Correa, for example, "The President became the head of a social alliance whose military forces had been victorious. He became the center of a system of mediations between interests. The strength of the Mexican President derives from his capacity to hold together a whole set of forces that are constantly changing" (1982:59). Few successful Mexican leaders take political stability for granted.[19]

Landsberger and Hewitt 1970; Rello 1986b; Restrepo and Eckstein 1979; Singelmann 1978; Stavenhagen 1975; and Weyl and Weyl 1939.
19. As Purcell and Purcell put it (1980:195), "The Mexican state is a "balancing act because it is based on a constantly renewed political bargain among several ruling groups and interests representing a broad range of ideological tendencies and social bases." This contrasts with an earlier emphasis on the solidity of Mexican political institutions (e.g., Hansen 1974; Huntington 1968).

The Role of Interlocutors

In spite of growing rural inequality, the Mexican state presided over relative social peace in the countryside after the Cárdenas reforms. Even after the PRM became the Institutional Revolutionary Party (Partido Revolucionario Institucional) [PRI]) in 1946, past reforms left a vast reserve of political, economic, and ideological resources with which to manage and preempt unrest. In the decades that followed, most rural mobilizations were kept within the bounds of the established order, with the notable exceptions of the Jaramillistas in Morelos and the radicalized movements in Guerrero and Chihuahua in the 1960s. The repeated emergence of these regional exceptions to the rule was crucial for encouraging reformist state managers to attend periodically to the question of rural political legitimacy.[20]

The Mexican state is adept at social control precisely because it usually attempts to deal with potential sources of instability while they remain localized or inchoate.[21] "Dealing with" implies the well-known formula of co-optation when possible and repression when necessary, but what is often referred to as "co-optation" sometimes involves substantive, albeit conditional, concessions (as noted in chap. 2). In order to bargain over the terms of such concessions, some kind of representation is necessary, whether genuine or self-appointed. State actors whose mission is to manage stability need counterparts to deal with: *interlocutors.*

In Mexican political discourse, interlocutors are intermediaries who manage to represent potential or actual social or political forces, including movements that are not incorporated into existing channels. State managers see unchanneled pressures as a serious threat; the term "México bronco" ("wild Mexico") is still used to hark back to the insurrectionary period. Those state actors most concerned about legitimacy are continually either searching for or creating interlocutors, even while other policy currents may be pursuing more coercive strategies.

20. The first important independent peasant movements during this period were led by the General Union of Workers and Peasants of Mexico (UGOCM), founded in 1948 (De Grammont 1989a), followed by Rubén Jaramillo, assassinated in 1962 (De Grammont 1989b), and the Independent Peasant Central (CCI), founded in 1964 (Bartra 1985; Moguel 1989). The state eventually managed to divide both the UGOCM and the CCI into pro- and antigovernment wings. In the 1960s, rural civic movements in Guerrero were repressed, later pushing peasants to take up arms (see Bartra 1985; Mayo 1980).

21. The case of Guerrero's armed resistance was a notable exception, and politicians at the time berated the governor for needless provocation rather than political negotiation. See note 20.

The search for interlocutors usually succeeds, not because "the state" monolithically co-opts or represses, but because those often-subordinated policy currents most concerned about legitimacy frequently retain some power resources to bargain with and thereby manage a "partial solution." Reformist initiatives toward social movements are often preemptive rather than direct responses to already mobilized groups because they may be prompted by state actors' perception of *rising*, or increasingly likely, instability. The importance of perceptions helps explain why regional pressures can have national policy implications.

Reformists' capacity to deal with legitimacy problems depends on the balance of power within the state. Yet even though they may lack influence during extended periods, they are often down but not out. Conflict between policy currents in Mexico is rarely resolved with the total victory of one side or the other. Part of the essence of the post-revolutionary state is its "something-for-everyone" approach for those within the ruling coalition. If political stability is a continuous bargain, then all parties to it must continue to have a stake.[22]

To shift the balance of power within the state, reformist policy currents sometimes encourage social mobilization. These social forces in turn perceive the increased opportunities for winning concessions. But such pressures also provoke reactions from opponents inside and outside the state.[23] The resulting conflict is rarely resolved until the national political context changes. In Mexico this happens when the presidential administration (*sexenio*) changes, hence the oft-noted alternation between "activist" and "consolidating" presidents.[24]

At least until the late 1980s, the presence of a broad range of policy currents within the "legitimate" political arena in spite of swings in balance of power within the ruling coalition made it less likely that the political system would freeze and lose its capacity to adapt to

22. President De la Madrid ignored this basic rule of the political game when he essentially expelled the "democratic current" from the PRI in 1987, provoking the most important overt split ever in the "revolutionary family." The 1988 nationalist electoral challenge was far from inevitable, since the elite dissidents probably could have been accommodated by a president more adept at balancing competing policy currents.

23. This dynamic began as a politico-military process during the armed phase of the revolution but was "institutionalized" by the reformist governors of the 1920s (Benjamin and Wasserman 1990).

24. Purcell and Purcell (1980:222) make the important observation that the "swings of the pendulum are not between two fixed ideological positions. Changes in institutions and in the relationship between the public and private sectors tend to be cumulative. The new strata of institutions and relationships laid down by one President form the basic materials with which his successor must work, even if his style of doing so is different."

change. Within each presidential administration, this broad range of policy currents, even if their weight was unequally distributed, also made shifts in political direction possible *within* a given sexenio. The presidential political project can change in important ways in the course of an administration, especially during the period of competition over the succession.[25]

President José López Portillo (1976–82) entered office leaning clearly to the right but then launched a domestic political opening, began to shift to a more nationalist foreign policy in 1979, continued with more nationalist and distributive social and economic policies in 1980 and 1981, and ended his term by imposing exchange controls and nationalizing private banking in 1982. The decision to adopt the Mexican Food System (SAM) strategy was an integral part of this shift. To understand this change in policy direction, one must go beyond individual quirks or immutable electoral cycles and analyze the shift in the balance of forces within the state in terms of competing policy currents.

New Waves of Rural Reform, 1970–1982

The Mexican state has occasionally ignored warning signs, allowing mobilization to lead to political instability. The 1968 student movement was widely perceived as legitimate, demanding the government's compliance with official ideals, but the president repeatedly chose force over negotiation, culminating in the bloody October 2 massacre. Political crisis management had failed, eventually weakening conservatives and making possible new cycles of reformist efforts to renew mass political legitimacy in the course of the 1970s and 1980s.[26]

25. Teichman (1988:92) observes that "as competing teams pressure the president for support of their respective programs, policy inconsistency may result as the president is swayed by one team or another or implements contradictory parts of each program." See also Loaeza 1981; Smith 1979; Story 1985; and Sanderson 1983.

26. The repression of the 1968 student movement cost the state an unprecedented loss of political legitimacy because it had violated "the correspondence between the uses of force and the rules which specify when it can and should be used" (Przeworski 1985:141). The state's revolutionary image was fundamentally tarnished in the eyes of broad sectors of the population, not just students. For example, the PRI won less than a majority of the potential electorate for the first time in the presidential elections of 1970 (i.e., less than abstention plus opposition). See, among others, Basañez 1981; Hellman 1983; Saldívar 1981; Shapira 1977; Stevens 1974; Huacujo and Woldenberg 1983; and Zermeño 1978. Some analysts emphasize the 1968 student movement's roots in reform efforts earlier in the

State actors differed in their responses, both in how they perceived the origins of the legitimacy crisis and on how to resolve it.[27] Hard-liners, associated with Gustavo Díaz Ordaz's administration (1964–70), did not see negotiated concessions as the appropriate response to the challenge, putting short-term control first. This orthodox current continued to respond to dissent with repression, and some of its partisans continued on into the Echeverría presidency (1970–76).

Luís Echeverría, in contrast, recognized the importance of negotiated solutions. His revived "nationalist populist" policy current coincided with the traditional hard-liners in that the legitimacy crisis did not indicate the need for fundamental political change. His prescription was quite different, however, using economic and political concessions as well as repression. His approach was both nationalist and statist, advocating increased international economic and political autonomy, more social spending, greater state intervention in the economy, and ideological confrontation with the private sector. The nationalist populists saw themselves in the Cardenista tradition and tried to revitalize the political system's traditional mechanisms of controlled interest representation.

The "modernizing reformists" also emerged, coinciding with the nationalist populists in economic and foreign policy but differing in their recognition of a need to make qualitative political reforms. Although the leading figures were older liberals, many young officials constituted a clear radical wing and had been veterans of or sympathizers with the student movement—the "generation of '68." These reformists sympathized both with legalizing opposition activity and with opening up official mass organizations to democratic participation. At first the government was seen to tolerate mass organizing outside the official corporatist structures, in part to counterbalance their autonomy from the president. By 1973, however, worker and peasant movements grew beyond official expectations, and the government again focused on broadening the base of the official mass organizations.[28] The modernizing reformists were contained during the Echeverría period, but their influence was felt at key points throughout the 1970s and 1980s.

1960s, such as Cárdenas's National Liberation Movement and Madrazo's failed attempt to open up the PRI (e.g., Moguel 1988).

27. As discussed in chapter 2, these sketches of policy currents are ideal types. In practice, many individuals shifted from one to another or combined elements of different approaches.

28. Many student activists had chosen not to join the new administration and instead went to the fields and factories to continue to support increasing grass-roots opposition.

In the countryside, the Echeverría government was confronted with signs of political and economic crisis. In the state of Guerrero, ongoing repression since the 1960s had driven peasants pressing for municipal democracy and higher producer prices to take up arms.[29] Nationally, a crisis of the peasant economy combined with an increased willingness to engage in collective action to undermine the corporatist framework, launching a new cycle of more autonomous mobilizations in the 1970s and 1980s.

A convergence of economic and political factors led to a nationwide wave of peasant mobilization. First, the agricultural growth model followed since the 1940s, with its subordination to industry and its emphasis on irrigated export production, had begun to weaken by the mid-1960s. Producer prices and agricultural investment both fell, weakening food production and decapitalizing the peasant economy.[30]

Second, the decades of conservative land reform policy began to exhaust the political capital left from the Cárdenas era. President Díaz Ordaz's agrarian policy combined record levels of distribution of *non-arable* land with a political discourse that proclaimed the end of land reform. This undermined one of the principal pillars of political compliance among the landless: the hope of someday having one's own plot of land, and therefore a steady income. The CNC was particularly weakened as the traditional "proper channels" closed.

Pressure on the land mounted, meanwhile, on three distinct fronts. Population increases on ejidos meant that the children of land reform beneficiaries had too little land for subsistence. Wage workers in export-oriented agribusinesses began to demand enforcement of the agrarian reform laws, since landownership ceilings were widely flouted. Indigenous communities increasingly protested widespread and violent displacement by large ranchers, who turned fertile cropland into inefficient pasture, primarily to feed Mexico City's growing demand for beef, as well as for export to the United States.

When land invasions broke out in highland states in 1972, they met with a contradictory response by the Echeverría administration. The

---

29. See Bartra 1985; Balanzar et al. 1982; Gómezjara 1979; and Mayo 1980.
30. For the range of perspectives on Mexico's food crisis during this period see, for example, Appendini and Salles 1980; Barkin and Suárez 1985; Boltvinik and Pessah 1981; Cartas and Bassoco 1987; Castell Cancino and Rello 1981; CEPAL 1981, 1982; Barkin and DeWalt 1988; Esteva 1980, 1982, 1983; Goodman et al. 1985; Grindle 1977, 1981, 1986; Hall and Price 1982; Hewitt de Alcántara 1976; Johnston et al. 1987; Luiselli and Mariscal 1981; Meissner 1981; Montañez and Aburto 1979; Mújica 1980; Paré 1977, 1982; Rama 1985; Redclift 1981b; Reynolds 1978; Sanderson 1981, 1986; Spalding 1984; Wionczek 1982; and Yates 1981.

repression of the 1968 student movement had led to a new rhetoric of populist reform and political "opening" that increased the likelihood of the government's making at least some concessions for the sake of renewing popular legitimacy. Almost every state felt the pressure of land hunger, with tens of thousands taking part in hundreds of large-scale land invasions. Rank-and-file participants were frustrated with the decades-long process of working through bureaucratic channels. Some actions spontaneously took on a somewhat insurrectional character, and the two armed peasant movements in Guerrero resonated politically throughout Mexico. Pressure from below forced the radicalization of the official peasant organizations in some areas, while in others new independent movements bypassed pro-government federations. At least a dozen regional movements rooted themselves in independent organizations that managed to survive the mass movement's later ebb.[31]

The central demand was for land. Because the primary issue was the enforcement of agrarian law, conflicts were shaped by their local specificity. The bureaucratic processing of the political "solutions" to the conflicts promoted classic "divide and conquer" tactics. Nonland issues were also raised, ranging from producer and input prices to municipal democratization, trends that would grow in the future. Because of this inherent decentralization, the mobilization was less a clearly national peasant movement than the simultaneous convergence of many local and regional struggles. The result was a powerful political presence with no single national expression, but with a multiplicity of urban-based political currents competing for leadership of the peasant movement.

Pressure from below led to a populist shift in official agrarian policy in 1973, which in turn encouraged further mobilization. Landlords' evasion of agrarian law was officially recognized as a serious problem for the first time, and nonviolent grass-roots movements could find allies in a wide range of government agencies. Some government reformists tried to limit repression and in some cases even encouraged land invasions. Negotiation, sometimes involving substantive concessions, became central to the government's attempt to keep the mass movement within acceptable bounds. Mainstream

31. For further studies of Echeverría period agrarian conflicts, see Astorga Lira and Hardy 1978; Avila 1986; Bartra 1985; Canabal 1982, 1984; Castell Cancino and Rello 1981; Gómezjara 1979; Gordillo 1980, 1988a; Granados 1977, 1978; Levy 1977; Robles and Moguel 1990; Montes de Oca 1977; Rello 1986; Ramos García et al. 1984; Robles 1981; Rubio 1987; Sanderson 1981; Székely 1977; and Warman 1980b.

agrarian politicians gained sufficient influence within the government itself to aspire to the nation's highest offices.

The Echeverría administration internalized much of the leftist critique of past agrarian and agricultural policy and responded with a wide range of new rural development programs. But commercial agriculture had matured under government protection, and by the 1970s large producers were powerful and well organized.[32] From the point of view of reformists within the state, it was politically easier to isolate intermediaries than to confront agribusiness interests directly, leading to the official definition of inefficient and inequitable rural markets as a key obstacle limiting rural progress. Since subsidies and market regulation delivered substantive benefits at less political cost than land redistribution, market regulation and employment creation through public works became rural development priorities.[33]

The many ways the state increasingly intervened in the countryside shared one characteristic: government agencies, with their own institutional interests, increasingly displaced the CNC, the traditional "demand manager," as the key agent in the state-peasant relationship. Independent competition pushed the official peasant organizations briefly to radicalize their rhetoric, but given the limited amount of land actually redistributed, they had little to offer the landless other than hope. At the same time, conservative "developmentalists" managed to continue promoting both extensive ranching and subsidized tractor use, two key causes of rural unemployment (Fritscher 1985).

Whereas the state responded to the landless largely with promises, its approach to the better-endowed smallholders was different, especially for those considered to have the economic potential to contrib-

32. Grindle put it well (1986:189): "Through its policies to modernize agriculture, the state helped create the very economic elites that subsequently became central to the maintenance of certain kinds of agricultural policies. . . . In many cases what emerged from this was an implicit or explicit bargain between the agricultural entrepreneurs and state elites to continue and even invigorate past support for capitalist expansion. . . . Thus, . . . successful state policies did much to create a structure of power and influence that eventually limited the range of options available to the state for changing conditions in rural areas."

33. On the official challenge to local bosses (*caciques*), see the strong public statements by PRI leader Jesús Reyes Heroles, cited in Bartra 1985. The government pursued several major efforts to reform rural income distribution, some of which would later be revived in the early 1980s as part of the SAM. The official food marketing agency, CONASUPO, began to carry out a wide range of innovative rural development programs. For the most insightful analyses, see Esteva 1979 and Grindle 1977. Another government program, PIDER, carried out short-term employment creation projects under the banner of "integrated rural development" (Cernea 1983; Lacroix 1985; Lindheim, 1986; Page 1989). PIDER projects had little lasting effect at the national level, but several experiences led to important local-level changes (e.g., Fox and Hernández 1989; Fox 1992a).

ute to internal and export markets. The state's greatly increased intervention in certain agricultural sectors (e.g., coffee, tobacco, sugar) succeeded in revitalizing part of its rural social base, in spite of the creation of a "conflictive dependency" (Bartra 1985:117).[34]

Legal and institutional changes also reshaped the agrarian scene. The 1971 reform of the Agrarian Code presented a new, "integral" vision of the ejido as an economic as well as a political institution, making peasant-managed rural development an official priority for the first time since the Cárdenas era. Toward the end of the Echeverría administration agrarian policy focused on the rushed attempt to collectivize eleven thousand existing parceled ejidos, to consolidate political and economic control. Because it was imposed by and for the state, the effort almost universally failed.[35]

In the context of this emphasis on "organization" as the post-redistribution phase of the reform, the Agricultural Credit Law was amended in 1975 to encourage the formation of regional associations of small producers for the first time since the 1930s. The Agrarian Reform Ministry (just promoted to cabinet status) then began to encourage "second- and third-level" organizations.[36] These new legal forms attempted to bring community-based producer groups together around some common economic interest (credit and input provision, processing, marketing).[37]

34. This selective corporatist investment policy helps us understand why the CNC was able to retain some peasant support. Competing pressures from above and below provoked tension between regional and national CNC authorities during the Echeverría period (Hardy 1984). Open internal conflict emerged again in 1990, over the new issue of direct elections of CNC leaders (*La Jornada*, 19-V-1989).

35. On ejido collectivization during this period, see Székely 1977; and Warman 1980b.

36. "Second-level" was defined as bringing together two or more local producer groups, such as ejidos, indigenous agrarian communities, or private production societies and cooperatives; "unions of ejidos" (UEs) were the most common. "Third-level" organizations brought together two or more second-level groups and were known as "rural collective interest associations" (ARICs).

37. Almost three thousand ejidos (11 percent of the total) were organized into 181 UEs during the Echeverría administration, according to data from the Secretariat of Agrarian Reform. Official registration was a prerequisite for most collaborative economic activity, but most of the group registrations were imposed from above by one government agency or another. The official agricultural bank was very active, since enterprising officials could "unload" large loans easily if they concentrated many producers together into large, usually agroindustrial projects. The size and technical sophistication of these projects made bureaucratic control easier, creating many opportunities for political and economic abuse of power. Because of this top-down approach, many UEs formed during this period soon existed only on paper. In the longer run, however, the outcome would be different. The legal framework created for multicommunity, peasant-managed enterprises, as well as the "developmentalist" legitimacy conferred on these "higher" forms of organization, left an institutional resource that would be taken advantage of by grass-roots producers' move-

Persistent farmworker movements in the northwest had nevertheless managed to keep land redistribution on the national agenda. Echeverría was eventually pressured into ceding large tracts of illegally concentrated land to thousands of landless peasants in the heart of some of Mexico's fertile irrigated districts, spurring a powerful private sector countermobilization and contributing to a major political and economic crisis surrounding the 1976 presidential transition.[38] Like most such populist measures, this major concession to a militant regional peasant movement was too little, too late to build a political alternative that could pursue further land redistribution beyond the presidential transition.

Echeverría pursued short-term economic solutions to fundamentally political problems. He failed to carry out a tax reform, which would have been necessary to sustain his redistributive policies. Instead, his use of subsidies to attempt to defuse political conflict led to increased debt, inflation, and eventually economic crisis (Newell and Rubio 1984:196–98). The official rhetoric of Echeverría's "shared development" strategy was sufficiently reformist to disrupt longstanding alliances between political and economic elites but too limited in practice to strengthen worker, peasant, and community organizations enough to permit the populists to construct a viable alternative set of political alliances. The result was the most serious presidential succession crisis since 1940. Most important, Echeverría chose a successor who appeared to promise stability.

López Portillo came to power from a position of weakness. His link to Echeverría and his previous training as a financial administrator limited his own base within the political system. In spite of Echeverría's widely heralded "political opening," the party system had remained closed, and those few parties that were legal did not present opposition candidates in 1976, depriving López Portillo of the political legitimacy associated with facing an electoral opponent. The International Monetary Fund (IMF) stabilization agreement signed by the outgoing president ruled out the option of a reformist economic policy.

The domestic and international pressures generated by the 1976

---

ments in the 1980s (Fox and Gordillo 1989). Fernández and Rello's (1984) definitive survey shows that 287 UEs were actively functioning as of 1981.

38. On the Sonora movements, see Gordillo 1988a, 1988b; Ibarra Mendivil 1989; Otero 1986, 1989; Rello 1986a; and Sanderson 1981. For related analyses of Echeverría's conflicts with the private sector see, among others, Basurto 1982; Basañez 1981; and Saldívar 1981.

crisis led López Portillo to move to the right, while at the same time trying to conciliate forces within the political system. Former members of the teams of both previous presidential administrations were included early in the administration. In economic policy, the priority was to reestablish investor confidence and growth, which was accomplished largely within the orthodox framework of the IMF agreement, followed by increased reliance on the petroleum industry as the motor of the economy.[39]

Although macroeconomic policy moved to the right, the more liberal currents within the administration gained room to maneuver in the political arena. The 1977 political reform was designed to broaden the base of the regime by including more opposition parties in the electoral system and giving amnesty to political prisoners.[40] The economic pressures on the right were balanced by granting political legitimacy to "responsible" opposition parties on the left. The political reform served to blunt the left's criticism of economic policy, while recognition of the Left gave the administration greater freedom to maneuver in its dealings with the Right. During 1978 and 1979 López Portillo wavered, fully carrying out neither the nationalist-populist nor the more orthodox neoliberal economic policy recommendations.

The president's policy discourse stressed the link between petroleum, food, and national sovereignty. The 1977 announcement of Mexico's massive oil reserves created great expectations about the possibility of finally overcoming underdevelopment. In the view of both populist and liberal policymakers, however, agriculture was the oil boom's Achilles' heel, since the autonomy and foreign exchange to be gained through oil could be lost through increasing dependence on imported food. But the 1976 crisis and its aftermath had narrowed their freedom to maneuver and prevented them from making food

39. On the López Portillo administration's conflicts over economic policy between the two principal contending currents, the "nationalists" and the "liberals," see Cordera and Tello 1981; Labastida Martín del Campo 1979; Maxfield 1990; Newell and Rubio 1984; Teichman 1988; Tello 1984; and Whitehead 1980, 1981.

40. For one of the most important statements of the rationale for the 1977 Political reform see the secretary of the interior's Acapulco speech, where he said, "Today civil society must struggle to become ever more political society, and in this way prevent the state from losing contact with and imposing itself on society" (*Unomásuno*, 6-II-79). He also called for trade union autonomy as part of the political reform process, which did not win Reyes Heroles allies in the official labor movement (*Unomásuno*, 19-IV-79). He was replaced shortly thereafter, preventing the extension of the opening. On the political reform, see Fernández Christlieb 1979; Gómez Tagle 1982, 1984; González Casanova 1985; Middlebrook 1981, 1986; and Rodríguez Araujo 1981.

policy a national priority until halfway through the administration. López Portillo's initially defensive stance strengthened those policy-makers who had great faith in the dictates in international comparative advantage, advocating the exchange of oil for food.

Rural Development Policy and the 1976 Transition

The presidential transition had a decisive effect on the peasant movement. Echeverría's policy of occasionally responding with substantive concessions had greatly increased the incentive to run the risks inherent in rural collective action. In contrast, López Portillo's agrarian policy began with generous compensation for those whose land had been expropriated, and the new official rhetoric stressed the importance of bettering rural incomes instead of redistributing property. Peasant mobilizations previously considered legitimate were no longer tolerated, and many of the newly formed independent groups found their tactics were met with repression rather than negotiation.[41]

The initial political weakness of the regime permitted the conservative semiofficial media to blame worker and peasant movements, along with the past populist concessions to them, for the 1976 economic crisis. Agribusiness interests waged a massive campaign to persuade the public and the elites that the agrarian reform had failed and that the peasants and their allies within the government were the cause of Mexico's growing dependence on imported food (Gordillo and Rello 1980). As further land redistribution became politically inviable, many observers concluded that rural reform in general would be impossible, predicting that López Portillo's early support for a proposed pro-business Agricultural Development Law (Ley de Fomento Agropecuario [LFA]) would mean a reversal of agrarian reform. The compacting of inviable smallholdings and increased support for capital-intensive, export-oriented agriculture were promised as the way out of the crisis. This pro-agribusiness policy current's political base was in the operational apparatus of the government's agricultural agencies and the state governments, as well as in the business organizations of large and medium-sized commercial farmers and ranchers.[42]

---

41. On the post-1976 fall in peasant mobilization, see table 1 below and Aguado López, Torres, and Ibarra 1983, as well as Alcántara 1981; Camahji 1979; and Rubio 1987. Mobilization also declined in part because the Echeverría government had made substantive concessions to some of the most powerful movements.

42. One of the agriculture secretary's major goals, for example, was to accelerate the mechanization of Mexican agriculture with expensive imported tractors, in spite of the vast

The Agrarian Reform Ministry announced that the security of private property was a top priority and that the land reform would be finished by the end of the administration.[43]

López Portillo's early actions in the agricultural sector concentrated on administrative reform, fusing the two competing ministries that had dealt separately with irrigated and rain-fed sectors of agriculture into a single Ministry of Agriculture and Water Resources (SARH). This began a shift in the balance of bureaucratic power away from the irrigation engineers in favor of the equally technocratic agronomists (Arce 1987). The terms of trade between agriculture and industry, meanwhile, fell significantly between 1977 and 1979. The real value of the government's support prices for basic grains dropped from 85 percent of their 1960 value in 1977 to 76 percent in 1979 (DGEA 1982). From the beginning of his administration, however, López Portillo had assigned a special team of advisers the task of searching for food policy alternatives, in the presidential tradition of keeping open a wide range of options.

By 1978 the economic recovery was in full swing, and by 1979 the oil boom had taken off. The 1979 increase in the world market price of petroleum gave an added boost to expectations for Mexico's economic future. The last IMF debt installment was paid in advance, freeing economic policymakers from its oversight. Developmentalist technocrats launched ambitious plans for rapid industrialization with a new national plan in 1979, projecting sharply increased public spending to stimulate growth and employment.[44]

As economic constraints eased, the president could give greater attention to the pending legitimacy issue. The electoral system had long served to legitimate the renewal of the political elite with each presidential transition (Smith 1979). When López Portillo ran for office unopposed in 1976, however, the image of the presidency in general and the candidate in particular was damaged. As the noted intellec-

---

body of evidence showing that it would aggravate rural unemployment and sharply bias benefits toward large producers. Public criticism forced the project to be scaled back, but it still led to massive waste and corruption (*Unomásuno*, 12-I-79, 8-IV-79, 15-IV-79; Rodriguez 1980:10–11).

43. Agrarian Reform Secretary Antonio Toledo Corro raised the white flag symbolizing the end of the agrarian reform over several states. The former John Deere distributor promised his private sector allies "unlimited respect for your properties and investment" (*Unomásuno*, 28-IV-79; Bartra 1985:135; Fritscher 1985).

44. On the Mexican government's "penchant for planning" during this period, see Blair 1981. State-led "modernization" was also pursued through administrative reform (Bailey 1980, 1988; Del Carmen Prado 1984). On administrative reform in Latin America more generally, see Hammergren 1983.

tual Pablo González Casanova put it (1979:13), in 1976 "the electoral system no longer involved the choosing [*elección*] of the president."

The 1977 political reform introduced limited political party pluralism, but it became clear that increasing abstention was as much a threat as either left- or right-wing opposition party challenges, rising from a record official 38 percent in 1976 to reach 50 percent in the 1979 midterm congressional elections.[45] The president grew increasingly concerned with both increasing abstention and the rise of the Right.[46]

As oil income flowed in, social demands mounted. The official labor union leadership began to openly criticize economic policy in 1979, pushed to the left by the combination of restrictive wage policies, democratic rank-and-file mobilization, and the increased political space for independent left competitors. The PRI labor congressional delegation suggested that instead of encouraging the independent Left with the political reform, the PRI "should radicalize its [own] positions" (Casar 1982:35). Official labor leaders took much more radical positions on agrarian reform and food policy than the official peasant organizations, calling for food self-sufficiency and sparring over which group should organize farmworkers (*Unomásuno* 14, 15, 16-VII-79). Strike activity increased, and by 1980 and 1981 even the official unions rejected the government's wage ceiling, winning higher increases than planned (Bizberg 1984:173). Bizberg argues that "an unwritten pact, whereby the labor movement agreed to postpone its demands until the national economy recovered, was ended unilaterally" (183).[47] Some official peasant movement cadre members argue

45. The 1979 congressional elections were the first held under the new election rules, which were intended to increase voter participation. The right-wing National Action Party (PAN) won 11 percent and the newly legalized Communist party won 5 percent, significantly less than the record-breaking rate of abstention (*Dí*, August 1982).

46. According to presidential adviser Cassio Luiselli, López Portillo chose the 1980 package of nationalist reforms as a "political way out" (*salida*), a shift intended to restore some of the system's revolutionary luster. In this view, the president saw himself as a stabilizer, moving the country to the right after Echeverría, then compensating in the other direction when "he felt the country move to the right." He reported that the president lamented privately that "there is no social spirit; we have to shake this country up." In contrast, many of López Portillo's critics focus on his nationalist populist turn as evidence of an ego out of control, alluding to images of a high-stakes gambler (e.g., Gabriel Zaíd, cited in Newell and Rubio 1984:227). It does appear that personal prestige mattered a great deal to the president, and it accounted in part for his tendency to evade politically costly decisions by trying to be "all things to all people."

47. While the populist union leadership pushed for more of the same, liberal reformists were calling for a less top-down approach in the labor movement. Manuel Camacho, for

Table 1. Levels of peasant mobilization, 1976–1982 (yearly)

Year	Number of actions	Percentage
1976	328	14.4
1977	256	11.2
1978	272	11.9
1979	276	12.1
1980	299	13.1
1981	328	14.4
1982	521	22.9
Total	2,280	100.0

Source: Aguado López et al. 1983:50–51.

that a similar phenomenon unfolded within the CNC, that by 1979 and 1980 the leader needed to "show something" for their patience.

Even though rural social problems worsened as the decade drew to a close, the government did not face clear signs of increased peasant mobilization. In 1977 peasant mobilization had fallen sharply compared to 1976. Repression had increased dramatically, from 81 peasants reported killed in 1976 to 242 in 1977 (Alcántara 1981:70, 72). National levels of mobilization were still relatively low in 1979 and early 1980 (see tables 1 and 2). Optimistic reform advocates nevertheless contended that the SAM decision was a response to peasant demands. José Del Val (1981:173–74) was among the few contemporary observers to argue that the SAM decision was made in the context of the peasant movement's *weakness*, when most struggles were local, defensive, and isolated. Table 1 shows that aggregate national levels of mobilization did not increase significantly until *after* the SAM strategy was launched, suggesting that peasants were more willing and able to mobilize because their actual and perceived chances of winning increased after reformists gained influence at the top.

The lack of an articulated national peasant opposition or a notable increase in the numbers of mass actions does not mean that pre-SAM peasant mobilization was irrelevant to the March 1980 policy decision. The SAM decision was preceded by qualitatively important advances in the peasant movement. A massive and militant movement of indigenous peasants had successfully expelled ranchers from a vast

---

example, later to become one of the principal architects of President Salinas de Gortari's "social concertation" strategy, then argued in his classic study of the labor movement (1980:167) that "a strong nation requires a strong society."

Table 2. National press reports of peasant mobilizations (monthly), January 1979–March 1980

1979		1979		1980	
January	11	July	6	January	7
February	10	August	10	February	10
March	11	September	10	March	7
April	11	October	10		
May	9	November	9		
June	14	December	5		

Note: Table 2 shows the results of a survey of reports of peasant mobilization that appeared in five major Mexico City daily newspapers in the course of the fifteen-month period preceding the announcement of the SAM decision. "Mobilization" was defined as incidents of collective action, such as marches, blockades, land invasions, mass conferences, and public building occupations. Actions involving leadership alone, such as "denunciations" or paid newspaper announcements, were excluded from this definition. It should be noted that the national press is not a reliable source for aggregate numbers of incidents of protest; it reports only an unknown fraction of the actual number of events. The quantification of reported incidents is nevertheless useful for two reasons. First, it provides an indicator, albeit approximate, of changing *relative* levels of mobilization. Second, these Mexico City newspapers are the principal source of information about rural unrest for most national policymakers. The Ministry of Interior (Gobernación) keeps its own accounts, but its confidential reports rarely circulate among other high-level policymakers, since Gobernación is often in active political competition with other ministries, and frankness about unrest would be a sign of weakness that adversaries could turn to their advantage. As a result, changes in publicly *reported* levels of mobilization have their own political weight. This is important here because explaining national policy decisions involves dealing with *perceptions* of rural social unrest as well as estimates of actual levels.
Sources: Excelsior, El Universal, Unomásuno, El Día, Novedades.

region of the state of Hidalgo, leading to a military state of siege (Avila 1986; Schryer 1990). Among smallholders, there was a broad movement among bean producers, who pushed for higher prices and created their own autonomous group within the CNC (León 1986). The CNC's official National Council of Indigenous Peoples (CNPI) also began to gain autonomy and make its own demands.[48] Most significantly, a broad range of regional and national organizations came together at the founding meeting of the National "Plan de Ayala" Network (CNPA). What began as a defensive mobilization to block the government's proposed relocation of Zapata's remains began to put peasant demands back on the national agenda.[49]

48. For an account of one of the turning points, the CNPI's Third Congress, see *Unomásuno*, 21, 25, 27-VII-79). For overviews of Mexican indigenous peoples' movements, see Mejía Piñeros and Sarmiento Silva 1987 and Sarmiento Silva 1981. See also the alternative CNPI's documents (1982).
49. The "Plan de Ayala" refers to Zapata's call for land reform. The relocation of

Reformist policymakers may well have seen in these events the possibility that still-regional mobilizations could grow to threatening proportions, but that is quite different from defining a government decision as a *response* to movements that were strong enough, and growing fast enough, to *"require"* concessions. The SAM decision represented a victory for those within the state who advocated dealing with some of the economic causes of rural discontent, to forestall more serious political problems in the future.[50]

The Turn toward Reform

López Portillo's March 18, 1980, announcement of three major decisions was a symbolic turning point in his assimilation of the nationalist-populist approach, which would eventually culminate in the 1982 bank nationalization. Having succeeded in encouraging both private and state capital accumulation, the president focused on renewing the mass legitimacy of the political system, and his own prestige in particular.

First, he announced that Mexico had decided to withdraw from negotiations for entry into the General Agreement on Tariffs and Trade (GATT), on the grounds that it would compromise Mexico's capacity for making autonomous economic policy.

Second, he announced the famous oil *tope* (ceiling). Oil exports would increase from 1 million barrels per day to a maximum of 1.5 by 1982, after which they could increase up to 10 percent, depending on the market. This position reflected a compromise between conflicting positions within the administration, but one that favored the Secretary of Industry's position, which was widely perceived as more

---

Zapata's remains from his rural home to Mexico City symbolized urban elite domination of the peasantry. The CNPA at its founding may well have seemed to threaten broader opposition than it eventually mustered, since semiofficial and left party-linked peasant organizations quickly distanced themselves from the smaller groups of more militant agrarian radicals. During the SAM period, the CNPA won two major amnesties for political prisoners as well as regular audiences with government agencies. After leading several impressive mass mobilizations between 1981 and 1984, the CNPA was weakened by disunity and repression. Histories of the CNPA include Bartra 1985; Canabal 1983; Flores Lúa, Paré, and Sarmiento 1988; García 1989a, 1989b, 1989c, 1990; Robles and Moguel 1990; Montes 1982; Robles 1981; Rubio 1987; and the CNPA documents published in *Textual* (1980–1984). For useful case studies of CNPA members in Chiapas, an especially conflictive state, see Harvey 1989, 1990b; Moncada 1983; and Odile and Singer 1984.

50. The SAM's principal architect warned other policymakers very clearly in the course of lobbying for his proposal that the state's inattention to peasants since 1976 was favoring "a tendency that *could soon lead* to discontent and repression" (Luiselli 1980:95; emphasis added).

nationalist than the state oil company's advocacy of rapid export growth "at all costs."[51]

Third, López Portillo announced that Mexico would invest some of its oil income in the countryside to regain national food self-sufficiency. The increased international autonomy Mexico had won in the course of its economic recovery would not be compromised by increased dependence on imported food. The political impact of this reform policy package was heightened by its calculated announcement on the occasion of the forty-second anniversary of Cárdenas's nationalization of the oil industry.

The response was overwhelmingly positive across the political spectrum, ranging from many of the president's left critics, to the traditional political apparatus, to major voices in the private sector. López Portillo had previously taken the unusual step of encouraging a public debate on GATT entry, even though (or perhaps because) the majority of his cabinet appeared to support it. Organized small and medium-sized protectionist manufacturers, together with nationalist intellectuals, mobilized opinion against it, and the rejection of GATT therefore could be argued to have been a response to organized social groups.[52] Since effective public input into presidential decision making is so rare in Mexico, the GATT decision was hailed as a democratic opening to the participation of civil society in decision making.[53]

The president's image and that of the political system more generally were deeply bound to Mexican nationalism. The government had already began to pursue a much more active and autonomous foreign policy after the appointment of Foreign Secretary Jorge Castañeda in 1979, especially in Central America. The GATT and oil production

51. On oil policy, see Székely 1983 and Teichman 1988. The decision remained ambiguous, since the 10 percent margin was for post-1982 *annual* increases. Although it was not announced until several months later, the López Portillo administration was at the same time decreasing its share of oil exports to the United States. The government was also shipping oil to the new revolutionary regime in Nicaragua on very generous terms.

52. On the GATT decision, see Mares 1985 and Story 1982, 1986, among others. The decision appeared to be nationalist and ideological, but it also reinforced "the intention to place all bets on one commercially viable product for exports: oil . . . [and] hardened the conviction to support the overvaluation of the peso that had already begun to affect commercial flows in 1979" (Newell and Rubio 1984:219).

53. See Pereyra 1982:164–65. Heberto Castillo, one of the principal nationalist critics of the "petrolization" policy of oil-led growth, contended that the March 18 measures showed that, like the original oil nationalization, "organized popular criticism can show the way for the nation" (*Proceso*, 24-III-80). In an article titled "The Decisions of a Hot March," the preeminent private enterprise magazine *Expansión* held that "each of these three issues relates to the others, and together they define, in large part, the future Mexico will see in the year 2000" (16-IV-80).

decisions shifted from the 1977–79 policy of increasing exports by gradually opening the economy to an attempt to explicitly politicize foreign economic policy (Mares 1985:694). The 1979 spurt in world oil prices, the Nicaraguan revolution, and López Portillo's perception of President Carter of the United States as ineffectual combined to convince him that Mexico could exercise significantly increased international bargaining power.

The SAM strategy not only promised greater national autonomy but, as indicated below, also promised to renew the state's legitimacy in the countryside. The SAM decision had been preceded by the 1979 expansion of COPLAMAR, the National Plan for Depressed Zones and Marginal Groups, which targeted resources to meet the basic human needs of the rural poor (see chap. 6). With a new Agrarian Reform Secretary, even the land distribution process was quietly and selectively revived.[54]

The wave of nationalist and welfare-oriented measures indicates that the state was paying more attention to the need to respond to the combination of eroded mass political legitimacy and increased economic expectations driven by the oil boom.[55] This change in policy emphasis was by no means consistent, however, and did not extend to all arenas of government activity, most notably the limited electoral reform. The administration *as a whole* did not reverse direction and become wholly reformist, but the March 18, 1980, announcements constituted a shift in *net* policy emphasis.

This shift in the center of gravity within the state involved the par-

54. Nationally, the number of families receiving land in 1980 doubled compared with 1979, doubling again to 93,000 in 1981 (implying that if actually executed up to half a million people would benefit from titling). The number of "executions" of agrarian reform resolutions followed a similar pattern (according to Agrarian Reform Secretariat data cited in *Informe de Gobierno*, 1984:563). As Bartra put it (1985:140), after 1980 López Portillo decided he wanted to be seen as "the last agrarian president" rather than the first post-revolutionary "antiagrarian president." See also Fritscher 1985. In the case of the Huastecas region of Hidalgo, where repression had been particularly severe, SAM planners reported that they intervened with the Agrarian Reform Ministry and the governor on behalf of thousands of squatters seeking to legalize their de facto mass repossession of land lost to armed ranchers. It appears that partial concessions ended up dividing the Hidalgo movement, however (Avila 1986).

55. Related distributive reforms included the 1980–82 Global Development Plan, which called for state-led economic growth along with increased attention to social welfare. The ambitious "Education for Everyone" plan also promised to significantly broaden access, launched the National Institute for Adult Education, and greatly expanded bilingual education for Mexico's large indigenous population. On the latter issue, see Hernández 1979. The Social Security Institute's mass coverage of the population increased dramatically beginning in 1979 (Mesa Lago 1989). For the urban labor movement, real wages rose 2.4 percent in 1981, after an accumulated fall of 14.1 percent since 1976 (Bizberg 1984:168).

tial absorption of policy options developed by nationalists and reformists, both inside and outside the state. They had the advantage of having a project with an ideological coherence much prized by policymakers. The project found support from among the post-1968 liberal reformists as well as from the more traditional populists.[56] Yet those policies that were taken from this project were assimilated from above, without the organized popular participation in policy formulation and implementation that some of its proponents considered essential.

The Choice of the SAM Strategy

Bad weather suddenly exposed the underlying agricultural crisis to the nation. Drought cut Mexico's harvest short in 1979, so that essential grain imports had to more than double. The national transportation infrastructure was strained to the breaking point. Thousands of railroad boxcars bringing United States grain went unaccounted for (leading to a reported U.S. $100 million in late fees). Grain imports had risen from 1.4 percent of national consumption in 1970 to 10 percent in 1975 and 36 percent in 1979 (U.S. Department of Agriculture, cited in Schumacher 1981a). Mexico's image as an autonomous regional political force and a burgeoning industrial power, faced only with the problem of "administering the abundance," was seriously tarnished.

Concerned about the growing food crisis, presidential adviser Cassio Luiselli took advantage of an informal Sunday get-together to convince the president that he had a dramatic new plan to deal with Mexico's growing agricultural problems. First, it would keep agriculture from becoming a drag on the oil boom's dynamism. Second, it

56. The reform project was most coherently articulated in the influential book *La disputa por la nación*, which outlined Mexico's choice between nationalist versus internationalist market-oriented development paths (Cordera and Tello 1981). Its authors' career paths clearly chart the way policy ideas from outside dominant policy currents can be taken up by reformists within the political system. While Cordera was a respected university economist and left social democratic leader of the group of opposition deputies from the Unified Socialist party of Mexico (PSUM), Carlos Tello was a structuralist Cambridge school economist associated with the Echeverría government. A longtime close associate of López Portillo, he rose to become Mexico's first minister of Planning and the Budget when the post was created in 1977. He fell from power after losing a debate over economic crisis management, only to rise again later as the architect of the nationalization of the banks, reigning as Mexico's "superbanker" for the last three months of the López Portillo administration (see Maxfield 1990; Tello 1984).

could be combined with other policy reforms to greatly bolster the president's national and international image. The SAM was still in the idea stage in February, far from being a complete policy package, but when the president called Luiselli and his staff in and asked if they could have a policy for him right away, Luiselli, a former academic economist turned policy entrepreneur, seized the opportunity and naturally said yes.

On March 5, 1980, the president convened his cabinet to present them with the Mexican Food System strategy. He set the tone of the meeting by giving full support to the plan before his skeptical and competitive ministers had a chance to criticize it.[57] The president publicly announced the SAM strategy thirteen days later, proclaiming that domestic consumption needs, not international market forces, should determine Mexico's food policy.

Although the need to respond in some way to the growing food crisis was largely determined by pressures and possibilities created by structural factors, the SAM decision itself was brought on by political conflict between contending policy currents within the state. The SAM's diagnosis of the causes of the food crisis reflected an assimilation of key elements of the radical critique of past government bias in agricultural resource allocation, though leaving aside the more overtly conflictive problem of land tenure.[58]

The SAM's architects were strategically situated in the office of the presidency. Many were from the "generation of '68," combining nationalist liberal and technocratic tendencies. López Portillo's initial turn to the right had meant that most personal and political allies

57. His first words were: "Before soliciting your opinions, I would like to underline the importance of this joint, coordinated effort, because almost all of you present here have participated in some way. Being aware that there have been certain petty jealousies, certain attitudes that have not understood what this is all about, I would like to emphasize that since the beginning of this regime we have marked food and energy as our priorities. In the latter it is often said that the state is the producer, and has been successful at it, but it is not so in the case of food." After expounding on the importance of the SAM's "rational, logical approach," which promised to convert needs into demands and "authenticate a real alliance for production with the peasants," the president returned to the importance of a united effort. "We must make a team effort, leaving behind . . . administrative insularities and bureaucratic fiefdoms; let's try to show the people of Mexico an effort that is on the agenda and that for me is fundamental: the unmet priority, food" (transcript of president's private speech, mimeo).

58. For the official diagnosis of the agricultural crisis, see the many SAM documents published in 1980; Luiselli 1980a, 1982; and Montanari 1987. On the SAM more generally, see especially Arteaga Pérez 1985; Díaz Polanco 1981; Durston 1981; Esteva 1981, 1983a, 1987; Goodman et al. 1985; Mestries 1981; Meissner 1981; Montes de Oca and Rello 1981, 1982; *Nueva Antropología* (entire issue, May 1981); Redclift 1981c, 1984; Rello 1980, 1981a, 1981b, 1982; and Spalding 1985.

from out-of-favor policy currents were relegated to low-profile positions. The president's role, both subjectively and objectively, was to mediate between contending policy currents, yet he also intervened in this competition by allocating political resources to the contenders. Private access was one of those resources, and it could be granted to out-of-fashion reformers at no political cost.

The president's advisers' rapid transition from analysts to makers of policy was marked by a heavy dose of pragmatism. They suddenly had to choose between more versus less politically feasible policy instruments, as well as to negotiate and compromise with unsympathetic agencies and policy currents. Most notably, the actual policy package that was announced several months after the initial decision largely ignored several issues originally considered crucial by its planners, including greater control of transnationals in the food system, massive government investment in peasant-managed agroindustries, a significant conversion of potentially arable pasture to crop cultivation, extensive nutritional education, and increased participation in policymaking by small producers.[59]

Once the 1979 crop failure created the impulse to do something about food policy and the oil-debt boom provided the wherewithal, three factors converged to favor the choice of what emerged as the SAM policy package: its promise of a quick production increase; its emphasis on income distribution rather than further land reform; and its reliance largely on existing implementing agencies to carry it out.[60]

The Production Imperative

Traditional agricultural policies had clearly favored large-scale, capital-intensive, irrigated production of industrial, luxury, and export products (see chap. 4). In contrast, the central SAM policies increased grain support prices; significantly increased spending on subsidized credit, crop insurance, and agrochemicals for nonirrigated

59. Redclift (1981b, 1981c) speaks aptly of SAM "Mark I" and SAM "Mark II" to distinguish between the original diagnosis and the policy package. See also Warman 1980.
60. Secretary of Agriculture Francisco Merino Rábago's lack of a coherent alternative food policy increased the SAM strategy's prospects for approval. The secretary recognized the possibility of rural political problems. After the 1979 drought he acknowledged that "almost ten million rain-fed hectares are practically abandoned, and the lack of action in these areas could cause social unrest, which at some point could endanger everything" (*Unomásuno*, 12-VII-79). After he had adjusted to the SAM strategy, he described it as "the guarantee of continuity for the development and social peace. . . . Mexico is betting its future on the SAM" (*El Día*, 2-IV-1981).

grain producers; expanded subsidies of staple food marketing and processing; and increased urban and rural consumer food subsidies.

The promise of increased food production served the interests of a much broader range of state actors than the relatively small group of SAM policy planners. The nationalist appeal of the idea of food self-sufficiency permitted the construction of a broader coalition both inside and outside the state, based in the liberal and left intelligentsia, entrepreneurial state managers, and the official labor movement. Three factors were crucial to this alliance building.

First, Mexico's growing dependence on imported food was considered a serious problem by technocratic modernizers and state enterprise managers. The 1979 Industrial Development Plan projected that if the trends of the 1970s continued, by 1985 Mexico would be spending 50 percent of its oil income on food imports, rising to 73 percent in 1990 (cited in Luiselli 1980a:91). The growing loss of foreign exchange meant that oil income would increasingly be spent on consumption rather than investment, and the career expectations of both macroeconomic policy planners and managers of state-owned industries were tied to the state-led investment boom outlined in the national development plans of 1979 and 1980. In the view of two of SAM's principal supporters within the cabinet, the secretaries of finance and of industrial development, agriculture had become a major economic bottleneck, and increased attention to production was therefore essential (*Unomásuno*, 26–VI-80).

Second, the U.S. government's 1979 decision to embargo grain sales to the Soviet Union strongly reinforced the position of those policymakers who advocated food self-sufficiency on national security grounds. The position of those favoring comparative advantage had already been weakened by the U.S. protectionist protest against Mexican agricultural products—the "tomato war" (Mares 1987; Sanderson 1986). Not only had the United States shown that it would not hesitate to use food as a political weapon, but the Mexican press also reported that the United States had offered to trade grain for oil (e.g., *Unomásuno*, 9–VI-79). This created the impression that the United States might use its grain exports as a bargaining chip to influence oil policy, which was the linchpin of Mexico's burgeoning international economic and political power.[61] The economic efficiency gains prom-

61. The nationalist political climate even permitted the generally conservative Agriculture Ministry to try to shift the blame for the 1979 crop shortfall by suggesting that U.S. government weather manipulation may have caused the drought (*Excelsior*, 28-VI-80).

ised by reliance on international comparative advantage appeared to be more and more politically vulnerable. The SAM announcement on the anniversary of Mexico's proud 1938 nationalization of U.S. and British oil interests was directed at international as well as domestic political audiences.[62]

Third, the SAM strategy offered a fresh approach to the problem of grain production. Food self-sufficiency had been officially promoted as a national goal since 1973, but the SAM strategy promised a bold new means of achieving it (Esteva 1981, 1987). Weakened by the first two factors mentioned above, the policy current that favored reliance on capital-intensive, irrigated agribusiness had just spent the first half of the administration presiding over a worsening of the situation. With a strong base in the official agricultural apparatus and the large producers' organizations, the conservative, pro-agribusiness current at first opposed the SAM strategy, but then members realized they could gain by trying to turn it to their advantage.[63] They too had a dramatic new proposal, the Agricultural Development Law, but it did not by itself promise any quick turnaround of the production problem. The moment in the six-year presidential cycle was ripe for dramatic new initiatives, and it promised to increase production before the end of the administration, and without great political cost.

The SAM's modern cast was crucial to winning the president's full support. Its overall conceptual framework, the "systems approach" for analyzing the food chain from the production process through marketing, processing, distribution, and consumption, was based on innovative macroeconomic and management research. The initiative was bolstered by the growing power of the agronomists within the SARH, whose institutional interest was in promoting a state-administered technical solution to the problems of rain-fed agriculture.[64] Their strategy stressed increased smallholder productivity, drawing technical inspiration from the "Plan Puebla" regional experience of broadened access to credit and fertilizer use (see chap. 4). The SAM also envisioned a significant increase in the area under cultivation, based

62. A subtler aspect of the threat posed by the possible use of food as a weapon should also be noted; not only would the conditioning or withholding of food shipments have been seen as an attack on Mexico's sovereignty, but food shortages could have destabilized the leadership in power as well.

63. For example, Agrarian Reform Secretary Antonio Toledo Corro later lobbied to continue the traditional policy bias in favor of irrigated zones in the name of the SAM, announcing that "self-sufficiency in basic grains lies principally in the nation's capacity to sow basic crops in irrigated zones" (*Expansión*, 1-X-80).

64. See Arce's insightful analysis of this process (1987).

on detailed studies that documented extensive underutilization of rain-fed cropland (e.g., PRONDAAT 1976; Turrent Fernández 1987).

Income Distribution versus Agrarian Reform?

The second principal factor contributing to the SAM's political feasibility was its focus on income distribution rather than reform of rural property relations.[65] The populist, technocratic, and liberal reform currents that gained influence midway through the López Portillo administration, including the SAM planners, avoided issues of land tenure. The Echeverrista populists had been defeated ideologically in part because their collectivist attempt to update the agrarian reform project from the antifeudal struggles of the 1930s was so top-down that it resonated with the failures of state-socialist agriculture. The president had drawn his own lessons from the turbulence of the Echeverría period, privately explaining to Luiselli, "I don't want to push the agrarian issue because we'll set fire to the countryside and in the end we won't get anything done." In the context of the government's access to apparently ever-increasing oil revenue, an approach that was costly but promised to defuse significant, if primarily latent, social tensions without threatening property owners became a desirable alternative. At the same time, the technocratic agronomists had their "apolitical" solution—increased use of agrochemical inputs—under their control.

The SAM's "modern" approach also proposed the promotion of integrated agroindustries, organized according to production systems in the ejido as well as the private sector. The political and demographic constraints on further conventional land distribution pointed to the need, in the view of SAM planners, for a new vertical agrarian reform that would redistribute capital in the form of ownership of agroindustries. The government faced peasant movement pressures specifically on production issues, especially after the 1979 drought. Mobilizations increasingly focused on the state's responsibility to encourage agricultural production. Although many were still concerned with land tenure, peasant smallholders also organized for more resources and less abusive treatment from government rural develop-

65. The strategy did not involve income *redistribution* because that would have implied a zero-sum transfer of resources from one sector of the population to another. The SAM was paid for with oil and foreign debt, which complicates any analysis of the incidence of the fiscal burden.

ment agencies.[66] The veto power of large landowners and their public and private sector allies blocked the demands of the landless, but the state was much more vulnerable to the demands of mobilized small producers. The state depended on its strategic political alliance with the 2.8 million families to whom it had granted land-use rights. The SAM's production incentives promised at least a partial response to many producer demands. In this context, early versions not only explicitly called for "increasing the bargaining power of peasant producers"[67] but even proposed an "alliance" with farmworker unions (Luiselli 1980a:95–101).[68]

The SAM stressed that national production policy should be determined by consumption needs. SAM analysts estimated the number of seriously malnourished people at nineteen million, two-thirds of them in the countryside. Hunger was seen as caused by uneven income distribution; the issue was therefore one of increasing the "effective demand" of the malnourished as consumers. Consumption by smallholders could be increased by supporting their capacity to produce. For those who lacked sufficient land even for subsistence, the answer was to be subsidized access to a "basic market basket" of essential foods.

While reformist policymakers saw the SAM as pushing the limits of the politically possible, their conservative competitors within the state, in alliance with large private farmers and ranchers, pursued their own political project, the Agricultural Development Law (LFA). The LFA provoked one of the most important legislative conflicts of López Portillo's administration.

The law was initially proposed by private agribusiness but was significantly modified to represent the long-standing "statizing" project of the SARH. Both saw security for private property and corresponding increased private investment as the answer to Mexico's agricultural problems, but the final version of the law also gave the SARH itself vastly expanded new powers, such as greater capacity to determine land-use patterns (LFA, section 5; Rello 1981b). The law

---

66. Bartra 1991; Fox and Gordillo 1989; Fox 1992; García 1989; Harvey 1989, 1990b; and Hernández 1989b, 1990c discuss this issue further.

67. In this area the SAM found some allies in one of the few relatively pro-peasant enclaves within the SARH, the Department of Producer Organization (Rello 1981b). For a microanalysis of the dynamics within this enclave, see Arce 1987.

68. This latter point was especially radical, given the state's rigid intolerance even for collective bargaining in agriculture—it dropped out quickly. On the economic and political situation of farmworkers, see among others De Grammont 1986; López Monjardin 1987, 1991; Nagengast and Kearney 1990; Paré 1977; and Wright 1990.

set the legal framework for the SAM policy package, including the SARH's rain-fed districts and the "shared risk" crop insurance plan.[69] The Left opposed the law primarily because it legalized joint ventures between private capital and ejidos. Ejidos would contribute their land and labor, while private entrepreneurs would invest their land and capital, legitimizing the hitherto illegal but widespread practice of renting ejido land. The leadership of the new production units would be chosen by votes weighed by property, not by individual membership.

The LFA project united two distinct sets of interests, conservative state developmentalists who saw their task as one of "planning" production, with antiejido private sector ideologues and agribusiness interests. The law promoted a de facto division of decision making whereby private agribusiness could consolidate its control over irrigated land and the SARH would increase its powers over dryland producers (Rello 1981b). Through its new rain-fed districts, the SARH's agroclimatic calculations would be the basis for telling peasants what they should grow and how (Arce 1987).

In retrospect, the LFA served as a symbolic promise not to touch property relations more than it presaged a rollback of the land reform. It ratified the unequal status quo in land tenure, in contrast to the SAM's pro-peasant, antiagribusiness ideology. The LFA's regulations, which determined how it would be implemented, made joint ventures difficult to establish.[70] Apparently mere "bureaucratic" obstacles turned out to have, as they usually do, much more political content.[71] Perhaps most important, an ejido could form joint ventures

---

69. Independent peasant organizations and leftist intellectuals were among the first to oppose the proposed law, but the official PRI labor union congressional delegation also came out strongly in opposition at first. See their major manifesto titled "The Association between Ejidatarios and Private Landowners Risks Reviving Latifundismo" (*El Día,* 11-XII-80; also in *Nueva Antropología,* May 1981). The law was nevertheless approved in December 1980 with the support of the CNC (*Unomásuno,* 11-XII-80). On the LFA debate see also Del Val 1981; Díaz Polanco 1981; Fritscher 1985; Gómez Tagle 1981; Ibarra Mendivil 1989; and Rello 1981b.

70. Few of the much-discussed joint ventures were ever actually formed. The first production unit formed under the LFA was found three years afterward to be in corrupt disarray, as a result of top-down imposition for public relations purposes (*Unomásuno,* 31-V-84).

71. From Cassio Luiselli's point of view, the "rival" LFA "had one dynamic and the SAM had another. The president never thought they would find such contradictory responses in society and politics. He said he didn't see a contradictory relationship between the two if we drew up the regulations well, to unite authentic small proprietors and ejidatarios, to prevent the big fish from swallowing the small one. We made up the regulations and the thing didn't move from there. In the best of cases, not much happened with

only as a group, by a vote of two-thirds of its members (the original proposal had allowed subgroups to join). The regulations appear to have been the result of a compromise the president imposed on contending policy currents. Although the reformists in the SAM and COPLAMAR opposed the law in private, once it was on the president's public agenda, with the full support of the secretaries of agriculture and of agrarian reform, they lacked the power to block it. Yet after they lost that battle, SAM and COPLAMAR planners were invited to participate in drawing up the regulations that would shape the effect of the law in practice.[72]

Because of the closed nature of Mexican policy debates and intrastate struggles, policymakers presented a common front at the time, and the law's opponents on the inside could not attack the LFA once it had the president's full support.[73] This did not mean, however, that the LFA and the SAM were part of the same political project. For the LFA and the SARH, peasants were at best junior partners, whereas the SAM's discourse held them up as the principal protagonists in food production (Fritscher 1985:73). In retrospect, they represented

---

the law. Few production units were created, and they were very artificial." Private sector LFA sympathizers confirmed that the law's operational mechanisms made joint ventures very difficult, particularly since long-term investment projects were blocked.

72. An internal SAM document details the differences between the SARH's LFA proposal and a version of the law that was considered acceptable to SAM planners. The SAM planners' most important disagreements were with SARH measures that would: permit joint ventures to be formed with noncontiguous production units; allocate voting rights by economic weight rather than individual membership; allow joint ventures between state enterprises and private producers; and allow ranchers to sow grain on land legally considered pasture. With this proposal, large ranchers and their allies within the SARH and among state governors tried to turn the SAM's attempted pro-grain approach to their advantage. Many large ranches would legally be subject to redistribution if they admitted including cropland suitable for farming; the LFA provision appeared to free illegal estates from size ceilings if they grew crops on some of the land. In Chiapas, ranchers won the right to sow up to 20 percent of their land with grain (Rutsch 1981). The SAM diagnosis had highlighted ranchers' control of vast expanses of tropical cropland, and this measure legitimated its continued waste. SAM planners privately advocated the redistribution of this grossly underused cropland, but the governors and the rancher interests of Chiapas and Veracruz were far too powerful. Redclift (1981b) highlighted this problem early on.

73. The conflict between different policy currents was so intense that one of the most powerful proponents of the law, the new Agrarian Reform Secretary, García Paniagua, even made serious threats against LFA opponents at the highest levels. At the height of the SAM's prestige he publicly supported it in part because of the "social peace" argument: "We want Mexico to be at peace forever, and if we want to preserve it, we cannot forget that if the abundance belongs to a few, then the many will want to take it away from them" (*Proceso*, 4-VIII-80). A rigid corporatist, García Paniagua reportedly forced one of the few LFA opponents in the CNC, reformist Beatriz Paredes (later governor of Tlaxcala), to publicly retract her criticisms.

competing policy currents, and the president's compromise allowed each to try to block elements of the other's project.[74]

The priority for the SAM planners was political viability. In their focus on income rather than property, access to generous producer subsidies was in practice limited almost exclusively by crop rather than by size or type of producer. Chapter 4 documents this point in detail. This something-for-everyone approach resulted from the combination of the well-organized veto power of private agricultural capital and its allied policy currents with the need to encourage commercial as well as peasant producers to sow basic grains quickly.

More Money, Same Structure of State Intervention

The third factor that converged to favor the adoption of the SAM strategy was its reliance on existing state agencies to carry it out. Yet SAM planners had no formal authority over this inherited apparatus. With less than three years remaining in the presidential term, food policy reformers lacked the time and the political resources to build effective alternative operational mechanisms. Those policy areas where they did so were notable exceptions and did not involve displacing an existing government agency (Austin and Fox 1987). The SAM, with its high profile and presidential blessing, was already perceived as a threatening bureaucratic competitor, not only by the SARH and its agencies but also by the head of the Planning and Budget Ministry (SPP), Miguel de la Madrid.[75] The SAM planners felt they had to move quickly into the political space briefly opened up by access to the president's policy agenda in early 1980 while making as few powerful enemies as possible.

74. Many independent peasant organizations and left intellectuals charged that the SAM strategy was only a cover for channeling subsidies to large producers and undermining prospects for further land reform. They therefore saw the LFA and the SAM as complementary rather than contradictory—"two sides of the same coin" (e.g., CNPA in *Proceso*, (14-IV-80). SAM planners did little to dispel this impression with their recommendations regarding sub-subsistence producers, which they defined as those with less than two hectares of low-quality rain-fed land. They explicitly recommended "compacting areas so that some of them could become viable producers, while the rest would be subjects of employment and consumer subsidy policies" (SAM 1980b, para. 60). How this displacement would be carried out was far from clear, but the LFA was much more anti-*minifundio*, calling for private plots under five *irrigated* hectares (or the equivalent) to be "in the public interest" (i.e., subject to expropriation) (LFA, arts. 63–70). Although nothing so ambitious as the "compacting" of sub-subsistence producers was actually attempted by the state, they were largely bypassed by the producer incentives (see chap. 4).

75. The SPP was responsible for the Global Development Plan, and the SAM's multisectoral plan for the food system was perceived as an imposition. Note the president's language in his March 5, 1980, cabinet meeting cited above.

If the SAM planners wanted the strategy to have a truly national impact in the short term, they had to deal with the existing food system establishment. The implementing agencies for credit, crop insurance, technical assistance, seed, fertilizer, grain marketing, processing, and distribution policy were already a powerful presence in the countryside. These agencies had been increasing their role in the food system for decades, and their mission was to control agricultural decision making (Arce 1987). They soon realized that the new strategy meant more resources for them, while the SAM reformists would be unable to challenge their control over how food policy was actually carried out. In any case, the SAM strategy was a presidential priority, which ruled out overt opposition. The agencies were ready and able to introduce the production incentives essential for progress toward the national self-sufficiency goals required for economic and political success.

The SAM strategy promised not only to increase production, but to revitalize the historic state-peasant alliance as well. Given the time pressure, the main national alternative to the existing agricultural agencies was the PRI's corporatist peasant organizations. Limited to electoral patronage and agrarian affairs, they had shown little capacity to manage or promote production efforts effectively, however. Since the official peasant groups were increasingly unrepresentative in much of the country and were unable to offer a project to revitalize their own organizations, not to mention grain production, SAM planners saw them as largely irrelevant (Luiselli 1980a:95). The official peasant organizations failed to take advantage of the SAM decision as a political opportunity for their own revitalization, and at most they saw the SAM as a new flag to wave over their traditional activities.[76] SAM planners were willing to deal directly with more autonomous producers' organizations, but at that time only a handful were sufficiently consolidated to carry out development projects beyond the community level. SAM policymakers therefore generally bypassed the offical peasant organizations and relied on state enterprises in their attempt to deliver productive resources to previously ignored peasant producers.

Conclusions

The SAM initiative emerged as part of a broader presidential project to revitalize the state's political legitimacy, in spite of widespread

---

76. According to Luiselli, the leader of the CNC at the time "didn't understand, didn't want to understand, and it didn't matter to him to understand. He was content with the rituals. This did great damage because it removed the SAM's capacity to mobilize through the CNC."

post-1976 predictions that the state had definitely lost its capacity for reform. The state's official self-image of the time is instructive: "The Mexican state has a mass base because of its economic and social powers. It is a strong state that directs, coordinates, and guides, not like a cork that floats among opposing and contradictory currents, the indecisive object of pressures" (Federal Election Commission 1979; cited in Gómez Tagle 1982:238).[77] In other words, both autonomy and capacity matter, at least for official discourse.

Some food-policy analysts see the Mexican state as growing ever weaker over time, under inexorable pressure from the long-term secular trends toward the internationalization of the Mexican economy (Barkin 1990; Sanderson 1986). This book recognizes the power of these external pressures but asks different questions about Mexican state action. The "internationalization of capital" approach to Mexican agriculture helps to explain the predominant "more of the same" policy outcomes but does not account for important exceptions. As I will argue, those exceptions can convey important lessons about future possibilities for policy reform. The internationalization approach, an extreme example of a society-driven explanation of state action, is unable to account for precisely how, why, when, or to what degree state actors *do* actively intervene in key markets.[78] The SAM's vulnerability to the 1982 economic crisis has been widely noted, which

77. As Luiselli put it, "The idea of the [presidential] project, a project that failed in the end, was to modernize; to modernize politics through pluralism and the political reform, to modernize through the administrative reform, and through those first efforts to bring petroleum wealth to the marginal groups, to broaden the social base of the state's legitimacy."

78. Both Barkin and Sanderson recognize that the SAM strategy was an exception to the dominant pattern. Barkin (1990:13, 36, 136) sees the effort as an important example of a "food first" strategy that could have worked much better had it had political support and been seriously carried out. But neither explains the degree—albeit limited—to which SAM did differ from conventional policy in practice, or why it went further in some areas than others. Sanderson (1986:260–62) acknowledges many of the institutional obstacles detailed in this book, but he also gives much more emphasis to the continuing powerful influence of export agribusiness over basic grain policy. He does not fully explain why these constraints were partially overcome in certain key policy areas, however. Crop support prices, import restrictions, and consumer subsidies are hardly the most targeted of policy instruments, as will be discussed in the following chapters, but in the case of maize they did manage to insulate a major part of the rural economy from international markets. For example, only a relatively autonomous state could set a domestic crop support price for maize at more than twice the international price in 1980 and 1981 (calculated in Goicoechea 1990). Moreover, the SAM's key economic weakness was not its unwillingness to attack export-oriented agribusiness, since Mexico could have become self-sufficient in basic grains *without displacing export-oriented irrigated agriculture at all* (Barkin 1990:122–23; Turrent Fernández 1987: 308). Barkin (1990:123) further stresses that grain production in irrigation districts is the direct result of inefficient water subsidies and recommends that these lands be shifted to higher-value export production.

reinforces arguments that stress the determinative weight of external constraints. We should not forget, however, that the internationalization of the economy through high oil prices and low real interest rates greatly *increased* state autonomy from 1978 to 1981. One of the most interesting questions is how state actors decided to exercise their relative freedom from conventional international and fiscal constraints when they had the chance. While most discussions of the SAM highlight its many built-in economic weaknesses, this book stresses how political initiatives and institutional inertia interacted *before* the structural constraints closed in.

The SAM's initial goal was "to alter (if not reverse) the transfer mechanisms that decapitalize the [agricultural] sector, and for the state to establish targeted subsidies and policies that favor the most backward groups and regions" (Luiselli 1980a:94). The presidential decision alone was far from sufficient to restructure resource allocation in practice, however. The availability of resources, combined with political constraints, encouraged the choice of a positive-sum, generalized subsidy approach, and the presidential cycle built in irresistible pressures for immediate production results. Competing policy currents were then able to defeat much of the SAM's reformist intent in the course of policy implementation.

The SAM's top-down origins fundamentally limited the possibilities for distributive reform. In Luiselli's words, the strategy was "from the drawing board, from above, and that was its original sin."[79] Since the policy shift was not a reflection of the articulated demands and mobilized power of those previously excluded from the benefits of food policy, it was unlikely that they would receive a much larger share of SAM-period food policy resources. The SAM's capacity to carry out its reform project depended largely on the peasant movement's capacity to push the policy opening further, yet it was launched following three years of underrepresentation of the peasant movement. The reform's limits, in both design and implementation, reflected the political weakness of the social forces that were supposed to benefit, which in turn limited the influence of the reformist policy current within the state.

Thus an interactive analysis that "unpacks" both state and society allows us to capture the dynamic and relational character of state

79. Quoted in Fox and Marsh 1986. As Rello also observed at the time (1981b:14), the SAM's "Achilles' heel is that it was born as a state project, and it is not being converted into a peasant project before the enemies of the peasantry take it over and distort it."

capacities for reform. The strengths or weaknesses of pro-reform forces both inside and outside the state are shaped by their strategic interaction with each other and with their adversaries. In the case of at least one significant SAM-period food policy, however, the dynamic interaction between reformists and emerging social forces was nevertheless able to pry open new policy space and to push back the inherited constraints on the politically possible. The chapters that follow analyze the conditions under which the reformist thrust was carried through—given that it usually was not.[80]

80. Few policy analysts publicly recognized that the SAM's impact was not inevitably predetermined. In addition to Esteva 1981 and Rello 1981b, Huacuja was an important exception, contending early on that "while the limits of its time span may be set by the coming change of presidential administration, its achievements, results, or failures will be able to be measured only by its instrumentation and by the way peasant organizations respond to its call. *The only certainty is that the project has unleashed a new struggle over the agricultural surplus in rural Mexico*" (emphasis added; Huacuja 1980:39).

4

Implementing Food Policy: Interests and Inertia

Most SAM programs turned out to be more of the same. State agencies did extend some services to previously excluded peasants, but they also continued to deliver most of their resources to traditionally favored agroexport, urban, and bureaucratic interests. The SAM began to carry out a distributive reform, but without redistribution. Most important for the future, the *process* of state resource allocation remained largely unchanged—quite compatible with rural elites and largely closed to peasant participation.

Why was the apparently pro-peasant food reform strategy so difficult to put into practice? This chapter begins with an analysis of the political context of policy implementation, framed in terms of the incentive structures faced by agencies involved in the food system. The discussion then turns to the three categories of programs that formed the core of the SAM strategy: first, subsidies for producer *inputs*, aimed at increasing grain yields in nonirrigated areas; second, higher government producer *prices* meant to increase the area sown and the amount of grain marketed, together with a marketing support program aimed at improving effective access to these support prices; and third, subsidized retail food *distribution* programs, directed at providing a "basic market basket" of essential foods to the urban and rural poor. The conclusion evaluates which groups benefited from the SAM and why.

This chapter argues that the SAM strategists' limited leverage over the implementing apparatus prevented them from altering the incentive structures most state agencies faced, and hence from changing the power dynamics of the resource allocation process "on the ground." Food policy reformers' leverage was limited because most agencies carrying out agricultural policy continued to be dominated by policy currents that favored "production first" rather than "pro-peasant" strategies. As one nongovernmental rural development organization put it at the time: "Who was left in charge of the SAM? Here comes the big 'but.' The institutions that deal with the peasants continue to be the same ones that for years have shown their incompetence and corruption. . . . The president's advisers launched a gigantic program (SAM) without taking into account that many of the enemies of their 'good intentions' are inside the bureaucracy" (IMISAC 1981:32).

The SAM decision was made with full presidential backing, but at the crest of his six-year term; there was too little time left for the SAM strategists to try to take over the massive and complex agricultural apparatus. The producer incentive programs were based on a positive-sum approach: they extended benefits to potentially surplus-producing peasants as long as the oil-debt boom permitted a massive increase in the total resources dedicated to agriculture. Only two little-known but relatively large-scale grain marketing programs explicitly attempted to shift the rural balance of power by increasing the economic bargaining power of rural producers and consumers relative to powerful intermediaries, and they are analyzed in detail in the two chapters that follow.

The mixed results of food policy implementation reflect the broader tension within the Mexican state between accumulation and legitimation priorities. The "production first" policy current pursued the accumulation of both private capital and "public" power over agriculture, while the "pro-peasant" policy current stressed the importance of pursuing more nationalist economic goals through means that broadened the state's political base at the same time. As discussed in the previous chapter, the uneven contest between these contending policy currents within the state was reinforced by the imbalance between their allies within civil society. Yet some of the struggles unleashed by the reform initiative led to important changes in the terms of this conflict.

The Political Context of Policy Implementation

Although the decision to pursue self-sufficiency in basic grain production was made at the presidential and cabinet levels, most SAM programs were carried out by well-established, relatively autonomous state agencies. The SAM strategy was thus based on the assumption that key agencies and enterprises could reverse a long-standing policy bias favoring commercial, irrigated agriculture over rain-fed peasant production. The prospects for reform implementation would depend largely on policymakers' capacity to change the incentive structures that conditioned bureaucratic behavior.[1] The behavior of most state agencies was consistent with "rent-seeking" arguments as they sought to increase their own resources and power, but their motivations were more complex, and the exceptions do not fit.[2] The challenge is to develop an approach that can account for both continued elite bias and those exceptions that mattered.

The SAM planners explicitly recognized and attempted to reverse the negative *consequences* of the dominant model of development for peasant agriculture. Their attention, however, was focused more on macroeconomic resource flows than on the resource delivery process itself and the discretionary power of bureaucrats.[3] Having promoted large-scale, irrigated production of luxury and export crops for decades, existing agencies and enterprises were limited as possible vehicles for changing the dominant thrust of state agricultural policy in favor of rain-fed peasant agriculture by two interrelated factors: the development agencies' systematic linkages with private rural elites and institutionally embedded technological and class biases.

Development Agency Biases

State agricultural development agencies first grew to national importance as part of the 1934–40 agrarian reform. Ejidos were then new and fragile, and most reformists felt they needed firm state guidance. Even when reformists dominated national policy-making during

---

1. As Heaver points out in his World Bank study of the politics of the implementation of rural development projects (1982:iv–v), "New programs and projects must take into account bureaucratic politics, and provide an incentive, in terms of perceived personal advantage, for the bureaucrats [involved] at each level. . . . [B]ureaucrats, like peasants, are rational. It is not often that ignorance and apathy are determinants of behavior, but that existing incentive systems make it in officials' rational self-interest to be apathetic in pursuit of development goals." Although the interpretation offered here found that the dominant incentives encouraged a perpetuation of the causes of underdevelopment rather than mere "apathy," close attention to the incentive structures each actor faces is crucial.

2. See Grindle's (1991) discussion of these limitations to the "rent-seeking" literature.

3. See Lipsky (1980) on the influence of "street corner bureaucrats" over distributive policies. On the power of policy implementers more generally, see Grindle 1980 and Grindle and Thomas 1989.

the Cárdenas presidency, their power was insufficient to guarantee that ostensibly pro-ejido development agencies would act in their interests. Pressure from above was needed, along with pressure from below, to curb corruption and abuses of power.[4] After the conservative shift within the state in 1940, however, agrarian reform beneficiaries lost most of their national allies, leading to the consolidation of pervasive alliances between public and private sector elites at regional and local levels.[5] The new national policy bias in favor of private agriculture was reinforced by the unchecked interpenetration of anti-peasant interests throughout the state apparatus.

"Developmentalist" state interventions that favored the growth of capital-intensive commercial agriculture led to the consolidation of a powerful constituency in favor of that policy, which restricted the state's capacity to act when later confronted with some of the social and economic results.[6] In order to expand agricultural production in support of urban industrialization, state intervention widened the gap between large and small producers. As a result, increasingly organized and assertive entrepreneurial producers developed the autonomy and the capacity to block or co-opt most subsequent reform initiatives. The state was not simply a monolithic entity that lost bargaining power in relation to the growing power and consciousness of commercial producers, however. A "single-actor" view of the state does not fit the Mexican experience, for two reasons. First, a shift in the balance of forces *within* the state preceded its key role in modernizing traditional elites and creating new ones. Second, this shift encouraged agricultural entrepreneurs and intermediaries not simply to constrain

4. Simpson (1937:348–54) details the influence of local landlords, opportunistic new elites, and the pervasive corruption of local and national agrarian reform officials. Even Weyl and Weyl's highly optimistic account (1939) offers similar evidence. As North and Raby conclude (1977:38), the Cárdenas government "found it impossible to even maintain discipline among those entrusted with carrying out the most fundamental aspects of its program [such as agrarian reform]." Rello (1987:47) notes that even the most organized peasants were only temporarily able to curb the Ejidal Bank's "tendency towards bureaucratization and authoritarianism." Cárdenas appears to have been aware of the problem, declaring that worker and peasant organization was "indispensable for the enforcement of the country's laws" (cited in North and Raby 1977). He also supported radical rural teachers to offset the power of conservative officials and landlords at the local level (dozens of teachers were assassinated). This effort to provide federal allies for peasant organizing against corruption within the state itself was an important precursor of the "sandwich strategy" detailed in chapter 6.

5. For an extreme example, note the experience of the collective ejidos in the Yucatán; see Brannon and Baklanoff 1987.

6. Grindle's comprehensive comparison of Mexico, Colombia, and Brazil (1986) indicates that this was a common pattern in Latin America.

the state apparatus, but to penetrate it as well. The explanation of antipeasant policy bias thus involved both state and societal factors.

Within the state, the counterreform of the 1940s also strengthened those agencies that defined their institutional missions in terms of the rapid promotion of large-scale, capital-intensive private agriculture. The post-1940 political subordination of the reformist policy current within the state led to a technological turning point as well, defeating those scientists and engineers involved in developing agricultural technologies more appropriate for peasant producers.[7]

The staffs of the production-oriented agencies were then trained in technologies that were appropriate and profitable only for large-scale enterprises or under irrigated conditions. By 1980 their long-standing technological biases left them unprepared to encourage rain-fed peasant production even had they wanted to. The lack of ready and reliable appropriate technologies, as well as the historical lack of investment in rain-fed agriculture, meant that the SAM's emphasis on short-run harvest increases encouraged production agencies to rely on their traditional clientele, the large-scale, often irrigated farmers.

The technological bias against peasant agriculture was compounded by a class bias in the social composition of agency staff. Because they lacked access to higher education, few peasants, and even fewer indigenous people, achieved mobility within the state apparatus. As a result, most of the strategic agency operational staff tended to come from provincial middle- or upper-class backgrounds, often related to traditional landowners and caciques. The most influential agency personnel also often shared the widespread and powerful middle- and upper-class prejudices against peasants in general and indigenous people in particular.[8]

The integration of public and private rural elites often shaped the impact of rural development policy at the regional level, where agribusiness, ranching, and commercial interests wielded powerful positive and negative incentives that influenced the activities of federal agencies as well as local and state governments.[9] Through both elec-

7. On the crucial issues of public investment in infrastructure (irrigation) and applied research, most notably on seeds (improved maize versus hybrid wheat), see Barkin and Suárez 1985 and Hewitt de Alcántara 1976. For an example of the research tradition that was marginalized, see Hernández Xolocotzi 1988.

8. As much as a quarter of the rural population is at a sharp disadvantage in communicating with government officials, virtually none of whom speak indigenous languages. At least 10 percent of the total Mexican population do not speak Spanish as a first language.

9. This pattern contrasts sharply with the national political class, which was quite socially distinct from the private sector (at least until the late 1980s). See Smith 1979.

toral and nonelectoral channels, regional elites actively participated in making personnel decisions for most federal agencies in the provinces, often with state governors on their side. The job security of agency staff members often depended, therefore, on their continuing support for antipeasant policies.[10]

In areas where peasant organizations were weak or unrepresentative, there was no effective counterweight to pressure state agencies and enterprises to reduce bias and corruption in carrying out policy. Electoral competition was rarely a viable means for holding officials accountable. Faced with the powerful political and economic incentives wielded by rural elites, implementing agencies had little reason to modify their long-standing production and politics-first priorities. Clientelistic benefits reached some peasants, but rarely the kind of support for rain-fed smallholders that would permit them to invest to increase their productive capacity or to increase their bargaining power in often oligopolistic markets. The principal development agencies also lacked incentives to encourage the development of community-managed economic enterprises, since such organizations could well generate pressures to allocate resources more equitably, honestly, and efficiently. The following review shows that most SAM producer and consumer programs left longtime agricultural agency resource allocation priorities and processes undisturbed.[11]

The SAM in Practice: An Overview of Agency Activities

The SAM planners viewed Mexico's food problems through the lens of an integrated food systems approach: their diagnosis and policy recommendations were based on a conceptual framework that un-

10. Interviews with policymakers about anticorruption efforts in the government agricultural bank, for example, reveal how far rural elites have penetrated the state apparatus at the local and regional level. In theory, the regular rotation of regional bank managers was to have lessened the managers' opportunities to develop local allegiances that might have interfered with the equitable implementation of policy. When these managers arrived at their new assignments, however, they often relied on nonrotating second- and third-level officials whose assistance was necessary to the bank's functioning, and hence to the career of the new manager. These local agency officials were frequently key actors in the local power structure, however, and they traded their knowledge and contacts for policy influence. As a result there was a great deal of continuity in policy bias, regardless of the rotation of the top managers.

11. The analysis that follows is limited to staple foods, particularly maize and beans, but the state role in many key industrial and export crops was at least as large (especially coffee, sugar, tobacco, fibers, and forest products). Vegetables and most fruits were the exception, with the state role limited primarily to providing subsidized irrigation and credit.

Table 3. Grain system-related market shares of state-owned enterprises (SOEs) as of 1979

Activity	SOE	Share
Inputs		
Credit	BANRURAL, FIRA	SOE share of formal agricultural credit—75.4%. BANRURAL share of total—52%. FIRA share of private credit—48.6%.[1] BANRURAL share of area harvested—27.4%.[2] Maize share of BANRURAL area harvested—43%.[3]
Agrochemicals	FERTIMEX	Share of fertilizer production—100%. Share of imports—100%. Import share of national consumption—20%.[4] Distribution through SOEs—53%.[5] #1 national insecticide producer, #2 herbicide producer.
Seeds	PRONASE	Share of certified maize and bean seed production—90%. Certified wheat—43%. Certified Sorghum—10%.[6]
Tractors	SIDENA, FTA	SIDENA-Ford market share—30%.[7]
Crop insurance	ANAGSA	Share of basic grain area insured—49%.
Technical assistance	SARH, BANRURAL, FIRA, CONASUPO	Share of area sown with maize covered—48%.[8]
Direct Production		
Grains	PRONAGRA	Share of national rice production—6%.[9]
Commercialization		
Procurement	CONASUPO	SOE share purchased of national maize production sold—23.1%. SOE share of maize demand—33.1%. SOE share of grain imports—100%. Import share of national maize consumption—9.8%.[10]
Warehousing	ANDSA, BORUCONSA (CONASUPO)	CONASUPO share of national warehouse capacity—40%.[11] ANDSA share of CONASUPO capacity—68%.[12] BORUCONSA share of national CONASUPO maize purchases—73%.[13] Share of BORUCONSA maize received with PACE transportation subsidy—19.8% (1978–1979).[14]
Wholesaling	IMPECSA (CONASUPO)	SOE coverage of national food retailers—15.8%.[15]
Retailing	DICONSA (CONASUPO)	SOE share of national retail market for basic consumer goods—9%. Coverage: 7,500 towns, 25 million consumers.[16] Rural share of number of DICONSA outlets—71.7%.[17]
Processing		
Grains, oilseeds	ICONSA (CONASUPO)	SOE share of national oilseed milling capacity—10.5%. SOE share of vegetable fat production—10%. SOE share of wheat milling—7.4%.[18] ICONSA share of basic food product market (Alianza brand)—6%.[19]
Maize	MINSA (CONSUPO)	SOE share of maize flour production—27%.[20]

Table 3. Continued.

Activity	SOE	Share
Bread	TRICONSA (CONASUPO)	SOE share of Mexico City bread production—40%.[21]
Milk	LICONSA (CONASUPO)	SOE share of national milk production—17%. Share of imports—100%. Import share of national consumption—11.8%.[22]
Animal feed	ALBAMEX	SOE share of mixed feed market—6% (fourth largest producer).
Formulated foods	NUTRIMEX	No data.

Sources: Austin and Fox 1987:63–64.   [1]Patron Guerra and Fuentes Navarro 1982.   [2]SARH 1982b.   [3]*Informe de Gobierno* 1981.   [4]Based on FERTIMEX data.   [5]FERTIMEX 1980.   [6]SARH 1981.   [7]*AMIA Boletin,* January 1981.   [8]*Informe de Gobierno* 1981.   [9]Cabrera Morales 1982; *Informe de Gobierno* 1982.   [10]CONASUPO 1982a.   [11]CONASUPO 1980.   [12]SPP 1981.   [13]CONASUPO 1982a; *Informe de Gobierno* 1981.   [14]Rubio Canales 1982.   [15]CONASUPO, *Sistema C,* November–December 1981.   [16]CONASUPO, 1980.   [17]*Informe de Gobierno* 1981.   [18]CONASUPO 1982a.   [19]*Sistema C,* May 1982.   [20]CONASUPO 1982a.   [21]*Sistema C,* March 1982.   [22]Santoyo Meza and Urquiaga 1982.

derstood access to agricultural inputs, food production, marketing, processing, and distribution as part of a single system. Based on this approach, they identified key points at which the state could and should intervene to achieve self-sufficiency in basic grains. As indicated in table 3, the Mexican government was active in almost all stages of the grain system, with the exception of direct production. Although the SAM affected all the agencies involved in the grain system, this discussion focuses only on the enterprises of national scope directly involved in the rural development process.[12]

12. A state enterprise is an agency that engages in economic activities and often enjoys relatively great autonomy from the rest of the state apparatus. The Mexican government's use of state enterprises as policy instruments increased dramatically during the 1970s and early 1980s (Barenstein 1982). The number of federal and state-level state enterprises grew from 96 in 1970 to 966 in 1982 (excluding the banks and their properties, which were nationalized in that year). Almost one-third of these enterprises were involved in the food system (*Mercado de Valores,* September 13, 20, 1982). The food system is defined as encompassing the broad range of productive activities and inputs needed to produce and transform food and transport it to the final point of consumption. The literature on state-owned enterprises has tended to divide enterprises into traditional sectoral categories, such as agriculture, manufacturing, and commerce. This segmented approach is inadequate for analyzing food policy implementation, which, explicitly or implicitly, involves action (or inaction) across sectoral categories (Austin 1984). For more detail on all the state enterprises involved in the grain system, see Fox 1986 and Austin and Fox 1987.

Production Input Subsidies

The core of the SAM strategy consisted of production incentive programs aimed at producers in between those commercial farmers who already benefited from agricultural policy and the huge number of sub-subsistence peasants who were unable to produce a surplus for the national market, at least in the short run. Following the U.N. commission CEPAL's typology of Mexican agricultural producers, these in-between groups were "surplus-producing peasants" and "transitional smallholders," together accounting for 20 percent of total producers and nearly 50 percent of Mexico's arable land (CEPAL 1982).[13] Both groups tended to produce maize surpluses, responding to producer price incentives on a scale that affected national grain markets.[14] Because a significant number of these producers had not previously had access to government production services, they were considered an ideal target group for the SAM incentives aimed at increasing the amounts of grain produced and marketed. While greater access to agricultural inputs would increase their productivity

13. The study by CEPAL (CEPAL 1982) thoroughly revised the 1970 agricultural census data in terms of Chayanovian class categories, and it remains the best national classification of Mexican agricultural producers. "Peasants" are defined as producers who employ less than twenty-five wage-days of labor annually; the class fractions of the peasantry include sub-subsistence, subsistence, stable (*estacionario*), and surplus-producing (*excedentario*). The peasantry as a whole accounted for 86.6 percent of total producers, with 57 percent of the CEPAL's standardized unit of arable land. More than half of all producers, 56 percent, were sub-subsistence peasants who had to complement their meager harvest with wage labor, usually through migration, in order to survive. Surplus-producing peasants were defined as those who had more than twelve standardized hectares of rain-fed land; this group accounts for 8 percent of all producers and 22 percent of arable land. "Transitional" producers were not considered peasants because they employed between twenty-five and five hundred wage-days of labor annually. They still relied primarily on unpaid family labor, however, and therefore were not clearly capitalists either. Capitalist producers, 2 percent of the total, were those who employed more than five hundred wage-days of labor annually. Capitalist producers controlled 21 percent of the arable land; transitional producers, 22 percent; and the peasantry, 57 percent. Surplus-producing peasants accounted for the greatest share within the peasantry, with 28 percent of the total arable land. Peasant and "transitional" producers include private as well as ejido and agrarian community forms of land tenure (the agrarian reform sector accounts for approximately half of Mexico's arable land).

14. Two-thirds of all peasants produced maize, compared with less than 13 percent of capitalist producers (CEPAL 1982). At least 30 to 40 percent of Mexico's maize crop is retained for family consumption and does not enter the market. This percentage varies with the size of the harvest, since output and sale prices change while family consumption needs remain relatively constant. When prices fall, producers may either sow less or sell less, but either way less maize enters the market. On the wide range of maize production processes more generally, see Montañez and Warman 1985.

per unit of land, the increased value of the government price would bolster the incentive to market more of the harvest.[15]

Government Credit and Crop Insurance: BANRURAL and ANAGSA

Agricultural credit, like agriculture in general, was historically subordinated to the demands of import-substitution industrialization. In spite of agriculture's contribution to the "Mexican miracle" of sustained economic growth, credit growth during the period 1940–70 was significantly less than the growth of agriculture in general or of the rural population. Agricultural credit then increased 15 percent annually in real terms between 1970 and 1975, in response to declining production combined with mounting peasant mobilization, but the new recognition of agricultural problems was insufficient to overcome years of bureaucratic bias and inertia in the agricultural credit institutions, and the production results were limited. In 1975 three lending agencies were consolidated into the National Rural Credit Bank (BANRURAL).

The importance of official credit has always been directly linked to a fundamental feature of Mexico's agrarian reform; since ejido land was "inalienable," it could not be mortgaged for private bank loans. Ejidatarios therefore had few choices, and they made up 87 percent of the bank's clients. As the major source of government-funded credit for small producers, BANRURAL was one of the most powerful state enterprises in Mexico. FIRA, the other source of government-funded agricultural credit, is discussed in the next section. BANRURAL's importance is political as well as economic, since its network of over six hundred branch offices made it one the state's principal arenas of interaction and negotiation with peasants. As Rello (1980) writes: "BANRURAL is the public institution that, since the Cárdenas era, has had the greatest influence in the countryside. It is the principal agrarian policy instrument in relation to the ejido, the corporatist apparatus par excellence, the clear sectoral leader and an institution that has enormous power at the regional level."

Only 33 percent of maize producers had access to formal credit in 1978, according to a large-scale survey carried out by BANRURAL's

---

15. For those with access to underutilized land, the increased price would also create the incentive to put more into production.

training department.[16] The study also found that the bank gave first priority to producers with ten to twenty hectares, second priority to those with five to ten, and third priority to those with two to five hectares. Thus credit was extended primarily to relatively well-endowed peasants most likely to produce a surplus for the market.

According to the survey, 80 percent of the peasants did not know the bank's loan requirements.[17] Almost half a million producers were estimated to have stopped working with the bank, equivalent to 72 percent of the producers then receiving government crop loans. In 30 percent of these cases, the bank decided to stop lending money. But in the majority of cases (52 percent) producers decided it was not in their economic interest to work with government loans, even though they rarely had alternative sources of formal credit (INCA Rural 1984a:73). These producers reported that they either lost money, were kept uninformed about the state of their accounts, or received credit too late for it to be useful. One might also infer significant losses through corruption.

BANRURAL usually delivered its credit in up to four disbursements, largely in the form of inputs rather than cash. Although the survey did not find the quality of these inputs to be a major problem (except for seeds—see below), it did find that 40 percent of producers surveyed considered BANRURAL input prices to be significantly higher than those prevailing in the market (INCA Rural 1984a:80–83). The official rationale was based on BANRURAL's ostensible economies of scale in the purchase of inputs, but it appears that BANRURAL operated with far higher margins than the private sector in much of the countryside.

Through its staged credit delivery procedures, BANRURAL exercised as much oversight as possible over the production process, requiring a large body of field inspectors who wielded a great deal of often arbitrary power over producers (Rello 1987). Since the producers had very little control over the price, timing, or composition of the inputs BANRURAL prescribed, this paternalistic credit de-

---

16. The survey was carried out in 1978 but published by INCA in 1984. It should be noted that official surveys are very likely to understate results that reflect negatively on the government.

17. The study attributed this lack of knowledge to weak outreach efforts and to "distorted information" about the bank's operations. Such "distorted information" included the perception of 71.8 percent of borrowers that working with the bank is a "slow, difficult" bureaucratic process (INCA Rural 1984a:72).

livery procedure significantly limited maize productivity.[18] Most of BANRURAL's critics attributed its difficulties to bureaucratic padding and widespread corruption, and indeed both were serious problems.[19] The corruption of BANRURAL field inspectors was legendary, but the fraud was widely understood to reach up to the highest levels of the bank.[20] As the former SAM era director of BANRURAL reported from his jail cell: "The diversion of funds in the bank is well documented. But the embezzlement was attributable to the system as a whole, not to me or any particular official. It was everyone's crime, or everyone's political action, from the president of the republic on down" (cited in Scherer García 1990:50).

The World Bank (1983, 1:19) attributed BANRURAL's problems to institutional "weakness," but an alternative interpretation claims the key problem was its strength. These critics suggest that BANRURAL's fundamental problems went beyond bureaucracy and corruption, contending that its domination of peasant producers systematically blocked their capacity to generate a surplus. In this view BANRURAL led a state effort to deal with the agricultural crisis by enhancing control over production and increasing peasants' dependence on the state and integration into the market (e.g., Tejera Gaona 1981). Ever since the 1943 law that permitted lending to subgroups within ejido communities, BANRURAL actively *dis*organized peasant producers to benefit its own political and economic interests. The resulting pattern of bureaucratic control, low productivity, overdue loans, and further bureaucratic control created a vicious circle of inefficiency.[21]

18. Productivity was also limited by the inflexible technological package often imposed by BANRURAL. Because of Mexico's great variety of agroclimatic zones, technological packages requiring credit must be locally appropriate in order to be more economically worthwhile than traditional production methods that require less cash outlay. On agroecological variation in Mexico, see Toledo et al. 1989.

19. Internal BANRURAL budget plans for 1983, for example, indicated that administrative costs amounted to 72 percent of the total amount of loans that year. In 1984 the Mexico City offices alone consumed 29 percent of the budget, leaving 71 percent for the regional banks that actually lent the money (*Informe de Gobierno*, 1984:335).

20. At a national meeting of the union of BANRURAL workers, nine out of thirteen regional leaders supported the contention that "BANRURAL protects officials who are guilty of fraud. Behind every [corrupt] field inspector there are two or three executives of the institution who commit illegal acts, but it is the field inspector who gets punished" (*Excelsior*, 31-III-85).

21. The experience of BANRURAL in the control of peasant cotton production in the north-central La Laguna region perhaps offers the best documented example of its systematic efforts to increase state control of peasant producers (Aguilar Solís and Araujo 1984; Hellman 1983; Rello 1987). For detailed case studies in other regions, see Brannon and

Because of BANRURAL's leverage over grain production, it was one of the first state enterprises the SAM planners consulted. The SAM architects wanted to find out if BANRURAL was flexible enough to increase the credit available in time for spring 1980 planting decisions. The bank quickly carried out a pilot project to see how the input and incentive package worked; the response was encouraging, and the agency moved ahead. When the SAM was announced in March 1980, annual interest rates were immediately reduced to 12 percent for all maize and bean producers, and below-market rates were available for other crops as well. Given that inflation was over 20 percent, interest rates were negative in real terms, for irrigated as well as rain-fed producers.

Total BANRURAL lending in 1980 increased 15.8 percent over 1979, after inflation. After another increase of 8.8 percent in 1981, total financing then fell 16.5 percent in 1982 (Pessah 1987). The area financed in 1980 increased 49 percent over 1979, reaching a total of 4.8 million hectares. In 1981 the area then increased 31.5 percent to 6.3 million hectares, and in 1982 it grew another 15 percent to an all-time high of 7.2 million hectares.[22] The number of producers receiving credit also increased significantly under the SAM: BANRURAL claimed it served 17 percent more producers in 1980 than in 1979, a rise from 1.24 million to 1.45 million. In 1981 the number rose 33 percent to 1.65 million (SARH 1982a:468).[23] The aggregate data on BANRURAL

Baklanoff 1987; Gordillo 1988a, 1988b; Mogab 1984; and Székely 1977. Ironically, the ruling party subsequently paid a high political price for its decades of control and corruption in the Laguna region. In a dramatic turning point early in 1988, the peasants of the region bitterly rejected the official presidential candidate and warmly welcomed his center-left opponent, in one of the first indications of his potential electoral strength. Investigative reporting later discovered that major abuses of power in BANRURAL underlay the protests (Nauman 1989). More generally, this incident highlights the importance of viable electoral competition for challenging corruption and bias in rural development policy implementation.

22. The area covered in 1982 increased when the total financing dropped because the amount of credit lent per hectare fell significantly in real terms (Pessah 1987). In 1983 the area financed fell 16.5 percent to six million hectares (*Informe de Gobierno*, 1984:528). The area covered by BANRURAL loans as a share of the total area rose from 17.7 percent of the total area in 1979 to 26.4 percent in 1981. Coverage peaked at 36.5 percent in 1982, falling back to 30.2 percent in 1983 (*Informe de Gobierno*, 1984:520, 528). These data are not very precise, since they are based on gross estimates of the area sown, but they do indicate the overall trend of sharp growth, with an apparent post-SAM fallback to greater coverage than before 1979. Agricultural lending temporarily recovered again in 1984 and 1985 (Myhre 1989). It then fell extremely sharply in the late 1980s (De la Mora Gómez 1990).

23. These data are not reported in the De la Madrid adminstration *Informes de Gobierno*, the official government annual reports, suggesting that they are probably in-

financing under the SAM thus indicate sharp growth between 1980 and 1982.[24]

Short-term crop loans increased much more than agricultural investment loans, financing increased production but not necessarily higher productivity. Since Mexican agricultural credit analysts generally agree that investment loans were largely unavailable to small producers, however, and since they tended to subsidize the substitution of capital for labor (i.e., mechanization), this was probably a positive trend in distributional terms.[25]

Although total lending increased dramatically, the distribution of credit between different loan categories indicates that the SAM period slowed, but did not reverse, the pro-livestock bias in credit allocation known as the *"ganaderización* of credit" (Pessah 1987). Overall, crop loans during 1980–82 received a smaller share of total agricultural and livestock credit than they had in 1977–79, contrary to the SAM strategy's emphasis on basic crops.[26]

Within the cultivated area financed with BANRURAL credit, however, the *share* devoted to maize and beans did increase significantly. The 1977–79 average share for these staple crops was 53.5 percent of area financed, whereas the 1980–82 average was 63.8 percent. The total area of maize and bean production financed increased from 1.8 million hectares in 1979 to 3.0 million in 1980, 4.4 million in 1981, and 4.2 million in 1982. The *rain-fed* share of the area financed also grew, from an average of 67.9 percent during 1977–79 to 78 percent

flated. In the case of the area financed, for example, the official figures were revised significantly downward between the SARH's 1980–82 annual reports and the *Informes de Gobierno* published under the De la Madrid government.

24. According to World Bank estimates (1983, 3:33), BANRURAL's share of total agriculture-related fiscal subsidies reached 41 percent in 1981.

25. In this context the World Bank noted that subsidized investment loans introduce "a strongly capital-intensive bias, with very adverse effects on the growth of employment" (World Bank 1983, 1:17). Short-term crop loans accounted for 70 percent of total lending in 1980, 73 percent in 1981, and 79 percent in 1982. The share of agricultural investment loans fell correspondingly, from 24 percent of the total in 1980 to 19 percent in 1982 (Reyes 1982). Although a fully pro-peasant credit policy would have broadened access to investment loans, achieving this probably would have been much more difficult than extending access to short-term crop loans.

26. The share of short-term credit allocated to crops accounted for 61.7 percent in 1980, rising slightly to 64.7 percent in 1981. The livestock share, however, rose from 16.3 percent in 1977 to 26.7 percent in 1980, falling slightly to 23.4 percent in 1982. Within the category of long-term credit, the crop share fell from 73.8 percent in 1977 to 58.2 percent in 1980, rising only to 60.3 percent in 1981. Only in 1981 did crop credit increase more than did livestock credit. In real terms, between 1977 and 1981, livestock investment credit rose at an annual rate of 35 percent, whereas crop loans increased at a rate of 16.6 percent. Agroindustrial loans increased at an annual rate of 56.1 percent (Reyes 1982:6–7).

during the SAM period. In 1982, however, even though rainfed areas accounted for over three-fourths of the area financed, they received only half of the loans (Pessah 1987).

Although BANRURAL financed more rain-fed grain production than ever before, *coverage* of each crop loan decreased. In constant prices, the average credit quota per hectare of maize sown was 16 percent higher during 1977–79 than during the 1980–82 SAM period. But in 1978, 76 percent of producers already thought that BANRURAL allocated insufficient credit to cover maize production costs, forcing 22 percent to borrow from other sources (INCA Rural 1984a: 94–95). This chronic underfinancing and the resulting dependence on informal credit prevented many peasants from breaking out of the cycle whereby usury and patron-client relations extract the peasants' surplus.[27] As Pessah (1987) observed, "In effect, more farmers were getting less; that may have reduced their ability to adopt the full technological package contemplated in the SAM strategy."

In conclusion, BANRURAL responded to the change in national food policy by significantly increasing the availability of agricultural credit. Until the SAM, credit growth increasingly benefited luxury and industrial crops and livestock instead of basic grains. In 1981 rates of growth shifted somewhat in favor of rain-fed basic grains. The change in relative rates of growth, however, did not involve any redistribution away from the previously privileged sectors, which continued to receive substantial real increases. In spite of increased attention to rain-fed maize and beans, livestock remained more important relative to crops generally than at the beginning of López Portillo's administration (Reyes 1982). Since small producers lacked access to most investment loans, a substantial portion of the vastly increased lending apparently went to producers who had alternative sources of formal credit and whose solvency reduced their need for the highly subsidized interest rates.[28]

Privileged producers and unaccountable bureaucrats took priority over redistribution of credit allocation. Because there was no change

27. Systematic research on the relation between formal and informal credit in Mexico is lacking. Swaminathan (1990) reviews the issue.

28. Soon after the SAM decision, Rello wrote: "It is not an accident that BANRURAL is the public institution that has been most actively interpreting the SAM in its own way. . . . In effect, BANRURAL is the SAM's greatest obstacle and most formidable enemy, the state apparatus that would have the most to lose if the essence of the new strategy were carried out, particularly the proposed greater peasant participation in managing the production process" (*Unomásuno*, 20-IV-80).

in the balance of power between credit administrators and recipients, there was no new incentive for BANRURAL officials to carry out their jobs honestly. One could therefore hypothesize that the scale of institutionalized corruption grew at least in proportion to increased budgets.[29]

The problem of broadening effective access to credit was directly linked to the issue of crop insurance. Producers who received BAN-RURAL crop loans were required to carry official crop insurance. The increase in credit provided by BANRURAL therefore drove the growth in insurance coverage by the state-owned enterprise ANAGSA. Under the SAM, ANAGSA reduced its annual premiums from 20 percent to 3 percent for rain-fed maize, beans, rice, and wheat as well as for irrigated maize and beans on plots up to twenty hectares. With the Finance Ministry covering the cost, both the area insured and the amount of coverage increased dramatically.[30]

The SAM period created a political environment that permitted ANAGSA to succeed in its decade-long effort to get the Congress to pass a new Agricultural Insurance Law. The law's provisions included the principle of "hectare lost, hectare paid" instead of the previous inflexible all-or-nothing loss rule. Coverage was also extended to the producer's estimated entire outlay, including the investment in labor costs for the first time (*El Mercado de Valores* 41(5), 2-II-81). Before this law, coverage began only if 75 percent of the seed germinated, and then it insured only 70 percent of the crop costs in irrigated zones and 50 to 60 percent in rain-fed areas. For the first time, ANAGSA insurance covered BANRURAL loans in full for lost crops, reportedly increasing the latter's recovery rate significantly; one ANAGSA source claimed that the new law increased BANRURAL's recovery

29. As a later *Excelsior* editorial observed (27-IV-84): "It is important for BANRURAL to transcend a past whose darkness has little legend and much reality. Deficiencies and corruption in rural finance have been so tolerated as to favor the formation of large fortunes, which continue to weigh on our economy as one of the factors that most created inequality."

30. ANAGSA insured 4.6 million hectares in 1980, jumping 54.1 percent over 1979 coverage. Area insured increased another 48.4 percent in 1981 to 6.9 million hectares, rising 10.6 percent again in 1982 to a record 7.6 million hectares (*Informe de Gobierno*, 1983:454). The maize *share* of area insured also increased sharply, from 30.6 percent in 1979 to 41.8 percent in 1980 and 49.3 percent in 1981, falling back to 40.3 percent in 1982 and 31.8 percent in 1983. Since these reduced shares were of a much greater total area covered, maize area insured in 1983 remained higher than it was before 1980 (*Informe de Gobierno*, 1983:454). Note that these official figures are significantly lower than the apparently inflated López Portillo era data (e.g., SARH 1982a, 3:439–63).

rate from 65 percent to over 90 percent. This involved shifting much of the subsidy burden to ANAGSA, however.[31]

To cope with the massive increase in coverage, ANAGSA made adminstrative and procedural adjustments, including regional decentralization. ANAGSA also increased its supervisory capacity, since its procedures required that it ascertain each stage of investment that might be claimed as a loss. According to a former top ANAGSA administrator, the supervision of credit use by both BANRURAL and ANAGSA reduced the opportunities for corruption through false claims. Local leaders of even pro-government peasant organizations, however, claimed that BANRURAL and ANAGSA officials continued to collaborate in refusing to report crop losses unless they were paid by the peasant claimants, an extremely common practice known as the "crop loss industry" (e.g., *Excelsior*, 5-II-85).

As with BANRURAL, ANAGSA's activities grew significantly in quantitative terms, but there is no evidence of any shift in the distribution of power over the resource allocation process. Before, during, and after the SAM period, ANAGSA was a lightning rod for peasant protests over charges of corruption and other abuses of its power over peasant producers. In one of the few regional studies of the implementation of SAM production incentives, Haber and Nochodom (1985) found that "ANAGSA was unanimously cited by [peasant] respondents as the largest single problem in agricultural service delivery."[32]

In addition to ANAGSA's services, BANRURAL also directly administered a new high-profile type of crop insurance. The Shared Risk Fund (FIRCO) was a created in 1980 and was, in the words of a SAM strategist, "100 percent SAM." It attempted to encourage traditional rain-fed producers to adopt higher-technology production methods by

31. Consistent measurement of either relative or absolute fiscal subsidies during the oil-debt boom is virtually impossible (and not only in agriculture). According to World Bank estimates, for example, ANAGSA received 5.9 percent of food-related fiscal subsidies in 1981, after BANRURAL, CONASUPO, and FERTIMEX (World Bank 1983, 3:33). In contrast, internal SAM documents indicate that ANAGSA received the second-largest share of SAM input subsidies during the peak 1981 spring-summer crop cycle (its 26.5 percent was second only to PRONASE [seeds] and significantly more than BANRURAL's 16.5 percent).

32. During President De la Madrid's tepid "moral renewal" campaign, ANAGSA's reputation deteriorated to the point that the director felt compelled to deny that his agency was "a symbol of corruption." He claimed that more than one hundred employees had been fired and rejected the frequent charge that "the entire staff of ANAGSA is corrupt" (*Excelsior*, 22-XI-84).

insuring the investment cost in case of crop failure. The concept of shared risk went beyond traditional crop insurance schemes because it guaranteed the estimated likely value of the harvest, not just the cost of purchased inputs, thus covering the producer's opportunity cost. The goal was for the state to assume the risks inherent in adopting new technologies in areas particularly vulnerable to erratic weather conditions. FIRCO participants were to receive seed and fertilizer at discounts greater than the already large national SAM input discounts.

The "shared risk" program was a central pillar of President López Portillo's intended renewal of the historic "state-peasant alliance," and it was important to the SAM's public relations effort. FIRCO implementation was nevertheless extremely limited. Some producers complained that if any aspect of the rigid requirements for the techno-logical package were applied differently, coverage would be with-drawn. According to a former SARH official who dealt with producer relations, FIRCO promoters were made financially responsible for er-rors that led to crop losses, which did not encourage *them* to take risks. FIRCO insurance was also less attractive than it could have been because of the SARH's technical package, which was not neces-sarily locally appropriate but still had to be adopted exactly as spe-cified in order to receive insurance coverage. FIRCO coverage reached a high point of 78,000 hectares in 1981, a mere 1.37 percent of the area covered by conventional ANAGSA insurance (ANAGSA 1982: 43).[33]

According to a former top ANAGSA official, BANRURAL had dif-ficulty administering the shared risk program, often encouraging pro-ducers to sign up with ANAGSA rather than take the time to set up another account with FIRCO. SAM created FIRCO through BANRURAL rather than through ANAGSA because some planners saw ANAGSA as too inflexible, while others were wary of its reputa-tion for corruption. On neither count was BANRURAL a significant improvement. Former SAM director Cassio Luiselli considered FIRCO "an area of SAM's complete failure."[34]

33. FIRCO coverage then dropped almost 50 percent in 1982 to only 35,000 hectares. FIRCO received an estimated 2.7 percent of total agriculture-related subsidies in 1981 (World Bank 1983, 3:33), an extremely high amount given the small area covered.

34. Quote cited in Fox and Marsh 1986. Two former SAM policymakers mistakenly imply that FIRCO "operated" the entire production input policy, underscoring the vast distance between the macroeconomists and those directly involved with policy implementa-tion (Cartas Contreras and Bassoco 1987:322).

Government-Supported Commercial Credit: FIRA

The Central Bank's Agricultural and Livestock Investment Guarantee Fund (FIRA), like BANRURAL, provided government-funded credit to agricultural producers. Whereas BANRURAL lent directly to producers, FIRA offered a rediscounting facility to the private banking system, which in turn lent largely to commercial producers. Because the commercial banking system usually avoided dealing with small producers, it was difficult for them to obtain access to FIRA-supported loans. If they did, however, they retained far more control over the production process than when borrowing from BANRURAL.[35] Under the SAM, FIRA-supported banks offered 12 percent interest rates to all maize and bean producers, the same as BANRURAL. Both the number of recipients and the value of credit allocated by FIRA increased significantly. While continuing to favor larger producers, FIRA did increase both the relative and the absolute amounts lent to ostensibly "low-income" producers under the SAM.[36]

FIRA defined "low-income" as those recipients earning an annual net income of less than one thousand times the daily regional minimum wage; "middle-income" was defined as between one thousand and three thousand times the daily minimum wage annually. Since most of the rural population was either unemployed or underemployed (defined as earning less than the minimum wage annually), the "low income" cutoff was actually far above average rural income.[37]

FIRA field agents admitted that they commonly erred by as much

35. Note the pioneering experience of the Coalition of Collective Ejidos of the Yaqui and Mayo Valleys. After several years of struggle against BANRURAL's opposition to their efforts to develop peasant-managed economic enterprises, the coalition found an alternative source of credit with less interference in internal economic and political affairs by borrowing from then-private commercial banks supported by FIRA. See Benjamin and Buell 1985; Castaños 1987; Coalición de Ejidos 1982, 1985; Gordillo 1988a, 1988b; and Otero 1989. FIRA was an alternative only for large, consolidated organizations of small producers, however, since only they were attractive clients for commercial banks.

36. Between 1979 and 1980, the number of FIRA borrowers increased 79 percent. The share of producers FIRA considered "low income" increased 66.6 percent, but the number of higher-income producers also increased 44 percent. The total number of borrowers in 1981 was twice that of 1979, and for the first time the number of high-income recipients fell in relative terms. Not coincidentally, FIRA created a new category of credit recipients ("Other Types of Producers"), which consituted an admission that its "middle income" category had actually included a substantial number of high-income producers. This new high-income category received 15 percent of FIRA credits in 1981, rising to 28 percent in 1982 (FIRA 1983:46).

37. A BANRURAL study reported that two out of three rural adults lacked regular employment. Out of 7.25 million peasants, more than 5 million were underemployed (58.2 percent) or unemployed (10.9 percent) (cited in *Proceso*, 129, 23-IV-79).

as 20 percent in their estimates of "beneficiary" income. Since it was in the producers' interest to underestimate net income in order to receive lower-interest loans, the actual implementation of the income categories was very sensitive to local relations between producers and bank officials. The differentiation of government-subsidized commercial interest rates by producer income was also extremely slight, varying between 26 and 29 percent for crops other than maize and beans during a period when inflation rose from 30 percent in 1981 to over 65 percent in 1982.

FIRA credit allocated to basic grains increased 156.5 percent between 1979 and 1981, more than for other crops. In relative terms, it rose from 21 to 30 percent of total lending. FIRA also developed a medium-term maize and bean program designed to increase technical as well as financial assistance, involving 67,000 producers by 1982. FIRA was reputed to provide excellent technical assistance, in part because its commercial credit procedures permitted producers to retain some autonomy. Because of the rapid overall expansion in credit coverage, however, FIRA analysts estimated that only 25 percent of 1981 credits were actually supervised by FIRA, with the rest receiving technical assistance either from BANRURAL or not at all.

Before the SAM, FIRA had resisted efforts to increase attention to genuinely low-income producers with productive potential. According to an internal World Bank evaluation, FIRA "was accustomed to work primarily with larger commercial producers, and its management was not eager to extend business to smallholders." The SAM's increased economic and political support for smallholder agriculture may have led FIRA to extend somewhat greater attention to genuinely low-income producers, but FIRA's categories of producers are too broad to confirm this hypothesis. FIRA, like BANRURAL, was able to use the significant increase in SAM-related financial resources to add a new target group to its traditional clientele without significantly changing its dominant policy orientation or operating procedures.

Agrochemicals: FERTIMEX

Fertilizer is widely considered to be the crucial input for increasing maize productivity in Mexico, and most credit is used to buy fertilizer. Fertilizer is especially important for ever-smaller highland plots that have been farmed intensively for generations (*minifundios*). According to a 1977 SARH survey, 53 percent of the total area in maize was sown with fertilizer (*Econotécnia Agrícola*, February 1979:9).

SAM director Cassio Luiselli drew from the Plan Puebla's emphasis on increasing rain-fed smallholder grain production as a policy model. A university-based regional agricultural development program, Plan Puebla was criticized as a "green revolution" program based on promotion of inappropriate high-yielding seed varieties in its early years (CEPAL 1981; De Janvry 1981; Redclift 1983). Since the green revolution had failed to produce major advances in rain-fed maize seed, however, Plan Puebla later emphasized increasing productivity through greater use of fertilizer in combination with greater plant density on small plots, usually less than ten hectares (Felstehausen and Díaz-Cisneros 1985).[38]

The state enterprise FERTIMEX monopolized production; it was also the country's number one insecticide producer and the second largest herbicide producer. Fertilizer was distributed through both public and private agencies, but it was BANRURAL that was largely responsible for administering the SAM-period fertilizer subsidies.[39]

The SAM's production input policies discounted fertilizer and insecticide prices 30 percent for rain-fed basic grain production.[40] These subsidies, like those for seed, were also avaliable to irrigated producers with less than forty hectares in 1980, lowered to twenty hectares in 1981 (SAM-SGTA 1981:3). These discounts for irrigated producers were among the few significant SAM input subsidies explicitly limited to a target group by size of producer. Twenty irrigated hectares was at least a medium-sized plot, since those few agrarian reform beneficiaries with access to any irrigation usually had five hectares or less. Large irrigated landowners, moreover, usually divided their land into smaller parcels registered in the names of family members or loyal employees, so many of them may have been able to take advantage of the discounts. The size limitation was to be enforced by local BANRURAL and SARH authorities, many of whom were dou-

38. Some Plan Puebla researchers eventually acknowledged the importance of effective and accountable institutional outreach to small producers, and the program evolved into a strategy for promoting regional development through producer organizations (Martínez Borrego 1991; Mora 1979; Niño 1985; Sánchez Hernández 1987).

39. The World Bank concluded that price controls on markups limited the incentive for private distributors to reach smallholders (1983, 2:41). This is a plausible result, but it would depend on assumptions about the actual effectiveness of price controls.

40. Fertilizer prices were 26 percent below production costs in 1981 (World Bank 1983, 1:7).

bly vulnerable to pressure for subsidies from large growers, on the one hand, and from their politico-administrative superiors, who wanted increased production at all costs, on the other.[41]

FERTIMEX responded to the SAM stategy with massive increases in the volume of fertilizer produced and distributed.[42] Total annual fertilizer sales volume increased 22.3 percent in 1980, rising 14.8 percent in 1981 and another 11.9 percent in 1982, reaching a record high.[43] According to FERTIMEX (1982a), the total area fertilized increased 9.5 percent in 1980, only 0.3 percent in 1981, and 22.5 percent in 1982.[44]

In the absence of detailed data on fertilizer use by crop or type of producer, a geographical breakdown is the best indirect indicator for approximating whether small producers gained increased access.[45] Andrade and Blanc (1987) carried out the most serious study on the subject, and they found that fertilizer use during the SAM period increased more rapidly in predominantly "peasant agriculture" states than where agriculture was predominantly "commercial," according to the CEPAL typology of producers cited earlier (CEPAL 1982). The 1980–82 growth rate for fertilizer use in "peasant states" was 89.3 percent, and for "commercial states" it was only 23.7 percent (excluding one outlier). As with other inputs, the rate of change bene-

41. Anecdotal reports indicate, moreover, that the SARH was allowed to authorize exceptions to the twenty-hectare maximum. One therefore cannot expect that it was strictly enforced.

42. The SAM period discounts created a powerful economic incentive to increase fertilizer use, and the challenge to FERTIMEX was to meet the demand. FERTIMEX's ability to respond quickly was hampered because its plants were already working at close to capacity. New plants require both large capital outlays and long construction periods. According to one high FERTIMEX official, "We learned of SAM's existence precisely on the eighteenth day of March 1980." Although a SAM planner claimed that the director of FERTIMEX had been consulted, the word was apparently not passed along to the operational level. FERTIMEX responded by increasing imports on the expensive spot market and by changing procedures to speed delivery and reduce inventory. The import component decreased over time, as oil-boom era heavy investments in fertilizer production began to come online. National production of finished fertilizers in 1984 was double that of 1980 (*Informe de Gobierno*, 1984:362).

43. Sales fell 15.5 percent in 1983 and rose again 11 percent in 1984, still 5 percent below the 1982 high (*Informe de Gobierno*, 1984:416).

44. This uneven rate of change may be accounted for by an increase in the average amount of fertilizer applied per hectare in 1981, probably because of the favorable rainfall, while 1982 applications probably increased because of the inflation-induced fall in the real price.

45. The most detailed geographical disaggregation available went no further than the state level.

fited peasants somewhat, but in absolute terms the resource allocation process did not change dramatically.[46]

It is likely that some subsidized fertilizer did "trickle down" to small producers who had not previously had access to it. Haber and Nechomod found that over 90 percent of small producers in the Pátzcuaro Rain-Fed District of the state of Michoacán received more credit and used more fertilizer than they had before. The share of those with increased access fell to 25 percent in the indigenous communities, where official credit was available for the first time. Peasants overwhelmingly cited the increased use of fertilizer as "the most important factor in increased production" (Haber and Nechomod 1985:109).

Nationally, however, the delivery of the subsidy in the form of a refund rather than as a direct reduction of the price may have limited peasant producers' access.[47] As discussed further below, an extensive Plan Puebla survey found that only 5 percent of maize producers knew about the discounts as late as 1982, even though many had signed the forms necessary to receive the refunds (Colegio de Posgraduados, Chapingo 1985).

Seeds: PRONASE

The SAM's input subsidy package included a 75 percent discount on "certified" hybrid basic grain seed, leading to a large increase in demand and a rapid production response by PRONASE, the National Seed Producer, the agency responsible for regulating the hybrid seed market by producing and selling its own varieties. PRONASE's output of certified seed increased dramatically during the SAM period, from 89,300 tons in 1979 to 183,300 in 1980, peaking at 235,200 tons in 1981. Demand collapsed after the SAM-period subsidies were removed.[48]

46. According to unpublished FERTIMEX data, the top ten principal fertilizer-consuming states did not change, although their combined share dropped from 73 percent during the period 1974–79 to 69.9 percent in 1981.

47. The wide range of actual SAM period fertilizer prices was implicitly acknowledged by the 1984 *Informe de Gobierno*, which listed the official price categories for 1980 and 1981 as "no data."

48. Seed production then began to fall, to 215,500 tons in 1982 and 138,800 tons in 1983. Most of the seeds produced were basic grains (wheat, maize, rice, and beans). PRONASE also produced significant quantities of other seeds, however, including soybeans, sorghum, oats, and barley. Maize seed production grew from a very low level before

PRONASE's close political identification with SARH may have accelerated its growth under the SAM, given the importance that increasing hybrid seed use had for SARH's commercially oriented policy agenda. The SARH and PRONASE shared a capital-intensive green revolution philosophy, and the scale of PRONASE's growth is indicative of SARH's capacity to "co-opt" the SAM in accordance with its long-standing policy orientation.

The medium-term impact of the SAM-period promotion of hybrid grain seed may have been negative.[49] The 1979 drought destroyed seed supplies before the SAM began. In 1981 the SAM subsidies induced peasants to sell their native varieties as grain, and then in 1982 frosts further damaged crops. The probable result was to reduce the variety of genetic stock available for future research into improved maize seed. This was particularly likely in those areas where government-imposed credit and insurance requirements obliged peasants to switch from their traditional self-reproducing varieties to hybrids, which must be purchased commercially. Since peasant demand for commercial seed depended on large subsidies, significant numbers of producers may have suffered a net loss in seed quality compared with the pre-SAM period, once those subsidies were withdrawn. The loss of locally adapted seed varieties developed over generations was one more step in the erosion of peasant producer autonomy in the face of integration into the market (Barkin 1987; Barkin and Suárez 1983).[50]

Technical Assistance: SARH

The SARH provided technical assistance primarily to those producers who received government-funded credit.[51] The total area cov-

---

the SAM period—8,000 tons in 1979—to account for a significant share of PRONASE production, with 52,900 tons produced in 1980 and 44,000 tons in 1981. Maize seed production then fell sharply to 17,100 tons in 1982, rising slightly to 21,300 in 1983 (*Informe de Gobierno*, 1984:520–21).

49. In the case of hybrid seed, an internal SAM evaluation found that the hybrid seed program "does not fit peasant needs, since it requires margins of risk and loss that only large-scale production can permit." The empirical basis for these comments is not specified, but they raise serious doubts about the program's impact.

50. Not all of PRONASE's activities were dedicated to promoting hybrid varieties. PRONASE's *criollo* maize program attempted to improve the productivity of local varieties; the program covered an estimated one million peasants and 2.5 million hectares by 1982. Although some reports were positive, an internal SAM evaluation of this program concluded that it "seems to be a failure. Simply consider that, out of ten seeds selected by peasant methods and ten from the PRONASE Criollo Maize Program, nine or ten from the first group germinate, while seven or eight from the second germinate."

51. Technical assistance is one of the few major production services provided directly by

ered by SARH technical assistance increased dramatically to a record 9.2 million hectares in 1981, 32.4 percent over 1980. These numbers are relatively high because "coverage" was defined as the area sown by producers who attended meetings led by SARH extension workers, not as the cropland actually reached by agronomists.[52]

During the late 1970s the SARH attempted to extend more control over nonirrigated areas, creating new "Rain-fed Districts" in an attempt to coordinate state services as well as to shape individual production decisions through administrative means (Arce 1987). Technical assistance played a key part in these efforts. Haber and Nechomod found that SARH extension workers were central to SAM implementation, since it was their job to convince often distrustful producers to increase their use of agricultural inputs. The SAM strategists, moreover, expected a great deal from these extension workers. Official SAM documents stated that they "would have to change substantially to keep in line with the SAM's strategies" (Haber and Nechomod 1985:98). Although extension workers had been recruited and trained to carry out tasks defined as strictly technical, they were now expected to undertake a major role in the SAM's attempt to improve the government's relations with producers.[53]

The response of the SARH extension agency varied between the state-level authorities and the field-workers. The state-level authorities refused to change their definition of rural development as a strictly technical problem, sharing the view of the dominant policy current in the SARH, "that peasants are basically incapable of developing the means to exploit their agricultural potential, and that this task is the responsibility of the centralized elite" (Haber and Nechomod 1985:99, 103). In contrast, the community-level extension agents acknowledged the constraints imposed by entrenched elites, including abuses in input distribution. The field-workers did tend to respond to some degree to the SAM shift in policy priorities, and in

the SARH rather than by a relatively autonomous state-owned enterprise, in addition to irrigation. On the traditional emphasis on irrigation policy, see, among others, Aceves Navarro 1988; Barkin and Suárez 1985; Cummings 1989; Greenberg 1972; Hewitt de Alcántara 1976; Wionczek 1982; and Yates 1981.

52. This level of "coverage" was not sustained, however, falling 17 percent in 1982 and then another 19 percent in 1983. The maize area reported covered by technical assistance also increased over 30 percent in 1981, but it fell 7 percent in 1982 and then another 20 percent in 1983 (*Informe de Gobierno*, 1984:523).

53. The SARH extension workers in the district under study did receive two SAM training courses. These courses did not include field agents of other key agencies, such as BANRURAL and ANAGSA, with whom the SARH workers had to coordinate if their efforts were to be effective (Haber and Nechomod 1985: 97).

Pátzcuaro, "SARH extension workers became increasingly effective in their capacity to aid peasants in the exploitation of government programs" (Haber and Nechomod 1985:113). In other regions, however, the few pro-peasant extension agents were successfully isolated by their bureaucratic superiors (Arce and Long 1987; Arce 1985).

Producer Prices and Grain Marketing: CONASUPO

The SAM's array of input subsidies was complemented by its emphasis on increasing the real value of the government's purchase prices for basic grains.[54] SAM strategists recognized that falling producer prices were one of the main causes of Mexico's increasing dependence on basic grain imports since the mid-1960s. Support prices were set by the Agricultural Cabinet, an interministerial coordinating body created at the beginning of the López Portillo adminstration that included the Ministries of Agriculture, Finance, and Internal Trade as well as CONASUPO, BANRURAL, and informally between 1980 and 1982, the SAM leadership.[55] As in the case of the Economic Cabinet, which set overall economic policy, the Agricultural Cabinet was led by the president. Once set, the "guaranteed prices" were paid to those producers who delivered their crops to CONASUPO reception centers.[56]

Before the SAM period, the Agricultural Cabinet generally received proposals for future crop price increases from the SARH; the increases usually met resistance from the Ministry of Commerce, since it would be obliged to increase urban consumer subsidies as a result. According to a former cabinet staff member, BANRURAL would tend to support SARH, and CONASUPO would fall somewhere in between. The SAM's full presidential backing led to its informal entry into the Agricultural Cabinet. In the case of prices, SARH might call for price increases of 20 percent, but SAM would call for 40 percent.[57]

54. For studies of Mexico's crop support price policy, Appendini and Almeida Salles 1981; Appendini 1988, 1992; Esteva and Barkin 1981; Barkin and Suárez 1985; Esteva 1979; Goicoechea 1990; Hall and Price 1982; Montañez and Aburto 1979; Renard 1981; DGEA/SARH 1982; and Vera Ferrer 1980, 1987.

55. In addition to coordinating the SAM, Cassio Luiselli also held the preexisting cabinet-level position of National Evaluation Coordinator.

56. Ostensibly, producers were not forced to sell to the government at the official price, but BANRURAL sometimes obliged borrowers to do so.

57. In response to Luiselli's proposals for increased crop support prices, the Finance Secretary asked: "And how much is the price of corn in the United States?" Luiselli replied

According to a former cabinet staff member, SAM became "a contender—the enemy to beat." This did not mean it won all the debates: early SAM position papers called for reductions of BANRURAL interest rates to only 3 percent rather than the 12 percent that was eventually decided on. But the SAM "arrived with a lot of political weight," shifting the center of gravity within the cabinet in favor of increased production incentives.

The SAM decision immediately increased CONASUPO's official support prices in 1980: 28 percent for maize, 55 percent for beans, 18 percent for wheat, and 24 percent for sorghum. Since inflation was 28 percent in 1980, however, these nominal increases basically slowed the decline of the real value of producer prices. Prices were raised again in 1981, leading to more significant real increases. Nominal prices were raised 47 percent for maize, 33 percent for beans, 31 percent for wheat, and 36 percent for sorghum, which meant real increases of 15 percent for maize, 4 percent for beans, 1 percent for wheat, and 6 percent for sorghum.[58]

The SAM period increases did not bring real grain prices back up to their previous highs. At first, the López Portillo administration had reversed the brief mid-1970s effort to increase maize prices, allowing them to resume their downward trend. The 1981 increase was significant, but still below even the 1976 high. Unexpectedly high inflation drastically undercut the value of the 1982 official maize price, which hit an all-time low. In spite of attempts to make the maize price more attractive, the oil-debt boom's inflation kept SAM-period maize prices

---

that the issue was not the U.S. price but rather employment and income in peasant production regions.

58. Agricultural Cabinet analysts recognized the powerful economic incentives that had encouraged the displacement of maize by sorghum throughout the 1970s. Internal cabinet documents show a debate about which maize/sorghum price ratio would effectively slow the displacement of maize. In 1980 the policy was that a 0.65 maize/sorghum ratio would be sufficient, but the "pro-maize" forces within the cabinet pushed this ratio down to 0.60 in 1981 and 0.59 in 1982. Even though the ratio changed, however, sorghum probably remained more profitable. For more on this aspect of the *ganaderización* of Mexican agriculture, see Barkin and Suárez 1985; Barkin and DeWalt 1985; DeWalt 1985; and Montañez and Aburto 1979. Sorghum is largely used for processed animal feed, 69 percent of which goes to egg and chicken production (Barkin and Suárez 1985:141). By the mid-1970s eggs and chicken increasingly became wage goods available to the organized working class rather than strict luxuries like most beef and dairy products. This means that, unlike the widespread and often violent displacement of peasant grain production by extensive cattle ranching, sorghum/maize competition does not involve a clear-cut conflict of interest between the very wealthy and the very poor; rather, it is between large segments of the urban population and rural net producers.

comparable to those of the 1975–77 period rather than recovering the high levels of the early 1960s.[59] Because of the overvalued peso, however, the 1980 domestic support price for maize was double the international price (Goicoechea 1990).

The SAM period price increases and the 1981 bumper crop led to a substantial increase in CONASUPO's share of national crop markets. CONASUPO bought increased relative as well as absolute amounts of basic crops after the 1980–81 harvest.[60] On the demand side, CONASUPO's grain market share was substantially larger because of increased imports. CONASUPO had a monopoly on Mexico's international grain trade, and it continued to import large quantities of grain throughout the first two years of the SAM period.[61]

Two principal factors might account for why CONASUPO continued to import when the SARH was claiming that the 1981 bumper crop had brought Mexico back to self-sufficency. First, CONASUPO did not trust the SARH production data, which were widely perceived as unreliable because of the political incentive to exaggerate. Second, some high-level CONASUPO policymakers had come to view the agency's primary task as regulating domestic markets through periodic imports, in contrast to its emphasis on rural development during the early and mid-1970s. This tendency was reinforced by the ex-

59. Many analysts argue that official support prices acted more as price ceilings than floors, as part of a policy that gave priority to the supply of cheap food for industrial development (see note 54, above). But it is not immediately clear why grain prices would have been higher in the hypothetical absence of low support prices. The crucial step in the logic is that official support prices are linked to administered price ceilings *farther down* the food chain—controlled intermediate and retail prices keep producer prices down. The official producer price for corn, even when low in relation to the costs of production, was still usually higher than the consumer price. Since the government paid the difference, it had an interest in narrowing the gap.

60. CONASUPO bought 18 percent of national maize production, 25.7 percent of beans, and 42.2 percent of wheat. CONASUPO buying continued to increase in the 1981–82 cycle, with 26.0 percent of maize, 42.9 percent of beans, and 41.6 percent of wheat. The government share of the sorghum crop increased greatly as well, rising to 35.9 percent in 1980–81 and 25.2 percent in 1981–82 (DGEA/SARH 1982:27). CONASUPO's crop share generally tended to increase in times of surplus, whereas scarcity tended to widen the official/private price differential. The geographic concentration of 1981 maize purchases was comparable to the 1977–79 average of 69 percent from the top five states (CONASUPO 1982b).

61. The original import crisis that followed the 1979 drought not only was a major factor encouraging adoption of the SAM strategy, it also led to a change in Mexico's grain import process. In 1980 CONASUPO created the Foreign Trade Coordinating Body in an effort to save money by using futures markets for Mexico's grain purchases. In 1981 CONASUPO purchased approximately one-third of its imports on the U.S. futures markets (Austin and Hoadley 1987). On Mexican agricultural trade, see also Cartas Contreras 1987; Link 1981; Mares 1987; Norton 1987; and Sanderson 1986, among others.

treme overvaluation of the peso, which made it appear relatively inexpensive to import.[62] The price of CONASUPO's resulting international debt would be paid in the mid-1980s, when accumulated financial costs became a much larger fiscal burden than current food subsidies.

Although the cause remains a matter of speculation, the fact is that Mexico incurred a record agricultural balance of payments deficit in 1981, with imports reaching U.S. $3.6 billion while exports languished at $1.7 billion. Agricultural imports, largely grain, actually increased 25 percent from 1980 to 1981, just as production was reaching record levels (Bank of Mexico, cited in Matus Gardea and Cruz Aguilar, 1987:135).[63] With the combination of a record harvest and imports in 1981, warehouses overflowed with a 1.95 million tons of maize stocks alone (CONASUPO 1982a). A large but unknown fraction of these reserves was lost owing to lack of adequate storage facilities.

Crop Procurement: BORUCONSA and PACE

CONASUPO received grain from large irrigated producers and imports via ANDSA, its large-scale grain handling subsidiary, while small and medium-sized grain producers who sold to the government delivered their crops to the smaller and more numerous reception centers operated by BORUCONSA, CONASUPO's small and medium-scale grain handling agency. BORUCONSA did not buy the crops itself; the CONASUPO central offices wrote the checks to the producers.

BORUCONSA's importance increased substantially because of the SAM's emphasis on basic grains and smallholder production. CONASUPO's increased market share, combined with the 1981 bumper crop, led BORUCONSA to increase the number and capacity of its reception centers.[64] The volume of maize purchased through BORUCONSA increased sharply during the SAM period, from an an-

62. Imports were also bureaucratically simpler, as well as potentially more vulnerable to high-level corruption through kickbacks and surcharges for large-volume purchases.

63. Increased elite consumption of processed foods accounted for part of those imports (Luiselli 1985:54), but the amounts were not large enough to explain the overall food trade deficit.

64. Between 1979 and 1981, the number of rural warehouses and reception centers increased 10.3 percent, from 1,528 to 1,686; total capacity grew 31.3 percent, from 1.49 to 1.96 million tons. By 1982 the number of reception centers rented or owned by BORUCONSA reached 1,726 (BORUCONSA 1983).

nual average of 1.17 million tons in 1977–79 to 1.65 million tons annually between 1980 and 1982. BORUCONSA purchases reached a record 2.6 million tons of maize in 1982 (*Informe de Gobierno*, 1984).

The number and geographical coverage of BORUCONSA reception centers were central determinants of effective access to the government's support price. The announced offer of a particular price at the warehouse gate did not necessarily mean producers in remote areas had access to that price. Effective access depended on how local grain and transportation markets worked: if local marketing channels were oligopsonistic, as they often were in regions lacking BORUCONSA reception centers, then isolated producers dependent on intermediaries for transportation could be assumed to lack access to government crop prices.

BORUCONSA was the institutional home of the Rural Marketing Support Program (PACE), the grain marketing program discussed in depth in the next chapter. Through PACE, BORUCONSA offered smallholders some of the crucial marketing services that often made private intermediaries more attractive buyers than CONASUPO, such as the loan of processing machines and bags. Most important, the PACE program offered nonirrigated corn and bean producers a rebate beyond the producer price to cover the costs of transporting rain-fed maize to the reception center.[65] The goal was to broaden effective access to the official price as well as to increase the de facto price paid to rain-fed producers. PACE also served institutional goals because it bolstered the incentive to sell through BORUCONSA, thereby increasing the enterprise's relative importance.

The PACE program expanded its coverage during 1979 and 1980, including rain-fed bean growers as well as nonejido grain producers for the first time. During the SAM, PACE grew to provide a wide range of marketing services to rain-fed grain producers in twenty-seven states. PACE's growth was reinforced by the SAM strategy, which in turn promoted PACE's increased attention to the SAM's target group.[66]

---

65. BORUCONSA could still not compete with several key nonprice services private buyers offered: payment in cash, purchase of the crop in the field; no discounts for quality or humidity problems; and informal credit in advance.

66. With strong political as well as economic support from the SAM, the percentage of BORUCONSA maize purchases that were covered by the PACE commercialization subsidy increased dramatically, from 17 percent of purchases in 1979 to 54 percent in 1980, rising to 58 percent in the huge 1981 crop and reaching 69 percent in 1982. The resources distrib-

Food Distribution: CONASUPO

Although the essence of the SAM was its focus on rain-fed basic grain production, it also had the goal of providing Mexico's estimated nineteen million malnourished people with access to a subsidized "basic market basket" of essential foods. This was to be carried out primarily through the rapid expansion of two existing consumer food subsidy programs: generalized food subsidies and state-run retail stores.

Generalized Food Subsidies

The government's global food subsidies on basic foods, such as tortillas and bread, were applied by selling subsidized intermediate goods such as flour and processed maize to private sector processors and distributors, who agreed to retail the basic foods at controlled prices in return for guaranteed supplies and a set rate of profit. These subsidies benefited a group of politically entrenched small and medium-sized industries as well as consumers in general, whether or not they were malnourished. SAM policymakers realized that this was an economically costly and inefficient way of reaching low-income urban consumers, and they worked on developing more targeted policy alternatives. They were also politically pragmatic, however, when faced with strong opposition from top Commerce Ministry and CONASUPO officials afraid of political pressures from the processing industry.

The most important generalized food subsidy was applied to Mexico's staple, the tortilla. According to a CONASUPO economist, the number of kilos of tortillas that could be purchased with the daily minimum wage rose from an average of 25.7 during 1977–79 to 31.8 during the 1980–82 SAM period, falling back to 28.5 in late 1983 (Ceceñas 1984:194). This implied a massive subsidy to cover the difference between the producer and consumer prices, which induced extensive illegal diversion of maize to animal consumption. Tortilla subsidies as a share of gross domestic product more than tripled, from 0.10 percent in 1980 to 0.36 percent (Ceceñas 1984:202). The overall cost of CONASUPO subsidies was not overwhelming, however, in either national or international comparative terms. Total subsidies of

---

uted through the rebate program increased in terms of constant 1978 pesos from 14.6 million in 1979 to 86 million in 1980 and 219 million in 1982 (BORUCONSA 1984).

CONASUPO operations averaged 2.53 percent of the federal budget during the SAM period, which compares favorably with Egypt and Sri Lanka's allocation of 15 percent of spending to consumer food subsidies (Lustig and Martín del Campo 1985:219, 221).[67]

Retail Food Distribution: DICONSA

The second principal food distribution policy instrument was the network of state-run retail stores, whose purpose was to regulate the market, reinforcing the administrative price controls through competition with the private sector. By offering basic foods of equal or slightly inferior quality at lower prices, the state's retail operations appear to have kept private sector prices lower than they would have been in an unregulated market, although reliable studies are lacking. Retail operations were managed by DICONSA, the largest branch of CONASUPO and one of the most extensive food distribution networks in the world.[68]

DICONSA officials estimated that their prices averaged 10 to 15 percent lower than market rates in the cities and 30 percent less in the countryside. There were three principal reasons for this difference. First, the urban stores sold more higher-margin nonbasic products than did the rural stores.[69] Second, private retail food prices generally

67. These generalized subsidies continued to serve as an important social buffer during the first years of the economic crisis. They were largely rolled back after the 1986 fall in the price of oil, leaving the targeted milk and retail operations, as well as a new urban food stamp program (*tortibonos*) (Fox 1991). Because of Mexico City's political sensitivity, tortillas continued to be cheaper there, receiving disproportionate consumer subsidies. On corn subsidy policies since the 1982 economic crisis, see Appendini 1992.

68. The milk subsidy was also very important, delivered through public and private retail channels as well as CONASUPO's own milk distribution branch, LICONSA. LICONSA targeted distribution of liquid milk (largely imported) to urban families earning less than twice the minimum wage (Rogers and Overholt et al. 1981). After growing significantly during the SAM period (Fox 1986; Austin and Fox 1987), LICONSA's social safety net program became one of the few to grow in spite of the post-1982 economic crisis, increasing coverage from 680,000 families in 1983 to 1.3 milllion in 1987 (LICONSA 1987:85, 97). Anecdotal evidence abounds of political conditioning of access to the program, but systematic studies are lacking. CONASUPO also operated a large wholesaling arm, IMPECSA, to supply low-cost basic commodities to small shopkeepers in return for their observance of controlled retail prices. IMPECSA also encouraged increased efficiency, to keep retail margins down. IMPECSA grew dramatically during the SAM period, probably reinforcing the government's political support among the numerous and politically significant small merchants. See CONASUPO publications *Sistema C* and *El Afiliado* (published for IMPECSA-affiliated shopkeepers). On the Mexico City food distribution system more generally, see Hewitt de Alcántara 1987 and Rello and Sodi 1989.

69. The urban poor do not depend principally on DICONSA outlets, nor are they DICONSA's principal clientele (Solís 1984).

tend to be higher in the more remote areas of the countryside than in the cities, both because transportation costs are greater and because of the prevalence of monopolies on extralocal goods, linked to informal consumer credit networks. Third, since approximately two-thirds of the nation's malnourished population was in the countryside, food policymakers deliberately prioritized rural areas to offset the negative impact of the SAM's increase in producer prices for rural consumers.[70] In remote villages, the presence of a government food outlet could play a major role in regulating consumer prices.

DICONSA's retail sales increased significantly in 1979 and continued to rise throughout the SAM period, falling off with the impact of budget cuts in 1983. Rural food distribution increased even faster than urban sales, as a result of a 1979 agreement between CONASUPO and COPLAMAR (See table 4). COPLAMAR, the National Plan for Depressed Zones and Marginal Groups, was a presidential agency that channeled oil revenue and international development agency funds into areas whose standards of living were determined to be the lowest in Mexico.[71] In 1979, before the SAM strategy was devised, COPLAMAR and DICONSA jointly identified a target population and planned a massive rural food distribution program. Top CONASUPO-COPLAMAR and SAM policymakers quickly became political allies, generally sharing a common view of Mexico's rural development problems, as discussed in chapter 3. They agreed that the state should intervene throughout the food system, regulating markets to benefit the majority of peasants hitherto excluded from the benefits of government policy and encouraging increased peasant organizations' bargaining power.

The rural food distribution program grew dramatically in both absolute and relative terms.[72] The organization of these stores also

70. Since DICONSA was not a profit-maximizing enterprise, it could meet its stated goal of reaching "financial equilibrium" and still apply part of the surplus generated in its urban stores to keep rural food prices relatively low.

71. COPLAMAR (1982) published comprehensive documentation of the problems of malnutrition, education, health, housing, and the geographic distribution of "marginality."

72. DICONSA estimated that it increased its share of the rural retail food market from 11 percent in 1980 to 17 percent in 1982 (DICONSA 1982a). Rural sales through the CONASUPO-COPLAMAR program increased 47 percent in real terms in 1979, 26 percent in 1980, 20 percent in 1981, and 19 percent in 1982. Budget cuts brought them down 40 percent in 1983. The rural share of sales grew from 10.5 percent in 1978, before COPLAMAR, rising to 18.3 percent in 1980 and 21.0 percent in 1982, as indicated in table 4. These percentages were even higher for the "superbasic" staple foods (grain, cooking oil, and sugar). The number of rural stores increased dramatically as well, from 3,311 in 1978 to 6,327 in 1980 and 9,049 in 1982. The rural share of total stores increased from 64 percent in 1978 to 80.8 percent in 1982 (*Informe de Gobierno*, 1983:178).

Table 4. Government retail sales of staple foods, 1978–1985 (Sales by CONASUPO distributors, in billions of 1978 constant pesos)

Year	Total sales	Urban share (%)	Rural share (%)
1978	10.789	89.46	10.54
1979	13.482	82.28	17.72
1980	15.899	81.69	18.31
1981	17.501	80.54	19.46
1982	14.869	79.00	21.00
1983	14.726	74.60	25.40
1984	15.140	72.29	27.71
1985	15.534	71.12	28.88

Note: These sales do not include the generalized basic food subsidies channeled through private sector processors and distributors.
Source: DICONSA 1986a:21.

changed: whereas before the SAM they were often granted as concessions to private merchants or run by state agroindustrial enterprises, with the SAM their management came under the direction of elected village committees. As detailed in chapter 6, the CONASUPO-COPLAMAR program changed DICONSA's procedures to promote citizen participation in policy implementation. Elected village committees chose representatives to form councils to oversee the activities in each of the two hundred warehouses that supplied the rural stores. The CONASUPO-COPLAMAR planners considered these councils a form of "coresponsibility" for the task of ensuring the timely delivery of subsidized food to the target groups. According to former CONASUPO-COPLAMAR planners and administrators, the program was most successful where local communities coordinated their actions at the regional level, taking the initiative to solve their problems. Local input into problem solving and determining needs greatly improved the flow of the subsidy to the target group, decreasing leakage due to inefficiency and corruption. The program survived the end of the SAM period in spite of opposition from elements within CONASUPO linked to local and regional elites whose interests were most threatened by increased community participation.

Who Benefited from the SAM and Why?

As the preceding overview indicates, most agencies and enterprises implementing food policy increased their activities significantly during the SAM period. Few, however, changed their basic policy orientation or the ways they carried out their functions. The oil-debt boom made the politics of resource allocation a positive-sum game: most agricultural agencies channeled resources to previously excluded peasants to some degree, but their traditional clienteles gained more in absolute terms from the massive flow of subsidies into the countryside.

The lack of reliable national-level documentation of the final destination of food and agricultural spending obliges analysts to rely on partial surveys and second-best indicators. Fortunately, two highly respected agricultural research teams carried out large-scale surveys of producer response, providing compelling evidence of the shortcomings of the implementation of the SAM strategy.

Researchers from one of Mexico's principal research centers, the Graduate College of Agriculture at Chapingo, conducted interviews with 1,670 Plan Puebla participants in 1982, after the SAM had been actively promoted for two years (Colegio de Posgraduados 1985). These maize producers were well integrated into regional markets, and many had been part of government rural development programs for at least fifteen years. For these reasons, they were among the peasants most likely to be familiar with the SAM's producer-incentive programs. Twenty-seven percent of the respondents had heard something about the SAM, but *only 5 percent* knew about SAM discounts for fertilizer and insecticides. Most producers surveyed had, however, been asked to sign the forms with which BANRURAL charged the reimbursements to the Budget Ministry. It is entirely possible that BANRURAL and FERTIMEX officials pocketed the refunded 30 percent of the input price. According to one of the directors of the study, "Most of the peasants never saw the money. The majority did not know about the program: they were just papers that came and went."[73]

SAM officials planned and evaluated the input subsidies from a macroeconomic point of view, placing their allocation in the hands of the same agencies that had traditionally abused their discretionary powers over input distribution. The planners may have considered the requirement that producers apply to receive the discount as a rebate a minor bureaucratic artifact, but this procedure ultimately increased officials' power over the ostensible beneficiaries of government policy.

The second survey was conducted by FIRA, the Central Bank's Agricultural Investment Fund. FIRA sampled its 1980 and 1981 "low- and middle-income" clients in order to evaluate its maize and bean

---

73. This general pattern was confirmed by Arce and Long's findings in Jalisco (1987), although in their case SARH extension agents shared a portion of the rebate with producers.

production efforts (Patron and Fuentes Navarro 1982). Only 46 percent reported that they had received the government's ostensibly "guaranteed" producer price or its equivalent for their maize and bean crops, and 70 percent of those who did were middle income. The study found a direct relation between access to inputs, degree of organization of borrowers, and income level. Whereas 70 percent of the producers reported that they had access to subsidized inputs, those who did not tended to be low income and not members of producer organizations. These findings raise serious questions about the distributive impact of the SAM producer incentives. FIRA credit recipients received some of the best technical assistance in the country and therefore were relatively well informed about available prices and input programs. As in the case of the Plan Puebla sample, if FIRA producers could not gain full access to SAM prices and discounts, then at the national level the degree of peasant access was probably much lower.

Irrigated producers, in contrast, took considerable advantage of the SAM's incentives to grow basic grains. This was to be expected with wheat and rice, which are largely irrigated crops in Mexico, but it also occurred with maize and beans, which are principally grown under rain-fed conditions. The irrigated shares of both maize and bean area harvested and volume produced increased between 1980 and 1982, indicating a strong response by irrigated producers to the SAM economic incentives.[74]

The SAM was never intended to displace luxury, export, and industrial crop production on irrigated land, especially given the importance of irrigated production for generating wage employment and export earnings. SAM strategists presented their rain-fed approach as complementary, rather than contradictory, to irrigated production.[75]

---

74. The irrigated share of the total maize *area* harvested increased from an annual average of 13.7 percent during 1977–79 to 15.5 percent during 1980–82, an aggregate increase of 11.5 percent in irrigated maize area harvested (Andrade and Blanc 1987). The irrigated share of the total *volume* of maize produced increased only slightly, from a 1977–79 average of 22.2 percent to a 1980–82 average of 23.3 percent. The total volume of irrigated production increased as well, with average annual SAM-period irrigated maize production increasing 27 percent over the period 1977–79. In the case of beans, the record 1980 and 1981 rain-fed production increases overshadowed the irrigated response, pushing the irrigated share down to 17.8 percent and 18.7 percent, respectively (*Informe de Gobierno,* 1984:531, 533). The 1982 drought brought the irrigated share up to 33.3 percent for that year.

75. The SAM strategy was based on years of agronomic research concluding that with an extension of area planted and increased productivity there was sufficient nonirrigated land for national grain needs (PRONDAAT 1976; Turrent Fernández 1987). These as-

The SAM's political feasibility was rooted in its promise to increase grain production without displacing politically influential irrigated producers (see chap. 3). Given this decision to avoid political conflict, most SAM producer incentives were to some degree available to irrigated producers.[76]

The significant real increases in the support prices and input subsidies for basic grains were available to all producers, regardless of access to water. Subsidized investment credit was available to any producer planting maize, though a tractor purchased with such a loan could easily be used to plant more profitable luxury crops the following year. The 30 percent discounts on fertilizer and the 70 percent discounts for hybrid seeds were officially available to most irrigated producers; there was little reason to believe that the SARH was strict about enforcing the twenty-hectare plot maximum for subsidized inputs.[77] Finally, irrigated producers, small as well as large, tend to be better organized, less isolated, and more politically influential than rain-fed grain producers. These factors probably increased their awareness of and access to SAM producer inventives.[78]

The production results from 1980 through 1982 indicate that, as designed and implemented, the SAM became a generalized grain production policy, losing its original emphasis on rain-fed peasant production. Although several important agencies extended their services to significantly more smallholders, they did not change the way they served their clients. Because of this, the new clients were among the first rejected when the post-SAM budget cuts restricted their activity. BANRURAL, for example, returned to its policy of lending only to those it considered creditworthy. Only the PACE and CONASUPO-COPLAMAR rural food supply programs considered the question of *power* to be essential to rural development and improving the peasants' standard of living. Only these two programs actively intervened

---

sumptions depended in part on displacing inefficient, extensive ranching from potential cropland, however, which would have aggravated sharp social and political conflict.

76. Note that the share of overall agricultural investment allocated to irrigation both decreased and became much more geographically dispersed by the beginning of the SAM period (Barkin and Suárez 1985:104), although this appears to have been the result of an independent trend, related to the exhaustion of the "easy" phase of large-scale irrigation projects.

77. Anecdotal evidence also indicates that the SARH may have used its control over water allocation to pressure producers to plant basic grains as well as more profitable crops, given the SARH's production-first interpretation of the SAM strategy.

78. An internal SAM subsidy study estimated that the 1981 costs of rain-fed maize production were subsidized 15.3 percent, while the costs of irrigated maize production were subsidized 11 percent.

to try to shift the rural balance of power away from local politicoeconomic elites and in favor of the peasantry.

Why was so much of the SAM more of the same? To a great extent, the strategy's potential was limited by the its architects' narrow political base early on in the policy process. There was a considerable difference between the SAM as a diagnostic critique and the SAM as a policy package. The original strategy of the SAM reformists, when they were still advisers trying to influence policy rather than official policymakers themselves, was much more structural than the SAM's short-term production incentives measures suggest. Key elements lost in the transition from intellectual critique to policy package included proposals for controlling the role of transnationals in agroindustry, the distribution of urban consumer food subsidies based on need, and an emphasis on the participation of worker and peasant organizations in the planning process, as discussed in chapter 3. The SAM planners did not have the political strength to push through most of their proposed qualitative changes, many of them essential to the strategy.

The effective delivery of targeted subsidies would have required fundamental changes in state enterprise structures, procedures, belief systems, and recruitment patterns that had been forged by decades of support for a prosperous and productive class of agricultural entrepreneurs. Most state enterprises were both unable and unwilling to deliver subsidies based on need, in part because of their own political orientation and administrative capacity and in part because of their direct relations with their traditional clienteles.

SAM planners were restricted in their capacity to encourage state agencies and enterprises to make structural changes that would have qualitatively changed the way they allocated resources in favor of peasant producers. With only two and a half years remaining in the López Portillo administration, fast production results were required, and the SAM leadership could not afford to jeopardize its relationship with the SARH and its related agencies by pressing hard for more targeted subsidies. The SAM's short-run political strategy was to proclaim "we are all SAM" rather than to encourage conflict between small and large producers, between peasants and ranchers, or between their respective allies in the state apparatus.

President López Portillo's blessing was a crucial bureaucratic-political incentive for the state apparatus to respond to the SAM strategy: all major policy currents were obliged to pay homage to the official goal of national food self-sufficiency, even though debate contined about its feasibility and the price required to pay for it.[79] Presidential support, however, did not extend to changing the structures or operating procedures of state agencies and enterprises, whose policy orientations were often inconsistent with the SAM. The SAM's high-profile emphasis on short-term production gains may have had the opposite effect, *reducing* incentives to carry out reforms to increase accountability to peasant clients or change the balance of power between the bureaucracy and the peasantry.

Food sector agencies, especially in the SARH, often claimed they were carrying out the SAM by simply changing the label on their traditional activities. The pre-SAM policy orientations of implementing agencies were more important than presidential backing in determining their response to the SAM strategy. The dominant policy current in the SARH emphasized large-scale commercial production and state control over smallholders, whereas the SAM planners were more interested in increasing production in ways that improved income distribution. Some state enterprise managers and many food system analysts, as well as peasant movement activists, contend that the SAM was, in effect, co-opted by the SARH. According to a SARH representative in the Agricultural Cabinet during the SAM period, for example, SARH secretary Francisco Merino Rábago opposed the SAM strategy behind the scenes until it received presidential support, at which point he "skillfully, little by little, limited the SAM's influence." Between the drawing board and the countryside, the SAM strategists' small organized base in both state and society left them little alternative other than to rely on the SARH and its allied agencies.[80]

79. Even De la Madrid, as head of the Planning and Budget Ministry (SPP), publicly supported the SAM, in spite of tensions and "turf" battles with SAM architect Cassio Luiselli. The SAM decision was made just as the SPP was developing its Global Development Plan, which was to "guide" the entire economy, including the food system. The president's 1982 nomination of Miguel de la Madrid as his successor did not bode well for the SAM's future. Nevertheless, even the De la Madrid administration did not challenge the political legitimacy of self-sufficiency as a nominal goal, speaking of "food sovereignty." On later national food policy statements, see De la Madrid 1987; De los Angeles Moreno 1987; and Jusidman 1987.

80. This problem was analyzed "from below" by one of a small group of SAM staff charged with relating to grass-roots peasant organizations: "The original SAM idea was new, based on the respect for the autonomy of the peasant organizations, accepting them as the principal actor in agricultural development. . . . What has happened in practice is that [this] is a direct challenge to the interests of the caciques, the intermediaries, and the landowners, who, through a complex network of relations with the government apparatus and vested interests that involves a good number of officials and local politicians, have tried to apply pressure to limit the SAM's capacity to reach its goal of supporting autonomous

CONASUPO's pre-SAM policy orientation, in contrast to that of the SARH, greatly aided food policy reform in the areas of crop purchasing and retail food distribution. CONASUPO's fundamental institutional mission was to ensure mass access to basic food supplies; it was therefore structurally predisposed to policies calling for greater state intervention in marketing. Since the Echeverría administration, CONASUPO had become one of the agencies most influenced by reformist policy currents intent on revitalizing the state's legitimacy in the countryside. The SAM's pro-peasant approach goals gave crucial political backing from the highest levels of the government to CONASUPO reformists who argued that an adequate diet was a basic right for all Mexicans.

Finally, a crucial factor that made the production input programs, the core of the SAM, lead to more of the same was the lack of participation by the target group, rain-fed peasants, in policy formulation or implementation. Organized participation by the target group in distributing of inputs would have increased the accountability of state enterprises used to dealing with their clients in a highly arbitrary fashion. A change in this balance of power would have created an incentive for state enterprises to allocate inputs more efficiently, equitably, and honestly. Such participation might have increased the life span of SAM-period changes in resource allocation patterns. Had new peasant credit recipients been integrated into BANRURAL allocation decisions, for example, they might have been less vulnerable to post-1982 budget cuts. Effective participation might have increased peasant bargaining power within the agency, which could have contributed to reducing corruption and decreasing the agency's vulnerability to cutbacks vis-à-vis other government spending priorities.

Instead, the oil-debt boom permitted reformist policy planners to

---

peasant organization. These are precisely the interests that are expressed in the concrete case of the SARH [here in the state of] Oaxaca. Through its actions, the SARH is trying to reduce the SAM to a simple package of cheaper inputs and a series of production goals for basic crops, which, although positive, are clearly insufficient to resolve the difficult problems of agriculture in Oaxaca. The SARH is trying to organize peasants to use the input package but reserving for itself the control of the process, reinforcing even more the institutional dependency of ejidatarios and comuneros, subordinating them definitively to the tutelage of the agronomists and field inspectors—an attitude that refuses to recognize that it is exactly [this kind of] antidemocracy and alienation that are the principal causes of the underdevelopment of agriculture in Oaxaca. To reduce the SAM to a series of technical measures means closing off the possibility that the organized peasants might appropriate the production process for themselves, reaching food self-sufficiency through self-management and the [resulting] capitalization of their own economic surplus" (Fernández Villegas 1981:2–3).

"buy" apparent compliance from agencies traditionally opposed to pro-peasant reform. The vast influx of resources allowed production-oriented agencies to continue to serve their traditional clientele—the larger, more commercially oriented producers—while at the same time increasing resource allocation to peasants. The SAM's political life was prolonged well into the 1982 "lame duck" period by the success of the 1981 harvest, but it encountered serious problems when adverse weather conditions and budget cuts resulted in the 1982 crop shortfall, leading to a new round of massive grain imports and corresponding negative publicity. Since the SAM had invested most of its political and economic resources in the pursuit of short-run production increases, the SAM strategy as a whole was discredited when those goals were not met in 1982. The SAM therefore paid a significant political price for its heavy emphasis on production, which had led to the early proclamation of food self-sufficiency in 1981.[81]

The generalized subsidy approach left the SAM strategy extremely vulnerable to the budget cuts that began in 1981 and 1982.[82] Most

81. Total production of staples (maize, wheat, beans, and rice) reportedly increased from a 1977–79 average of 13.6 million tons to a 1980–82 record average of 17.5 million tons. Annual rates of change were 39 percent in 1979, another 20 percent increase in 1981, and then a 19 percent drop in 1982. Production of maize in particular rose 46 percent in 1980 and another 18 percent in 1981, then fell 30 percent in 1982 (SARH, cited in Andrade and Blanc 1987:217).

82. The SAM's costs must be discussed in the context of the overall explosion in public spending that took place during the oil-debt boom years. The average annual agriculture and livestock budgets increased 15 percent in real terms during the SAM years, compared with annual increases of 10 percent during 1977–79. But other areas of spending increased to such a degree that agriculture's *share* of total spending *fell* during those years, from 8 percent of 1977–79 average annual spending to 7.7 percent during 1980–82. Agriculture's share of investment fell correspondingly, from a high average of 18 percent during 1977–79 to 16 percent during the SAM years (*Informe de Gobierno*, 1983). The World Bank (1983, 1:7) estimated that current fiscal transfers in 1981 amounted to 13.5 percent of agricultural GDP, about 1.3 percent of total GDP, and about 18 percent of total current transfers from the Treasury. Not all agricultural spending can be attributed to the SAM strategy, however, since much of nominal SAM-related spending was co-opted by the SARH.

Because of the SAM's food system approach, agricultural spending alone does not capture the SAM's full budgetary impact. The "food spending" category of the Mexican budget, created in 1978, shows an increase from 8.2 percent in 1979 to a SAM-period annual average of 9.6 percent of the total budget, peaking in 1981 at 10.8 percent. Any discussion of SAM costs must also take into account the increase in production that its incentives helped to stimulate. Andrade and Blanc (1987) estimate the production increase that can be attributed to the SAM and find that the incremental costs exceeded the value of the benefits, with a 1.39:1 cost-benefit ratio. They point out, however, that the value of savings from forgone grain imports would increase greatly with the use of a shadow exchange rate to compensate for the overvaluation of the peso. SAM-period food system spending cannot be considered to have increased greatly in terms of its share of total government spending, food agencies' activity levels fell in 1982 and 1983. The 1982–83 collapse in the real value of the government's support prices for basic grains was perhaps the most serious, hurting those least able to switch to more profitable crops, the peasant smallholders. After the SAM period ended, with most of its reformist architects in political disarray, the tendency among agricultural agencies was to return to previous patterns of resource allocation. For many peasants brought fully into the market for the first time, the abrupt loss of access to inputs may have had serious negative consequences, particularly for those who had been encouraged to abandon hardy native seed in favor of more "modern" varieties.

Conclusions

The SAM's production incentives were, for the most part, delivered by the same agencies whose alliances with privileged clients had furthered the decapitalization of the peasant economy over the preceding four decades. Some key SAM planners recognized this historical pattern, but they were unable to impose effective targeting of subsidies on the relatively autonomous implementing agencies. In the absence of a powerful national peasant movement to insist on efficiency and accountability, the actual distribution of SAM subsidies was largely left up to these same agencies.[83]

Although presidential backing was crucial to the initial SAM decision, it did not extend to active support for state intervention in rural power relations in favor of peasant producers and consumers. Because of the reformists' political weakness in the face of the production-first approach of competing policy currents, inside as well as outside the SAM itself, the strategy ended up emphasizing immediate production results at the expense of its original goals, which were more concerned with social change.

---

and any comprehensive discussion of SAM subsidies must take into account the macroeconomic context that permitted extremely wasteful subsidies to multiply for a wide variety of purposes less essential than food, such as gasoline, poorly planned industrial projects, and capital flight. On subsidy policies, see also Appendini 1992; Lustig 1982, 1984a, 1984b, 1986; and Gibson, Lustig, and Taylor 1987. On changing agricultural subsidy levels over the 1970s and 1980s, see Gordillo 1990.

83. Some regional smallholder organizations were able to pressure agricultural production-related agencies to improve their performance locally, but they were clearly the exception rather than the rule. Fernández and Rello (1984) document the state of producer organizations as of 1981. See also INCA Rural 1984b.

The only two programs that did retain this emphasis, PACE and CONASUPO-COPLAMAR, were both administered by CONASUPO and its branches. CONASUPO's institutional receptivity to food policy reform was augmented by a fairly broad consensus about the desirability of regulation of rural markets. Reformists clearly occupied a subordinate role within the ruling coalition, and they lacked the power to fundamentally change the allocation of land or production inputs. Both reformist and more orthodox policy currents did agree, however, that reforms that undercut the power of rural intermediaries, or caciques, would improve both peasants' living standards and the government's political image. Because marketing reforms potentially made fewer enemies than did challenges to the distribution of land and production inputs, and because of CONASUPO's historically hospitable institutional climate for reform efforts, SAM reformists were able to promote change in rural power relations through apparently pro-peasant regulation of grain markets. The next two chapters examine whether these programs really became exceptions to the dominant pattern of failed efforts at reform from above.

5

Reform Dynamics in Practice:
Public versus Private Intermediaries

If most of SAM-period food policy implementation was more of
the same, why was any of it different? Through both PACE and
CONASUPO-COPLAMAR programs, reformist food policymakers
intervened in rural grain markets in an explicit attempt to increase the
economic bargaining power of small producers and rural consumers
vis-à-vis local political and economic elites. PACE's manager defined
his program as "a marketing alternative that the state offers to agricultural producers as a social justice approach to promote self-sustained rural development" (Rubio Canales 1982:15). This chapter begins with a brief examination of rural grain markets and the role of
local elites, to explain why intermediaries became relatively vulnerable targets of food policy reform. The next section analyzes PACE's
origins and trajectory until 1980. The discussion then turns to the
political dynamics of PACE during the SAM, first assessing the program in action, then examining the political and institutional factors
that limited PACE as a vehicle for social reform.[1]

Competition and Rural Commodities

Before discussing the local politics of government grain procurement, it is important to briefly examine one of the key assumptions

---

1. This chapter is based on fieldwork conducted in the principal maize-producing areas
of Chiapas, Jalisco, and Chihuahua in 1984 and 1985. For more detailed regional case
studies, see Fox 1986.

behind the policy: Do elites really dominate rural grain markets? There is no one simple answer. Private sector critics of CONASUPO have pointed out that the subject has received remarkably little research attention from economists in Mexico and that most analysis has come from CONASUPO itself (Vera Ferrer 1987). Several distinct questions are involved. If one is primarily interested in understanding national markets, then the fraction controlled by local oligopsonists at the point of procurement may be relatively small.[2] Some regional grain markets undoubtedly do "work" in the sense of being fairly competitive, within parameters set by international prices and the uneven regulatory impact of state intervention. Even in remote areas, not all low procurement prices are attributable to lack of competition and of peasant bargaining power, since risk, transportation, and storage costs are often high (e.g., García 1978). That a hypothetically free market would therefore offer some producers less than official national procurement prices does not mean, however, that competitive market forces are the only determinant of those lower prices. Recall the large-scale FIRA study cited in chapter 4, which found that only 46 percent of rain-fed maize and bean producers received as much as the official price for their crops, depending on their level of income and group organization (Patron Guerra and Fuentes Navarro 1982).

We can find a middle ground between the dichotomous a priori assumptions of competitive versus oligopsonistic grain markets. Both exist. One may be more appropriate for understanding the economics of a given commodity at the national level, while the other may better describe the market as experienced from the bottom up by the rural poor.[3] Several barriers come between remote, low-income producers and national commodity markets.

The first barrier is transportation. The farther farmers live from paved roads, the farther they are from national markets. Moreover, when small-scale rural producers want to bring their crops to market, they rarely encounter a free market for transportation. One of the largest barriers to entry is the inaccessibly high cost of trucks for the vast majority of small producers (with the partial exception of those

2. For commodities whose buyers are highly concentrated, such as agroindustrial processers, the local procurement structure may not be the determinative link in the chain of intermediation, but the focus here is on maize and beans. For detailed analysis of feed-grain markets, see Barkin and Suárez 1985; Rello and Rama 1980; and Fox 1985b.

3. For some perishables, not even national markets are competitive. The cliental, credit-based dependence of small-scale urban food sellers on patrons who control bottlenecks farther up in the marketing chain parallels the situation of small food producers in the countryside (Hewitt de Alcántara 1987; Rello and Sodi 1989).

with significant migrant remittances or those who live near the northern border). At least as daunting is tight government regulation of the commercial use of trucks. Permits are required, especially for interstate commerce, and their allocation is marked by considerable extortion, often enforced by violence. According to the government-affiliated National Federation of Ejidal Transporters (FNTE), the Transportation Ministry, which allocated trucking permits, "benefited rural intermediaries because they denied permits to authentic producers." The federation further charged that the Federal Highway Patrol singled out ejidal truckers for extortion and violence (*Unomásuno*, 27-IX-83).[4] The threat of destroying a vehicle can be sufficient to keep most competitors out, especially in the absence of both insurance and the impartial administration of justice. As with coercion more generally, if it can be used with impunity it does not have to be used often to have its intended effect. This classic "rent-seeking" scenario of public-private collusion would by itself be enough to sharply constrain competition in key markets for the rural poor, but other factors must be taken into account as well.

In addition to the distorting effect of arbitrary government regulation of commercial transportation, several factors inherent in rural poverty combine to undermine the bargaining power small-scale producers have with intermediaries. A second major barrier is their frequent reliance on informal credit. Very few smallholders can cover their credit needs through public or private banks, as was shown in the previous chapter. Some have access to migrant remittances, but the rest must rely on informal moneylenders. One need not resolve the controversial debate over the relative "efficiency" of informal credit markets to find that they may well have a powerful spillover effect, undermining the bargaining power of small-scale producers in markets where they sell their products. Even if the interest rate is economically "efficient" in the sense of accounting for risk factors and lack of collateral, producers are often required to sell their crops to the moneylender at below market prices.[5]

The third barrier to truly competitive markets is seasonality. By definition, sub-subsistence producers run out of food before their crop is harvested. They often must turn to informal credit to survive,

4. According to the FNTE, of the thirty thousand truckers with official permits, fewer than 30 percent were producers, and only 18 percent were ejidatarios (*Unomásuno*, 26-IX-83, 10-VI-85).
5. For a useful comparative overview of the problem of "interlocking transactions" embedded in the land, labor, and capital markets facing the rural poor, see Hart 1986.

especially if wage employment is scarce. This crisis often obliges them to commit the sale of their crop before the harvest at below-market rates.

The fourth barrier is also related to the inherent seasonality of agriculture: the need for storage. Normally, prices fall to their lowest point in a given cycle at harvesttime. The only way for a producer to hold out until the price rises later in the season is to have access to storage. As with trucks, such infrastructure is expensive and therefore out of reach for most small-scale producers (especially in more humid areas). Both involve economies of scale and are therefore much more viable for organized groups of smallholders.[6]

These mutually reinforcing barriers to "free" competition structure the highly fragmented markets within which many of the poorest producers bargain with private buyers. Through the PACE program, the state attempted to reach out beyond its physical infrastructure and nationally announced price to offer more small producers a competitive alternative to private buyers.

Coyotes, Caciques, and the Politics of Rural Development Reform

Chapter 4 demonstrated that the relation between most food policy implementing agencies and their traditionally privileged clientele was largely undisturbed during the SAM period. Rural elites continued to benefit disproportionately both from the continuation of previous policies under new names and from the lack of effective targeting of most of the new production incentives. Rural power structures are not homogeneous, however, and certain types of elites were more vulnerable than others to reformist efforts to reorient development programs in favor of peasants, at least at the level of policy formulation. Policy currents differed over how much to support modern agribusiness, but both reformist and more orthodox technocrats agreed that oligopolistic rural traders were major obstacles to rural development in Mexico's poorest regions. The two programs that emphasized the SAM strategy's commitment to reorient the distribution of rural development resources by changing rural power relations focused on this more vulnerable target, explicitly attempting to increase peasant bargaining power in rural grain markets.

6. For an overview of crop storage issues in Mexico, see Mummert 1987.

Rural traders, known disparagingly as *coyotes*, are often embedded in a system of power relations known as *caciquismo* (bossism), especially in Mexico's poorest areas. Caciques range from the most traditional to the most modern in appearance, but the basis of their power remains the same: the mutually reinforcing domination of key political positions and economic activities, which prevents the effective operation of either competitive electoral democracy or free markets. As such, caciquismo has been essential to the operation of the clientelistic "divide and rule" approach that has dominated state-society relations in Mexico since the revolution.[7]

The importance of caciquismo to the Mexican state is rooted in the alliance of regional power groups that defeated the revolutionary peasant armies; the founding of the dominant party in 1929 was based on the exchange of support between the regional caciques and the new national political leadership. At that time political-military chiefs ruled entire states. Although the scope of cacique power has been reduced over time by the consolidation of the central state and the increased penetration of national and international market forces, traditional regional elites have proved remarkably capable of changing with the times, readily adapting to the state's corporatist interest groups and rural development agencies.

Fusing powerful interests entrenched in the state's bureaucratic and electoral apparatus with regional private sector interests, the system of rural caciquismo has two main facets. First, it frequently shapes a region's integration into the national economy. Rural elites often dominate regional input and product markets. Moreover, they are rarely strictly "private" economic actors; they influence the local implementation of national economic development programs through their control over information, agency staff appointments, and resource allocation. Second, caciquismo often shapes a region's integration into the national political system. In return for economic influence, regional caciques may deliver short-run political stability to national state actors. This political exchange is based on the caciques' capacity to isolate the population from national political alternatives

7. For the classic collection of case studies of rural caciquismo in Mexico, see Bartra 1975. Brading's collection (1980) offers a comprehensive historical overview. Schryer (1980) deftly shows how new local elites emerged and adapted readily to the postrevolutionary political system. Ugalde 1973 also focuses on the "modernization" of caciquismo in contemporary Mexico. On urban caciquismo in Mexico, see Cornelius 1973b, 1975; Eckstein 1977; and Ward 1986. See also Capriate 1972; Friedrich 1965, 1968, 1977; Paoli 1984; Salmerón Castro 1984, 1988; and Tuohy and Ronfeldt 1969. For cross-national comparisons, see Kern 1973 and Roniger 1987.

and on the co-optation or repression of autonomous local political or economic initiatives (Gordillo 1980:83–84).[8] Cacique power, then, is rooted in the capacity to mediate between the region and the national state and market. As one of the major caciques of the 1920s and 1930s put it, "The secret is to convince those in the center that one is strong in one's homeland and those in one's homeland that one is strong in the center."[9]

Both the PACE and CONASUPO-COPLAMAR programs explicitly attempted to weaken local marketing oligopolies, one key source of cacique power. While by no means all traders are caciques, almost all rural caciques do depend to some degree on marketing. Until the revolution and the agrarian reform that followed, control over land was the fundamental source of economic and political power in Mexico. Although the agrarian reform broke the political power of the traditional landowners in the areas where it was successfully carried out, the state did not follow up with pro-peasant intervention in the markets for production inputs, crops, or consumer goods. Control over these key markets displaced land as the principal source of economic power for local elites in most of Mexico, particularly outside the irrigated zones.

A wide range of actors had a stake in the state's regulation of what were officially recognized as inefficient and inequitable rural markets under the Echeverría administration (Bartra 1985:2). As was discussed in chapter 3, concerned policymakers had debated the reasons for the relatively low returns on rural development investments since the early 1970s (Grindle 1977, 1981, 1986). One policy current saw the problem as a technical one and advocated the increased use of modern production inputs. A second, *neoagrarista* policy current emphasized the need for renewed land distribution but encountered powerful resistance both inside and outside the state apparatus. A third reformist policy current sought to outflank the conservative resistance to land reform by focusing on the role of intermediaries in

8. The more traditional caciques even oppose the construction of rural roads, lest they lose physical control over access to their regions (Paré 1975; Székely 1977). The experience of the largely indigenous Huasteca region was a classic case of the cycle of market integration leading to violent takeovers of community farmland by ranchers (Avila 1986). In one of the few studies on the subject, Hoffman (1989:58) suggests that the general pattern following road building in isolated indigenous areas is first a strengthening of caciquismo, followed perhaps a decade later by a weakening of political, commercial, and transportation monopolies. See also Martínez et al. 1980.

9. Gonzalo Santos, leader of San Luis Potosí, cited by Aguilar Camín (1982:10). For a history of caciquismo in San Luis Potosí, see Falcón 1984.

blocking peasant efforts to accumulate capital for investment and on the need for more peasant organization.

CONASUPO became one of the agencies most influenced by reformist policy currents; President Echeverría named Jorge de la Vega Domínguez, an ally of the official peasant organization, as the agency's director. As an agency whose institutional mission was to ensure mass access to basic food supplies, CONASUPO was structurally predisposed to favor policy analyses that called for greater state intervention in marketing, since this would enlarge its own power and resources. In addition, it was one of the agencies most vulnerable to increasingly militant independent peasant mobilizations, which frequently engaged in nonviolent occupations of government offices and facilities. The threat of an even more radical alternative, the peasant-based guerrilla movement, added to the pressure, showing that some peasants were so alienated they were willing to take the risks inherent in openly confronting state power (see chap. 3). For the various institutional reasons discussed in chapter 2, CONASUPO put a premium on defusing social unrest through noncoercive means.[10] During this period, state reformists and peasant movements reinforced each other, leading CONASUPO to provide significantly more services and subsidies to rain-fed smallholders than ever before (Esteva 1979; Grindle 1977).

The relatively broad consensus among different policy currents on the relation between rural marketing and development made intermediaries more vulnerable targets of reformist initiatives than were large-scale commercial farmers or producers. Traditional intermediaries were considered to have a lower rate of investment than more modern entrepreneurs; their low productivity and seemingly high profit margins drove up urban food prices, which in turn forced employers to pay higher wages. The domestic market for national consumer goods industries was also constrained by low rural purchasing power, in part attributable to intermediaries' capacity to block peasant accumulation. From the point of view of state reformists, market regulation was economically important to prevent local monopolies from inefficiently allocating scarce development resources. Politically, market regulation could also help renew social peace at a relatively low political cost. Finally, at the ideological level, both the center and

10. Reformists in CONASUPO even on occasion provided food supplies to sustain land invaders, as part of the negotiating process whereby reformists tried to keep the peasant movement working inside the political system with a policy of conditional concessions.

the Left shared a nonneoclassical view that saw marketing activity as unproductive and rejected the legitimacy of profits from commerce. Grain traders are often referred to as "hoarders" in rural Mexico (*acaparadores*).

When reformists gained influence over rural development policy-making, as they did under Echeverría and in the latter part of the López Portillo administration, it was far easier for them to attack the way uncompetitive markets distributed income than to challenge the distribution of property. Thus it was in the area of market intervention, rather than production, that the SAM addressed power relations as an integral part of food policy reform.

The History of PACE

The announcement of an official national support price upon delivery to the government warehouse does not necessarily mean producers in remote areas have access to that price. As noted above, in remote areas far from government reception centers, small producers are often dependent on oligopsonistic intermediaries and frequently do not have access to the official price. The Rural Marketing Support Program (PACE) offered several marketing services to nonirrigated maize producers; these were extended to rain-fed bean producers as well in 1980 during the SAM.[11]

PACE was first launched in 1975, as part of CONASUPO's effort to respond to the most intense rural social upheaval since the 1930s and the concomitant crisis in the peasant economy (chap. 3). Until the early 1970s, CONASUPO purchased the vast bulk of grain for urban distribution from large producers or intermediaries. Reformists newly appointed to CONASUPO discovered that for peasants, access to government reception centers was difficult if not impossible. According to its official history, the idea of PACE was first conceived in the 1960s, when CONASUPO began building its small- and medium-scale rural warehouse network (BORUCONSA). The initial plan was to encourage peasants to reduce marketing costs by delivering their harvests jointly to government reception centers. PACE began to

11. Heath (1987, 1990) has done the most useful studies of the relation between maize production, marketing, and PACE. PACE was initially open only to ejidatarios, but under the SAM access was broadened to include any rain-fed producer. Although the program's name changed from Programa de Apoyo a la Comercialización Ejidal to Programa de Apoyo a la Comercialización Rural, the acronym remained the same.

move forward only halfway through the Echeverría administration, however, when the official peasant organizations, under pressure from their members, called for a national rural marketing program to support peasant communities in selling their crops (Rubio Canales 1982:3). CONASUPO responded by creating the PACE program, subsidizing the marketing costs of rain-fed maize producers as a pilot program in the 1975–76 winter crop cycle (BORUCONSA 1982c:13–15).

This pilot program was carried out in the states of Tlaxcala, Michoacán, Oaxaca, Querétaro, and Puebla, signing up over 27,000 producers in the first year (these states had experienced land invasions). By the next year the program was operating in twenty-seven states, signing up over 122,000 producers in 3,753 communities. Fewer than 10 percent of those who enrolled ended up participating, however, signaling a problem that would continue throughout the course of the program (BORUCONSA 1982a:18). Participation in the program was voluntary, and signing up did not force producers to deliver their harvest to the state. As indicated above, many producers resorted to informal credit, committing their harvest in advance at a price determined largely by the producers' extremely weak bargaining position.[12] In addition, given the wide seasonal fluctuations in supply and demand for grain, only producers with access to storage, or without severe cash-flow and survival constraints, could withstand pressures to sell to intermediaries.

According to Gustavo Esteva, one of the original high-level advocates of the PACE program within CONASUPO, the organized participation of the peasantry in grain marketing "could permit CONASUPO to have a transforming presence in subsistence communities." In his view the suppression of intermediaries would "destroy the economic base of the cacique power structure, which in many communities is the principal obstacle to development." The warehouse reception centers, together with rural clinics, consumer outlets, and other development services, would become development poles, beginning a process of self-sustained community development. He

12. This is mentioned by Heath (1990:43) and many others, but the process has received little systematic research attention. The continuing gap between those who signed up and those who participated may also have reflected the difference between the private market price and the government price. More flexible private buyers also offered many nonprice advantages over CONASUPO (Heath 1987). The participation gap may also have reflected the superficiality of the promotion process through which producers were enrolled; many may have signed up out of perceived obligation to government and ejidal authority.

noted, however, that the success or failure of the program, "including the possibility of putting it into operation, always depends on the balance of political forces" (Esteva 1979:239–42).

PACE planners saw two distinct policy currents within the CON-ASUPO apparatus, one antagonistic to the program and the other supportive of it. The "bureaucratic tendency" in CONASUPO was shaped by the agency's hierarchical command structure, which limited the responsibilities of each administrator to the tasks handed down from higher levels. This policy current within CONASUPO perceived PACE as additional work and treated program implementation as the responsibility of individual peasants rather than of organized communities. Early PACE planners predicted: "If PACE is operated bureaucratically, without the participation of the peasants it will tend to become corrupted, increasingly subject to personal decisions rather than authorized procedures. It will lose its reason for being, as well as the support of peasant organizations, since its actions will be carried out through orders from above rather than through commitments agreed to by the institution" (reprinted in Fondo de la Cultura Campesina [FCC] 1984, Annex 8, appendix 3:2).

The second policy current was identified by PACE planners as the "nonbureaucratic" or reformist policy current within CONASUPO, rooted in the agency's "institutional commitments with the peasants" (FCC 1984, Annex 8:5). As would be true of elements within CONASUPO-COPLAMAR years later, the "nonbureaucratic" tendency designed PACE, and rural development reform programs more generally, in an effort to make the government more responsive to peasants' needs and to promote peasant organizations.

The reformists had two key political resources. First, Echeverría's populist rhetoric established a new national political climate, creating an opening from above in response to a perceived erosion of legitimacy. Second, the reformists' bargaining power within the CONASUPO apparatus was bolstered by mounting peasant mobilization, both inside and outside accepted channels. The response of moderate reformists was to try to strengthen pro-government peasant organizations, which would both contain radical dissent and bolster their own influence within the state.

The reformist attempt to increase CONASUPO's accountability to its ostensible beneficiaries did not always fit neatly with the goal of strengthening official organizations. According to early PACE policy documents, reformist planners originally intended the program to bypass not only private intermediaries, but official peasant federation *gestores* as well—those who "manage" peasant demands (FCC 1984, Annex 8:4).[13] PACE's potential was sharply restricted, on the one hand, by the entrenched power of the traditional bureaucracy, within peasant organizations as well as in CONASUPO, and on the other, by the reformists' limited ability to promote extraofficial participation and mobilization.

CONASUPO reformists' capacity to struggle against their opponents within the system depended fundamentally on the legitimacy provided by the national political climate for reform. When the Echeverría regime ended in a renewed crisis of legitimacy, all policies associated with his populist approach were discredited and the national political climate changed dramatically. As a result, reform efforts were halted or reversed across the policy spectrum. PACE's "nonbureaucratic" tendency had barely had a chance to get off the ground.

When President López Portillo took office in December 1976, he sharply changed CONASUPO's direction, appointing one of his most conservative advisers as its director. Echeverría's rural reform efforts had become perceived as a key barometer of state–private sector relations nationally, and after the political and economic shocks of a sharp devaluation of the peso, intense capital flight, coup rumors, and an IMF stabilization agreement, the main priority of López Portillo was to restore a political climate favorable to private investment (see chap. 3). CONASUPO's rural food stores were shut down by the hundreds, and PACE was slated for complete elimination. Without resources, PACE was canceled in de facto terms, but its formal existence was maintained, reportedly because of peasant support (FCC 1984, Annex 8:5). This turned out to be important: once the balance of forces within the state shifted back toward distributive reform, PACE's continued formal existence permitted a rapid revival of the program.

After two years in office, López Portillo appointed Jorge de la Vega Domínguez, Echeverría's former director of CONASUPO, as Secretary of Commerce. De la Vega quickly put a former associate in charge of CONASUPO, creating a more hospitable climate for the revival of earlier marketing reform efforts, including PACE and rural food distribution. By 1979 the balance of power within CONASUPO began to shift, with both programs led by young political entrepre-

---

13. Possible conflict with official peasant leaders was foreseen, for example, since they controlled the lists of who was considered a legal ejido member, long an important source of power and patronage (FCC 1984, Annex 8, appendix 2:4).

neurs, state reformists who linked their personal ambitions to the fortunes of CONASUPO in general and to their reform programs in particular. PACE's pre-SAM revival can be attributed largely to internal CONASUPO and Commerce Ministry politics, but as chapter 3 shows, this maneuvering took place in a national political and economic climate that was becoming more hospitable to distributive reform efforts in general.

Until official national food policy changed with the 1980 SAM decision, PACE's plans for the 1980–82 period were simply to consolidate its existing operations (BORUCONSA 1979:24). Although it had reestablished itself institutionally, PACE's effective scope still encompassed only a few states. With the SAM, PACE grew to national importance, offering a wide range of marketing services to rain-fed maize and bean producers.

Top SAM strategists worked directly with PACE managers, reinforcing each other as conscious political allies in the struggle within the state for increased attention to peasant agriculture. Cassio Luiselli, architect of the SAM, said he "wanted to make PACE the counterweight to the idea that the guaranteed price discriminated against the worst off." One top PACE official recalled, "We hitched ourselves to the SAM. Where they went in, we followed. They went in to increase production, and we followed for the marketing phase." As he saw it, PACE became "an enterprise within an enterprise" inside BORUCONSA.

The Politics of PACE in Practice

PACE's stated goal was to change rural power relations by increasing peasants' bargaining power in the grain market. In theory, PACE could have achieved this in two ways. First, it could have provided access to marketing services in isolated and impoverished areas on an economic scale sufficient to improve individual peasants' bargaining position with intermediaries. Second, PACE could have potentially provided the political resources for peasants to organize their group participation in the market communitywide or regionwide, which would increase their bargaining power even if PACE incentives were not economically significant in themselves. As implemented during the SAM period, however, PACE did neither. Economic resources were channeled primarily to better-off peasants in high-surplus grain-producing areas in order to maximize the volume of grain delivered to

CONASUPO. The program did not penetrate deeply into isolated regions where its minor economic benefits could have had a greater relative distributional impact. Even when PACE benefits were available in more remote regions, there is little evidence that they accomplished the goal of increasing peasants' bargaining power with private intermediaries. In these regions, PACE alone could not break long-standing patron-client relationships that tied usurious loans to the delivery of the harvest or dismantle local transportation monopolies. Although PACE was relatively well targeted, in that intermediaries were not able to divert the bulk of the program's resources, it did virtually nothing to change rural power relations because it dealt with producers as individuals rather than as organized communities. This section looks at the strengths and weaknesses of PACE's implementation under the SAM and assesses the institutional and political constraints on the program as a vehicle of social reform.

PACE Implementation during the SAM

PACE boomed during the SAM. Maize sales to CONASUPO through the PACE program increased 400 percent between 1980 and 1981, accounting for 27.7 percent of the government's national maize purchases. The number of producers who delivered maize through PACE increased from 11,700 during the 1979–80 cycle to 109,000 during the record 1981–82 crop year. The value of PACE rebates increased 489 percent in real terms from 1979 to 1980, rising another 155 percent in 1981. The 1981 record grain harvest, the result of a combination of excellent weather and the SAM's production incentives, was the key factor explaining the magnitude of this increase. PACE's main effect was to bolster one of the key production incentives, the 14 percent real increase in the 1981 maize support price. The value of PACE bonuses represented an estimated 2 percent additional increase over the official price in 1979–80, rising to 2.5 percent in 1981–82.[14]

The PACE program's basic economic effect was to increase the incentive to sell to the state, but the marketing subsidies were small compared with the government price itself, which remained determinant. PACE participation therefore depended on the attractiveness of the official price. When the price was low, PACE loans of bags and

14. All PACE data cited are official internal figures from BORUCONSA's Rural Commercialization Support Department.

processing equipment may have served as a marginal incentive to sell to the government. If the market price was higher than CONASUPO's offer plus PACE, there were few incentives to do so.

PACE's most important service was its transportation rebate, beyond the government crop price, which was supposed to cover the costs of bringing the crop to the BORUCONSA reception center. PACE also offered rebates to cover initial processing and loading costs and the free loan of up to 150 eighty-kilogram bags.[15] Free initial processing services were eventually made available as BORUCONSA acquired the necessary equipment. The transportation rebates were differentiated according to the difficulty of road access as well as the distance between the plot and the reception center.[16] The basic bonus rate per kilometer of paved road was increased by 25 percent for graded, unpaved road (*terracería*) and by 50 percent for ungraded road (*brecha*) (BORUCONSA 1982b:16). Transportation costs are significantly higher on ungraded roads, not only because of the greater depreciation of the vehicles and the amount of time involved, but also because there is even less competition to provide these services in such areas. The farther from the paved road network, moreover, the less effective enforcement of official controls on commercial cargo fares.

Although in theory PACE was aimed at marginal surplus producers who otherwise would have difficulty obtaining the government crop price, in practice PACE's efforts tended to be concentrated in the areas of high surplus maize production. Three major surplus-producing states—Jalisco, Chiapas, and Chihuahua—accounted for most PACE activity in terms of both producer participation and the volume of maize covered by rebates. In these states most surplus rain-fed maize is grown by commercially oriented, relatively well endowed

15. The transportation rebates were the only ones that were increased annually to take inflation into account, in accordance with the official rates set by the Ministry of Transportation. Field research indicated that in 1984 these bonuses covered up to one-half to two-thirds of the real costs in Jalisco and Chihuahua, and about one-third of the real costs in Chiapas. The rebates for initial processing had not been increased since 1979 and therefore had fallen to less than 3 percent of the real costs, according to internal PACE estimates. Similarly, the bonuses for handling costs had not been revised since 1977 and had fallen to 10 to 15 percent of the real costs. Many producers considered these rebate levels insulting, and by 1984 the rebates may have cost more to administer than they paid out to producers. They went up significantly in 1989 and 1990.

16. This measure was changed in 1984 to the distance between the center of the ejido and the reception center, which resulted in significant rebate cuts in nominal as well as real terms for producers whose plots were removed from the center of the community. This cut was particularly pronounced for those villages that had a warehouse at the center, since it sometimes eliminated the bonus completely for distant members of that community.

small to medium-sized producers, although their agroclimatic endowments and conditions of production vary significantly.[17]

Initially, PACE was open to all rain-fed producers, large or small. Many grain traders were also producers, however, and those who were not could easily evade that requirement. As a result, especially after the large 1981 harvest drove the rural market price below the CONASUPO price, some deliveries of maize reached several hundred tons, according to top PACE officials (one thousand tons in at least one case). These amounts were far greater than any one rain-fed producer could harvest, even in the fertile regions of Jalisco and Chiapas. The 1981 record harvest resulted in serious congestion in the warehouse system and exacerbated existing abuses in the crop reception process, leading to increased pressure on BORUCONSA authorities to make its crop reception process more equitable. Overloaded warehouses generated conflict between small producers and private intermediaries over who would get priority access to CONASUPO reception centers. Private intermediaries often bought privileged access, leaving smallholders waiting for several days in long lines outside the warehouse gates. Such delays were extremely difficult for smallholders to withstand, especially since the cargo vehicle that was left waiting was usually rented. As a result, many were reportedly forced to sell their crop at 20 to 30 percent below CONASUPO's price to the private intermediary, who in turn would drive straight through the warehouse gate and sell the load at the official price.

In April 1982 a fifty-ton limit per producer was placed on the amount of grain that could be covered by PACE.[18] Producers could continue to sell unlimited amounts to CONASUPO, but only the first fifty tons delivered could receive PACE bonuses. A ten-ton limit was placed on beans. Even after the fifty-ton maximum was imposed, de-

17. Between 1977 and 1984 these three states accounted for an average of 59 percent of producer participation, ranging from a high of 90 percent in 1979–80, after the drought damaged harvests elsewhere, to a low of 41 percent in 1981–82, after the national bumper crop. In the same period, 67 percent of the grain delivered through PACE came from these three states.

18. This maximum may have been imposed in part by budgetary considerations, but the internal PACE memo announcing the decision stressed the importance of ensuring that the bonuses be distributed according to the program's goals. The memo, signed by Abraham Rubio Canales, manager of special programs (PACE), closed by saying that "the [measures] above are in response to the concerns you [PACE state coordinators] have expressed jointly with the regional payment coordinators, with the goal of avoiding the misuse of PACE forms." The measure was taken in spite of protests from large growers, especially from Jalisco, one of the regions where larger producers and intermediaries took greatest advantage of the program. The defeat of this effort, the memo, and the interpretation of several former PACE managers all indicate that the measure was taken primarily to improve PACE's targeting of rain-fed smallholders.

termined private traders often found ways of evading the limit. If a PACE field-worker did not know the region or its producers especially well, a private intermediary could sign up family members, employees, and clients, though usually only if the trader was a producer as well. At least in the three states where PACE was most active, however, many field promoters and producers agreed that the fifty-ton maximum did effectively limit intermediary access to PACE benefits.[19]

PACE's importance depended on the national grain self-sufficiency effort: its share of total grain delivered to BORUCONSA peaked at 69 percent in 1982, falling off to 43 percent in 1983. PACE was one of the many SAM-period programs that were cut back significantly after the 1982 change in presidential administration and the resulting changes in food policy priorities. Its formal existence was not in danger: the program was even cited in President De la Madrid's National Food Program, PRONAL, announced in October 1983. According to PACE managers, the program survived because it was already well known and was backed by the producers, as expressed by letters sent to BORUCONSA. Nevertheless, according to PACE officials, after the end of the SAM, the government was "letting [the program] die, but better a slow death than a rapid one." With the new administration's elimination of reformists from the cabinet, PACE was left without high-level allies, although it retained some support among the top directors of the CONASUPO central office.[20]

Institutional Constraints: PACE and the CONASUPO Apparatus

Since it began, PACE had had the same broad mix of stated goals: to protect the incomes of smallholders, to encourage them to enlarge grain production, to increase CONASUPO's share of the grain mar-

19. One must also take into account, however, that in the same year the real value of both PACE benefits and government prices fell dramatically, reducing the incentive for grain traders to overcome the increased barriers.

20. The amount spent on PACE rebates for the 1982–83 crop was only 14 percent of that spent in 1981–82 in real terms. Although PACE participation began to increase again in 1984, the best explanation appears to have been the effect of earlier promotion efforts combined with highly favorable weather, which produced a large crop, rather than the value of either the official price or PACE incentives. In 1983–84 rebate spending tripled in real terms, but it still reached only 41 percent of 1981–82 levels. PACE was later revived early in President Salinas's administration, perhaps because of its effective targeting and government reluctance to increase support prices overall. Rebates reached higher levels than ever before: an estimated average 9 to 11 percent of the official purchase price (depending on the maize variety). See BORUCONSA 1991.

ket, to expand CONASUPO's institutional ties with ejidos, and to support peasants' efforts to market their crops by offsetting their "traditionally disadvantageous bargaining position" in the face of "abusive practices by intermediaries and speculators" (BORUCONSA 1982b:16). These goals were not inherently contradictory, but they were not necessarily mutually reinforcing either. As with other SAM-period programs, the implementation-level goals and incentives determined how priorities were set for these multiple objectives and how fully they were accomplished. In the case of PACE, these institutional factors encouraged the program's implementation in the better-off, surplus-producing regions and discouraged any systematic effort to deal with producers as organized communities rather than as individuals.

BORUCONSA had been obliged to tolerate the rapid emergence of PACE as a relatively autonomous program because of the SAM's support for food policy reform. PACE continued to be constrained, however, by the larger institutional goals and priorities of BORUCONSA, as its host agency, and by those of CONASUPO more generally. PACE's geographic concentration was largely a response to pressures to maximize its quantitative impact, measured most clearly in terms of the volume of grain delivered through PACE and by the numbers of producers enrolled. Public PACE documents systematically tended to report the numbers of producers and ejidos enrolled without stressing the small percentage who actually delivered their crop via PACE at harvesttime.

The institutional incentives for short-term quantitative increases in purchases, in line with SAM's production goals, led PACE to focus on producers in areas where rainfall was reliable, yields were relatively high, and roads were good. CONASUPO's paramount institutional concern with increasing maize production and deliveries was also a key factor in allowing larger producers and intermediaries to take advantage of the program's subsidies until the imposition of the April 1982 rebate ceiling.

PACE operations were further limited to areas where CONASUPO had a comprehensive network of reception centers already in place. These centers were usually warehouses owned by CONASUPO, but they also included private buildings rented in times of good harvests. Mexico's warehouse network was extensive but far from adequate, leading to uneven coverage and therefore to uneven PACE penetration.[21] This infrastructure was also concentrated in areas of high sur-

---

21. The Ministry of Commerce estimated that Mexico's grain storage capacity covered only 75 percent of national needs (*Excelsior*, 30-VI-84), which undoubtedly contributed to

plus production, reinforcing PACE's tendency to put less emphasis on regions with greater poverty and isolation and less surplus production. The actual pattern of CONASUPO purchases was even more concentrated than the distribution of its reception centers, with five states accounting for between 55 and 90 percent of its purchases in the 1970s.

PACE's implementation in more remote areas was also constrained by limited resources for the key promotion stage (discussed further below). Because of BORUCONSA's limited support for the program, PACE officials had to carefully ration the resources dedicated to promotion. In their efforts to first increase, and then defend, their budget allocation to BORUCONSA's manager, CONASUPO central offices, and the Programming and Budget Ministry, PACE was able to obtain more resources for high-surplus areas than for outreach in lower-surplus regions. Regardless of whether PACE managers themselves had a redistributive orientation, promotion was hampered by other agencies who accepted the program on "statist" grounds, in terms of its capacity to increase CONASUPO's share of the national maize market.[22]

Finally, the political goals and orientations of PACE managers also shaped the program's implementation. In practice, few PACE managers saw the program as part of an effort to transform rural power relations. Ejidatarios were perceived by some as "naturally lazy," and prejudice against indigenous people was widespread. One manager stated, "If it weren't for Spain we'd still be wearing feathers." One state-level official in Chihuahua referred disparagingly to Tarahumara indigenous people who had come down from the mountains to the city as "half-civilized." These attitudes, widespread throughout most government rural development agencies, were often associated with the view that peasants' lack of formal education was the cause of rural poverty, rather than their lack of resources, rights, and power.

Nevertheless, most PACE managers knew the countryside well,

---

the independent estimate that 10 percent of the grain crop was lost annually (*Unomásuno*, 10-XI-84). CONASUPO'S grain losses were officially considered to be within the 2 to 4 percent range often regarded as technically acceptable, but since these figures were produced by the same agencies responsible for controlling losses, even high-level CONASUPO officials questioned their accuracy.

22. PACE's decreased resources after the SAM period probably affected promotion most seriously, in terms of the program's ability to meet its goals. By 1984 promoters' monthly salaries had fallen to M $20,000 (U.S. $130), without access to normal BORUCONSA employee benefits. This included travel expenses, which were high given the lack of vehicles for promoters. This scarcity of resources clearly affected the area promoters could cover as well as the number of assemblies held and attendance at them, especially in more isolated areas where PACE benefits could make the most difference.

traveled extensively, and had years of experience with the program. They were sensitive to increasing rural social tensions and considered PACE one appropriate way to deal with them. Lamenting the post-SAM cutbacks in economic support to the countryside, one manager said, "The Mexican government is creating the conditions for another revolution; there is not enough food, which forces the peasants to steal and to take up arms." In contrast to traditional populist reformers, most PACE managers did not attempt to address social tensions by reinforcing the traditional pro-government peasant organizations, nor did they systematically discriminate against members of any particular organization. As one manager put it, "I could care less what organization a peasant belongs to, as long as he doesn't have irrigation." Several felt that ejidos should be privatized in order to encourage production. PACE managers thus shared the "efficiency-oriented" preference common among state enterprises for bypassing the traditional corporatist organizations in dealing with peasant producers. They saw peasant participation as assisting in the implementation of agency tasks, not in terms of an active role in program decision making.

PACE managers were clearly reformists in that they were willing to make substantive concessions to peasants in order to reproduce the legitimacy of the political system. They were convinced that they had contributed significantly to improving the government's image in the countryside: "Before, CONASUPO's image was that we were a bunch of crooks, and we've changed that. They didn't know what CONASUPO was, and now they know. In fact, PACE is the only program that has gone into the countryside and left a direct benefit for the peasant. We don't take away a single peso—we give away the services. All the other agencies go out there to screw over the peasants."

Their brand of reformism was both "statist" and politically risk averse, leading them to deemphasize the potentially democratizing aspects of the PACE program. They adapted readily to the expected form of political discourse: PACE's official report of its SAM-period activities speaks of the importance of "self-management" and "collective action," of the "democratization" of BORUCONSA, and of serving the needs of the "marginal" population (BORUCONSA 1982a:46–67). In practice, however, PACE managers made no effort to promote peasant self-management in marketing, nor was the program aimed at serving the "marginal" population; much more attention was paid to the stated goal of "strengthening CONASUPO and

BORUCONSA operations by gaining the backing and majority consensus of the peasants" (BORUCONSA 1982a:64).

SAM-period PACE managers, in contrast to some of their predecessors during the Echeverría period and to their contemporaries in COPLAMAR, did not attempt to transform rural power relations through conflict with antipeasant forces inside and outside the state (chap. 6). They tended to agree with the specific goals of the PACE program and attempted to carry it out, but not as a vehicle for broader social change.

The Grass-Roots Politics of PACE Promotion

How did these institutional and political constraints affect PACE promotion at the grass-roots level of program implementation? It was the PACE promoters who actually brought the program to the countryside. They constituted the link between BORUCONSA and the peasants, and their actions therefore shaped the program's political effect on the ground.

PACE promoters worked within the existing community power structure; they did not try to change it. They were instructed to work with local authorities to set up community marketing committees to help with the delivery of the harvest. The official purpose of PACE outreach was "to make producers aware [of the program] so that they participate in an organized way in the marketing of their products and in the diffusion of the benefits available through PACE," according to the promoters' manual (BORUCONSA 1982a:75).

The promoter was to call special ejido assemblies, in coordination with the Agrarian Reform Ministry, which would be considered official only with more than 50 percent membership attendance. After an explanation of the program, the assembly would decide whether to sign up for access to PACE services. Actual participation was up to each individual, however, and did not mean the producer was obliged to sell to CONASUPO. As the PACE manual acknowledged, "Factors outside the control [of the producer] could impede the sale of part or all of the harvest" to CONASUPO (BORUCONSA 1982a:80).

The communities that accepted the program were to form a marketing committee, formally within the structure of the ejido, which would assist in the delivery of the harvest and represent the community to CONASUPO authorities. The tasks assigned to the marketing committee in the PACE promoter's manual, however, were almost all strictly operational. That is, its role was to help implement the program, relieving CONASUPO of certain logistical tasks, but the committee was not given the authority or means to *oversee* CONASUPO's performance. On paper, the group was "to participate in the solution of all the problems that the users of the program may develop," but mechanisms were not specified (BORUCONSA 1982a:82).

As Cernea (1983) points out in his study of the community participation methods of Mexico's PIDER program, unless the means, procedures, and authority for community participation in program implementation are clearly detailed in a "software" package, there is no reason to believe that such participation will be encouraged or even tolerated. In practice, PACE assemblies were largely for one-way communication. The community would be informed about the PACE program, and from there on the relationship would be primarily between the *individual* producers who signed up and the promoter and warehouse manager who handled the paperwork.

The role of the promoter was, in theory, to "be the liaison and the means of communication between the state and the producers," whose task was to "promote the creation and strengthening of the social infrastructure though which the ejidatarios, comuneros, or small property owners can obtain services from the state" (BORUCONSA 1982a:69). The promoters were to try to displace the intermediaries from the food chain to benefit both producers and consumers, and in the process they would "dynamize the institutional action of the CONASUPO system in the countryside" (BORUCONSA 1982a:69). "To dynamize" is usually taken to mean to make more efficient and responsive, which implies potential conflict with those forces inside and outside the state that prevent agencies from acting efficiently and responsively.

Given the crucial tasks they were assigned in theory, in practice promoters were not chosen or treated by the agency with the importance one might expect. Their remuneration was low, considered a mere "scholarship" (*beca*) by BORUCONSA, as a way to prevent access to regular employee benefits or possible unionization efforts. The "scholarship" category implied that they were students, as though they would soon receive a degree and change jobs. This status denied that rural development promotion was a skill that required consistent commitment to communities and years of experience.[23] Pro-

___

23. The status of the PACE promoters in practice was more a reflection of the political weakness of PACE within BORUCONSA than a choice by PACE's management as to the treatment of its field staff. When a BORUCONSA regional manager decided to carry out

moters from peasant backgrounds were consistently the most effective, but only six out of the twenty-five PACE field promoters interviewed were of peasant origin. Four had several years of experience working for BORUCONSA as elected community warehouse managers.[24] They were willing to work long hours for low pay, in part because of their social commitment to the program and their vocal opposition to private "crop hoarders," and in part because the position of promoter signified upward mobility. Not surprisingly, promoters who knew their communities, or peasant life more generally, were much more effective than those who were on their way to becoming bureaucrats or professionals, for whom the job was temporary and insufficiently middle class.

PACE managers did not encourage the promoters to take initiative beyond promoting and implementing the program, such as advising or organizing communities in marketing more generally.[25] Most promoters did not encourage community participation in PACE decision making. This failure was the central factor explaining why PACE did not shift the rural balance of power in favor of peasant producers.

---

last-minute inventories, for example, he felt free to commandeer promoters' time even at the height of the harvest, when they should all have been in the field (much to the chagrin of PACE managers in Mexico City).

24. BORUCONSA's warehouse "analysts" managed the storage, movement, and weighing in of grain delivered to CONASUPO. Reliable weights were especially important to small producers, who had long complained of cheating by coyotes. CONASUPO's public image to buyers depended on the honest implementation of these potentially sensitive tasks, and during the Echeverría-period peasant mobilizations and CONASUPO reforms, ejidos won the right to elect the managers of the warehouses in their communities. It is not known how many warehouse analysts were democratically elected in practice, but the position was unusual in that it ceded the hiring decision for a relatively privileged federal government job (e.g., cash income, access to technical training, and potential upward mobility for landless sons of ejidatarios) to the community as a whole and ostensibly removed it from the realm of traditional patronage. One indicator of the degree of community responsiveness in the election of warehouse managers was the frequency of rotation. In terms of the analytical framework develop in chapter 2, this potential channel for accountability constituted a gray area of mutual interpenetration between the realms of state and society. This created an access route for peasant pressure on CONASUPO, since elected managers were unlikely to oppose mass movements against the agency, such as the wave of nonviolent warehouse occupations for higher crop support prices in the mid- and late 1980s. Such mobilizations had maximum leverage just after the harvest, when the warehouses were full, and in states where the government was especially concerned about the rural vote. On the latter point, see Fox and Gordillo 1989 and Hernández 1992.

25. In one case, when communities in Jalisco protested about a change in PACE procedures that reduced their benefits because of rigid application of bureaucratically convenient norms, promoters played their role as liaison and brought the protests to the attention of their state coordinator. The promoters were the ones who had to bear the brunt of the complaints, and many sympathized with them. The PACE state coordinator discouraged any collective action by the communities and instead instructed the promoters to tell the communities to send letters to the Mexico City offices and patiently await a reply.

Lack of organized community action also fostered intermediary participation and corruption more generally.[26]

The organization of producers would have been more efficient even from BORUCONSA's view, given economies of scale; in theory PACE could have encouraged such cooperation by offering incentives for communitywide or multicommunity grain deliveries. PACE did occasionally make large-scale arrangements with unions of ejidos when they petitioned PACE, for example, lending bags and processing equipment and streamlining paperwork. But in none of the three states of greatest PACE presence was there any reported outreach to producer unions to encourage joint deliveries, at least during the SAM period. When the PACE program first began under Echeverría, cooperative deliveries had been an important part of its official goals and rationale. According to PACE operational officials who have been with the program ever since, the idea of cooperative deliveries never got off the ground. As one PACE manager explained it, "Our problem is that if we go around organizing peasants, then they're going to be pushing us to do this and do that."[27]

Conclusions

PACE confronted a perennial food policy problem. How can the public sector increase producer incentives without also increasing the

26. In the Babícora region of Chihuahua, for example, a BORUCONSA zone chief conspired with several warehouse managers to withhold grain bags during the peak harvest period, secretly selling them to private traders who took advantage of the tight market. These staff members were fired when the scheme was discovered by regional BORUCONSA authorities, but only more than two years after it began. In another case in Chihuahua, a PACE promoter who was selling enrollments in the program became an issue only when an independent local peasant organization pressured BORUCONSA to fire him. In spite of these instances of corruption, however, the perception of PACE, and of CONASUPO in general, was moderately favorable in Chihuahua, even among radical opponents of the government. As one militant peasant leader from the Babícora region, a veteran of fifty years of regional struggles, put it, "Nine out of ten peasants have been screwed over by the bank [BANRURAL], while maybe one in ten has had problems with CONASUPO" (see chap. 4).

27. There were additional reasons, beyond lack of promotion, why collective deliveries through PACE were rare. The experience of PACE managers was that collective deliveries were difficult to coordinate if producers had not organized their marketing jointly as well, which often required the cooperation of other agencies. Such cooperation was notably rare. Unless producers were organized into unions of ejidos with their own trucks, the logistical problems also became significant. Several unions of ejidos did deliver the crops on a large scale through PACE, probably helping to consolidate their existing bargaining power in the market, but they were the exception. This policy became more consistent later, when many more ejido unions had become consolidated economic actors (BORUCONSA 1991).

eventual price to consumers? The conventional approach, where the government pays the difference between the producer and consumer price, is often unsustainably expensive. Moreover, crop support prices are not the most equitable policy instrument because they inherently benefit better-off producers more. Larger producers have more to sell and often may harvest higher yields. Uniform crop support prices "treat unequals as equals," as Esteva put it (1979:233). In contrast, PACE offered an approach to grain procurement that took these problems into account, providing *non*price incentives to producers and also targeting them to the less well endowed.

As an antipoverty policy, however, PACE was limited by its very nature to producers who harvested a surplus above subsistence needs and who had access to the existing network of government reception centers. Producers who fulfilled those conditions were already relatively well off compared with the 78 percent of Mexican producers who produced less than enough for bare subsistence (CEPAL 1982:118). PACE spending was nevertheless much more closely targeted to smallholders than were most SAM-period food programs, since it was available only to rain-fed maize and bean producers. The 1982 imposition of the fifty-ton maximum on PACE grain delivery rebates, as a response to unintended intermediary intervention in the program, made it one of Mexico's most closely targeted small-producer subsidies.

The PACE program nevertheless faced an institutional imperative to allocate scarce resources for promotion and rebates in areas that would produce a significant return from the point of view of the larger state enterprise: large volumes of crop purchases. Because of this "statist" pressure, PACE activity was geographically concentrated in areas of reliable rainfall (*buen temporal*), where peasants were relatively better off, rather than in lower surplus-producing areas where the rebates would have made more of a difference to the producers.

The primary goal of BORUCONSA, PACE's host agency, was to increase its share of the grain market rather than to improve the producers' bargaining power in the market. Both inside and outside CONASUPO, the PACE program—and in particular the allocation of promotional resources—was primarily justified as an incentive to sell to the state rather than as a redistributive reform. In contrast to the CONASUPO-COPLAMAR experience to be analyzed in chapter 6, neither PACE managers nor field promoters tried to use the program to encourage broader social change; rather, they accepted the limited, institutional definition of the program's goals.

PACE treated the problem of oligopsonistic grain markets as if it were an issue of the relationship between two *individuals*, a buyer and a seller, when intermediaries' market power is based on their lack of effective competition. The only way peasants can have more than a marginal impact on marketing oligopsonies is for producers to organize sustainable alternatives that can compete effectively, and whose bargaining power can survive the vicissitudes of budgets determined in Mexico City. In areas where private intermediaries and their allies dominated the regional political system, however, small-scale peasant-managed marketing efforts were still extremely vulnerable to economic and political sabotage. Because of these constraints, alternative peasant-managed marketing channels would have the greatest chance for success if they were organized on a larger scale, at a regional level, as are ejido unions.

Although PACE was reformist in intent, and though much of its budget reached some small producers, it did not effectively intervene in the rural balance of power because it did not actively encourage *collective action* in defense of peasant interests relative to either the state bureaucracy or private grain traders. For the state, the problem of encouraging a "level playing field" in grain marketing was one in which the tension between accumulation and legitimation demands was low. One can conclude, therefore, that a politically feasible opportunity for more far-reaching reform was lost. In terms of the analytical framework outlined in chapter 2, the PACE reform did not set off a dynamic process of interaction between potential allies in state and society, failing to achieve the politically possible.

6

The Sandwich Strategy:
Opening from Above Meets
Mobilization from Below

Targeting with Accountability

The CONASUPO-COPLAMAR program opened up one of the most important opportunities for creating representative local organizations since Mexico's reforms of the 1930s.[1] Its national network of thousands of village stores supplied subsidized food to Mexico's lowest-income population. A reformist policy current tried to bypass and offset vested interests entrenched in the bureaucracy, internalizing social conflict within the state. This chapter analyzes the program's political dynamics from several perspectives, tracing the course of the village food store program in the 1970s and 1980s. The process of delivering the subsidy is then detailed, followed by an analysis of the grass-roots politics of implementation. Finally, contrasting scenarios of regional participation analyze how it shifted the local balance of bargaining power in favor of the majority.[2]

In practice, the program was carried out largely to the degree that

1. The consolidation of representative local organizations is the key factor that turns limited physical and economic resources into successful rural development efforts. Esman and Uphoff's (1984:15) cross-national study of over 150 local development associations, cooperatives, and other grass-roots organizations found that the ability to provide rural citizens with a means of participating in rural development decisions was "essential for accomplishing broad-based rural development."

2. This chapter is based on extensive interviews with active participants, ranging from national policymakers and middle-level officials to local program outreach workers, elected leaders of regional community food councils, and village-level participants (primarily from the states of Oaxaca and Guerrero, as well as from Michoacán, Nayarit, Puebla, Veracruz, Tabasco, and Coahuila).

peasant communities mobilized to support policy goals against reluctant bureaucrats. But peasant mobilization usually required active support from reformist policymakers in order to achieve results. Reformists within the state and autonomous social movements became "objective allies" in terms of the interactive approach developed in chapter 2. Their relations were marked by conflict as well as cooperation, but their strength was interdependent.

The CONASUPO-COPLAMAR program delivered a nutritionally important subsidy to thousands of Mexico's most impoverished villages. In contrast to much of the SAM strategy, the village stores not only survived but continued to grow after the end of the oil-debt boom. But the material impact of a consumer subsidy alone could do little more than help buffer a worsening situation of profound rural underdevelopment. The Peasant Stores also provoked long-term change in the institutional context that shapes rural development because they furthered democratic regional peasant organization in many areas. Autonomous peasant movements took advantage of the program's participatory procedures to build their own representative organizations, whose activities and scope went beyond the boundaries originally defined by policymakers.

The Origins of CONASUPO-COPLAMAR

CONASUPO's rural consumer food subsidy program was first launched, as was PACE, as part of the Echeverría administration's effort to renew the regime's political base among the peasantry. CONASUPO's distribution arm, DICONSA, began building a network of rural outlets in 1973 as part of the campaign by the reformist current within the agency to increase its capacity to regulate uncompetitive local markets.[3] After the 1976 change in administration, incoming president López Portillo then reversed CONASUPO's reformist orientation, closing hundreds of village stores weekly.[4] After two

3. See Grindle 1977:117 and Esteva 1979:236. In addition to beginning a network of rural DICONSA and cooperative stores, CONASUPO reformists tried to turn BOR-UCONSA's warehouse network into a distribution system as well. In theory, peasant communities would then gain control over both the buying and the selling ends of the marketing of basic foods (maize, beans, sugar, rice, cooking oil). By 1976 CONASUPO reported that its rural distribution network included over 400 cooperative stores, over 500 mobile units, more than 2,100 stores jointly run with other government agencies, and over 7,300 basic goods outlets (Austin and Hurless 1978:5).

4. See chapter 3. By 1977 there were only 751 rural stores left, accounting for only 5 percent of government retail food sales (DICONSA 1982a:1).

years of counterreform, however, López Portillo put Echeverría-era food policymaker Jorge de la Vega Domínguez in charge of the Commerce Ministry, which permitted reformist policymakers more freedom to maneuver in the arena of food marketing. The numbers of rural outlets began to increase again, but the key shift in official rural food distribution policy was in how they were organized.

Until the creation of the joint CONASUPO-COPLAMAR program in late 1979, most rural CONASUPO stores were run as concessions and the rest were "institutional stores," managed by other government agencies and supplied by DICONSA. To get a DICONSA concession, one had to offer a locale, working capital, and transportation. They were therefore run by the few already capitalized private entrepreneurs rather than by either DICONSA or the community. Because there was little profit to be made selling basic foods at subsidized prices, the concessioned stores either failed to carry essential foods or sold them at higher prices. As DICONSA officially reported,

> The enterprise's experience shows one essential operational problem: the guarantee of the final destination and price of the products in the rural stores, which because of their number and location complicates supervision. The operation of concessions, which face a market where the prices of basic products are three or four times the official prices in the cases of maize, sugar, and beans, *makes it practically impossible to avoid corrupt practices* involving the diversion of the products to other stores and industries or their sale at prices above those officially established. (DICONSA 1982a:3; emphasis added)[5]

The National Plan for Depressed Zones and Marginal Groups (COPLAMAR) was founded soon after López Portillo took office. In his inaugural speech he asked "the forgiveness" of the "disposessed and marginalized" people of Mexico, those who had not shared in the benefits of the revolution. He then named Ignacio Ovalle, a former high-level Echeverría-era official, to head the new agency, which combined several preexisting social welfare programs and was directly responsible to the president. Like most of the handful of Echeverría-era reformist holdovers, at first Ovalle received no support from the crucial policy-implementing agencies in carrying out his task. After al-

---

5. According to a top DICONSA official who studied the problems of the rural network at the time, they were usually run by caciques and, in the absence of supervision, were "worthless." The institutional stores were not much better. They were inaugurated with public relations fiestas but soon fell apart, "as small mafias formed around them within the agencies."

most three years without significant political or financial resources, mounting pressures from inside as well as outside the political system to "do something" about the "marginals" combined with the availability of increasing oil revenues to produce a decision that would put some substance behind the official rhetoric.[6]

The director of the Mexican Social Security Institute (IMSS), Arsenio Farrell, a close associate of the president, allied with Ovalle to design a massive program of rural clinics.[7] One of the president's principal rhetorical themes was to link food and energy issues in his discourse of national autonomy and economic development, but at that point virtually nothing had been done to give priority to food policy. The president approved the IMSS-COPLAMAR program but reportedly pointed out that it was difficult to improve rural health without food, leading Ovalle to quickly join with CONASUPO to present a plan for a new village store network.

The CONASUPO-COPLAMAR program was launched by an alliance between Ovalle, who brought extensive political expertise to bear, and Demetrio Sodi, DICONSA's general manager. Sodi's strong point was operational experience, having moved into government service after working for many years at the large private retail chain Aurrerá.[8]

Unlike many of the reforms of the Echeverría period, the COPLAMAR rural health and food programs were the result of cabinet- and subcabinet-level initiatives rather than direct responses to social pressures from below. The late 1970s was an ebb period for peasant movements with national presence (as shown in chap. 3). According to a former COPLAMAR official, although the president

6. According to one former top COPLAMAR official, the program was put on the national policy agenda in a 1979 cabinet meeting where López Portillo asked, "What has been done for the marginals?" His cabinet's inability to respond reportedly led the president to storm out of the meeting. This may have contributed to the demotion of the Secretary of the Budget, who was obliged to begin to allocate more resources for rural reform programs. Miguel de la Madrid joined the cabinet to take his place.

7. IMSS-COPLAMAR built over three thousand rural medical units and sixty rural hospitals by the end of 1982 (IMSS 1983:36). See Sherraden 1989a, 1989b for the most comprehensive analysis and Mesa Lago 1989 for an overview. For journalistic critiques of IMSS-COPLAMAR, involving charges of sterilization of low-income rural women, see Campbell 1984 and Ortiz Pinchetti 1981a.

8. According to a former Sodi aide, their combination of political and operational resources was crucial to launching the program. In this view both were young, dynamic "men of the system" who defined themselves as part of its "progressive wing, firmly believing that greater community participation was necessary." In the official reformist discourse, they thought that the peasants should become "the subjects rather than the objects of official action."

was "conscious" that the countryside was in difficult straits, the COPLAMAR decision was "completely top-down," with no direct pressure for such a program from peasant organizations either inside or outside the state. When asked why the decision was made, the same official responded, "Those in civil society are no fools. . . . 'Marginal' is the more elegant word for the exploited. They [the indigenous people of Mexico] have survived in spite of us for four hundred years."

One former middle-level COPLAMAR official offered a more analytical explanation of the decision:

> The intent was to try to control peasant discontent and independent peasant organization, to buffer it, or keep it within certain limits. The program didn't go into the most developed areas; instead it was targeted fundamentally to the poorer peasants. It is necessary to control this sector because it is the most discontented. They work the hardest to create their own independent organizations. . . . In this way the program tried to meet the old demands of the revolution, those of the peasants who never shared its fruits. . . . [After Echeverría] the state had to opt, on the one hand, for a line that respected the interests of the agrarian oligarchy, through slowing the pace of land redistribution, but on the other hand it had to offer some solution to the situation in the countryside, which was to offer a package of social programs.

In other words, officials with a long-range view of the need to forestall a *potential* increase in social unrest gained increased influence over policy-making in the context of the oil boom.

The Goals of the CONASUPO-COPLAMAR Program

CONASUPO-COPLAMAR's "preferred target population" was defined before the SAM decision, but it turned out to coincide closely with the SAM's target population. COPLAMAR's national surveys of living standards were used to determine objective need. Almost ten thousand rural communities were found to be eligible for the program's "basic market basket" of subsidized food, covering approximately twenty million people. CONASUPO-COPLAMAR stores were considered to have an effect on the population within a radius of five kilometers surrounding the community. The program was not intended to serve all low-income rural communities, because of operational constraints to those with more than five hundred inhabitants and year-round road access (DICONSA 1982a:1–4).[9]

CONASUPO-COPLAMAR planners carefully analyzed the problems that had frustrated earlier efforts to deliver subsidized food to the rural poor, and they decided it could be done efficiently and equitably if four conditions were met. First, the program needed *guaranteed supplies* of the foods considered essential. Shortly before the rural store network was established, the López Portillo administration had independently launched its "Alianza" line of basic foods, produced by both state and private enterprises for distribution as part of the administration's "Alliance for Production." This made low-cost processed foods widely available for both the urban and the rural network (e.g., milk, crackers, flour, pasta, and cooking oil).

Second, the network needed its own *storage network*, strategically located within reach of the target areas. DICONSA facilities had traditionally been in the state capitals, whose distance from the rural stores raised distribution costs and made diversion of subsidized foods to the private sector more likely. For the first phase, the Ministry of Public Works signed an agreement with COPLAMAR to build a network of two hundred warehouses in the target areas, each of which would supply several dozen village stores.[10]

Third, CONASUPO-COPLAMAR planners decided that one of the lessons of previous efforts was that the network needed *its own transportation network*. The Echeverría-period program ostensibly offered to reimburse communities for their transportation costs, but in many areas intermediaries monopolized access to vehicles. CONASUPO-COPLAMAR was able to buy over three thousand vehicles in the first two years of the program, greatly aiding both promotion of community organizing and the delivery of food (DICONSA 1982a:7). Unlike those in the PACE program, most COPLAMAR promoters had their own vehicles. The oil-debt boom made possible the creation of an independent infrastructure (i.e., warehouses and trucks). This gave reformist planners much greater control over operations than they had in the past, when they depended on the existing CONASUPO apparatus.

Fourth, planners agreed that *genuine community participation* in

9. Until the 1982 budget cuts, there were also major efforts to overcome even these limitations, using mules, boats, and light planes to reach several hundred of the most isolated villages.

10. Although the Public Works Ministry's lack of political commitment to the reform effort slowed the construction process and caused up to year-long delays in beginning village food deliveries, in most cases the program overcame these obstacles.

policy implementation was essential to guarantee the final destination and price of the food. They concluded from the experience with private concessions that "the only valid option was to involve the community itself in the supervision, and even the very management, of the operations" (DICONSA 1982a:4). Mexico's principal previous effort at integrating community participation into policy-making was with the World Bank–funded PIDER program, begun in 1973. In the case of PIDER, however, participation was encouraged only in selecting community-level public investments, not in carrying out the projects (and then only several years after the project was launched). As Cernea's detailed study noted (1983:25, 61), lack of community involvement in the control and monitoring of implementation was one of the key weaknesses of the program. Although in theory PIDER shared COPLAMAR's goal of encouraging participation in order to increase the accountability of government development agencies to their ostensible beneficiaries, it developed no means for consistently doing this (Cernea 1983:43, 69).[11]

Unlike PACE, CONASUPO-COPLAMAR was well on its way to becoming a program of national scope *before* the SAM decision. CONASUPO-COPLAMAR and SAM planners were part of the same policy current, sharing fundamentally similar conceptions of the state's role in the countryside and of their role as political actors within the state. From different points in the food chain, SAM primarily from the production process and CONASUPO-COPLAMAR from marketing, each attempted to attack Mexico's long-standing problem of rural poverty with what it viewed as structural reforms. The strategies were linked at the highest level, not only as part of the public face of the SAM's overall shift in food policy, but as part of the behind-the-scenes planning as well. Since one of the SAM's basic production incentives was to raise the official purchase price, it was especially important to offset the likely negative impact on rural consumers.[12]

---

11. In those cases where PIDER-related projects were carried out by agencies controlled by participation-oriented policymakers, PIDER investments did occasionally have a democratizing impact. During the Echeverría period, for example, the Community Access Road program was funded in part by PIDER and directed by Raúl Salinas de Gortari. Caciques often opposed the expansion of the road network into their regions in order to maintain their monopoly over links with the rest of the country (Paré 1975), and Salinas de Gortari reportedly channeled PIDER resources to independent peasant challenges to cacique domination. At times, Raúl Salinas would later take similar stands as head of DICONSA in De la Madrid's administration.

12. As the Price Commission of the policy-making Agricultural Cabinet contended in its 1980 internal proposal, "The increase in the guaranteed price will have a regressive impact

Not all SAM planners agreed that food distribution was an important area for policy intervention. Some of those from the more statist,
production-first current within the SAM staff presumed that mere
"circulation" was not important, justifying their position in debates
with COPLAMAR planners by citing Marxist classics to prove the
"determinative" nature of production versus consumption. In spite of
their apparent ideological orthodoxy, a residue of the Echeverría era,
these SAM staffers were politically moderate bureaucrats in practice.
Equally well versed in the classics, COPLAMAR strategists were both
ideologically pragmatic and more committed to social change in practice. They stressed the social and political obstacles to economic development and the consequent importance of building democratic
local poor people's organizations around their immediate material
needs.

Targeting Subsidy Delivery

CONASUPO-COPLAMAR, like PACE, was designed to increase
peasants' bargaining power with private intermediaries, but at a different point in the food chain. CONASUPO-COPLAMAR stores were
to compete with, not replace, the private outlets, selling basic foods at
an average 30 percent below the private price.[13] The effective regulatory effect would vary in practice according to the region's isolation
from urban markets, since the more remote the region, the more
likely it was that private traders could take advantage of monopoly
positions. Sub-subsistence producers and the landless often depended
on expensive informal credit for consumption, especially in the
months before the harvest. This dependence was often reinforced by
patron-client ties with caciques (as discussed in chap. 5). Effective
regulation of rural grain markets was therefore not simply an economic question of increasing competition; it would involve creating
credible alternatives to complex networks of social and political as
well as economic domination.

CONASUPO-COPLAMAR built its network primarily in maize-

---

on broad sectors of the rural population, since many do not produce enough maize to
satisfy their consumption needs. They therefore have to obtain maize in the market, at
prices which will surely rise significantly. *We therefore emphatically recommend that CON-
ASUPO, through its CONASUPO-COPLAMAR program, participate widely in depressed
areas, maintaining the current maize [sale] price there*" (emphasis in original).

13. Government evaluations clearly showed that the village stores complemented rather
than displaced the rural population's reliance on traditional marketing channels, especially
where public marketplaces were strong institutions.

deficit areas, largely in the central and southern parts of the country. PACE, in contrast, tended to concentrate in regions that produced a grain surplus. Whereas PACE's coverage was confined to areas with existing warehouse coverage, CONASUPO-COPLAMAR's independent storage network permitted it potentially to reach areas of much greater need than those traditionally served by government outlets.

CONASUPO-COPLAMAR's coverage of its target population, essentially the rural bottom third of the income distribution, was determined in part by the geographic extension of its network. Geographic selection was carried out largely by policymakers who used objective criteria of need rather than by administrators or politicians who would use the allocation process as part of the traditional patronage system. The pressures from the party-oriented wing of the political system were powerful, however, and could not be resisted entirely.

Placing the stores in areas of need was necessary but not sufficient for ensuring the delivery of basic foods to the target population at the official price. Regional CONASUPO and DICONSA officials faced powerful economic incentives to sell subsidized grain to private merchants, who in turn would resell it in remote areas for two or three times the official price. Since limited amounts of grain were available to the rural distribution program, diversion to private intermediaries left the village stores empty.

The community participation procedures were designed, however, precisely to create a political force for oversight that would counter the temptation for abuse at the operational level. A variety of factors intervened to determine the degree of community participation, as will be discussed below, but the important point here is that the delivery of CONASUPO-COPLAMAR's economic subsidy required the *collective action* of the community in defense of its immediate material interests.

As warehouse siting began, many traditional PRI legislators lobbied heavily for their favored clients and localities, and CONASUPO-COPLAMAR managers had to at least meet with them. Former managers claim that their districts were considered if they fit CONASUPO-COPLAMAR's criteria, but that petitioners were rejected when the area did not fit the official definition of need. This was largely possible because the decisions were highly centralized by national-level reformists in Mexico City rather than involving the official participation of politicians more directly responsive to traditional regional power structures, such as state governors. Governors did intervene, but only to a limited degree. According to one former top

COPLAMAR official, of the two hundred warehouse sites originally submitted for approval, nine were vetoed for political reasons, usually by governors who did not want the program's benefits allocated to villages of questionable loyalty.

Most of the warehouse sites were chosen in consultation with the National Indigenous Institute (INI), COPLAMAR's close political ally. COPLAMAR also consulted privately with autonomous regional peasant organizations about warehouse locations. One official directly involved with site selection estimated that about thirty of the locations were "politically chosen" in an attempt to provide economic resources and political legitimacy to nascent grass-roots peasant organizations. Some of these autonomous local movements were operating within the traditional PRI structure, but most avoided all political parties. The idea was to select areas where movement was already in progress to increase the likelihood that the program's procedures for democratizing DICONSA operations would be carried out. COPLAMAR policymakers intended the program as an opportunity for the consolidation of regional democratizing movements.

The economic implementation of the program—the delivery of the subsidy—was mixed even where significant community participation was achieved. In most cases the program was beset with shortcomings in both the quantity and quality of basic goods delivered.[14] Supplies of subsidized food were not limitless, even during the oil-debt boom, and peasant consumers were a new and not always welcome client group for CONASUPO operational staff. DICONSA judged the performance of its regional branch managers by sales and profit criteria, creating a powerful institutional incentive to favor urban stores over village stores when allocating scarce resources. The rural stores suffered financial losses whereas the urban stores generated a surplus, indicating that the program was supported in large part by internal redistribution within DICONSA. As will be discussed below, the managers rarely shared COPLAMAR's reformist orientation.

Bureaucratic disincentives were partially offset by DICONSA's rapid overall growth. Nationally, DICONSA food distribution increased sharply in both urban and rural areas during the oil boom. Overall sales increased by 47 percent in real terms in 1979, continu-

14. Price abuses were not found to be a serious problem. According to a 1981 internal DICONSA evaluation, store prices differed from official prices in only 2 percent of the outlets and in 5 percent of the warehouses, usually because of delays in inflation-related markups. Sales of basics were found to be conditioned on other purchases in 7 percent of the stores surveyed (to increase the store manager's commission).

ing to rise 26 percent in 1980, 20 percent in 1981, and 19 percent in
1982. The rural share of sales more than doubled, from 10.5 percent
in 1978 to 21.0 percent in 1982. When overall sales fell 40 percent in
real terms in 1983, the rural share held steady at 19.9 percent. The
number of rural stores increased dramatically as the CONASUPO-
COPLAMAR network expanded and the traditional concessions were
gradually phased out. The rural share of stores rose from 31 percent
in 1977 to 81 percent in 1982, when they numbered just over nine
thousand (*Informe de Gobierno,* 1983:178).[15]

The rural food store program not only survived the end of the SAM
period, it increased in relative importance within the enterprise.
COPLAMAR was too closely identified politically with López Portillo
to survive the 1982 presidential transition as a separate agency, but
the rural food distribution program continued to increase in importance in spite of the post-1982 economic crisis. By 1985 the number of village stores reached over thirteen thousand (DICONSA
1986a:23).[16]

The Politics of CONASUPO-COPLAMAR Implementation

Rural consumer food subsidies were effectively delivered only when
the CONASUPO-COPLAMAR program was able to change the incentive structure that shaped the behavior of operational-level policy
implementers. This change was induced by providing political and
economic resources to peasant communities to create *political counterweights* to offset the power that local elites traditionally wield over
the implementation of rural development policy. CONASUPO-
COPLAMAR changed the environment in which peasant communities decided whether it was worth the political and economic risks
of insisting on greater government accountability. As the analysis and
case studies that follow indicate, the effective delivery of the subsidy
was the *result* rather than the *cause* of political change.

The essential step in creating these countervailing forces was the
promotion of new, democratic community and regional-level peasant
organizations. This was a risky endeavor for reformist policymakers.

15. The SAM-period goal of rapidly expanding the network to reach twelve thousand by
the end of 1982 and fourteen thousand by mid-1983 was scaled back by the 1982 economic
crisis (DICONSA 1982a:11), although the network's growth sped up in later years.

16. DICONSA also estimated that it covered 16 percent of the retail market in basic
foods and reached 51 percent of the rural target population (*Unomásuno,* 4-I-85).

If "beneficiary" participation in implementing rural development was to be genuine, then policymakers could not be certain that the participants would use their new power only to follow a predictable and docile route through officially established channels. Many in COPLAMAR and some in DICONSA represented a policy current that was willing to take the risks inherent in promoting genuine community participation in order to offset the power of local elites and traditional antipeasant currents in the bureaucracy. They knew this would create political problems, though they may not have stressed them when originally trying to convince cabinet-level backers. They accepted that they would not be able to "solve" many of them. As one unusually frank official evaluation put it, "DICONSA faces permanent and continuing problems in relation to the communities, and it could not be any other way; the very essence of the program is to establish that dialectic. The goal is to keep these problems under the enterprise's control and to resolve what is necessary and possible" (DICONSA 1982a:17).

CONASUPO-COPLAMAR planners attempted to attack the political roots of rural poverty by creating a new bargaining relationship between the state and civil society. This approach was to create an officially legitimate channel for expressing peasant dissatisfaction, which permitted reformist policymakers to justify the participation strategy squarely within the framework of the established political system. At the same time, however, they attempted to change the political system by inducing the mobilization of a new social force to push for increased government accountability to the majority of rural citizens. Only through this *sandwich strategy* of coordinated pressure on the implementation agency from both above and below would reformist policymakers be able to promote social and economic change.

Officially, CONASUPO-COPLAMAR had the same approach to peasant organization as PACE did: peasants could improve their bargaining position if they participated in the market as organized communities with government support. Officially, the two programs worked neither directly through nor directly against the official peasant organizations. In practice, their approaches were quite different. PACE never tried to undermine the traditional corporatist peasant organizations, and it occasionally employed their cadre as field staff. CONASUPO-COPLAMAR, on the other hand, made a deliberate, behind-the-scenes decision at the highest levels to encourage peasant organization independent of the PRI. This was the result of an unusual alliance between radical and moderate reformist policymakers.

The "Radical Reformist" Tendency

One wing of the policy-making group behind CONASUPO-COPLAMAR's sandwich strategy was made up of university-trained officials who had been educated in the left-wing environment of post-1968 student politics in Mexico City. They still maintained networks of radical friends and colleagues who had resisted the temptation to join the system, and they were not afraid of them. For radical reformist policymakers, the Left was a key source of political support and policy ideas rather than a threat.

The post-1968 generation of radical reformist policymakers had pursued the "long march through the institutions," like many of their compatriots around the world. Many had been transformed by the system along the way, but others remained determined to pursue change from within. Their motivations were primarily political, based on their belief that social justice and greater democracy were both important and possible, and that they could be achieved by making the state apparatus more accountable to the citizenry through pressure from both inside and outside the political system. Because of their support for this sandwich strategy for democratizing the Mexican political system, these "radical reformists" would become the key link to the community organizers who promoted the program in the field.[17]

The "Moderate Reformist" Tendency

The CONASUPO-COPLAMAR leadership also included technically skilled administrators who were motivated primarily by personal career aspirations. They sought to advance their political futures

17. According to a top adviser to Raúl Salinas de Gortari (general manager of DICONSA from 1983 to 1988), the reason for the "democratization in these programs is part of a history which goes back further than López Portillo, even further than Echeverría, back to the [student] movements of 1968, when many of the people who participated, whose outlooks were affected by the movement, went out to work in the countryside after the 2 October [massacre]. There were two results. First, there was a political decision at the highest levels to take up the issue of popular participation in a democratic way, since the link between the base and the state had been dislocated or broken. That was one of the reasons the state tried to recover its social base by broadening democratization in certain policies and regions. Second, the people who went out to work in the countryside began to work at the grass-roots level to build independent, autonomous social movements. I think that in the case of CONASUPO-COPLAMAR there was a convergence between the government's political expectations and needs and an organizing process that was already going on. I don't think either that the organizing and democratizing happened spontaneously or that it came about as a result of the government's political posture; rather, the [reformist] position from above converged with a movement from below."

within the official hierarchy by getting credit for the efficient adminis-tration of a program that appeared to defuse social tensions.[18] They also realized that creating a constituency for the policy greatly im-proved the prospects for their own careers within the program. From the point of view of this wing of the CONASUPO-COPLAMAR lead-ership, there was an important instrumental reason for opening the program up to socially committed grass-roots activists: they needed to get the job done, in a short time. They may have had doubts about their newfound political allies, but they were pragmatic. As one SAM planner put it, COPLAMAR hired them "because they are folks who don't get corrupted, who know how to live in the countryside. It's not that we wanted to favor them, but they represent something. They weren't going to hurt Mexico—on the contrary."[19]

One moderate COPLAMAR official described the hiring of inde-pendent activists as a "necessary evil." He was relieved that once the initial job of promotion was done, he and other mainstream policy-makers would no longer need to depend on them. This kind of instru-mental logic led them to support mobilized but undemocratic peasant organizations. Some of these moderate policymakers, for example, channeled resources to Antorcha Campesina, a semiofficial paramili-tary group that has been accused by independent peasant groups of assassinating dozens of their members, especially in the state of Puebla.[20]

Grass-Roots Promotion

The effort began with the selection of organizers to promote the formation of Village Food Committees. According to extensive inter-

18. Some members of this current were from privileged family backgrounds and through the program came into intimate contact with Mexican poverty for the first time. According to more politicized COPLAMAR managers, some of their colleagues showed signs of "lib-eral guilt," which encouraged them to pursue their individual ambitions within a program that dealt with basic social problems.

19. According to one former mid-level COPLAMAR official, the logic was that "a PRI-ista isn't going to push harder than a guy who really goes out into the countryside, who goes around talking to each peasant. To begin to develop some trust the promoter had to spend at least three months out there to be able to begin to do his job. A PRIista isn't going to do it; they're going to draw their paycheck and then stay in the state capital the whole time, going out every once in a while to see what's up. Sometimes they'll make a deal with the cacique. The program needed the kind of person who could really put some substance into the program, and only leftists could do that."

20. See Martínez Borrego 1991. Some see possible future parallels with Peru's Sendero Luminoso, in terms of combining orthodox Leninism with coercion to build support in isolated indigenous areas.

views both with former CONASUPO-COPLAMAR officials and with grass-roots rural activist leaders, most COPLAMAR organizers saw the PRI more as part of the problem than as part of the solution. The vast majority of promoters were not, however, members of opposition political parties. The recruits tended to be nonparty activists who saw the consolidation of autonomous peasant organizations, rather than electoral politics, as key to greater social justice and the democratization of Mexican society.[21] One participant in the selection process estimated that 20 to 25 percent of the promoters hired were women—high compared with other rural development programs, but rather low considering the gendered concern for food supply problems at the household and community level.[22]

Both the radicals and the moderates within the CONASUPO-COPLAMAR leadership agreed that the program should support existing representative peasant organizations, in spite of their differences over how to handle the field staff. In some regions promoters were selected in consultation with existing community organizations. This process was coordinated with the geographic selection of some of the warehouse sites in areas where mobilization was already under way. Participants estimated that about 10 percent of the promoters—the original three hundred grew to approximately six hundred—were nominated by regional peasant organizations.[23]

The CONASUPO-COPLAMAR promoters were officially presented to the municipal president and ejido commissioners at the very

21. Many were drawn from the "social left," which included several low-profile, pragmatic political tendencies (most notably Línea Proletaria, among others). For an overview of the different currents on the Mexican left during this period, see Moguel 1987. On the recruitment procedures for field organizers, including the extremely sophisticated multiple-choice tests used for evaluating candidates, see Uvince Rojas 1982:88–110. The selection process required either social science training or rural development experience. In contrast, PACE field-workers were usually agronomists with little background in social or economic issues.

22. Very little precise information on women's participation in the program exists. In Oaxaca, one program adviser estimated that 30 to 40 percent of the elected store managers were women. As one might expect, women were significantly underrepresented at the leadership levels of the rural consumer movements.

23. According to one midlevel COPLAMAR official, "If you look at the speeches of López Portillo and the other leaders of the time, one of the central issues they refer to constantly was the cacique, the crop hoarder as an obstacle to rural development. The logic was for the program to confront the intermediary by encouraging the direct management of marketing by the peasants and their organizations. One criterion CONASUPO-COPLAMAR used in determining whether to hand over the administration of a warehouse to the peasants of a region was that they be organized, and that's where we sought to make agreements with independent organizations. In general the organizations accepted the entry of the program, but we had to make concessions, like hiring people proposed by the organization as warehouse workers and promoters."

beginning, but they rarely received a warm welcome. One former top-level COPLAMAR official estimated that 70 percent of the municipal and ejido leaders opposed the program. They were often part of the dominant power structure, since the electoral process in most rural municipalities and ejidos was not free and fair.[24] In some remote communities promoters had to meet with villagers clandestinely because of the threat of violence from caciques who insisted that all government programs be channeled through them. Although the promoters, as government employees, were relatively safe from cacique repression, the villagers were not.

The key task of the promoter was to organize community assemblies to choose the people who would represent the village in overseeing and managing DICONSA operations at the village and regional levels. In the case of PACE assemblies, the main purpose was to sign up as many producers as possible. The main purpose of CONASUPO-COPLAMAR assemblies, in contrast, was to create a new and democratic community organization in order to increase the accountability of government food agencies.

To install a village store, a community had to decide in a formal assembly to administer it according to the guidelines laid down by the CONASUPO-COPLAMAR promoter. The stores were set up on the principle of "coresponsibility." The community would take responsibility for managing the store, and CONASUPO agreed to supply it. The community would find the locale, and CONASUPO would put up the working capital to buy merchandise. If the community decided to set up a store, the first step was to "democratically elect" six villagers to a Village Food Committee to oversee its management. The assembly was also to elect a store manager, who would be paid a commission from sales. The commission was set at 5 percent of sales, although originally there was some confusion over whether this all went to the store manager or whether the assembly could allocate some of it (it varied in practice). The assembly agreed to prepare a locale for the store for other projects and to meet monthly to hear reports from the rural food committee about store operations. The community also agreed to send two representatives, usually the president of the Village Food Committee and the store manager, to monthly meetings at the regional warehouse that supplied the store (DICONSA 1982a; Uvince Rojas 1982).

24. On rural municipal politics, see López Monjardin 1986 and Fox and Hernández 1992.

The Village Food Committee representatives and the store managers who met monthly constituted the Consejo Comunitario de Abasto (Community Food Council). The councils were officially considered "one of the fundamental elements for making the CONASUPO-COPLAMAR program one of shared responsibility between the community and the institution" (*Sistema C*, September 1981:32). Their task was to oversee the operations of the warehouse and to make sure the surrounding village stores were supplied. These meetings involved reports from the villages, reports from the warehouse managers, and discussions of how to deal with operational problems. These councils and their meetings were the focus of the political conflict over the nature of the program. Not only were they the key point of contact between the state and newly organized consumers, but they encouraged the creation of a shared regional identity that had rarely existed before.

Participation in Practice

CONASUPO-COPLAMAR managers in Mexico City developed a sophisticated method for monitoring levels of participation in the program. They set up three separate information channels. First, they received the reports of the field staff and their supervisors, who followed both community participation and DICONSA provisioning performance. Second, they received copies of the official *acta de asamblea*, the document recording the results of the food council meetings. Mexico City administrators considered this their most important source of information, since the assembly was ostensibly led by elected peasant leaders rather than by government employees. Third, they received reports from the warehouse and DICONSA branch managers. One of the key struggles for the monitoring staff in Mexico City, according to one former member, was to "keep the branch managers' hands off the assembly reports," since they often attempted to tone down criticism of their performance.

Quantitative national indicators of participation serve as a useful starting point for analyzing the politics of the program. In the month of July 1982, 95 percent of the Community Food Council meetings planned were held. These meetings were attended by 42 percent of the representatives expected, of whom 53 percent were store managers and 31 percent were village committee representatives. The village store managers attended more regularly, in part because they earned their living from commissions and therefore had a direct stake in being supplied. Almost all the meetings were attended by COPLAMAR field staff, who often used company vehicles to bring community representatives to the meetings. Of those village committees represented, 88 percent reported that they were satisfied with the staff support from the promoters. Only 60 percent reported, however, that their petitions were "adequately attended" by the warehouse staff (DICONSA 1982a:13–14), reflecting the operational bureaucracy's resistance to dealing with organized clients.

The data indicate that the pattern of participation did not follow the simple pyramid projected on paper. Instead, almost all regional Food Councils met, whereas only 42 percent of village committees were represented. This indicates that participation was very uneven and was probably nonexistent in many areas. Many, perhaps most, of the Community Food Council meetings did *not* involve the mobilized participation of the majority of communities in those regions. These figures do suggest, however, that after only two years of operation the program had achieved notable participation in a significant minority of the villages targeted.

Although the CONASUPO-COPLAMAR program did not openly challenge the local power structure, it created the political opportunity for peasants to do so. There were of course many areas where the caciques themselves, or the official peasant organizations, managed to block or control the program, for reasons discussed below. But where representative, autonomous peasant groups were active, or where conditions were ripe for their formation, CONASUPO-COPLAMAR often contributed to their consolidation. Democratization usually generates friction, however, since authoritarian power structures are rarely weakened without conflict. The resistance generated came not only from the local power structures but from powerful interests within CONASUPO itself.

The Apparatus Reacts

The essence of the CONASUPO-COPLAMAR program was the creation of a new policy current within the state: the coordinated alliance between "reformist" Mexico City managers and politically committed field promoters (see fig. 1, below). This new coalition in turn allied with peasants and helped to organize them in their efforts to pressure the rest of CONASUPO to carry out the policy. The reform program would succeed to the degree that it was able to *internalize social conflict within the agency* and thereby change the incentive structure faced by DICONSA's operational apparatus. At the same time, the private and bureaucratic interests served by the agency's traditional urban bias continued in their positions of author-ity, and they did not remain passive in the face of this challenge.

The reaction of the CONASUPO apparatus to the village store pro-gram was crucial to determining what promoters could and could not do, as well as whether food actually reached the villages. The re-sponse of DICONSA branch managers, who were usually responsible for retail food distribution in an entire state, was central. They were in a position to interfere with promotion of the program, and they were also the ones who allocated resources between urban and rural stores at the state level. DICONSA management usually resisted the attempt to force them to share power over resource allocation with peasant communities, but the issue was to what degree and to what effect.

The typical branch manager "aspired to have a Le Baron [car] and to be a member of the Lions Club," just like a private business execu-tive, according to one director of the rural store program. Their insti-tutional priority was to generate sales and profits, which were con-centrated in nonbasic products and high-volume urban supermarkets. Village stores sold relatively small volumes of low-margin basic goods at a high unit transportation cost. There were few bureaucratic incen-tives to supply the village stores, though they were often sent surplus shipments of inappropriate urban merchandise (such as mayonnaise). In the view of one former Mexico City planner, the branch managers "were used to dealing with concessionaires, from the same social class, with whom they had an understanding. CONASUPO-COPLAMAR came along and said, 'now you're going to have to pay attention to a mob of ragged, dirty, smelly Indians, who are going to tell you what you're doing right and what you're doing wrong.' It was difficult for them to accept." The branch manager "could even be a cacique himself," according to one national DICONSA official with regional-level operational experience.

Branch managers used a wide range of tactics to block Community Food Councils, including such measures as gerrymandering ware-house districts to divide allied communities and preventing company trucks from being used to bring community leaders to meetings from outlying areas.[25] Branch managers were often hostile even to the most

25. Some would try to keep participation down by not paying for the day's meal. The more sophisticated branch managers would allow the trucks to pick most village represen-

politically cautious COPLAMAR promoters because they were considered an imposition from outside the CONASUPO apparatus. In some cases limited supplies were distributed only to favored and docile villages, in an attempt to divide the food council and create a clientele for the DICONSA branch manager.

Branch manager resistance was very frustrating to the reformist policymakers in Mexico City, but there was little direct action they could take against them from above. DICONSA branch managers were usually chosen by the CONASUPO director, in consultation with the state governors (see fig. 1, below). It was in the very nature of the regional power structures to be able to defend themselves from national-level reformist pressures. In this case the mechanism was usually an alliance between the governor, responsible only to the president, and the DICONSA branch manager, and not even the head of DICONSA could easily pressure a governor.[26]

The community organizing process unleashed by CONASUPO-COPLAMAR provoked resistance within the government at the national level as well. Opposition to community participation was concentrated in the Ministry of Commerce, which oversees CONASUPO operations, and in the state delegations department at CONASUPO's head office. The State Delegates represented the CONASUPO director, supervising the work of CONASUPO subsidiaries in each state.[27] Although their formal role was to coordinate CONASUPO activities, their main task was to manage the political relationship between the enterprise and the regional power structures, particularly the governors.[28] When CONASUPO-COPLAMAR began, the director of the CONASUPO delegations was a figure "always connected to the most

---

tatives up for meetings but would have them skip the "troublemakers." In some areas DICONSA branch officials intervened in the internal affairs of both village-level and regional committees, in order to install more pliable representatives. Branch managers in some states were able to block promoters from working with politically independent peasant organizations.

26. The assistant branch managers were sometimes more willing to hold dialogues with field organizers and peasant representatives, because some were named by CONASUPO-COPLAMAR from Mexico City. According to a former participant, however, "They were often isolated because they didn't really get along with the field organizers, even though they were both from COPLAMAR, and they didn't get along with the branch managers either. The manager didn't support them, and on top of everything the peasants were pressuring them. As a result, in many cases the assistant manager ended up allying with the manager against the organizers, calling them provocateurs, saying that they were doing political rather than technical work."

27. See *Sistema C*, May 1984.

28. See Grindle 1977:111–41.

traditional PRI power structure, who knew the game perfectly," according to a former COPLAMAR planner.

> He was one of the first who began to attack us, from the delegations office, because they began to have problems of so-called political control, with the stores in their states. Remember the pressures from the legislators to put the stores where they wanted? Imagine the pressures on the delegates from the governors and the heavy hitters in each state. It was a difficult situation for the delegates because they were supposed to be the managers of CONASUPO in each state, but they had no control over the program. It's within this logic that the firing of promoters began in 1981.

The Purges

The pressures on CONASUPO-COPLAMAR to limit its promotion efforts began to mount soon after the program was launched. Opposition came from the whole array of forces that benefited from CONASUPO's long-standing urban and industrial bias, as well as from those who simply feared democratic peasant organizing in any form. The complaints from governors, municipal presidents, ejido commissioners, and private traders eventually led to rumors of "communist infiltration" in the program. As one frustrated member of the liberal wing of COPLAMAR management put it, "Anything having to do with organizing peasants to defend their interests is called communist. Anyone who carries the constitution under his arm is called a communist."[29]

The purges began in Puebla. According to one former COPLAMAR planner, the branch manager "was very afraid of the peasants. He'd never seen one before, so he called in Gobernación to repress them." According to the Puebla Community Food Councils, he was particularly corrupt and authoritarian. After months of working through official channels and being ignored, several Community Food Councils united to bring greater pressure to bear on the branch manager. He considered them a dangerous political problem and blamed the promoters for the peasants' self-organizing. After a clear threat against the councils, the community representatives decided to take their complaints to the president in Mexico City, a traditional re-

---

29. The program's field promoters also included a handful of former political prisoners, beneficiaries of López Portillo's 1978 political amnesty. Their past records were used in an attempt to discredit the entire program.

course. Each individual then received more serious threats, and the president of one warehouse council reportedly was beaten by the top police official in the state in the presence of a DICONSA branch official (Ortiz Pinchetti 1981b:10). The trip to Mexico City was suspended.

By May 1981, 65 percent of the promoters in the central highlands states of Puebla, Mexico, Tlaxcala, and Hidalgo either had been fired or had resigned to protest "actions contrary to the philosophy of the program." As one promoter put it, "The problem is one of mentality and interests. The DICONSA administrators are against community participation; they are interested only in selling and maintaining their privileges." According to the president of the Community Food Council of Santiago Tezontlale, Hidalgo, the warehouse where President López Portillo first inaugurated CONASUPO-COPLAMAR with great fanfare, "CONASUPO is the big enemy of the program" (Ortiz Pinchetti 1981b:6–10).

The push for purges began at the national level with attacks from the head of the Commerce Ministry's state delegations office.[30] He found an ally in CONASUPO's director of state delegations, who was interested in using the program as an electoral tool. By mid-1981 Gobernación sent CONASUPO-COPLAMAR a list of the fifty employees who had to be fired. CONASUPO-COPLAMAR policymakers found the list a bit strange, since it included a mix of those who had an open political militancy, "who Gobernación would evidently have on file," along with others who had no such past, "for whom it was absurd to be on the list." This combination led CONASUPO-COPLAMAR managers to believe that "surely the list was drawn up by DICONSA people, who then gave it to Gobernación." One policymaker further suggested that Gobernación had no idea what was going on until reform opponents in CONASUPO alerted them.

The reformists at the top had to give in or lose their positions. The pressures grew to the extent that the director of DICONSA reportedly thought he was going to lose his job, but the director of CONASUPO intervened on his behalf. The top leaders of COPLAMAR, DICONSA, and SAM all lacked the rank to deal directly with Gobernación in this matter. Those negotiations were reportedly handled by

30. He was reportedly associated with far right wing circles, particularly the Opus Dei (a semiclandestine Catholic lay organization), and was the first to denounce the presence in the program of political prisoners freed under the amnesty, according to former COPLAMAR officials.

the director of CONASUPO, a technocrat who tolerated the program, and by the Secretary of Commerce. A close associate of De la Vega's reported that, given his presidential ambitions at the time, he was more concerned about appearing too leftist a "precandidate" than with defending the program.[31] As a result, according to one high-level defender of the program, it was "frozen" politically. Upon reflection, this former high-level policymaker further observed that "in this country they give you some room to maneuver. With López Portillo and Echeverría, there was much more dialogue, much more political space [than after 1982]. But that's all child's play when Gobernación says "stop it. . . ." The president wasn't afraid of CONASUPO-COPLAMAR, but Gobernación was. . . . After all, deep down, Gobernación is the conscience of the president, in the sense that it sets his limits. Sure, the president is in charge and can fire the Secretary of Gobernación, but Gobernación's political control is an obvious presence, you can feel that's where real political power is. *You can go up to a point, and if you go past it they just deal you a blow.* I did some very dangerous things" (emphasis added). The reformist policymakers had unleashed a political dynamic that pushed them up against the limits to reform from above.

CONASUPO-COPLAMAR managers decided to try to handle the political pressure through evasive action, without resisting directly. At first fifty members of the original field staff of three hundred were fired, but by the end of the SAM period four hundred of a total of six hundred were replaced, according to a former top manager of the rural program. Not all were fired, but many resigned because they were demoralized by the purges. Many had been skeptical of the government's commitment to genuine participation in the first place, and they saw the initial purges as a signal that the political space for it had closed completely.[32]

The remnants of the original staff fought a remarkably effective

---

31. According to a former high-level national food policymaker, "The end of the administration was catching up with us in a hurry, and the idea was to unleash a process of self-management in the stores, with cooperatives. . . . But De la Vega, the Secretary of Commerce, who had a lot of power over CONASUPO, was afraid of the CONASUPO-COPLAMAR trucks, afraid of the cooperatives. They said that COPLAMAR, DICONSA, and SAM were giving too much play to people who weren't from the state."

32. High-level policymakers also fell. After the program's first year the head of CONASUPO wanted one top CONASUPO-COPLAMAR manager to meet with delegations of protesting rural grain traders. He sent him a poll of their attitudes, out of concern for the program's potential cost to the traditional cacique-dominated rural electoral system. Even though he himself was clearly by no means a radical, he resisted what he called "a witch hunt. . . . They sent me my ticket to the embassy in Switzerland within a month."

rearguard action against their opponents within CONASUPO. Neither the radicals nor the liberals in the program were ever fully purged, and they defended themselves by moving away from explicit discussion of social change to a more technical, operational approach. "Promoters" became "operational supervisors" as the head of DICONSA managed the crisis by integrating COPLAMAR staff more closely into DICONSA's structure. As one of the managers of this change put it, "We had to learn how to handle groceries." Although reformists' greater involvement in operations gave them more information about the resource allocation process and potential leverage over it, the selection of new field staff was shifted to the regional level, allowing DICONSA branch managers to propose candidates for the first time. The defensive tone of one of the few frank official evaluations of the program reveals the political situation of CONASUPO-COPLAMAR management at the end of the SAM period: "The original essence and in fact the only formal goal of the whole program is to *guarantee the final destination and price* of the products. . . . It is never useless to insist that the entire strategy—especially the community participation—was designed to meet that goal, and *no other*" (DICONSA 1982a:19; emphasis in original).

In spite of the political conflict surrounding the program, the reaction of the traditional power structure inside and outside the CONASUPO apparatus was too little and came too late to roll back the regional mobilizations unleashed by the community participation process. The "operational supervisors" often toned down their efforts, but the momentum of mobilization, once under way, did not require "outside agitators" to keep it going in many areas. In those areas where promotion was not able to provide the political resources for communities to organize effectively, or where food distribution was less of a problem (as in many grain surplus areas), the new political constraints clearly blocked the consolidation of the program. But in many areas of pressing need, where communities had a history of organizing in defense of their own definition of their interests, the mobilization process was taken up by the communities themselves.

The Creation of Political Space: The Warehouse

CONASUPO-COPLAMAR's combination of community and regional participation turned simple warehouses into focal points of political conflict over the allocation of key resources. In general, few ostensibly "participatory" government-sponsored development programs integrate village-level with *regional* participation. Village-level participation alone, however, provides no leverage over huge state enterprises or powerful and violent regional elites. Since most state actors are reluctant to accept the legitimacy of autonomous peasant organizations and bargain directly with them outside the "proper channels" of traditional corporatist peasant organizations, the regional political space created by the Community Food Councils was unusual.

Key resource allocation decisions were made at the warehouse, including distribution of food, trucks, laborers, and working capital within its regional "area of influence." According to a wide range of former CONASUPO-COPLAMAR officials, independent grass-roots organizers, and elected peasant leaders, approximately fifty of the two hundred regional warehouses were effectively run by democratic Community Food Councils (as illustrated in fig. 1, far right-hand side). Perhaps another fifty regions were considered to be influenced by peasants' demands for accountability in policy implementation (fig. 1, center right).[33]

The program granted food councils the official power to nominate warehouse workers and truck drivers (DICONSA 1982b). They were considered "community employees," in part to prevent them from unionizing and demanding corresponding benefits and higher pay from DICONSA, but also to keep their job security dependent on their service to the communities. CONASUPO-COPLAMAR planners assumed that if they were DICONSA employees the communities would have little leverage to make sure that drivers and loaders did their jobs effectively. Where Community Food Councils were not effective, these jobs were allocated by DICONSA authorities as part of the traditional patronage system. In many regions, however, the councils exercised these rights and also fought for and often won the right to participate in hiring and firing DICONSA employees, such as regional warehouse managers and operational supervisors.[34] When several food councils managed to join together and share experiences, their demands sometimes focused on the branch manager or even

---

33. "Effective control" meant that the basic decisions made at the warehouse level were made by or in consultation with the Community Food Council. This does not mean all the stores in those regions were well stocked with quality goods, since many resource allocation decisions were made elsewhere in the CONASUPO apparatus.

34. For an official account of one such conflict (in the Huasteca region), see *Sistema C*, No. 23, July 1984.

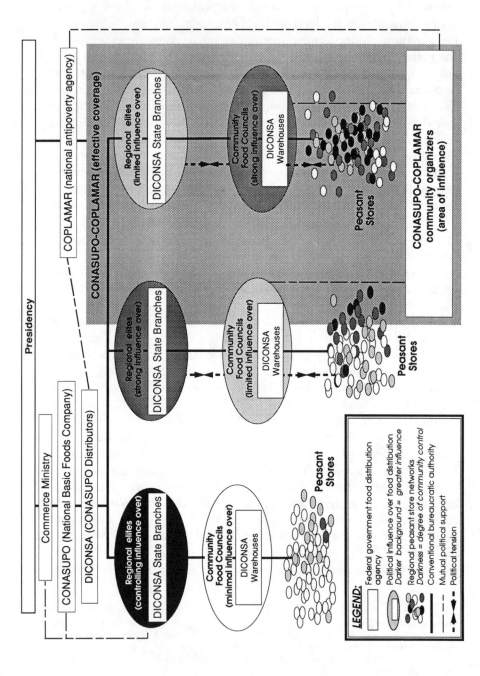

Presidency

Commerce Ministry

CONASUPO (National Basic Foods Company)

DICONSA (CONASUPO Distributors)

COPLAMAR (national antipoverty agency)

CONASUPO-COPLAMAR (effective coverage)

Regional elites (controlling influence over)
DICONSA State Branches

Community Food Councils (minimal influence over)
DICONSA Warehouses

Peasant Stores

Regional elites (strong influence over)
DICONSA State Branches

Community Food Councils (limited influence over)
DICONSA Warehouses

Peasant Stores

Regional elites (limited influence over)
DICONSA State Branches

Community Food Councils (strong influence over)
DICONSA Warehouses

Peasant Stores

CONASUPO-COPLAMAR community organizers (area of influence)

LEGEND:

Federal government food distribution agency

Political influence over food distribution
Darker background = greater influence

Regional peasant store networks
Darkness = degree of community control

Conventional bureaucratic authority

Mutual political support

Political tension

Figure 1. CONASUPO-COPLAMAR food distribution operations

higher up in DICONSA, obliging national program officials to intervene.[35]

Top food program managers were frequently torn between the institutional imperative to defend the enterprise's last word over its own
personnel decisions and their knowledge that the enemies of the Community Food Councils were often their enemies as well, in the context
of the struggle between policy currents within the state. The agency's
institutional imperative to control personnel decisions was not merely
a result of the pursuit of power for its own sake; it was also driven by
the Mexico City management's need to set limits to its conflicts with
its own operational staff. It could push them just so far. If top management sacrificed the careers of its middle managers in response to
every peasant demonstration or building takeover, the operational
staff members would themselves rebel, in conjunction with their allies
in state governments and elsewhere within CONASUPO. As a result,
only after especially intense regional mobilization would the branch
office itself be touched. If branch managers or assistant managers had
to be removed under Community Food Council pressure, they were
often simply transferred to another region.

Variation in Participation

There was great variation among community and regional responses to the CONASUPO-COPLAMAR program. The aggregate
data cited above indicate that participation did not "take off" in
much of the country (see fig. 1, left and center left). The evidence *does*
indicate successful community participation in a significant minority
of cases, however, and the case studies below will examine why. Participation worked in much of the south and southeastern part of the
country and failed in most of the north and central west, for three
types of reasons.

The first difference was economic. The demand for subsidized basic
food was not as strong because many northern and central-western
regions are surplus grain-producing areas. Pockets of deep poverty
persist, but food shortages and local monopolies are less of a problem
and migration is often chosen over community mobilization as a survival strategy.

35. The official documents that record food council demands, framed in terms of their
efforts to defend the program, repeatedly charge specific officials with corruption or abuse
of authority. The official DICONSA response was usually to insist that the councils provide
proof. In turn, the councils would call for official audits open to their participation.

The second difference was political, in that caciquismo still has a much more powerful hold over Mexico's poorest rural communities of the south. Even for those able to organize themselves autonomously at the village level, joint collective action with others against common enemies was much more difficult and dangerous. Basic freedoms of assembly and expression are not guaranteed. Especially for the more remote indigenous communities, semiofficial coercion is common and impunity is institutionalized. The political space opened up by the program was therefore much more important as a qualitatively new opportunity to permit communities to bargain together for the first time without risking serious repression.

The third difference, underlying the first two, was social and cultural. Participation in the program was most intense in areas where indigenous traditions of cooperative labor and community decision making by consensus continued to evolve. This was no coincidence. CONASUPO-COPLAMAR's participatory procedures were consciously designed by experienced, socially committed anthropologists to be compatible with communitarian indigenous traditions that still survive in many rural areas, in spite of increasing socioeconomic differentiation. In practice, conflicts between organized communities and the DICONSA apparatus often focused on culturally based differences over the participation process.

In Michoacán, for example, as elsewhere, the DICONSA bureaucracy tried to impose its interpretation of the participation procedures on the Purépecha communities. For most indigenous communities in Mexico the fundamental decision-making body is the general village assembly. DICONSA authorities did not accept this, preferring to involve only the elected community representatives. From the *comuneros'* (members of the indigenous agrarian communities) point of view, they all had the right to participate "with voice and vote." In their words, "neither the store manager nor the food committee is sovereign," and they contested foreign conceptions of representative delegation of authority with traditional direct democracy. For the DICONSA authorities, only prices and warehouse operations were acceptable topics for discussion. For the participants, the warehouse meeting served "to permit comuneros from different communities to meet, usually difficult because of the physical difficulties of access, to deal with whatever issue the majority decided to include in the order of the day" (Fuentes and Rossel 1982:78). Conflicting conceptions of participation provoked continual struggles over the nature and purposes of democratic collective action.

Participation in the food program was most intense in the indigenous areas of the south and southeastern states of Oaxaca, Guerrero, Veracruz, and Yucatán. Those central and center-western regions where participation emerged also tended to be primarily indigenous areas—most notably the Purépecha highlands, the Huasteca region of Hidalgo, and the northern Sierra of Puebla.

DICONSA's southeastern regional office, for example, successfully promoted participation in a significant minority of the Community Food Councils (before it was purged in 1982).[36] The councils were particularly important in the southeast because of the relative lack of regionwide peasant organizations. One of the first efforts in the country to bring together different food councils was in the Yucatán, in 1980. According to a former staff member, by July 1982 ten of the forty-two warehouses in the region were under conscious independent peasant control, defined as "clarity about the need to defend the warehouse as a political space."[37]

Because of the greater relative strength and impunity of cacique traders in the south, however, repression against the program was more severe than in any other area. Before the end of the SAM period, two community food activists reportedly were assassinated in Chiapas.[38]

The use of repression against peasant movements in Mexico has long been justified by the accusation of a revolutionary political challenge to the state. Although "security forces" often used this pretext whether or not such groups were actually involved, their presence did increase peasant movements' vulnerability to attack. COPLAMAR strategists tried to defend the program from repression by staying away from party politics. As in other areas, for example, the southeastern regional staff took pains to block efforts by small radical po-

36. The region covered the states of Yucatán, Quintana Roo, Campeche, Tabasco, and Chiapas.

37. The movement continued in the Yucatán, with ebbs and flows. In 1988, for example, a group of five hundred peasants from 280 villages occupied the main CONASUPO offices in the state capital. Even after they won the suspension of the branch manager on corruption charges, they remained in place until their other demands were met, including the firing of his lower-ranking "unconditional" subordinates and the renewal of maize supplies in the stores (*La Jornada*, 9-VIII-88).

38. The leader of an emerging statewide network of councils in Tabasco was found dead not long afterward. DICONSA authorities claimed it was suicide, but the victim's colleagues contended that he was murdered because of his community organizing efforts. After a year's lull, the organizing process began anew, and by 1985 the eleven councils in the state of Tabasco were united into a statewide network, together with three from northern Chiapas.

litical parties to take over food council mobilization, educating participants about how to retain their autonomy and avoid manipulation.
In other areas, differences emerged among the lower- and middle-level
COPLAMAR staff about whether to politicize the organizing process.
At first, for example, the center west was among the best-organized
parts of the country in terms of networking between regional food
councils, but internal divisions among the staff about the appropriate
role of radical political parties led to major setbacks. Whereas some
wanted to restrict the networking among food councils to issues of
food marketing, others were willing to sacrifice the program by using
it as an instrument for party building.[39] At the same time, any networking at all among food councils was perceived by higher-level
managers as a threat. In response, their purges successfully rolled
back most of the autonomous regional consumer mobilization in the
center-west region.[40]

Participation Scenarios: Community Food Council Experiences

The CONASUPO-COPLAMAR participation process followed
three scenarios in practice: no change in the local balance of power,
consolidation of an existing process of regional democratization, and
the catalyzing of a new regional counterweight to cacique power. The
first scenario, the continuation of the status quo, does not pose an
analytical problem. Failure is the norm for most top-down rural development reforms; the way local and regional politicoeconomic elites
appropriate the implementation of rural development programs is
well known. The second scenario, given the deliberate strategy of
CONASUPO-COPLAMAR planners to support existing or emerging
regional peasant movements, is not surprising either, once we have
explained how reformist policymakers reached positions of influence.
The third scenario is less obvious, since reformist initiatives were able

39. Reportedly, organizers from one semiclandestine radical group wanted to take over
the food council movement in the center-west in order to increase their relative weight
within their organization.
40. The center-west region extended from Sinaloa to Querétaro. COPLAMAR organizers convened five networking meetings between 1980 and 1982, involving up to twenty-
five of the thirty-five food councils in the region. Representatives from food councils in
Oaxaca, Puebla, and Veracruz came as observers, contributing to their own regional networking. Even though food council networking in the center west advanced earlier and
more quickly than in the south-southeast, it was generally more dependent on the external
organizers and therefore more vulnerable to the eventual purge.

to trigger the emergence of new social actors, and representative examples of these regional movements are analyzed in greater detail.

Scenario One: No Change

In the first scenario, CONASUPO-COPLAMAR did not provoke any change in local power relations. Branch managers in the north were particularly urban oriented, and most of the more committed community organizers were in the south, south-central, and southeastern parts of the country. This scenario covers two kinds of processes: where participation never "took off," and where it was launched but was then successfully blocked or repressed. After the attacks on the program in Puebla, for example, a leader of the Tetela food council reported: "Now we're worse off. Because of the shortages our stores don't have what the folks want, so we have to go to the cacique's store. He then takes advantage even more; he laughs at us: 'You [disrespectfully informal] have your CONASUPO store, don't you? Why don't you go buy there?' he says. And then he won't sell to us, or he'll sell at whatever price he wants because he's got us by the throat" (cited in Ortiz Pinchetti 1981b:9).

In much of the center and north, the councils simply followed the DICONSA managers' orders, and the rural program's trucks were controlled by private interests.[41] Where participation did not take off, the program either made no difference or may have even reinforced local elites by infusing fresh political and economic resources (fig. 1, left side).

Scenario Two: Consolidating Ongoing Change

In the second scenario the program helped to consolidate an existing regional peasant movement. This occurred primarily in areas that had been experiencing periodic waves of mass mobilization since the early 1970s. The "Tosepan Titataniske" Agricultural Cooperative (CARTT), for example, was already a regional force in northern Puebla before CONASUPO-COPLAMAR.[42] The name of the coopera-

41. The main exceptions in the north were in the contiguous states of Coahuila and Durango, which developed food council coordinating networks by the mid-1980s. One leading activist in the Laguna region estimated that its councils were "70 to 80 percent democratic."

42. The region had experienced intense mobilization in the mid-1970s in the form of land invasions and semiclandestine peasant organizing, which was defeated by army occu-

tive means "We Shall Overcome" in the indigenous Nahuatl language. The cooperative first organized regionally by developing its own consumer distribution network, in response to cacique monopolization of sugar in the region. It then extended its efforts to organize regionwide marketing of coffee and allspice, two of the principal smallholder cash crops in the region, which turned the cooperative into a major economic enterprise. COPLAMAR deliberately organized one of the first pilot Community Food Councils in the cooperative's area of influence, and it became one of the early "showcases" of community participation.[43]

The Community Food Councils also helped to revive a regional producers' movement that had stagnated. The "Lázaro Cárdenas" Union of Ejidos (UELC) in the western state of Nayarit, launched as a dynamic regional organization of dryland maize producers in 1975, had later been taken over by a hostile state government. The Community Food Council program permitted inchoate dissatisfaction to crystallize into discreetly organized region-wide opposition, as communities regrouped in the food council and prepared to redemocratize the UELC.[44] The revived community-based leadership was then able to confront the government-installed authorities, informally relieve them of power, ratify the change through elections, and revitalize the UELC's participatory regional economic development projects.[45]

---

pation early in the López Portillo administration (Ramos García et al. 1984). Land tenure could no longer be touched, but peasants could still attack cacique power through marketing. The "social energy" (Hirschman 1984:43) unleashed by the land invasions continued to express itself in the political space remaining, which turned out to be the alternative marketing efforts supported by sympathetic government rural development program officials from the Plan Zacapoaxtla (a spinoff from the Plan Puebla based in the Chapingo Agricultural University). For useful studies of the CARTT, see Martínez Borrego 1991; Mora Aguilar 1979; Masferrer Kan 1986a, 1986b; Sánchez Hernández 1987; and the long interview with its leaders in *El Día* (1-IX-84).

43. See *Sistema C*, September 1981. The CARTT also hosted a major national meeting of peasant organizations in 1985, where the UNORCA was formally constituted, the National Union of Autonomous Regional Peasant Organizations (*El Día*, 6-IV-85).

44. The CONASUPO-COPLAMAR promoter later became a key UELC staffer. Early on, he brought fifteen ejido leaders to visit the most dramatic success story of peasant-managed regional development in Mexico at that time, the Coalition of Collective Ejidos of the Yaqui and Mayo Valleys of Sonora (CECVYM). The CECVYM had grown to national political and economic importance, showing that the ejido sector could produce efficiently if organized democratically and autonomously (see chap. 7). This direct exposure to a practical alternative vision of the future inspired the community leaders to broaden and deepen their efforts to revive the peasant movement in the region.

45. For further studies of the UELC, see Fox and Hernández 1989; Hernández 1990c; and Fox 1992a. CONASUPO-COPLAMAR also contributed to the consolidation of the following preexisting regional movements: the Regional Union of Ejidos and Communities of the Hidalgo Huasteca (URECHH), the regional movement associated with the Ejido

Scenario Three: The Creation of Regional Political Space

Many of Mexico's rural people identify more closely with their particular village or kinship network than with broader ethnic, political, or class categories. The village stores and the warehouse meetings often brought together people who had not perceived common interests before. In this third scenario, a new social actor emerged.

Regional identities are politically contingent, even where people belong to the same ethnic group. Although regions may be clearly defined in terms of agroecological zones, social history, economic activity, or political boundaries, one cannot assume that the inhabitants consider themselves to share common interests. They are frequently locked in long-standing conflicts with neighbors who are equally oppressed in class and ethnic terms, often over land and other resources linked to survival.[46] Regional identities are primarily social constructs and therefore cannot be assumed. Where the warehouse and its food council became the focus both of shared material interests and of collective action, the rural food program created a new regional civic identity.

The case studies that follow are all examples of movements that united dozens of diverse communities on a broad regional level to an unprecedented degree (e.g., fig. 1, far right-hand side). They are representative of the estimated one-fourth of the food councils that managed to actively represent the interests of the majority of their communities. The movements were all independent of political parties, although two of the three regions had previously experienced opposition political activity in some areas. The three regional movements developed varying levels of mobilization and organization, but they

---

Batopilas in the Laguna region, the Morelos state network of food councils, which arose in part out of the Emiliano Zapata Union of Ejidos, the Coalition of Ejidos of the Costa Grande of Guerrero, and the Worker-Student-Peasant Coalition of the Isthmus of Oaxaca (COCEI), among others.

46. For detailed studies of local identities and violence in Oaxaca, see Dennis 1987; Flanet 1979; Greenberg 1989; and Parnell 1988. Nagengast and Kearney's analysis (1990) of the "social construction" of ethnicity is especially useful, showing the process through which Mixtecos come to define themselves ethnically, beyond their membership in a "corporate community," through their experiences as migrant farmworkers. Ideas about what it means to be Mexican are also complex in indigenous Oaxaca. For example, an informal sample of Zapotec voters offered a revealing reason for supporting the 1988 nationalist presidential candidate: "Because he's Mexican." Poor, and tired of six years of economic crisis, they blamed it on a succession of presidents who, in addition to being seen as white (i.e., "Spanish"), could not "really" be Mexican because otherwise they would have better defended their interests and those of the nation.

all were triggered by the opportunity created by the CONASUPO-COPLAMAR program and then extended their democratizing efforts to deal with other pressing rural development issues.

Tlapa, Southeastern Guerrero

Tlapa is the commercial and political center of the Montaña region of Guerrero, which is divided into temperate highlands and semiarid midlands. Most of the population is indigenous, including Tlapanecos, Mixtecos, and Nahuas, and the rate of monolingualism is relatively high. Less than 10 percent of the population in the region had access to safe drinking water (COPLAMAR 1982). Few government services extended to the countryside, where virtually the only cash to complement meager subsistence plots came from crafts such as palm weaving, providing a daily income of perhaps fifty cents (U.S.). Many hamlets in the region were relatively undifferentiated in social terms, retaining access to land as well as traditional forms of democratic decision making.

Even though Tlapa had fewer than ten thousand inhabitants, it defined the surrounding region through its economic and political domination. Paved roads linked the region to the national transportation network only in the late 1970s. Each of the several municipal centers in the region rotated local political leadership among several wealthy, usually nonindigenous families, sharing power over the many surrounding villages. These same families dominated the terms of economic exchange between the villages and the national market, controlling both the provision of key inputs, such as credit and fertilizer, and the sale of local products such as fruit and palm hats and sleeping mats. They controlled the local offices of the state and federal agencies as well.

Peasant mobilization in some pockets of the region predated CONASUPO-COPLAMAR, but the program permitted a qualitatively new scope and degree of regional consolidation. The Montaña region was not deeply involved in the peasant-based guerrilla movements that erupted in response to similar problems in other parts of the state of Guerrero in the late 1960s. As elsewhere in the state, earlier peasant movements in the region had developed around the two key issues of municipal democratization and better terms of trade for agricultural inputs and harvests.

In 1968 a peasant movement for local democratization within the ruling party won the town elections in the midland municipality of

Huamuxtitlán, but they were anulled by the governor. Armed peasants protested by occupying the town hall, but they were expelled by the army. As radicalized villagers who had managed to get an education began to come back from Mexico City, many as schoolteachers, the democratization movement regrouped and eventually defeated the caciques in municipal elections in 1977, peaking in 1982–83.

In the highland area of Montaña, meanwhile, opposition political activity peaked in 1979 with the founding of the Council of the Peoples of the Montaña in Tlapa. The Council was founded primarily by indigenous bilingual teachers and was associated with the first local Mexican Communist Party congressional candidate, a long-standing teachers' movement leader. One of their principal demands was the establishment of a network of CONASUPO stores in the villages of the region (*Unomásuno*, 20-V-79).[47]

These two cases show that very different subregions, the highlands and the midlands, both dominated by Tlapa, had experienced village-based movements for greater local political autonomy from traditional authorities since at least the late 1970s. Both were locally based, electorally oriented, and connected to outside allies, but these two efforts were not coordinated, nor did their influence extend within the region far beyond their respective municipalities. The CONASUPO-COPLAMAR program provided political and economic resources for the consolidation of a fully regionwide representative peasant organization for the first time.

The CONASUPO-COPLAMAR warehouse in Tlapa came to serve sixty-two village stores. Both existing local movements mobilized to take advantage of the program, since it responded to the needs of their members and at first was relatively open to participation by non-PRI groups. Supporters of a local independent peasant organization, the Popular Front of La Montaña, for example, came to control nine of the stores in the midlands.

The first president of the Community Food Council in Tlapa was Professor Juan Miramón Cantú, a senior bilingual teacher who was well respected in villages throughout the region because of his several

---

47. The PRI was declared winner of the election, which was marred by fraud and violence. Community activists were reportedly beaten and dragged through the streets of their villages by the mayor's hired men (*Unomásuno*, 12-VII-79). By 1983 the movement managed its first electoral victory, in one of the most remote highland municipalities, Alcozauca, under the banner of the Unified Socialist Party of Mexico (PSUM). The opposition local government later established an innovative "maize bank" to stabilize local markets (Toledo, Carabbias, and Provencio 1992).

decades of work on their behalf. He was not a member of either of the two subregional political movements, but he was open to both of them. He opposed using government services as a tool for maintaining the traditional cacique power structure. As he saw it, "Folks might be PRIista, they might be Communist, or they might be PANista, but they all eat tortillas just the same. . . . Our idea is to organize people to work to develop their communities, not for electoral politics."

The DICONSA apparatus in Guerrero was linked to the group that dominated the state government, one of the most entrenched and conservative in Mexico. The warehouse was supplied regularly, but little food reached the village stores. The Community Food Council's polite complaints were ignored by the branch headquarters. Instead, the director of Gobernación for the state called the Mexico City CONASUPO-COPLAMAR managers claiming that "a Communist teacher was using the program to lead an armed uprising to take over the state capital." The Mexico City managers found out that peasants in La Montaña were indeed led by a teacher, but that they had proof of corruption in warehouse operations that had been ignored for six months.

The DICONSA assistant branch manager had put his lover in charge of the Tlapa warehouse, and she had been selling maize and sugar destined for the village stores to private traders who resold it in the region for triple the price. Professor Miramón himself caught a well-known private trader in the act of unloading a truckload of maize from the warehouse. He did not blame the merchant, however. As he saw it, "He's a trader, and he tries to deceive people as do all traders; it's the system they have, taking the peasants. The warehouse manager knows the rules of the system. Why does she dare to sell maize to merchants? Who is the guilty one? By what right did she sell the maize, knowing that it is for a program in which maize isn't sold to private traders? It was a serious fight."

CONASUPO-COPLAMAR managers came personally from Mexico City to resolve the dispute, acting as intermediaries between the state authorities and a fifty-member peasant commission. They found the warehouse manager guilty. Both the warehouse manager and the assistant branch manager were reportedly fired. This kind of Mexico City intervention in disputes between DICONSA and communities was not unusual, but it often required what the reformist policymakers perceived as a high political cost.

The region's village stores continued to have supply problems. One store reported in 1985 that it had been without beans for three months, and the quality of the food remained low (*Unomásuno*, 20-V-85). The food council had nevertheless managed to win several political battles. By 1985 most of the local DICONSA personnel were named by the communities, including the warehouse manager. After a long struggle, the food council won the right to send warehouse trucks to bring community representatives to the monthly council meetings, not just the store managers as DICONSA had originally insisted. As Professor Miramón put it, "The store manager is nothing more than the errand-boy [girl] of the community. The community constitutes the authority, the elected leaders and the elders, they are the ones who know the community's problems best. We've managed to achieve a high level of participation, bringing more folks down, maybe three hundred, four hundred, five hundred at a meeting. We're the ones who've pushed this forward, and the branch [office] hasn't been able to stop us."

The Tlapa Community Food Council also created a production support network to extend its bargaining power beyond food distribution. The original COPLAMAR plan called for creating crop production support groups as well as food distribution committees, to permit peasants to negotiate regionwide with government agricultural agencies. COPLAMAR was unable to carry out this plan nationally, in spite of its historical and ideological roots in a similar Cárdenas-era idea. In the closing months of the López Portillo administration, one agency formed as part of COPLAMAR, the Pacto Intersectorial (Interagency Agreement), prepared for the end by literally giving away several hundred trucks to autonomous peasant organizations. Promotion of marketing cooperatives had been part of the COPLAMAR strategy all along, but it was carried out forcefully only at the end. According to one manager, "The number of trucks we gave each warehouse depended on the size and force of the organization, its bargaining capacity, and who was there. It was all negotiated. In the central offices, where we did this, 75 percent of the people were progressive, so before sending trucks to a CNC-controlled warehouse, obviously we'd send them where there was an independent group. It was logical. You can also do a lot from behind a desk, you know." With the uncertainty created by the presidential transition, there was only limited follow-up, but the idea was nevertheless taken up by Community Food Councils in a few areas where COPLAMAR's original policy statement circulated. The Tlapa food council began pushing for better treatment from the government bank in 1981 and started to get more fertilizer for many of its member communities. BANRURAL continued to deliver fertilizer too late for it to be useful, however, causing crop losses that were then ignored by the government insurance company.

By 1984 food council leaders had formed a Production Consultation Committee with local Agrarian Committees in twenty-four communities, about one-third of the region. They managed to negotiate an interest-free grant from the state government to buy fertilizer directly from FERTIMEX, bypassing the government bank.[48] Even though COPLAMAR no longer existed as an agency by that time, as far as the peasants of La Montaña were concerned the government had made a commitment to them, and the program's ideas were transformed into action. The experience of organizing and bargaining regionally around distribution spilled over into the arena of production. The autonomy conceded by DICONSA unleashed a dynamic that permitted a third of the region's communities to win greater autonomy from BANRURAL.

Pinotepa, Southwestern Oaxaca

Oaxaca ranks at the bottom in terms of state poverty levels in Mexico. Over 80 percent of rural producers lack sufficient land for subsistence (CEPAL 1982:119). The coastal population of the Pinotepa region is largely indigenous, including Mixtecos and Amuzgos as well as people of African descent. Caciques are more violent, peasants are reputedly more assertive, and landownership is more conflictive than in most of the state's central mountains and valleys.[49]

Until the opportunity created by the Community Food Council, the area had not previously experienced a regionwide peasant movement (aside from a few individuals who were on the fringes of the Guerrero guerrilla movement). The movement was linked indirectly to other grass-roots movements of the early 1980s, especially rural teachers'

---

48. The new governor was more open-minded and pioneered a new kind of crop loan on trust that did not require collateral (*crédito a la palabra*), with the support of an innovative nongovernment development organization, COPIDER (Comité Promotor del Desarrollo Rural).

49. The established national newspaper *Excelsior* described these regional caciques, after the murder of a PRI state congressman reputed to defend peasant interests: "Like feudal barons with gallows and knives, since time immemorial they have taken over the best lands in the districts of Pinotepa Nacional, Jamiltepec, and Juquila" (7-XII-85). On violence and land conflicts in this region, see Flanet 1979:64; and in a nearby region see Greenberg 1989.

efforts to democratize their union.[50] The organizing process began in 1981, reaching from the warehouse, located along the coast in Huaxpaltepec, up into the surrounding mountains. Cacique repression cost the lives of several local leaders, according to survivors and relatives. As a result, peasants active in community affairs had to work their fields with ancient rifles, if they had them, slung over their shoulders. The hired gunmen were well known, but were free from government prosecution.

The region's history and polarized social conditions had a major impact on the regional movement's understanding of the nature of the CONASUPO-COPLAMAR program. According to Don Ramiro Aparicio Torres, one of the early leaders of the food council, "This program wasn't born because the government wants to be nice, but because there was a lot of discontent in the countryside. Folks were getting angry; we saw what the League and Lucio were doing [early 1970s guerrilla groups]. The government said it had to give something to the peasants. They've got advisers, so they gave us COPLAMAR, which covers food and health care. . . . If they would carry it out, it would be a good program."

The distribution program in Pinotepa was beset with problems that appeared to be simply operational but actually reflected the region's low priority in the eyes of the DICONSA branch headquarters. Still, in spite of recurrent shortages, local consumers reported that the program did lower prices for some staples and significantly reduced the travel time required for shopping. For Aparicio, however, the most important achievement was the creation of a democratic regional organization. The program's delivery of benefits required regular mobilization, including frequent protests and the occasional occupation of DICONSA's Oaxaca branch headquarters itself.

The Pinotepa regional food council did not recognize DICONSA's authority over its warehouse personnel. The council leadership was not seen as the final authority either, since by tradition the community assemblies have the last word. The food council won the right to fire inadequate warehouse managers, but it was not perceived to make a significant difference. According to Aparicio Torres, "We can change the personnel with pressure, but the replacements are always the same. It's as though they had a factory to turn them out. If they don't work, then out they go." He considered the program to have

50. For the most comprehensive analysis of the Oaxaca teachers' movement, see Cook 1990a, 1990b.

been afflicted by a combination of "bureaucratism" and "bad intentions," which he saw as two distinct problems in spite of their apparent similarities. "With bureaucratism there are delays, a lot of paper pushing, but there are interests behind bad intentions. We've met with DICONSA, we've pressured them through the proper channels. For example, they don't send us beans when the concessioned stores do have them. Or they keep our trucks tied up in repairs for months to have an excuse not to send us our products. The problem isn't our lack of effort, it's their lack of will, and that's why I think there are interests involved."

In 1981 the council began sending representatives to national gatherings of autonomous grass-roots producer organizations, as well as participating actively in the statewide Oaxaca network of food councils, in order to learn how to set up peasant-managed enterprises directly from the experiences of other organizations. By 1985 the first priority of the food council leadership was to organize grass-roots support for a democratic union of ejidos, in order to have a legally recognized producers' association from which to launch cooperative marketing and investment projects. They named it the "Peasant's Awakening" Ejido Union and linked up with the National Union of Autonomous Regional Peasant Organizations (UNORCA).

The Central Valleys of Oaxaca

Many peasants from the Central Valleys surrounding the state capital region farm small parcels of relatively fertile land, but few have sufficient access to land for full employment. Although most members of this largely Zapotec population speak Spanish, many as a first language, most of the region's villages conserve community traditions of cooperative labor exchange and consensus building. The warehouse served a large clientele, estimated at one hundred thousand, with greater buying power than in the more remote areas of the state.

The Community Food Council in the Central Valleys grew to assert itself not only regionally, but also statewide and eventually at the national level as well. The Central Valleys surprised CONASUPO-COPLAMAR managers; participation in warehouse management was one issue, but increasingly autonomous statewide and later national-level mobilization was an unexpected outcome.

The Central Valley communities responded quickly to the opportunity to participate in the CONASUPO-COPLAMAR program. Some communities in the region had experienced land invasions in the early

1970s.[51] Particularly widespread protests over PRI manipulation of municipal elections also swept the state in 1977 and 1980–81.[52] The late 1970s also saw a rise in community protests about loss of control over their natural resources, particularly forests and water. Don Arcadio Morales Zárate, who would later lead the Community Food Councils on a national level, represented his village in a conflict over water use between irrigated smallholders and urban authorities and industries.

Strong opposition from the nearby DICONSA branch headquarters accelerated the Central Valleys food council's consolidation by providing a clear-cut and convenient enemy for communities to focus on. Because the branch headquarters supplied all the warehouses in the state, the Central Valleys occupied a strategic location for promoting statewide mobilization. The first networking efforts were clandestine, since the branch manager had forbidden them.

Fourteen food councils came together for the first time in July 1981, in response to a movement by CONASUPO-COPLAMAR truck drivers for rights to union benefits (especially social security insurance).[53] In March 1982, late in the SAM period, the Central Valleys led nineteen of the twenty-five Oaxaca food councils in the first effort at establishing a statewide coordinating body to negotiate with DICONSA for more and better merchandise and for freedom to organize as they chose. They first met on the eve of a planned visit by President López Portillo to inaugurate one of the new CONASUPO-COPLAMAR warehouses. According to Morales, "Seeing the anomalies that DICONSA always uses to try to fool the campesinos, filling one warehouse full of merchandise to try to make it seem as though all twenty-five are the same, we all decided to close the warehouses seventy-two hours beforehand, so they wouldn't have a chance to fill

51. The leading organization in the Central Valleys in the mid-1970s was the Worker-Peasant-Student Coalition of Oaxaca (COCEO). See Paz Paredes and Moguel 1979; Yescas Martínez 1982; and Zafra 1982.

52. See Martínez Vásquez 1990 and Martínez Vásquez and Arellanes 1985.

53. Insurance was of special importance to them, since drivers were continually exposed to extremely difficult driving conditions as well as the possibility of armed robbery (drivers often carried the stores' cash payments to the warehouse). Even though the food councils usually nominated the drivers, as "community employees" their interests did not always coincide. DICONSA was unwilling to take them on as full employees, arguing that the food council would lose its means of holding the drivers accountable for their performance. The drivers and food councils usually offered mutual support in their protest actions, but the drivers wanted union benefits while the food councils did not want to find themselves turned into formal "bosses." Reportedly, close collaboration between the two movements was not furthered by the involvement of a militant Trotskyist political party in the drivers' movement.

them up at the last minute. The trucks stayed in the lots outside the warehouses. We were going to let Lic. López Portillo in, we were going to let him inaugurate the warehouse, but we wanted him to be able to see what the real conditions were" (*El Día*, 24-III-84).[54]

As a result of this protest, national and regional DICONSA authorities signed a formal agreement in May 1982 with seven warehouse council presidents, representing the twenty-five Oaxaca councils. The agreement committed DICONSA to "cover the needs of the basic market basket of goods with opportunity, quantity, and quality, with written notice of exceptional cases of scarcity." After dozens of tons of products that had been delivered to the communities already spoiled were dumped outside the state DICONSA headquarters, the enterprise agreed to reimburse the village stores for the losses. In an apparent compromise, the agreement also committed DICONSA always "to respect the community organization and the Community Food Councils, along with the decisions of the General Assembly, when they are adjusted to the guidelines set out by the program. The councils also commit themselves to respect the enterprise's personnel decisions." The councils won the right to solicit and participate in evaluations of DICONSA personnel, however, as well as the right to hold formal meetings without the presence of DICONSA employees.[55]

The years 1982 and 1983 were a crucial transition period for the emerging statewide network, which protested continuing supply problems and called for regular audits. A planned occupation of the branch office failed when DICONSA authorities, together with the state police, cracked down. The first statewide network fell apart. The leadership soon regrouped, however, and founded the Oaxaca Food Council Coordinadora (coordinating network) in October 1983. The new organization was less open, limiting its vulnerability to govern-

---

54. The formal agreement among the food councils was as follows: "If we do not obtain a favorable response to the issues raised, it is sadly necessary for us to close the warehouses for seventy-two hours, from March 18 to 22, as a means of protesting the lack of compliance with the agreements made by the different executive offices of the program, state, regional, and national. We would like to point out to you that we are the ones most interested in the program's proper functioning, we are the marginal ones, those who have so often been deceived by so many programs and unfulfilled promises. That is why, if the COPLAMAR project wants to help poor peasants, it is necessary, from the beginning, to correctly solve the problems that have afflicted the program from the start." Representing 430 of the 550 communities that then had peasant stores, the nineteen food councils included Ayutla Mixe; Constancia del Rosario; Chalcatongo; Coixtlahuaca; Cuajimoloyas; Huajolotitlán; Huaxpaltepec; Ixtlán de Juárez; Juchatengo; La Reforma; Laollaga; Matatlán; Oaxaca; Sn. Andres Hidalgo; Sn. José del Chilar; Tamazulapam; Tecomaxtlahuaca; Tlaxiaco; and Yanhuitlán ("Pliego Petitorio," 15-III-82, mimeo).

55. Internal DICONSA document, May 7, 1982.

ment interference in its internal affairs. By 1985 the Coordinadora claimed to represent 856 communities and over 1.4 million low-income rural consumers.[56]

In 1984, after another round of intense mobilization, DICONSA signed an accord to supply the stores with at least 50 percent preferred Mexican white maize, instead of 100 percent low-quality yellow maize. The white maize tortilla is a cultural as well as a nutritional staple in indigenous regions of southern Mexico, though bread or yellow maize is more acceptable elsewhere. CONASUPO gave urban food processing industries priority access to white maize, however. The maize distributed in DICONSA channels was almost always U.S. yellow number 2 grade. Up to 10 percent of the volume delivered was dust and impurities. As Morales saw it, "Even in the poorest community there is money for quality maize. . . . They treat us like animals."

After several months it became apparent to the Coordinadora that DICONSA was not going to abide by its agreement. DICONSA failed to meet its commitment in part because it lacked the political clout within CONASUPO. CONASUPO's delegations and commercialization departments were closely allied with politically influential urban food processing interests, and they still controlled the allocation of white maize. Because of DICONSA's inability to provide sufficient quantities of adequate maize, the Coordinadora began to look for alternative sources. It set aside land to grow its own maize for the stores and sought ways of buying preferred white maize directly from other peasant organizations, but it proved very difficult to bypass CONASUPO.

Although the Coordinadora originally met with strong resistance from operating levels of DICONSA, it had some supporters in the Mexico City office. The Coordinadora's obvious popularity among peasants and local political and agrarian authorities, its nonpartisan political stance, and its alliance with a new national network of other grass-roots regional organizations forced both the state and national governments to treat it with unprecedented respect.

One of the high points in the Coordinadora's history was when it hosted the August 1984 meeting of the new national network of regional peasant organizations (formalized in 1985 as the UNORCA, the National Union of Autonomous Regional Peasant Organizations). Thirty-eight organizations from fifteen states attended, including a

---

56. For the Coordinadora's own chronology of its 1982–85 activities, see *El Día* (24-III-85).

high turnout by Oaxaca local elected officials (*El Día*, 18-VIII-84). The UNORCA was the principal national advocate of the strategy of blocking traditional mechanisms of surplus extraction by changing the political as well as the economic "terms of trade" between regional organizations and both the state and private markets. The UNORCA network represented an important new political gray area in the Mexican countryside, bringing together both nominally official and independent organizations (Fox and Gordillo 1989). Many UNORCA producer groups were reinforced by allied Community Food Councils.[57]

Some national DICONSA officials who tolerated or even supported the Coordinadora early on lost their enthusiasm when it began to promote the first national network of food councils, with the goal of coordinating bargaining strategy on behalf of thousands rather than hundreds of organized communities. Over three hundred delegates attended, representing 110 regional councils and over 4,200 communities from eighteen states, at that time approximately one-third of the food councils nationally (see table 5).[58] In public terms, relations with officialdom were still good. The historic "Encounter" (Encuentro) was organized largely by and for the peasants and their chosen advisers, although there were some minor efforts at infiltration by middle-level DICONSA officials.[59] The event had such legitimacy that it was scheduled to be formally "closed" by speeches from the conservative governor of the state as well as the general manager of DICONSA. As the hour for their arrival approached, nervous organ-

---

57. National-level coordination between producer and consumer groups did not last into the late 1980s, in part because they had different interests regarding the maize price issue. Given this conflict, as well as ethnic differences, the degree of unity they did achieve was remarkable.

58. Peak participation at any one time was on the second day, with 106 councils representing 4,162 communities. For a summary of the results, see *El Día* (31-VIII-85).

59. In the experience of Valentín González Martínez, representative of the Council from San Felipe, Guanajuato, for example, "We came to this Encounter called by the Coordinadora of councils from the state of Oaxaca because we think that the advances they've achieved in this state are really important. We see that they are different from the interests that others seek in this program, the branch managers and the operating chiefs, and I reaffirm this with the presence of a group of [DICONSA] operatives from the Guadalajara region, who have come to sabotage this meeting. They are trying to divide people, to keep the representatives from our region quiet. I think that this is absurd, because we are the ones who live in the countryside, we are the ones who feel the suffering—we don't need their guidance. Maybe they were able to get in because of the large number of people here; it wasn't possible to keep it closed, but the truth is that it doesn't matter to us. Let them know! Those of us who are making these petitions, or who are looking for possible alternatives to solve our problems, we're doing it publicly, as is our constitutional right."

Table 5. Representation at the First National Meeting of Community Food Councils

State	Community Food Councils per state
Oaxaca	26
Veracruz	16
Puebla	14
Tabasco	13*
Michoacán	10
Coahuila	6
Zacatecas	5
Guerrero	3
Morelos	3
Yucatán	2
Nayarit	2
Tlaxcala	2
Guanajuato	2
Aguascalientes	2
Querétaro	1
Jalisco	1
Durango	1
Nuevo León	1
Total (18 states)	110

*This number probably included some representation from Chiapas, since at the time the Union of Councils of the State of Tabasco included three from neighboring warehouses of northern Chiapas.
Source: "Asistentes a la Primera Reunión Nacional de Consejos Comunitarios de Abasto, del 16 al 19 de julio de 1985 (Guelatao, Oaxaca)" (unpublished document).

izers realized that their final plenary deliberations were far from over.[60] Rather than keep the officials waiting (and risk the chilling effect of their presence on the debate), they decided to suspend the meeting shortly before their arrival. With great fanfare, the governor and general manager of DICONSA then formally "closed" the meeting, and as soon as the officials left the plenary session resumed.[61]

The national meeting in Oaxaca was followed by several others in Puebla, Veracruz, and Morelos over the following year, but no other

60. The last day's session had gotten off to a late start, owing to the success of the previous evening's Guelaguetza festivities (Oaxaca's customary celebration of its diverse regional ethnic dances).

61. The message from Raúl Salinas de Gortari, general manager of DICONSA, was very supportive: "Today is a true show of triumph. A few years ago, even a few days ago, many officials were predicting the total failure of this program. . . . There were one, ten, twenty, a thousand detractors of this program who asked: Why are we giving this to peasants? They live off household production; why are we going to pay for the transport, why are we going to let them participate in the decisions, why are we going to listen to them if we know how to administer? The answer has been, and continues to be: because we are here to serve the Mexican people, and because we believe more in the organized community than in the consolidated bureaucracy" (*El Día*, 31-VIII-85)

would be as large, or have as much official legitimacy.[62] The Third National Encounter brought together the more consolidated core of the movement, including 84 councils from 3,664 commuities in ten states. New statewide networks had come together in Morelos, Puebla, Veracruz, Guerrero, and the Laguna region.[63] The national food council movement ebbed after 1986, but a significant minority continued to increase their capacity for oversight, self-management, and alternative marketing projects at the warehouse level.[64]

After the Guelatao meeting, the Oaxaca network grew increasingly militant, sufficiently confident to attempt a protest caravan to Mexico City in November 1985. The demands were familiar: inadequate food supplies, an alleged campaign of repression, and the firing of the Oaxaxa branch manager. The march was stopped in a high pass above the city; the Interior Ministry got directly involved. The Coordinadora had overextended itself. Some participants argue that the leadership grew more confrontational than the rank and file, both alienating powerful former elite allies and creating a gap that permitted later division and demobilization by DICONSA officials. The Oaxaca movement was down but not out, however. Shortly before the Third National Encounter, twenty of the Oaxaca councils joined together in one more major statewide action, a successful nine-day mass occupation of the branch headquarters in the state capital.[65]

The Coordinadora did not limit itself to rural consumer demands. Most of its members were producers as well as consumers, although few had the resources to harvest a net annual surplus.[66] In 1984 the

62. For accounts of later meetings between the national leadership of the councils with DICONSA, see *La Jornada* (5-IV-86, 6-IV-86).

63. "Informe de la Comisión Nacional de Enlace" (Report from the National Liaison Commission); unpublished document, no date.

64. The two warehouses along Guerrero's coast developed especially important experiences with self-management. In the case of the Alcholoa warehouse, in 1988 the entire operation was formally transferred to SIRAC, the distribution arm of the Coalition of Ejidos of the Costa Grande, which had created the food council from its beginnings in 1982. The SIRAC supplies a region of twenty thousand families. See Cobo and Paz Paredes 1991. A nearby self-managed food distribution experience was also led by a producers' organization, the Regional Ejidal Union of the Costa Chica (URECCH). See Espinoza and Meza 1991.

65. DICONSA reportedly agreed to the following demands: to suspend six important branch officials pending an audit; to give each warehouse investment capital; to deliver fifty-eight new trucks; to let the councils decide which garages should handle vehicle maintenance and repairs; and to study the possibility of transferring the warehouses to direct administration by the councils where feasible (*La Jornada*, 27-III-86).

66. The official Coordinadora statement to "the National Forum in Defense of the Ejido" reads: "Even if our organization was born as as organization of consumers in response to a government institution (CONASUPO), since the beginning it has been linked to

group decided to use its capacity for mobilization to win greater autonomy from BANRURAL. As elsewhere, the government agricultural bank in Oaxaca systematically delivered fertilizer too late in the season to be useful (see chap. 4). In response, the councils used community-supplied capital and DICONSA trucks to deliver eighteen thousand tons of fertilizer throughout the state at approximately 60 percent of the price charged by the government agricultural bank, sparking the rapid formation of the twelve-thousand-member Unión Libre Campesina (Free Peasant Union) in 1985.[67] In spite of operational problems owing to lack of administrative experience, the network still outperformed the government bank. As the Coordinadora grew more militant, DICONSA authorities withdrew access to government trucks, abruptly undercutting the new fertilizer program and promoting increased "divide and rule" efforts.

Other Community Food Councils around the state, such as the one in Pinotepa, followed the Central Valley experience closely to see how they too could create self-managed producers' organizations.[68] By late 1986 at least three Oaxaca food councils had "spun off" nascent autonomous regional producers' organizations. Their goal was to use increased bargaining power to retain a larger share of the value of what they produced for the market. These efforts were particularly important because of the food councils' lack of legal status and therefore greater vulnerability to changes in government policy and loss of elite allies. By 1990 the "social energy" unleashed by the food coun-

---

rural producers and their demands and aspirations; in fact, the vast majority of the members of the councils are ejidatarios and comuneros. It is therefore important that we not be seen as an organization of nonproducers. Although we understand that our form of association is not one taken into account by the official legal forms for producer groups, we are one, and one of our goals is to move toward constituting unions of ejidos and comunidades, as is already happening with the "Unión Libre Campesina de los Valles de Oaxaca," which recently obtained its registration. We say that we are an organization linked to the ejido and the comunidad because from the beginning we have struggled to lower the price of fertilizers and other inputs through the free distribution to the producers' plots, which we have achieved with our own transportation. We are an organization linked to the ejido because we understand that organization for food supply should be a complementary and fundamental task for producers, since the control of the products that peasants consume is basic, so that the few centavos we earn do not escape us" (from a speech presented to "La Jornada Nacional en Defensa del Ejido," Mexico City, August 5–8, 1985, mimeo).

67. Several DICONSA operational supervisors were very loyal to the Coordinadora, and their support proved important. Others sowed internal conflicts.

68. The union's legal registry proved to be an important stumbling block. According to advisers to the union, some administrators in the Agrarian Reform Ministry opposed it because they were allied to regional private sector elites, while others were unsympathetic because it was not government initiated.

cils found a new expression through a remarkable wave of mobilization by smallholder coffee producers throughout Oaxaca.[69]

Why Participation in Oaxaca?

Of the estimated one-fourth of the Community Food Councils that
managed to significantly democratize the rural food distribution process by the end of the SAM period, half were in Oaxaca. The objective need for subsidized maize and the sociocultural importance of the
tortilla have been suggested as explanations for the success of mobilization in Oaxaca. Indeed, since the vast majority of Oaxaca's citizens
are sub-subsistence rural producers, access to subsidized basic foods
such as raw maize, beans, cooking oil, salt, and sugar can have a
significant impact on the quality of their lives. The program was most
important to the very poorest. Debt peonage, for example, is still
widespread among coffee estate workers along the coast (*jornaleros
acasillados*), so alternatives to inflated food prices at company stores
were especially important (Vera 1990). But these factors were compa-
rably present in other regions in which CONASUPO-COPLAMAR
participation did not take off. The neighboring state of Chiapas was
equally in need, for example, and indigenous traditions of community
and ethnic self-government survived as well, but relatively few food
councils were consolidated there.[70] One must therefore also look for
factors specific to the Oaxaca experience.

Oaxaca's last century appears calm in comparison with the peasant
rebellions elsewhere in Mexico. Oaxacan peasants participated little
in the armed phase of the revolution, and when they did it was usually on the side of local caciques (Waterbury 1975). Most had managed to retain some rights to their community lands. Yet if we step
back to the colonial period, we find a long history of revolts against

69. The Oaxaca State Coordinadora of Coffee Producers (CEPCO) represented over
20,000 families by 1991, and many key leaders and organizers were veterans of the food
council movement (Fox 1992b; Moguel 1991; Hernández 1990c). CEPCO joined with important regional movements from Guerrero, Veracruz, and Chiapas to form the National
Coordinadora of Coffee Organizations (CNOC). See Ejea and Hernández 1991.

70. Few Chiapas councils participated in national movement-building efforts. Some networking did take place within the state, however, including a meeting of six food councils
in Tapachula in late 1982 (*El Pozol*, 1(2), December 1982). Three food councils in the
northern part of the state also participated in the Tabasco state network because their
warehouses were supplied by the same branch office. Strong ejido unions were also developing in that area in the early 1980s. On the range of relationships between peasant movements and the state in Chiapas during this period, see Harvey 1989, 1990a.

government abuses. The rebellions were largely brief, spontaneous, and limited to single villages. They involved consensus building by the entire community—men, women, and children—who fought to defend some degree of village autonomy within a system they knew they could not change. The colonial state's principal goal was to keep rebellion from spreading, and the process bears a striking similarity to the contemporary give-and-take between the state and rebellious communities.[71]

Behind this traditional defense of local autonomy is a complex web of communitarian institutions. The still widespread *tequio* system of unpaid obligatory community labor, for example, was often used to build the village stores themselves (e.g., Vera 1990). The roles of rural food committee and store managers also often fit smoothly into the traditional civil-religious authority system known as *cargos*, which organized essential village services such as water, agrarian matters, and parent-teacher associations as well as religious festivals.[72] The cargo system ran parallel to the formal municipal authorities, whose main task was to settle local disputes and to represent the community to outside institutions.[73]

Oaxaca's unusual structure of municipal political authority was also an important factor that aided the rapid consolidation of the Community Food Councils. Oaxaca is divided into 570 municipalities, far more than any other state. Since they are usually the size of a village, and since many villages are relatively internally democratic, municipal authorities tend to be much more responsive to the interests of the community than they are in the rest of Mexico. Municipal authorities often proved to be important allies of the food program, rather than opponents as elsewhere. Organizers recalled that as many as 120 to 130 municipal presidents attended meetings during the Coordinadora's peak.[74]

71. Thirty-two separate peasant rebellions in the Central Valleys of Oaxaca were recorded between 1689 and 1806 (Taylor 1979:176–77). The colonial state responded to these challenges with what Taylor calls "a calculated blend of punishment and mercy. . . . Colonial leaders were anxious to end revolts by negotiation and especially to keep them from spreading. The Spaniards' fear of regional insurrections was apparently quite real" (1979:120).

72. See, for example, Segura 1982 and Stephen 1991. For an overview of ethnicity in Oaxaca, see Barabas and Bartolomé 1986.

73. See, for example, Bailón 1984 and Dennis 1973, 1987. On indigenous rights and municipalities in Oaxaca more generally, see Díaz Gómez 1988; Domínguez 1988; Equipo Pueblo 1987; and Ornelas López 1989.

74. Government attempts to limit municipal autonomy have met strong resistance. National political parties, including the PRI, have very little real presence at the municipal level

The particularities of caciquismo in Oaxaca also played an important role in encouraging community participation. Because of the mountainous terrain and the lack of all-weather roads, transportation is extremely difficult and many communities lack self-sufficiency in food. Most of the rural population retains access to some land, but most must migrate or engage in craft production to survive. In Oaxaca, cacique control over retail village food distribution was considered a particularly onerous burden by most rural consumers. In contrast, in other areas of Mexico caciques exercise their power primarily through their control over land, municipal political power, or crop marketing and production inputs. The felt need was there, the cacique was a common enemy, and once CONASUPO-COPLAMAR became an option, the route to change was clear.

The differences in the implementation *process* in Oaxaca were at least as important as the differences in background conditions, however. The food program was carried out with an especially strong connection to the grass-roots in Oaxaca. The location of the warehouses and their surrounding regions took Oaxaca's complex ethnic map into account, to encourage unity rather than division. The bilingual teachers, who had built a powerful grass-roots network through the state, also lent crucial political support to the program.[75] The program also had more experienced, community-based promoters on staff in Oaxaca than elsewhere, including an unusually high proportion who were of peasant origin and were already recognized as community leaders. Many shared a conscious commitment to encouraging the consolidation of regionwide democratic organizations that would go beyond issues of food distribution alone.

Conclusions

Personnel and programs often change abruptly in the course of Mexico's presidential transitions, and it was by no means clear that

in Oaxaca, although many authorities may nominally be party members. See, for example, Bailón 1984, 1990; Díaz Montes 1989; López Monjardin 1986; and Martínez Vázquez and Arellanes 1985. Unlike Chiapas, where the municipalities are large enough to be of interest to caciques, most are far too small to concern political bosses. Oaxaca's most notable movement for local autonomy and democracy in the municipal arena is in Juchitán (Rubin 1987; 1990).

75. They were also important actors in the statewide teachers' movement for union democracy. Recall also the point made in Chapter 3, that greatly increased emphasis on bilingual education was one important component of the 1979–80 policy shift in favor of legitimation-oriented programs.

CONASUPO-COPLAMAR would survive the end of López Portillo's administration. Both SAM and COPLAMAR went down with him, but the rural food distribution program quietly became DICONSA-Rural, and it continued to increase in importance in spite of the continuing economic crisis.[76]

The program survived for three principal reasons. First, its efficient capacity to target subsidies to the poorest of the poor reduced its vulnerability to attacks from increasingly ascendent technocrats. Second, the success of the participation process had generated a powerful constituency for the program's survival and, indeed, expansion. Third, the "coresponsibility" approach fit with the new administration's rhetorical emphasis on regional decentralization and "democratic planning."[77]

The liberal policy current that oversaw the fate of social programs during the 1982 presidential transition was also sensitive to the potential political cost of withdrawing the state's commitment to supply food to thousands of organized communities. They saw the Community Food Councils as a means of keeping discontent within limits rather than as a threat to political stability. On the contrary, they considered it essential to have interlocutors to negotiate with in areas of potential and ongoing social unrest. As Carlos Salinas de Gortari wrote before his rise to power (1982:42), "A state that does not permit the participation of its citizens runs the risk of losing not only instrumental efficiency, but also its very legitimacy." As incoming President De la Madrid's new Secretary of Programming and the Budget, Carlos Salinas de Gortari participated in the decisions about which social programs to keep and which to cut.[78]

The political continuity in program leadership was only part of the explanation of why DICONSA-Rural survived. As one top reformist policymaker put it, "My ideological battle was to show that it is cheaper to take up the flag of popular struggles than to confront them head on. In other words, it is cheaper than buying arms." If these "legitimate" channels were closed off after participation had been

76. Many top DICONSA officials consciously tried to salvage what they could of the SAM and COPLAMAR reform projects, in spite of the clearly dominant conservative tendency within the new administration. At least twenty upper- and middle-level SAM planners found jobs in DICONSA after the SAM offices were unceremoniously dismantled at the end of the López Portillo administration, with the clear understanding that they would be able to pursue their reform goals from within DICONSA.

77. For discussions of the rural food distribution program by key former top managers, see Peón Escalante 1988 and Sodi de la Tijera 1988.

78. Some food distribution officials suggested that the naming of Raúl Salinas de Gortari to lead DICONSA was not unrelated to Carlos Salinas's long-term political plans.

launched, peasant communities might then have sought less orderly means for redress of their grievances.[79]

Because the food councils assumed that the program would continue, they did not mobilize a mass movement to defend it during the presidential transition. From above, the perceived political price for closing the program was therefore *hypothetical*, in the sense that it required a prediction of the medium-run impact on the state's political legitimacy in the countryside. The program survived in part because moderate reformists, who preferred to negotiate with autonomous social movements rather than repress them, had sufficient influence to defend the program in the high-level behind-the-scenes policy debates. They gained this influence in part, however, because the program had generated a constituency. This is typical of subsidy programs, in Mexico as elsewhere, but it was unusual in that the constituency was politically autonomous, was pluralistic, and represented the poorest of the poor.

It is not surprising that participation was highly uneven. The program was captured by regional elites in some areas, and in others, elites saw through the program's technocratic facade, counterattacking from both inside and outside the CONASUPO apparatus and expelling reformists from program staff. But the purge was not complete, and it was too little, too late; hundreds of peasant communities had already taken up the organizing process themselves as the implementation of participatory procedures developed its own dynamic. As Don Arcadio Morales, leader of Oaxaca's statewide network of food councils, put it, "The company has been punishing operational supervisors because they think they are the ones who are organizing us. That's where we don't understand each other, because we thought that the promoters were supposed to organize communities to set up stores. But it is we who have organized ourselves, not because some supervisor or employee goes around motivating us, but because of our own needs" (*El Día*, 24-III-84). Community organizing became much less overt in the more conservative context of the new administration after the staff purges, obliging the grass-roots movements to occupy the available political space on their own.

Peasant communities were most capable of taking advantage of opportunities to create their own representative and autonomous re-

79. As the president of one food council from an area beset by cacique violence put it, "The promoters don't teach us how to make revolution, but they are helpful. They orient us about how to get what we need. And if we can't get it that way, we know there are other ways" (i.e., more militant direct action).

gional organizations where they had a prior history of collective action. They found no sharp boundary between policy "sectors," such as "production" versus "marketing." Once given the opportunity to engage in collective action over food distribution policy, they used that political resource to begin to bargain over the whole range of rural development policies that affected them.

It made no sense to villagers for the trucks that supplied their stores to go back down the mountain empty. The Oaxaca and Guerrero cases clearly showed the tendency of autonomous rural consumer organizations to spark the formation of like-minded producer associations. Trucks, warehouses, and organizational resources used for distributing food could just as easily be used to haul fertilizer or cash crops, permitting peasants organized first as consumers to try to become independent of both intermediaries and government agricultural agencies.

Although government and academic policy planners often think the production process determines rural development prospects, for the largely indigenous communities of southern Mexico the freedom to organize was primary. The CONASUPO-COPLAMAR experience could be considered, in Hirschman's terms, an "inverted development sequence." He drew attention to what he called "'wrong-way-round, or 'cart-before-the-horse' development sequences" because "they demonstrate how certain forward moves, widely thought to be indispensably required as first steps in some development sequence, can instead be taken as second or third steps. From prerequisites and keys to any further progress, these moves are thus downgraded to *effects*, induced by other moves that, so it turns out, can start things going. Perhaps these other moves will be within easier reach of certain societies and cultures than the dethroned 'prerequisite'" (Hirschman 1984:1; emphasis in original).

Once the state created an institutional "access route," organized peasants not only occupied the space but tried to broaden it as well. The Community Food Councils created such an "acccess route," as discussed in chapter 2, in two ways. First, they constituted a legitimate channel for focusing collective action to increase the state's accountability to the rural poor. Even when organized rural consumers also mobilized to defend their interests as producers, their demands still tended to remain within the boundaries of those broadly considered legitimate. Their tactics may have been radical, including mass direct action, but their goals did not challenge the basic foundations of the regime, nor did they raise demands that were inherently "un-winnable," given the balance of forces, such as serious enforcement of land reform legislation or an end to impunity for security forces. The Community Food Councils thus opened up an access route in the sense that they provided leverage in both directions: peasants could pressure the state, but the state also structured their demands by limiting the range of "winnable" struggles.

In conclusion, the CONASUPO-COPLAMAR experience suggests that the driving force for more accountable distributive reform is the reciprocal interaction between state reformists and social movements. This outcome depends fundamentally on two key factors. The first is the *capacity of social movements for democratic mobilization*, defined in terms of representativeness and demands for greater government accountability. Their capacity to defend themselves from the twin threats of repression and co-optation depends largely on their autonomy from external interference in their decision making. This capacity depends on shared goals as well. The rural poor may seem from the outside to be a relatively homogeneous group with clear common interests, but they are sharply divided internally by class, ethnicity, gender, sense of place, kinship, and clientelistic loyalties. In this context, the food distribution program forged new regional identities by simultaneously targeting common enemies and offering influential allies. This was an important step toward the "thickening" of rural civil society.

To survive, democratic rights must be won, not granted. But winning them depends on access to the freedom, information, and resources to organize. The second key factor, therefore, is *the degree to which reformists, strategically situated within the state, have the capacity to undertake democratizing initiatives*. Reformist policy currents, made up of state actors who express their concern for long-run political stability through a willingness to bargain with relatively autonomous social movements, must be strategically placed to be effective. Unless they control implementing agencies at both the national and local levels, it is unlikely they will have leverage over the allocation of significant economic or political resources. The most important economic resource they can supply is an immediate material incentive for grass-roots collective action, which usually requires operational control over policy implementation. The most important political resource they can offer is to create space for democratic mobilization by providing some protection from both public and private sector repression.

In practice, the program was carried out largely to the degree that peasant communities gained leverage over reluctant bureaucrats. Most traditional officials were clearly enemies of the program, while some reformists were "objective allies" of the peasant movement, in spite of frequent friction. Grass-roots mobilization was often aided by active support from reformist policymakers, but its agenda and scope were not limited to the boundaries originally defined from above. Most important, *peasants took advantage of the program's resources and participatory procedures to build their own representative organizations.*

The rural food distribution program embodied a new approach to distributive reform in Mexico. In the past, access to most antipoverty programs was conditioned on clientelistic political subordination. In contrast, not only did CONASUPO-COPLAMAR tolerate pluralism, it created meaningful electoral processes and encouraged the emergence of new, representative social actors.

7

Lessons for Understanding
Political Change in Mexico

The rise and fall of the Mexican Food System (SAM) demonstrated both the limits and the possibilities of reform from above. The SAM experience showed, first, that national grain self-sufficiency is a feasible though expensive goal and second, that it is possible for the state to develop new "positive-sum" patterns of bargaining with the rural poor if it is willing to accept the legitimacy and representation of autonomous peasant movements. Strategically placed reformists used their access to power to support new social actors, marking the emergence of more pluralistic relationships between state and society. Many autonomous, representative regional peasant organizations that consolidated during the SAM period's relative political opening survived and later grew into important forces for rural democratization.

Most of the reform package failed to lead to lasting change—as one might expect—but an unusual opening from above was partly appropriated by mobilization from below. Reformist policy currents, without prior support or pressure from increased mass protest, partially democratized an important arena of state action: rural food distribution. By occupying and expanding the newly opened political space, peasants mobilized to turn Community Food Councils into a new access route for the rural poor to push for accountable implementation of development policy. A distributive reform thus became a *political* reform, as Przeworski (1986:58) defines it: "A modification of the organization of conflicts that alters the prior probabilities of realizing group interests given their resources."

This reform's combination of change and continuity challenges both state- and society-centered explanations of state action. As chapter 2 shows, society-driven explanations have difficulty explaining state initiatives that change the organization of important social groups, while societal responses which in turn leave their imprint on the state are not easily explained by state-centered frameworks. This book develops an interactive approach to state-society relations, emphasizing the institutions that mediated these interactions and explaining how those institutions were themselves transformed. Shifts in the balance of power within the state interacted recursively with changes in the correlation of forces within society.

This chapter reviews the major findings and conclusions of the book, and then turns to the more general problematic of reform from above. This discussion focuses on the dilemmas faced by reformist "entrepreneurs" within the state and on the possibility that their efforts to mobilize a social base of support for reform will have unexpected outcomes. The chapter concludes with an assessment of an emerging new set of more pluralistic bargaining arrangements between the state and autonomous social organizations, some of whose roots lie in the unexpected outcome of partial democratization in the CONASUPO-COPLAMAR food distribution program.

Explaining both Continuity and Change in the SAM Period

The Mexican state's institutional structure and political culture were shaped by revolutionary social conflict, periodically giving certain state actors the capacity to take autonomous initiatives to renew political legitimacy. This concern for political stability was embedded in the state through institutionalized incentives and opportunities for policymakers to advocate creating channels for negotiation with social movements. Agencies dedicated to the administration of social conflict were often the key institutional base for reformist state actors—those who preferred to respond to mass demands with negotiation rather than repression. As discussed in chapter 2, this dynamic created structurally selective access routes for social forces to bring pressure to bear on the state, while at the same time shaping patterns of social mobilization.

The institutional foundations for Mexico's several decades of relative rural social peace were first built in the 1930s, when state reformists allied with grass-roots peasant movements to carry out a massive redistribution of land. Because of this legacy, peasant mobilization never posed more than local, or at most regional, political problems for the regime for nearly forty years. Beginning in the early 1970s, however, the traditional corporatist peasant organizations grew increasingly ineffective at channeling and controlling peasant demands. The peasant movement's growing autonomy and militancy highlighted the need for new forms of representation to keep mass demands from threatening the regime's legitimacy in the countryside. Instead, reformist responses largely reproduced authoritarian populist approaches.

Political and economic crisis in 1976 led the state to turn away from the peasantry. Repression increased and mobilization ebbed. Grass-roots movements were too weak to "require" a reformist response. By 1980, however, some reformist policy currents sought new ways to revive distributive efforts and open up some political space in order to maintain political stability in the long run. They managed at times to bypass the official party and to create opportunities for social movements to increase their autonomy from the state, thereby changing the boundaries of political bargaining.

The SAM's 1980–82 national grain self-sufficiency effort provided only limited economic benefits for the rural majority, but its *political* impact was much greater and more enduring. The shift in the balance of forces within the state during the latter half of the López Portillo administration permitted strategically located food policymakers to encourage a *sandwich strategy* of mutually reinforcing pressure from above and below. These unusual initiatives increased the capacity of autonomous peasant movements to weaken regional power structures in some areas, pushing back "structural constraints" to a small but significant degree. Access to food was recognized as a right of citizenship. The relative political opening permitted hundreds, perhaps thousands, of peasant communities to define and pursue their interests more autonomously, leading to the consolidation of a wide range of representative regional organizations.

After the economic crisis beginning in 1982, even autonomously organized peasants were still too weak to shape the national political agenda; they had little say over how Mexico should handle the nation's persistent economic problems, and attempts to defend the gains of the past had little effect on national policies (with the partial exception of basic grain crop support prices).[1] The SAM nevertheless

---

1. Some might argue that basic grain support prices were an exception, since their value did not collapse if we compare them with the general inflation rate (Martínez Fernández

represented a major turning point in the transition from agrarian to agricultural issues as the principal terrain of conflict between the state and the rural poor. With this growing politicization of production and consumption demands in the countryside, some of the more consolidated and autonomous organizations managed to win significant concessions. In spite of often being on the defensive, autonomous regional peasant organizations became a national presence in the increasingly fluid bargaining arrangements between state and society in Mexico in the late 1980s and early 1990s.[2]

The history, structure, and mission of the Mexican state's massive food trading agency, CONASUPO, contributed to an institutional predisposition to view access to food as a political right and to encourage peasant allies to organize and fight for that right. This redistributive bias certainly did not guarantee that reformist policy currents would dominate in practice. In fact, reformists were usually limited to policy formulation; they were able to make a difference only on those rare occasions when they actively intervened in implementation. Within CONASUPO, the balance of power between reformists and allies of the traditional regional power structures shifted back and forth throughout the 1970s and 1980s, with powerful technocratic cadres found on both sides. At issue was how far the agency would ally with peasants as opposed to intermediaries and industrialists in its regulation of national and local grain markets. The conflict be-

---

1990). Increased mobilization of both peasants and better-off farmers kept the pressure on the government through the mid-1980s, reinforcing the shift in the political terrain of rural conflict from land tenure to producer demands (Hernández 1992). If we compare producer prices with the costs of production, however, we can see the dramatic effects of the rollback of most input subsidies, which on balance sharply reduced incentives for basic grain production (Gordillo 1990; Salinas de Gortari 1990). Farmers with irrigation, however, continued to pay only 11 percent of their water costs (Cummings et al. 1989:32). The share of the budget assigned to rural development fell from 13.4 percent in 1982 to 8.1 percent in 1985 and only 5.6 percent in 1988 (Carrasco Licea and Hernández y Puente 1989). Imports combined with tortilla subsidies partially buffered the impact on urban consumption, but per capita *rural* maize consumption fell from 239 kilograms per year in 1980 to only 161 in 1988 (Cummings et al. 1989:3). After receiving little attention since 1982, maize received renewed support in 1990, when nominal support prices were increased 40 percent, largely because of its political sensitivity. On post-1982 agricultural policy, see also Appendini 1988, 1992; Barkin 1989; Calva 1988; De la Mora Gómez 1990; Gordillo 1990; Heath 1985, 1988; Hewitt de Alcántara 1992; Martín del Campo 1988; Montañez 1988; Pérez Haro 1990; Robles and Moguel 1990; Ros and Rodríguez 1987; Salinas de Gortari 1990; SARH 1990; Sosa 1990; and Zepeda Patterson 1988.

2. For analyses of the changing trends in the peasant movement in the 1980s more generally, see Bartra 1989a, 1990; Flores Lúa, Paré, and Sarmiento 1988; Fox and Gordillo 1989; A. García 1989, 1990; E. García 1989a, 1989b, 1989c, 1990; García de León 1989; Gordillo and Block 1988; Harvey 1989, 1990a, 1990b; Hernández 1989a, 1989b, 1990a, 1990c, 1992; López Monjardin 1988; Rello 1988; and Sarmiento Silva 1989.

tween reformists and their opponents was shaped both by changing pressures from below and by the shifting balance of forces within the state between policy emphasis on private accumulation versus public legitimation.

Many food policy analysts contended that the SAM policy package would change little: both the Left and the Right political opposition saw it as a mere palliative that would not touch the crisis of the peasant economy that underlay the twin crises of agricultural production and hunger. Although they proposed diametrically opposed solutions, contending left and right critiques agreed that property relations, not income flows or institutional change, were fundamental. The Right argued that only a reversal of the agrarian reform would secure the large-scale private investment necessary to solve the production problem. Much of the Left stressed that only an extension of the agrarian reform at the expense of capitalist agriculture and ranching could alleviate rural hunger.

The SAM strategy emerged from a political stalemate over rural property relations. Large private agribusiness, ranching, and commercial interests, in alliance with conservative government "developmentalists," were sufficiently powerful to block a significant extension of the agrarian reform, but they were too weak to reverse it politically.[3] The 1981 Agricultural Development Law was a political victory for the public and private sector advocates of a "top-down" capital-intensive approach to agricultural development, but continued behind-the-scenes resistance by high-level reformists rendered it largely symbolic in practice (particularly when compared with much more conservative later amending of agrarian law). At the same time, peasant movements and their allies inside and outside the state lacked the power to put a major extension of the agrarian reform on the political agenda. The threat of their response to a reversal of the reform nevertheless gave them a certain veto power that paralleled that of the Right. Ever since the political crisis surrounding President Echeverría's 1976 land redistribution, with a few regional exceptions, left-

---

3. Long-standing economic, political, and demographic pressures have clearly undermined the economic viability of the reform sector, but even by the end of the 1980s it was still largely intact in political and legal terms (with the notable exception of extensive ejido and indigenous lands forcibly occupied de facto by ranchers). In spite of intense domestic and international pressures, as of 1990 President Salinas still rejected the overt privatization of ejido lands. His 1991 constitutional reform permits joint ventures, rental and the ostensibly voluntary sale of ejido lands.

and right-wing pressures vetoed each other's attempts to deal with the food crisis through a national change in land rights.

In the midst of this political standoff on the agrarian question, the oil-debt boom created the opportunity for reformist policymakers to maneuver in the area of changing *income* flows. The SAM strategy attempted to channel subsidies to nonirrigated peasant production essentially by increasing incentives for *all* grain producers who produced for the market and had effective access to state services. The SAM's generalized, "something-for-everyone" subsidy strategy was both its strength and its weakness, broadening its political viability in the short run while increasing its later vulnerability to charges of wastefulness when the 1982 economic crisis obliged incoming President De la Madrid to tighten budget constraints. Even if they had wanted to, SAM planners lacked the political power to impose effective targeting of subsidies on most of the relatively autonomous food policy implementing agencies. In the case of urban consumer food subsidies, perhaps the single most expensive part of the SAM policy package, reformers did develop more targeted policy alternatives, but they were politically defeated by more powerful policymakers who did not want to pay the political costs of the transition to a more efficient system. Generalized urban food subsidies actually grew after the SAM ended, to buffer the effects of the first years of the crisis, until they were scaled back at the end of the decade.

Most of SAM period food policy, in practice, was more of the same. Chapter 4 shows that increased grain production incentives were largely delivered by the same agencies whose alliance with large farmers, ranchers, and intermediaries had helped bring on the food crisis in the first place. President López Portillo's full political backing for increased food production did not translate into direct support for the reformers' social change agenda. Although SAM planners spoke of increasing peasant bargaining power and producer participation in formulating and implementing policy decisions, and of the "vertical" extension of the agrarian reform through peasant-managed agro-industrial enterprises, in practice only the PACE and CONASUPO-COPLAMAR marketing programs emphasized social change.

The ambiguous role of political change in the SAM is highlighted in the following public strategy statement: "Today the Mexican state can act from a broad, strategic perspective, inducing actions, concerting popular alliances to transform, finally, long-standing needs into active demands" (SAM 1980b:para. 2). Here the state asserts its willingness and capacity to "induce" change, but the kinds of "demands" it wants to activate are open to interpretation. The statement could be understood to refer to the importance of holding the agricultural apparatus accountable to rural citizens or, more likely, it could simply refer to the importance of attacking hunger by increasing the purchasing power, the "effective demand," of the poor as individual consumers. One approach implies political and institutional change, the other does not.

Some SAM technocrats defined their project strictly in terms of macroeconomic and agricultural change, taking the institutional parameters for granted. Even had they had more power, many of these economists and agronomists would have been quite willing to leave the agricultural apparatus unchallenged. The implementation experience, however, underscored what peasant communities knew all along: the "operational levels" of rural development agencies transform the decisions made in Mexico City into what the state *does*, and they pursue their own political and economic interests rather than simply carry out orders from above.

On the production side, reformists did manage to promote some institutional change through ad hoc bypassing of the conventional bureaucracies that dominated SAM implementation. The more reformist food policymakers were able to channel economic and political support to several autonomous peasant-managed economic enterprises whose development had national implications. The consolidation of large self-managed agricultural enterprises, such as the Coalition of Collective Ejidos of the Yaqui and Mayo Valleys (CECVYM), showed that the agrarian reform sector could be organized both productively and democratically, an example that would have an important "spread effect" among peasant organizations in the years to follow.[4]

One of the most important national opposition agrarian organizations also managed to link up with reformist policymakers. The Independent Federation of Peasants and Farmworkers (CIOAC) had been

---

4. "The root of the agricultural crisis is neither exclusively with the government nor with the peasants, but rather is a problem of their relationship with each other, one as ruler and the other as ruled" (Coalición de Ejidos Colectivos de los Valles Yaqui y Mayo 1985:10). On the CECVYM, see Benjamin and Buell 1985; Castaños 1987; Gordillo 1988a, 1988b; and Otero 1989. In turn, the CECVYM became a role model for many of the groups that later formed the National Union of Autonomous Regional Peasant Organizations (UNORCA). Formed in the mid-1980s, by the end of the decade UNORCA had become one of the principal national networks within the peasant movement. See Fernández Villegas 1991; Fox and Gordillo 1989; Gordillo 1988b; Harvey 1990b; and Hernández 1989a, 1989b, 1990a.

a leading force in the land invasions of the early 1970s, shifting its emphasis to farmworker unionization and strikes in the mid-1970s.[5] By the SAM period, the CIOAC had developed an approach that tried to balance work with farmworkers, land petitioners, and small-holders. Food policy reformers were unable to create sufficient political space for the CIOAC to win collective bargaining rights for farm-workers, but they did leverage a substantial government loan for the CIOAC to create a national credit union for smallholders. The loan was made possible by a new degree of tolerance of what SAM planners called "constructive criticism."[6]

In the absence of a truly national peasant movement capable of demanding equity, efficiency, and accountability, however, the pattern of allocation of crucial production inputs changed little. As chapter 4 shows, most of the SAM-period programs with reformist intent had no lasting impact and at best temporarily shifted resource allocation patterns somewhat in favor of nonirrigated grain producers. Some regional elites may well have been strengthened by this infusion of resources. In spite of the SAM's clearly pro-peasant intent, most of the food policies carried out in its name put the fox in charge of the chicken coop.

The Dynamics of Rural Reform

The political opening from above was small but significant. The opening was small because it was limited to those few regions and policy areas where reformists effectively intervened in the implementation, as well as the formulation, of rural development policy. It was

5. The CIOAC began as the left wing of the CCI, founded in the early 1960s (see chap. 3). Originally aligned with the Mexican Communist Party, by the early–mid-1980s the CIOAC had become more autonomous. On the CIOAC's farmworker organizing in the 1970s and 1980s, see De Grammont 1986; Flores Lúa, Paré, and Sarmiento 1988; López Monjardin 1991; and Nagengast and Kearney 1990.

6. The loan reportedly was granted without political conditions, and the CIOAC did not give up its independent stance. According to a former high-level SAM planner: "There was a great guy behind the CIOAC, Ramón Danzós Palomino, and that made a difference. He is a true peasant leader, who lived through the struggles and the repression. He is a man with great political wisdom, and he had all the sympathy of the president. The president didn't consider him to be an opponent of the system, but rather a man who was in a phase of constructive opposition and honest struggles. . . . Danzós could go to the office of the Secretary of the Treasury and there was no problem. There was a very special climate. . . . The country was in a good mood. The CNC itself complained." By 1984 the CIOAC's credit union reported thirty-six thousand members, having won over many former CNC members (*El Día*, 16-III-85).

significant because it offered useful political and economic resources to representative and autonomous peasant organizations. Where this opening helped the consolidation of regional peasant organizations, it shifted the balance of power between peasant communities and rural politico-economic elites.

Because of CONASUPO's institutional predisposition toward reformist initiatives, there was more room for political maneuver and innovation in food marketing policy than in the allocation of productive resources. Private intermediaries were also more politically vulnerable targets than were large farmers and ranchers. Opening up markets was controversial, but not nearly as politically charged as land redistribution.

Where grain traders exercised monopoly powers, state intervention attempted to offer a competitive alternative. The PACE and CONASUPO-COPLAMAR marketing programs, both of which grew dramatically in the SAM period's "pro-peasant" political environment, explicitly attempted to increase peasant bargaining power vis-à-vis rural intermediaries. Neither program distributed a subsidy of overwhelming economic importance in itself, although the consumer food subsidy may well have had a significant nutritional effect among the most impoverished populations. As chapters 5 and 6 show, each program had the potential to challenge entrenched local elites' domination of both state and market by promoting democratic organizations of the rural poor, yet only one led to lasting change.

The PACE grain marketing support program failed to intervene in the regional balance of power because it did not encourage collective action to overcome high entry costs and offset the power of politically influential private grain traders. In contrast, the CONASUPO-COPLAMAR village food store program deliberately relied on creating democratic regional consumer organizations to challenge the impunity of private and bureaucratic interests entrenched in the state itself. The CONASUPO-COPLAMAR experience put into practice a system of formal democratic rules for community participation in implementing food distribution policy. These rules were created by a reformist policy current within the state that sought to create new channels of communication and negotiation for the hitherto disfranchised peasants of Mexico's most impoverished rural areas. In those areas where this process took off, the regional democratizing impact spilled over into other arenas, particularly the formation of large-scale democratic producers' organizations.

This reformist policy current accepted the partial democratization of a significant arena of government activity, involving two distinct tendencies: the moderates and the radicals. The moderates were "men of the system," whereas the radicals' presence within the state was a direct result of the far-reaching impact of the 1968 student movement. This Mexican version of the "long march through the institutions" was an important example of what Migdal (1990:2) calls the "recursive relationship between state and society." Although the moderates saw democratic procedures as useful for the success of the program, and therefore for their careers and their bargaining power within the state, the radicals were more ideologically motivated, valuing democratization in and of itself. In other words, democratizing food distribution was a means for the moderates and an end for the radicals.

In the course of SAM period food policy implementation, these reform tendencies were strong only within CONASUPO-COPLAMAR and the SAM planning apparatus itself. They were usually united in their conflict with the traditional corporatist and more technocratic policy currents dominant in most other rural development agencies. The moderate-radical distinction is nevertheless analytically and politically important. Without the radicals, their social vision and their networks of organizers, CONASUPO-COPLAMAR would never have been able to promote an effective partial democratizing of food distribution. Without their moderate allies, however, the radicals would never have had the access to political legitimacy and economic resources that permitted them to sustain CONASUPO-COPLAMAR's "opening from above" in the face of the inevitable counterattack from the cacique power structure.

Reformists provided two key resources for the consolidation of regional peasant organizations. The first was political legitimacy, which limited the violent repression often directed against democratic community organizing efforts, particularly among indigenous people. The regional power structures whose political and commercial monopolies were threatened by the program fought back from both inside and outside the CONASUPO apparatus. Most of the field staff were purged, but the program and its constituency survived. The second key resource the program contributed was transportation. With its own trucks the CONASUPO-COPLAMAR program could both supply the village stores with subsidized food—an immediate incentive for mass participation—and regularly bring together large numbers of community delegates to create an organization that was both region-wide and genuinely representative of the majority of villagers.

It is not surprising that by itself this top-down initiative failed to create genuine community participation. Most regional Community Food Councils were at best consultative and failed to play their intended role as autonomous, "coresponsible" partners in food distribution. They became mere instruments of the CONASUPO apparatus in many areas, presenting no challenge to entrenched elites. This pattern of elite "capture" of the official channels for poor people's representation is what one would expect, given Mexico's history of rural reform programs. But unlike traditional populist reforms, CONASUPO-COPLAMAR did not systematically condition material benefits on political subordination. A significant minority of Community Food Councils gained the capacity to articulate their interests autonomously, with the help of coordinated support from national program managers and committed outreach staff. Where participation was widespread, the food councils became powerful democratic counterweights that weakened entrenched elites both inside and outside the massive government food company.

Democratic regional food councils emerged primarily in areas with traditions of autonomous collective action. CONASUPO-COPLAMAR's participatory procedures were put into practice predominantly in areas where indigenous forms of community self-government survived, providing the basis for democratic social mobilization in response to the opening from above. Although participatory traditions may have survived at the village level, however, only rarely had poor, isolated communities been able to overcome powerful internal and external obstacles to *regionwide* organization.[7]

In the context of a rural society riven with cross-cutting cleavages, in many areas the warehouses created a new set of shared regional interests, allies, and enemies. Where loyalties rarely extended beyond family and village, the warehouse generated a regional identity that greatly encouraged social mobilization.

---

7. Regional organizations are critical for democratizing rural development. In much of Latin America, the entrenched power of allied public and private sector regional elites is the principal obstacle to broad-based rural development. Regional organizations that can represent the majority of the rural population are therefore crucial for opening up closed markets and political systems, promoting more accountable development policy. Regional peasant organizations are also especially important because they have the potential to combine the clout of a larger group with the responsiveness of smaller associations. Village-level groups are easily isolated by their enemies, and national peasant organizations are usually democratic only insofar as they are made up of representative regional building blocks. "Regional" is used here to describe a membership organization that develops a second level of decision making "above" the village (i.e., elected regional executives, community delegate assemblies, etc.). On the issue of internal democracy within regional peasant organizations, see Fox and Hernández 1989 and Fox 1992.

By the end of the SAM period, at least fifty of the two hundred CONASUPO-COPLAMAR warehouses were under the control of autonomous peasant organizations, half of them in Oaxaca, Mexico's most impoverished state. This partial democratizing of one important arena of government rural activity survived beyond the end of the SAM period and on into the deepening economic crisis. The program had generated its own organized constituency, increasing the political cost of any state attempt to renege on its commitment to supply low-cost food to low-income rural consumers. Chapter 6 shows that by 1985, for between one and two million of Mexico's poorest rural people, the food councils were among the first genuinely mass-based, regionwide representative organizations of any kind.

Reform from Above and Mobilization from Below

The Community Food Councils became a new, two-way institutional access route that connected state and social actors. From above, state reformists structured new patterns of representation within rural society. From below, these new opportunities for participation became autonomous channels for interest articulation that in turn left their imprint on the state.

More generally, the comparative case analysis supports the argument of chapter 2 about the interdependence between state and society in implementing distributive reform. The Mexican state's capacity to go beyond proclamations and carry out distributive reforms depended on its ceding power to autonomous, representative social organizations. Democratizing the development process inherently involves conflict, both between state and society and within the state itself. The state's capacity to reform therefore depends on its internalizing social conflict.[8]

The Mexican state's capacity to preempt, channel, or respond to new social and political pressures is largely determined by the ebbs and flows of the strength of the reformists within it, even though they are usually subordinated to more powerful policy currents. In the 1970s and 1980s, reformists' precarious power rested on two contra-

---

8. As Gordillo put it (1988a:233), "State apparatuses, especially those that have priority economic tasks, are at the same time arenas of social conflict, the material condensation of a determined correlation of forces, and social actors with their own interests. The internalization of social conflict is an especially pronounced characteristic of agencies that deal with rural affairs, since they play a key regulatory role in the context of the absence of representative sectoral organizations and explosive growth of government economic functions."

dictory bases. First, they gained strength relative to competitors within the state by promising to renew the legitimacy of the system as a whole, in spite of the short-run costs of displacing interests entrenched in the regional and corporatist power structures. Second, reformists gained allies among organized social forces, both official and independent, by promising substantive concessions. Lacking a strong base within the state, they could not and cannot displace antidemocratic regional or corporatist power structures on their own; they need pressures from "objectively allied" social movements that may well define themselves as opposition.

State reformists therefore run a risk. They are concerned with finding "interlocutors," because they understand Mexican history to have shown that social pressures that cannot find channels of expression are the greatest long-run threat to political stability. Their premise is that mobilization is "healthy" if negotiated solutions can be found to keep it within the system, meaning that some authoritarian elements are worth sacrificing to keep mobilized peasants coming back to the bargaining table. The reformists' view of stability therefore requires some degree of conflict with caciques. But caciques rarely give up without a fight, and they are often more important to the political system in the short run than are the reformists themselves. Caciques are deeply embedded within the state; when they mobilize the system feels it. The electoral apparatus in particular depends on traditional control mechanisms to produce the reliable and overwhelming majorities in the countryside that became so central to the PRI's electoral strategy in the 1980s.[9] Cacique allies at all levels of the state apparatus stand ready to intervene should reformists cross an unmarked (though shifting) line, as the political purge of the CONASUPO-COPLAMAR program showed.

From the point of view of the state, reform dynamics can be understood in terms of political entrepreneurship—the willingness to take risks. The successful management of the inherently uncertain transition to a more open political system requires investing political capital—taking chances in order to promote strategic interaction that re-

---

9. The electoral impact of the rise of autonomous producer and consumer organizations in the countryside is still not clear. Some of the social and economic organizations have turned their attention to municipal politics. In some cases electoral success may have come at the expense of a loss of autonomy (e.g., CARTT in Puebla, UELC in Nayarit), while those less willing to negotiate their votes continue to face widespread fraud and violence (e.g., Guerrero). On the rural side of the 1988 national election, see Fox 1989, 1990a; Hernández 1989a, 1989b; and López et al. 1988. On rural electoral violence, see Americas Watch 1990.

shapes the terms of conflict. If reformist state actors are to displace the authoritarian rural elites who stand in the way of distributive reform and long-term political stability, they must risk promoting the mobilization of social forces they cannot necessarily control. If reformist state actors are willing to tolerate such autonomy, they can offer important support to peasants against their common enemies.

This reform dynamic is abstracted in figure 2, which depicts the conflict sparked by a political opening for social movements created by the combination of some degree of protection from repression and a reform program they consider to be in their interests.[10] The regional power structures then counterattack, because the "objective alliance" between national reformist and autonomous social movements threatens their economic and political survival. As a result of this counterattack, the conflict between peasants and caciques is internalized within the reform implementing agency itself, most likely leading to a partial veto of the policy in question. The issue is how much is vetoed. The outcome of the conflict is politically contingent, depending on how long national reformist pressure from above, combined with rural social movement pressure from below, can be sustained in the face of the inevitable counterattack.

The regional power structures are not, in this scenario, under frontal attack; they are being challenged only in the arenas where reformists control policy implementation. Authoritarian elites are too entrenched in the political and economic system to be displaced in more than a minority of the geographic areas involved, even in the policy arena in contention. If pressure from above is at all effective, however, the likely result will be the formation or consolidation of autonomous regionwide peasant organizations. Even if the reformists then fall from power or their program is eliminated, regionwide democratic counterweights to the elite power structure can survive and perhaps continue to shift the balance of power in favor of the rural poor.

The specifics of this sandwich strategy are unique to Mexico, but the more general process of triangular conflict between reformists, entrenched authoritarian elites, and autonomous social movements is not. More generally, for interaction between social movements and state reformists to broaden distributive policy implementation, pressure from below must both weaken reformist policymakers relative to the poor while simultaneously strengthening them relative to those

10. This is the same process portrayed in terms of actual institutions in figure 1 (chap. 6).

With pressure from both above and below, the sandwich strategy creates political space and shifts the balance of power between authoritarian elites and movements for rural democratization

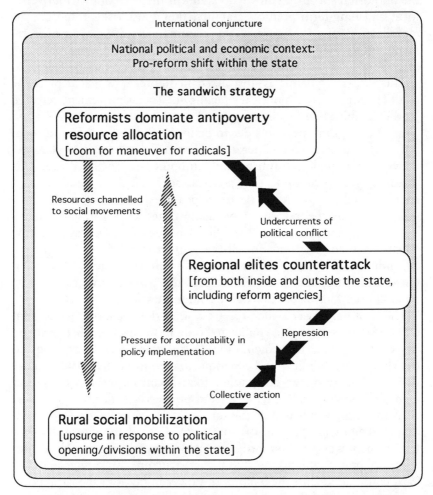

- *Possible outcome: Increased government accountability in contested policy arena, spreading to other issues*

- *Probable outcome: Increased peasant capacity to articulate interests, as autonomous, representative organizations consolidate*

Figure 2. The political dynamics of rural reform

competing policy currents that are less concerned with social equity and broad political legitimacy.

Similar processes can be observed in reform efforts ranging from the early 1960s antipoverty programs in the United States to reformist state governments in India or the combination of political opening and economic restructuring in the Soviet Union. What seems to vary the most may be the role of competitive elections, either as explanations for the reformist initiatives, as in the U.S. War on Poverty programs, or as channels for creating mobilized allies for elite reformists, as in the Soviet Union.

Concertación Social: Liberalization or Democratization?

The anomalous flexibility of the Mexican political system, confronted with unprecedented economic and political challenges since the early 1980s, defies conventional categories of political analysis. In contrast to countries where electoral competition structures the conflict over distributive reform, Mexico's food policy reform of the early 1980s was attempted *before* the official party's hegemony met any electoral challenge other than abstention.[11] The political party system continued to lag behind the "thickening" of civil society, but it became qualitatively more competitive as of the hotly contested presidential election of July 1988.[12] The context for distributive reform politics in the early 1990s was therefore shaped not only by continuing mass underemployment and sharply constrained government budgets, but also by the ongoing electoral challenges to the official party from both Left and Right. As a result, the Mexican state entered a period of transition toward a new set of political and economic arrangements, still in the process of definition. Important official policy currents clearly recognized that the traditional corporatist controls were obsolete, and they sought alternative channels of interaction between the state and society.[13] Liberalization does not necessarily lead

11. For explanations of distributive reform that stress the interaction between electoral competition and social mobilization, see Piven and Cloward 1977 on the United States and Ascher 1984 on Latin America.

12. For a range of analyses of the controversial three-way race, see, among others, Cornelius, Gentleman, and Smith 1989; González Casanova 1989; González Graf 1989; and Monsiváis 1989. For a comprehensive overview of recent party competition in historical context, see Molinar 1991.

13. President Carlos Salinas de Gortari asserted in his inaugural address (1988:9): "There is a new political Mexico, a new citizenry with a new political culture; the expres-

to democratization, however. As Stepan points out (1988:1–7), the liberalizing of the state's relations with civil society is distinct from the increased freedom for political parties to compete for political power.

The early 1980s food policy experience left an important legacy for policymakers. After 1982, when intense austerity pressures mounted, the challenge for those concerned with income distribution was to manage the transition away from the traditional reliance on generalized subsidies while strengthening the more targeted social programs that supported what was left of Mexico's social safety net. In this context, the rural food distribution program had delivered what was perhaps Mexico's most successful targeted subsidy (to the poor, that is). An environment of relative tolerance for pluralism and autonomy permitted the creation of effective citizens' oversight mechanisms, making it the first national experience with what would later be called *concertación social*, a new relationship between "mature" interlocutors in state and society.[14]

Under unprecedented pressure in the electoral arena, the government appeared to cede new space in the nonelectoral sphere as this evolving new bargaining process raised hopes that at least some development agencies would become more open and accountable. Where social organizations were sufficiently powerful, the state sometimes relaxed its insistence on the overt political subordination of organized citizens in exchange for material concessions.

By the mid-1980s, perhaps the most important new concertación experience was the largely positive-sum negotiations between the state and Mexico City's postearthquake housing movements.[15] The state began to demonstrate a limited but still unprecedented willingness to

---

sion of that culture demands the transformation of political channels. . . . My administration will offer a response to citizens' demands for pluralism and effective participation."

14. "Mature" is in quotation marks in the official original (Ramos 1985:5).

15. The government's low-income housing agency (FONHAPO) was quite akin to DICONSA in its reformist orientation (Aldrete-Haas, 1990, 1991; Annis, 1988; CIDAC 1991). The literature on the political aftermath of the earthquake is vast (see especially Monsiváis 1987), but on the specifics of housing policy see, among others, Mecatl, Michel, and Ziccardi 1987; Eckstein 1988; and special thematic issues of *Revista Mexicana de Sociología*, 51(2), April–June 1989; *Estudios Demográficos y Urbanos* 2(1), January–April 1987; *El Cotidiano*, 2(8), November–December 1985. The postearthquake housing negotiations came to be led by one of the most important architects of *concertación*, then Secretary of Urban Development and Ecology Manuel Camacho (later appointed Mayor of Mexico City during the Salinas government). For a sense of his approach to political analysis, see Camacho 1980. UNORCA pressure on FONHAPO also led to an innovative rural housing program (Gordillo 1988a; Fox and Hernández 1989; Hernández 1990c).

cede legitimacy to autonomous citizens' groups by establishing both formal and informal concertación social agreements. Although more traditional corporatist pactmaking also came under the rubric of concertación, the more open and pluralistic variant made some inroads in agricultural production policy, urban social services, and public sector labor relations.[16]

The reformist policy current advocating a more pluralistic style of concertación social appeared to represent a countertendency subordinated to the neoliberal current that dominated macroeconomic policy and the "dinosaurs" who continued to handle most of the electoral system. The more pluralistic reformists did not challenge macroeconomic or electoral strategy, but rather attempted to buffer their political impact. They ceded key spaces for the consolidation of representative social organizations while at times attempting to limit their growth or recover lost political ground.[17] At the same time, however, more traditional policymakers used the new rhetoric and funding of concertación social in an effort to revive and modernize the corporatist political apparatus. The best known of these "traditional" concertación agreements was the successful national anti-inflation pact between the government, business organizations, and the official labor unions (Ejea 1989).

President Salinas promised to modernize Mexico's economic and political system, seeking to revive citizen confidence by bypassing both the political opposition and the traditional corporatist political apparatus. He brought distributive spending increasingly under the high-profile umbrella of the Programa Nacional de Solidaridad, or PRONASOL (National Solidarity Program). PRONASOL was widely credited with helping to revive the official party's electoral fortunes in 1990 and 1991 (although its impact is difficult to disentangle from

16. Inspired by UNORCA policy alternatives, the agriculture sector's official "destatizing" plan involves bargaining with public, private, and social sector actors over the nature and pace of transferral of these operations to producer organizations. As of 1990, the most broad-based and democratic of these experiences was in the coffee sector, where the state faces a powerful national network of autonomous producers' organizations (Ejea and Hernández 1991). Many members of this network, especially in Oaxaca and Guerrero, trace their origins back to the Community Food Councils of the early 1980s.

17. Perhaps the government's most important concession to social pressures for democratization in the late 1980s was the partial opening within the official teachers' union in April 1989. The massive mobilization led the government to sacrifice one of the ruling party's most important and authoritarian "dinosaurs." The democratization of several large, state-level union locals was consolidated, and though the new national leader was not democratically elected, she acceded to a more open and pluralistic bargaining process. See the insightful analyses in Pueblo/Información Obrera 1990.

the influence of reduced inflation and the beginnings of economic growth).

After Mexico's electoral earthquake of 1988, the president could not afford to continue his predecessor's policy of largely ignoring the poor. In lieu of a full transition to democracy, the main policy alternative was to buffer the social and economic crisis that had helped to drive the 1988 political opposition.[18] But with continuing economic austerity it was inefficient for the state to distribute social spending through traditional channels; their intermediate layers and corporate sectors still consumed huge amounts of revenue before services actually reached those poor people who managed to gain access. The president needed a "postpopulist" option, an electorally and economically efficient mechanism for buffering the effects of years of crisis. Social spending grew, but was targeted through channels that would have the largest possible positive impact on the state's public image. To make sure that high-impact basic services were actually delivered, PRONASOL either bypassed or reoriented many traditional government agencies, decentralizing delivery to reach more people while centralizing control in practice. They got results; both the president and PRONASOL had quite positive 1991 opinion poll ratings, much higher than the official party.[19]

PRONASOL delivered services to large numbers of people within a short period of time.[20] Like earlier umbrella programs, PRONASOL is more a strategy for policy reform than an operational office, since it

18. At least by the end of Salinas's first three years, in spite of ad hoc and partial concessions to the political opposition, the electoral process continued to be sharply biased and marred by serious irregularities. Most contested outcomes were still determined by post-ballot civic mobilization. Whether the continuation of fraud was the result of a presidential decision or a reflection of his weakness vis-à-vis traditional political elites remains an open question. For overviews of the August 1991 elections, see among others, Alcocer and Morales 1991 and Loeaza 1991.

19. According to the *Los Angeles Times* (Oct. 22, 1991), for example, by late 1991 83 percent of Mexicans thought that Salinas was doing a good job, even though only 36 percent said they were better off than when he took office. More than half of those who said they supported Salinas mentioned PRONASOL as one of the reasons. One-third of those interviewed said they or a family member had benefitted personally from a PRONASOL project. Those who called themselves *priistas* also increased, from one in three in 1989 to almost one in two. The validity of polling in Mexico remains controversial.

20. PRONASOL's target groups are: the urban poor, poor peasants, and indigenous people. Its various programs focus on health, education, food distribution, potable water and sewerage, electrification, street paving, housing, and specific supports for peasant producers, women, and indigenous peoples. Its early accomplishments in the construction of physical infrastructure have been especially notable, delivering electricity, piped water, and paved streets to literally thousands of communities. See PRONASOL 1991a, 1991b.

mainly coordinates and reorients existing agencies. The question remains, then, to what degree the *process* through which services are delivered actually changed. Many different implementation mechanisms were used, but most PRONASOL funding was federal revenue-sharing distributed via block grants to state and municipal governments.[21]

PRONASOL proclaims its ostensibly nonpartisan character. PRONASOL is clearly politically motivated, however, in that it is designed to renew the regime's legitimacy, and it skillfully targets disproportionate resources to electorally contested areas.[22] But this does not necessarily mean that access to the program's benefits is systematically politically conditioned or corporatist in the traditional sense. Indeed, most opposition municipalities receive funding. An argument could even be made that PRONASOL rewarded communities for their past electoral opposition, in that the government must compete to win back their support, or at least acquiescence. This is not necessarily new, however, since Mexican state managers have a long tradition of sophisticated combinations of "carrot and stick" responses to political challengers. In practice, the range of antipoverty policy scenarios is quite varied, as it was under the SAM and COPLAMAR umbrella programs, and much more empirical research is needed to accurately explain a policy process in transition.

Some smaller PRONASOL programs clearly did attempt to put the official discourse into practice, especially those carried out by the National Indigenous Institute (INI). With PRONASOL funds, the INI created a series of economic development funds that attempted to turn local investment decision making over to autonomous regional councils of indigenous organizations. In contrast to most PRONASOL programs, where the state created its own interlocutors, these regional funds attempted to bolster existing representative social

---

21. The gaps and overlaps in the public data make it difficult to determine the relative size of each funding channel or the numbers of beneficiaries.

22. See Dresser's (1991) comprehensive critique, and Moguel 1991. Haber (1989) analyzes an important case in detail. In the month before the August 1991 midterm elections, for example, PRONASOL spending rose 31 percent over previous months (*Christian Science Monitor*, Sept. 3, 1991). On PRONASOL's massive public relations campaign preceding the August 1991 national legislative elections, see Gómez Leyva 1991. For journalistic accounts of direct electoral use of PRONASOL funding, see, among others, Beltrán del Rio 1990a, 1990b; Correa 1990; and Corro 1991. PRONASOL's geographical choices in its regional development programs are revealing, since they target electorally contested areas such as La Laguna (Coahuila/Durango), eastern Michoacán, the isthmus of Tehuantepec (Oaxaca), the state of Mexico, Tierra Caliente of Guerrero and the Oaxaca coast.

organizations. Preliminary field research found a significant minority of the funds to be notably pluralistic.[23]

On paper, PRONASOL carried on the spirit of "co-responsibility" put into practice by CONASUPO-COPLAMAR.[24] As with the rural food distribution program, the record of actual power-sharing was mixed. The food councils had been somewhat protected from partisan politicization, however, because they predated effective electoral competition. PRONASOL's pluralist potential faces a greater threat of partisan manipulation from a ruling party increasingly uncertain about its future. Did PRONASOL's combination of more efficient social spending with skilled electoral targeting reinforce the pattern of liberalization without democratization?

Political analysts in Mexico debate the significance of these new patterns of *concertación social* between the state and social movements, especially given the regime's lack of fundamental change on the electoral front. Pluralistic patterns of distributive reform remain the exception rather than the rule. Perhaps the regime's willingness to cede legitimacy to autonomous citizens' groups while manipulating voting outcomes was an attempt to prolong official party rule by dividing the opposition. But this liberalization could also have emerged in *spite* of the lack of an electoral opening, and its future may depend on the relative weight of factions within the regime which favor further political opening. Competing policy currents have different goals, but whatever their political intent, it will prove increasingly difficult to keep the electoral and nonelectoral spheres separate in the future.

More pluralistic antipoverty policy may simply represent the modernization of corporatism, or it may constitute a step toward the gradual democratization of the relationship between state and society. Because of the unpredictability of Mexican politics, the question re-

23. The funds build directly on the CONASUPO-COPLAMAR experience, and Figure 2 describes INI-PRONASOL dynamics equally well. The regional councils were sufficiently pluralistic to provoke the governor of Chiapas to jail the top INI officials in the state on trumped-up charges of corruption. It is rather unusual in Mexico for federal officials to become political prisoners. As one indigenous leader put it, "Their only crime was to work with everyone, whether or not they are sympathizers of the government" (*La Jornada*, March 21, 1992). In the state of Oaxaca, out of 20 regional funds, at least 11 included autonomous groups, while 3 excluded independent organizations (as of 1991). Many of these regional councils were themselves remarkably pluralistic, as official and nongovernmental groups learned to share power with each other for the first time. See Fox 1992b.

24. As PRONASOL's director claimed, Solidarity's "new dynamic . . . breaks with bureaucratic atavism and administrative rigidity. Public servants increasingly share a vocation for dialog, agreement, *concertación* and direct, co-responsible work with the citizenry, which also assumes an increasingly active and leading role in the actions intended to improve their standard of living" (PRONASOL 1991b:23).

mains open. Will liberalization lead to democratization in Mexico? The outcome may be uncertain, but an interactive process is under way. Democratization in Mexico will depend on how conflict between authoritarian and reformist policy currents within the state interacts with the efforts of opposition political parties and autonomous social actors to broaden and deepen their roots in society.

Glossary

acaparador   hoarder (disparaging term for private crop buyer)

ANAGSA   Aseguradora Nacional Agrícola y Ganadera, S.A. [National Agricultural and Livestock Insurance Company, Inc.]

ANDSA   Almacenes Nacionales de Deposito, S.A. [National Warehouses, Inc.]

ARIC   Asociación Rural de Interés Colectivo [Rural Collective Interest Association]

BANRURAL   Banco de Crédito Rural [Rural Credit Bank]

BORUCONSA   Bodegas Rurales CONASUPO, S.A. [CONASUPO Rural Warehouses, Inc.]

cacique   local political boss

CARTT   Cooperativa Agropecuaria Regional "Tosepan Titataniske" (Puebla) ["We Shall Overcome" Regional Agricultural Cooperative]

CCI   Central Campesina Independiente [Independent Peasant Central]

CECVYM   Coalición de Ejidos Colectivos de los Valles del Yaqui y Mayo (Sonora) [Coalition of Collective Ejidos of the Yaqui and Mayo Valleys]

CEPAL   Comisión Económica para América Latina [Economic Commission for Latin America, United Nations]

CEPCO   Coordinadora Estatal de Productores de Café de Oaxaca [Oaxaca State Network of Coffee Producers]

CIOAC   Central Independiente de Obreros Agrícolas y Campesinos [Independent Farmworkers and Peasants' Central]

CNC   Confederación Nacional Campesina [National Peasant Confederation]

CNOC   Coordinadora Nacional de Organizaciones Cafetaleras [National Network of Coffee Producer Organizations]

CNPA   Coordinadora Nacional "Plan de Ayala" [National "Plan de Ayala" Network]

CNPI   Coordinadora Nacional de Pueblos Indios [National Network of Indian Peoples]

229

Coalición de Ejidos de la Costa Grande de Guerrero [Coalition of Ejidos of the Costa Grande (region) of Guerrero]
COCEI Coalición de Obreros, Campesinos, Estudiantes del Istmo [Coalition of Workers, Peasants and Students of the Isthmus (of Oaxaca)]
COCEO Coalición de Obreros, Campesinos, y Estudiantes de Oaxaca [Coalition of Workers, Peasants, and Students of Oaxaca]
Comité Rural de Abasto Village Food Committee
comunero member of an agrarian community
comunidad agraria agrarian community [official category of land tenure, restoring ancestral use-rights to indigenous communities]
CONASUPO Companía Nacional de Subsistencias Populares [National Basic Foods Company]
Consejo Comunitario de Abasto Community Food Council
COPLAMAR Coordinación General del Plan Nacional para Zonas Deprimidas y Grupos Marginados [National Plan for Depressed Zones and Marginal Groups]
coyote disparaging term for commercial intermediary (e.g., private crop buyer)
DICONSA Distribuidora CONASUPO, S.A. [CONASUPO Distributors, Inc.]
ejidatario member of an ejido
ejido official category of land tenure, granting use-rights to agrarian reform communities which are usually parcelled to individual families
FERTIMEX Fertilizantes de México [Mexican Fertilizers]
FIRA Fondo de Garantía y Fomento para la Agricultura y Ganadería [Agricultural and Livestock Investment Guarantee Fund]
FIRCO Fideicomiso de Riesgo Compartido [Shared Risk Fund]
FNTE Federación Nacional de Transportistas Ejidales [National Federation of Ejidal Transporters]
IMPECSA Impulsora de Pequeño Comercio. S.A. [Small Commerce Promoter, Inc.]
IMSS Instituto Mexicano de Seguro Social [Mexican Social Security Institute]
INCA Instituto Nacional de Capacitación Agropecuaria [National Agricultural Training Institute]
Informe de Gobierno Government Report (annual)
INI Instituto Nacional Indigenista [National Indigenous Institute]
LFA Ley de Fomento Agropecuario [Agricultural Development Law]
LICONSA Leche Industrializada CONASUPO, S.A. [CONASUPO Industrialized Milk, Inc.]
PACE Programa de Apoyo a la Comercialización Ejidal (later changed to "Rural") [Ejido (later Rural) Marketing Support Program]
PAN Partido de Acción Nacional [National Action Party]
PIDER Programa de Inversiones en el Desarrollo Rural [Rural Development Investment Program]
PNR Partido Nacional Revolucionario [National Revolutionary Party]
PRI Partido Revolucionario Institucional [Institutional Revolutionary Party]
PRM Partido de la Revolución Mexicana [Party of the Mexican Revolution]
PRONAL Programa Nacional de Alimentación [National Food Program]

PRONASE   Productora Nacional de Semillas, S.A. [National Seed Producer, Inc.]

PSUM   Partido Socialista Unificado de México [Unified Socialist Party of Mexico]

SAM   Sistema Alimentario Mexicano [Mexican Food System]

SARH   Secretaría de Agricultura y Recursos Hidráulicos [Ministry of Agriculture and Water Resources]

SIRAC   Sistema Integral Regional de Abasto y Comercialización (Guerrero) [Integrated Regional Food Distribution and Marketing System]

SPP   Secretaría de Programación y Presupuesto [Planning and Budget Ministry]

SRA   Secretaría de Reforma Agraria [Agrarian Reform Ministry]

UELC   Unión de Ejidos "Lázaro Cárdenas" (Nayarit) ["Lázaro Cárdenas" Union of Ejidos]

UGOCM   Unión General de Obreros y Campesinos de México [General Union of Mexican Workers and Peasants]

Unión de Ejidos "Despertar Campesino" (Oaxaca) ["Peasants' Awakening" Ejido Union]

Unión Libre Campesina (Oaxaca) [Free Peasants (Ejido) Union]

UNORCA   Unión Nacional de Organizaciones Regionales Campesinas Autónomas [National Network of Autonomous Regional Peasant Organizations]

URECCH   Unión Regional de Ejidos de la Costa Chica (Guerrero) [Regional Union of Ejidos of the Costa Chica]

URECHH   Unión Regional de Ejidos y Comunidades de la Huasteca Hidalguense [Regional Union of Ejidos and (Agrarian) Communities of Hidalgo's Huasteca (region)]

Bibliography

Aceves Navarro, Everardo. 1988. "Uso y manejo del agua en la agricultura mexicana." *Comercio Exterior* 38(7), July.

Aguado López, Eduardo, José Luis Torres, and Gabriela Scherer Ibarra. 1983. "La lucha por la tierra en México (1976–1982)." *Revista Mexicana de Ciencias Políticas y Sociales* 113–14, July–December.

Aguilar Camín, Héctor. 1982a. "La transición política." *Nexos* 51, March.

———. 1982b. "A través del túnel." *Nexos* 60, December.

Aguilar Solís, Samuel, and Hugo Andrés Araujo. 1984. *Estado y campesinado en la Laguna: La lucha campesina por la tierra y el excedente*. Saltillo: Universidad Autónoma Agraria Antonio Narro.

Alcántara, Sergio. 1981. "La capacidad de respuesta del campesinado mexicano." *Revista del México Agrario* 14(1), January.

Alcocer, Jorge, and Rodrigo Morles M. 1991. "Mitología y realidad del fraude electoral." *Nexos* no. 166, October.

Aldrete-Haas, José Antonio. 1990. "The Decline of the Mexican State? The Case of State Housing Intervention (1917–1988)." Ph.D. diss., Department of Urban Studies and Planning, Massachusetts Institute of Technology.

———. 1991. *La deconstrucción del estado mexicano, políticas de vivienda 1917–1988*. Mexico: Alianza.

Alford, Robert R. 1975. "Paradigms of Relations between State and Society." In Leon Lindberg et al., eds., *Stress and Contradiction in Modern Capitalism*. Lexington, Mass.: D. C. Heath.

Alford, Robert R., and Roger Friedland. 1985. *Powers of Theory: Capitalism, the State, and Democracy*. Cambridge: Cambridge University Press.

Algara Cossio, Ignacio, and David Winder. 1985. "Rural Community Development in Mexico: Issues and Trends." *Community Development Journal* 20(2).

Alisky, Marvin. 1974. "CONASUPO: A Mexican Agency Which Makes Low Income Workers Feel Their Government Cares." *Inter-American Economic Affairs* 27(3), Winter.

Alonso, Jorge, ed. 1985. *El estado mexicano*. Mexico: Nueva Imagen/CIESAS.

Alvarez, Sonia E. 1989. "Politicizing Gender and Engendering Democracy." In Alfred Stepan, ed., *Democratizing Brazil: Problems of Transition and Consolidation*. New York: Oxford University Press.

Alves, Maria Helena Moreira. 1985. *State and Opposition in Military Brazil*. Austin: University of Texas Press.

Americas Watch Report. 1990. *Human Rights in Mexico: A Policy of Impunity*. New York: Americas Watch.

Amnesty International. 1986. *Mexico: Human Rights in Rural Areas*. Exchange of Documents with the Mexican Government on Human Rights Violations in Oaxaca and Chiapas. London: AI Publications.

ANAGSA. 1982. "Estructura, organización y funciones de la aseguradora nacional agrícola y ganadera." Mexico: COPIDER-Harvard Workshop.

Anderson, Charles. 1965. "'Reformmongering' and the Uses of Political Power." *Inter-American Economic Affairs* 19(2), Autumn.

Andrade, Armando, and Nicole Blanc. 1987. "SAM's Cost and Impact on Production." In James Austin and Gustavo Esteva, eds., *Food Policy in Mexico: The Search for Self-Sufficiency*. Ithaca: Cornell University Press.

Andrade, Armando, and Manuel Martínez. 1980. "La consulta y participación de los productores agropecuarios en las programas de desarrollo." In *Sociología del desarrollo rural*, vol. 2. Memoria. Mexico: Universidad Autónoma de Chapingo.

Annis, Sheldon. 1988. "What Is Not the Same about the Urban Poor: The Case of Mexico City." In John P. Lewis, ed., *Strengthening the Poor: What Have We Learned?* Washington, D.C.: Overseas Development Council.

Appendini, Kirsten. 1988. "El papel del estado en la comercialización de granos básicos." In Jorge Zepeda Patterson, ed., *Las sociedades rurales hoy*. Zamora: Colegio de Michoacán.

——. 1992. "De la milpa a los tortibonos: La reestructuración de la política alimentaria en México." United Nations Research Institute for Social Development. Mexico: Colegio de Mexico.

Appendini, Kirsten, and V. Almeida Salles. 1980. "Precios de garantía y crisis agrícola." *Nueva Antropología* 4(13–14), May.

Arce, Alberto. 1985. "La asistencia técnica de un distrito de temporal: Entre la 'grilla' y la política." In Sergio Alcántara and Enrique Sánchez, eds., *Desarrollo rural en Jalisco: Contradicciones y perspectivas*. Mexico: Colegio de Jalisco/CONACYT.

——. 1986. "The Administration of Agrarian Policy in a Less Developed Country: The Case of the SAM in Mexico." Ph.D. diss., Department of Sociology, University of Manchester.

——. 1987. "Bureaucratic Conflict and Public Policy: Rainfed Agriculture in Mexico." *Boletín de Estudios Latinoamericanos y del Caribe*, no. 42, June.

Arce, Alberto, and Norman Long. 1987. "The Dynamics of Knowledge Interfaces between Mexican Agricultural Bureaucrats and Peasants: A Case Study from Jalisco." *Boletín de Estudios Latinoamericanos y del Caribe*, no. 43, December.

Arteaga Pérez, Javier. 1985. "El Sistema Alimentario Mexicano (SAM): Una perspectiva política." *Estudios Sociológicos* 3(8), May–August.

Ascher, William. 1984. *Scheming for the Poor: The Politics of Redistribution in Latin America.* Cambridge: Harvard University Press.

Aspe, Pedro, and Paul Sigmund, eds. 1984. *The Political Economy of Income Distribution in Mexico.* New York: Holmes and Meier.

Astorga Lira, Enrique, and Clarisa Hardy. 1978. *Organización, lucha y dependencia económica: La Unión de Ejidos Emiliano Zapata.* Mexico: Nueva Imagen/CIDER.

Austin, James. 1982. "Strategies and Mechanisms for Urban and Rural Subsidization: The Case of CONASUPO." In Neville Scrimshaw and Mitchell Wallerstein, eds., *Nutrition Policy Implementation.* New York: Plenum.

———. 1984. "The Visible Hand." Research Paper: Seventy-fifth Anniversary Colloquium Series. Presented at the Harvard Business School Seventy-fifth Anniversary Colloquium on World Food Policy Issues, April 8–11.

Austin, James, and Michael Buckley. 1983. "Food Marketing SOEs: Mexico and Venezuela." Working Paper, Division of Research, Harvard University Graduate School of Business Administration, December.

Austin, James, and Gustavo Esteva. 1985. "SAM Is Dead—Long Live SAM." *Food Policy* 10(2), May.

———, eds. 1987. *Food Policy in Mexico: The Search for Self-Sufficiency.* Ithaca: Cornell University Press.

Austin, James, and Jonathan Fox. 1987. "State-Owned Enterprises as Food Policy Implementers." In James Austin and Gustavo Esteva, eds., *Food Policy in Mexico: The Search for Self-Sufficiency.* Ithaca: Cornell University Press.

Austin, James, and Kenneth L. Hoadley. 1987. "State Trading and the Futures Market: The Experience of CONASUPO in Mexico." In Bruce Johnston, Cassio Luiselli, Celso Cartas Contreras, and Roger D. Norton, eds., *U.S.–Mexico Relations: Agriculture and Rural Development.* Stanford: Stanford University Press.

Austin, James, and Robin Hurless. 1978. "CONASUPO '76." Harvard University Graduate School of Business, School of Public Health.

Avila, Agustín. 1986. "Etnia y movimiento campesino en la Huasteca Hidalguense." In Agustín Avila and Alma Cervantes, *Procesos de organización campesina en las Huastecas.* Mexico City: Facultad de Economía, UNAM/DICONSA.

Aziz, Alberto, and Jorge Alonso. 1984. *Reforma política y deformaciones electorales.* Mexico: CIESAS.

Bachrach, Peter, and Morton Baratz. 1962. "Two Faces of Power." *American Political Science Review* 56(4).

Bailey, John. 1980. "The Presidency, Bureaucracy and Administrative Reform in Mexico: The Case of the Secretariat of Programming and the Budget." *Inter-American Economic Review* 34(1), Summer.

———. 1988. *Governing Mexico, 1976–1988: The Statecraft of Crisis Management.* New York: St. Martin's.

Bailey, John, and John Link. 1981. "Statecraft and Agriculture in Mexico, 1980–1982: Domestic and Foreign Policy Considerations." *Working Papers in U.S.–Mexican Studies* 23.

Bailón, Moisés Jaime. 1984. "Elecciones locales en Oaxaca en 1980." *Nueva Antropología* 7(25), October.

———. 1990. "Los problemas de Morro Mazatlán: La lucha por el control de una agencia municipal en el estado de Oaxaca." *Estudios Sociológicos* 8(22), January–April.

Balanzar, Efrén, et al. 1982. "La lucha coprera en la costa de Guerrero." *Textual* 3(10), December.

Baldwin, David A. 1979. "Power Analysis and World Politics: New Trends versus Old Tendencies." *World Politics* 31(2), January.

Banco de México. 1980–1984. *Informe anual.* Mexico.

Barabas, Alicia, and Miguel Bartolomé. 1986. *Etnicidad y pluralismo cultural: La dinámica étnica en Oaxaca.* Mexico City: INAH.

Barberán, José, et al. 1988. *Radiografía del fraude: Análisis de los datos oficiales del 6 de julio.* Mexico: Nuestro Tiempo.

Barenstein, Jorge. 1982. *La gestión de empresas públicas en México.* Mexico: CIDE.

Barkin, David. 1987. "SAM and Seeds." In James Austin and Gustavo Esteva, eds., *Food Policy in Mexico: The Search for Self-Sufficiency.* Ithaca: Cornell University Press.

———. 1989. "Resolving the Dilemma of the Internationalization of Mexican Agriculture." Paper presented at the Fifteenth Latin American Studies Association (LASA) International Congress.

———. 1990. *Distorted Development: Mexico in the World Economy.* Boulder, Colo.: Westview Press.

Barkin, David, and Billie Dewalt. 1985. "La crisis alimentaria mexicana y el sorgo." *Problemas del Desarrollo* 16(61), February.

———. 1988. "Sorghum and the Mexican Food Crisis." *Latin American Research Review* 13(3).

Barkin, David, and Blanca Suárez. 1983. *El fin del principio, las semillas y la seguridad alimentaria.* Mexico: Océano/CECODES.

———. 1985. *El fin de la autosuficiencia alimentaria.* Mexico: Océano/CECODES.

Bartra, Armando. 1980a. "La revolución mexicana de 1910 en la perspectiva del magonismo." In Adolfo Gilly, et al., *Interpretaciones de la revolución mexicana.* Mexico: Nueva Imagen.

———. 1980b. "Crisis agraria y movimiento campesino en los setentas." *Cuadernos Agrarios* 5(10–11), December.

———. 1985. *Los herederos de Zapata. Movimientos campesinos postrevolucionarios en México.* Mexico: Era.

———. 1989a. "Prólogo al libro de Gustavo Gordillo: *Estado, mercados y movimiento campesino.*" *Pueblo* 12(144–45), May–June.

———. 1989b. "La apropiación del proceso productivo como forma de lucha." *Pueblo* 12 (143), April.

———. 1990. "Modernidad, miseria extrema y productores organizados." *El Cotidiano* 36.

———. 1991. "Pros, contras y asegunes de la 'apropriación del proceso productivo.'" *El Cotidiano* 39, January–February.

———. 1992. "Darse abasto: Diecisiete tesis en torno a la autogestión en sistemas rurales de abasto." In Cynthia Hewitt de Alcántara, ed., *Reestructuración económica y subsistencia rural*. El maíz y la crisis de los 80. Geneva: UNRISD.

Bartra, Roger, ed. 1975. *Caciquismo y poder político en el México rural*. Mexico: Siglo XXI.

———. 1982. *Campesinado y poder político en México*. Mexico: Era.

Basáñez, Miguel. 1981. *La lucha por la hegemonía en México, 1968–1980*. Mexico: Siglo XXI.

Basurto, Jorge. 1982. "The Late Populism of Luis Echeverría." In Michael L. Coniff, ed., *Latin American Populism in Comparative Perspective*. Albuquerque: University of New Mexico Press.

Beals, Ralph L. 1975. *The Peasant Marketing System of Oaxaca, Mexico*. Berkeley: University of California Press.

Beltrán del Río, Pascal. 1990a. "Solidaridad, oxígeno para el PRI, en el rescate de votos." *Proceso* no. 718, August 6.

———. 1990b. "El memorandum de Pichardo, prueba de que el Pronasol es para servir al PRI." *Proceso* no. 730, October 29.

Benítez Zenteno, Raúl, ed. 1982. *Sociedad y política en Oaxaca, 1980*. Mexico: IIS/UABJO, Oaxaca.

Benjamin, Medea, and Rebecca Buell. 1985. "Coalition of Ejidos Report." Research Report, San Francisco Institute for Food and Development Policy.

Benjamin, Thomas. 1985. "Leviathan on the Zócalo: Recent Historiography of the Postrevolutionary Mexican State." *Latin American Research Review* 20(3).

Benjamin, Thomas, and Mark Wasserman, eds. 1990. *Provinces of the Revolution: Essays on Regional Mexican History, 1910–1929*. Albuquerque: University of New Mexico Press.

Bennett, Douglas, and Kenneth Sharpe. 1982. "The State as Banker and Entrepreneur: The Last Resort Character of the Mexican State's Economic Intervention, 1917–1970." In Sylvia Ann Hewlett and Richard Weinert, eds., *Brazil and Mexico, Patterns in Late Development*. Philadelphia: ISHI.

———. 1985. *Transnational Corporations versus the State: The Political Economy of the Mexican Auto Industry*. Princeton: Princeton University Press.

Bennett, Vivienne, and Jeffrey W. Rubin. 1988. "How Popular Movements Shape the State: Radical Oppositions in Juchitán and Monterrey, Mexico, 1973–1987." Paper presented at the Fourteenth International Congress of the Latin American Studies Association (LASA), New Orleans. March 17–19.

Berger, Suzanne, ed. 1981. *Organizing Interests in Western Europe*. Cambridge: Cambridge University Press.

Bergsman, Joel. 1980. "Income Distribution and Poverty in Mexico." World Bank Staff Working Paper no. 395, June.

Beyer, Janice, John Stevens, and Harrison Trice. 1983. "The Implementing Organization: Exploring the Black Box in Research on Public Policy." In Richard Hall and Robert Quinn, eds., *Organizational Theory and Public Policy*. Beverly Hills, Calif.: Sage.

Bhaduri, Amit. 1986. "Forced Commerce and Agrarian Growth." *World Development* 14(2).

Bizberg, Ilán. 1984. "Política laboral y acción sindical en México (1976–1982)." *Foro Internacional* 25(2), October.

———. 1990. *Estado y sindicalismo en México*. Mexico: Colegio de México.

Blair, Calvin. 1981. "Economic Development Policy in Mexico: A New Penchant for Planning." In Richard Erb and Stanley Ross, eds., *United States Relations with Mexico: Context and Content*. Washington, D.C.: American Enterprise Institute.

Block, Fred. 1987. *Revising State Theory: Essays in Politics and Postindustrialism*. Philadelphia: Temple University Press.

Boege, Eckart, and Pilar Calvo. 1975. "Estructura política y clases sociales en una comunidad del Valle del Mezquital." In Roger Bartra, ed., *Caciquismo y poder político en el México rural*. Mexico: Siglo XXI.

Boltvinik, Julio, and Raúl Pessah. 1981. "La asignación de recursos públicos a la agricultura en México, 1959–1976." CEPAL/MEX/SAC/73, February 10, unpublished.

Bonfil, Guillermo. 1982. "El estado, indigenismo y los indios." In Jorge Alonso, ed., *El estado mexicano*. Mexico: Nueva Imagen/CIESAS.

Booth, John, and Mitchell Seligson. 1984. "The Political Culture of Authoritarianism in Mexico: A Reexamination." *Latin American Research Review* 19(1).

BORUCONSA. 1979. "Presentación de bodegas rurales CONASUPO." Asesoría Técnica. October.

———. 1982a. *Normas para la operación del PACE*. Mexico: BORUCONSA.

———. 1982b. *Manual del promotor PACE*. Mexico: BORUCONSA, Gerencia de Programas Especiales.

———. 1982c. *Memoria, programa de apoyo a la comercialización rural, 1976–1982*. Mexico: BORUCONSA, Gerencia de Programas Especiales.

———. 1983. "Utilización de bodegas propias y ajenas." BORUCONSA, Subgerencia de Programas Especiales. March, mimeographed.

———. 1984. "Programa de apoyo a la comercialización rural (PACE)." BORUCONSA, Coordinación General de Regiones. September, mimeographed.

———. 1991. *Encuentro campesino de experiencias y alternativas para la comercialización del maíz*. Jalisco, June 8–10. BORUCONSA.

Brachet de Márquez, Viviane. 1984. "Proceso organizacional y políticas estatales: Un acercamiento metodológico." *Estudios Sociológicos* 2(1).

———. 1985. "State and Society in Mexico: The Politics of Family Planning and Pollution Control." Paper presented at the 13th International Congress of the Latin American Studies Association, Albuquerque, April.

Brading, David A., ed. 1980. *Caudillo and Peasant in the Mexican Revolution*. Cambridge: Cambridge University Press.

Brannon, Jeffrey, and Eric N. Baklanoff. 1987. *Agrarian Reform and Public Enterprise in Mexico: The Political Economy of Yucatán's Henequen Industry*. Tuscaloosa: University of Alabama Press.

Bright, Charles, and Susan Harding, eds. 1985. *Statemaking and Social Movements: Essays in History and Theory*. Ann Arbor: University of Michigan Press.

Brignol, Raúl, and Jaime Crispi 1982. "The Peasantry in Latin America: A Theoretical Approach." *CEPAL Review* 16, April.

Briseño, Juan. 1986. "Migración y violencia en la Huasteca Hidalguense." *México Indígena*, no. 13, November–December.

Caballero, Emilio, and Felipe Zermeño. 1981. "SAM: Utopía y realidad." *Economía Informa* 77, January.

Cabrera Morales, Jorge. 1988. *Que es Pronagra?* Mexico: Pronagra, November.

Callaghy, Thomas M. 1989. "Toward State Capability and Embedded Liberalism in the Third World: Lessons for Adjustment." In Joan M. Nelson and contributors, *Fragile Coalitions: The Politics of Economic Adjustment*. New Brunswick, N.J.: Transaction Books.

Calva, José Luis. 1988. *Crisis agrícola y alimentaria en Mexico, 1982–1988*. Mexico: Fontamara.

Calvo, Pilar, and Roger Bartra. 1975. "Estructura de poder, clases dominantes y lucha ideológica en el México rural." In Roger Bartra et al., *Caciquismo y poder político en el México rural*. Mexico: Siglo XXI.

Camacho, Manuel. 1980. *La clase obrera en la historia de México: El futuro inmediato*. Mexico: Siglo XXI/IIS/UNAM.

Camahji, Arturo. 1979. "No todo en el campo es orégano, Panorama de la lucha campesina 1977–1978." *Nexos* 14, February.

Cammack, Paul. 1989. "Review Article: Bringing the State Back In?" *British Journal of Political Science* 19(2), April.

Camp, Roderic. 1984. "Generals and Politicians in Mexico: A Preliminary Comparison." In David Ronfeldt, ed., *The Modern Mexican Military: A Reassessment*. Monograph Series 15. La Jolla: University of California, San Diego, Center for U.S.–Mexican Studies.

———. 1985. "The Political Technocrat in Mexico and the Survival of the Political System." *Latin American Research Review* 20(1).

Campbell, Federico. 1984. "En hospitales móviles se esteriliza a mujeres indígenas de Chiapas." *Proceso* 405, August 6.

Canabal, Beatriz. 1982. "La organización campesina independiente en la década de los sesenta." *Textual* 3(10), December.

———. 1984. *Hoy luchamos por la tierra.* . . . Mexico: Universidad Autónoma Metropolitana-Xochimilco.

Canak, William L. 1984. "The Peripheral State Debate: State Capitalism and Bureaucratic Authoritarian Regimes in Latin America." *Latin America Research Review* 19(1).

Cantú, Arturo. 1982. "El estado programador." *Nexos* 51, March.

Capriate, Jorge Alberto. 1972. "The Political Culture of Marginal Elites: A Case Study of Regionalism in Mexican Politics." Ph.D. diss., Stanford University.

Cardoso, Fernando Henrique, and Enzo Faletto. 1979. *Dependency and Development in Latin America*. Berkeley: University of California Press.

Carnoy, Martin. 1984. *The State and Political Theory*. Princeton: Princeton University Press.

Carr, Barry. 1985. "Mexican Communism, 1968–1981: Eurocommunism in the Americas?" *Journal of Latin American Studies* 17.

Carrasco Licea, Rosalba, and Francisco Hernández y Puente. 1989. "Atender al campo: Prioridad inmediata." *La Jornada*, August 7.

———. 1990. "La agenda para el campo." *La Jornada*, January 15.

Cartas Contreras, Celso. 1987. "The Agricultural Sector's Contributions to the Import-Substituting Industrialization Process in Mexico." In Bruce F. Johnston, Cassio Luiselli, Celso Cartas Contreras, and Roger D. Norton, eds., *U.S.-Mexico Relations: Agriculture and Rural Development*. Stanford: Stanford University Press.

Cartas Contreras, Celso, and Luz María Bassoco. 1987. "The Mexican Food System (SAM): An Agricultural Production Strategy." In Bruce F. Johnston, Cassio Luiselli, Celso Cartas Contrers, and Roger D. Norton, eds., *U.S.–Mexico Relations: Agriculture and Rural Development*. Stanford: Stanford University Press.

Casar, Amparo. 1982. "El proyecto del movimiento obrero organizado en la LI legislatura." *Estudios Políticos* 1(1), October.

Castaños, Carlos Manuel. 1987. *Organización campesina: La estrategia truncada. . . ."* Chapingo: Futura.

Castell Cancino, Jorge, and Fernando Rello. 1981. "Las desventuras de un proyecto agrario: 1970–1976." In Rolando Cordera, ed., *Desarrollo y crisis de la economía mexicana*. Mexico: Fondo de Cultura Económica.

Ceceñas, Javier. 1984. "La industria del maíz en México: Análisis de precios y subsidios." Thesis in agricultural economics, Autonomous University of Chapingo.

CEPAL. 1981. "Caracterización de la política agrícola mexicana en diferentes períodos de los años veinte a los años setenta." CEPAL/MEX1052, June 26, unpublished.

_____. 1982. *Economía campesina y agricultura empresarial*. Mexico: Siglo XXI.

Cernea, Michael. 1979. "Measuring Project Impact: Monitoring and Evaluation in the PIDER Rural Development Project—Mexico." *World Bank Staff Working Paper* no. 332, June.

_____. 1983. "A Social Methodology for Community Particition in Local Investment: The Experience of Mexico's PIDER Program." *World Bank Staff Working Paper* no. 598, August.

CIDAC. 1991. *Vivienda y estabilidad política, alternativas para el futuro*. Mexico: Diana/Centro de Investigación para el Desarrollo, A.C.

Cleaves, Peter S. 1974. *Bureaucratic Politics and Administration in Chile*. Berkeley: University of California Press.

_____. 1980. "Implementation amidst Scarcity and Apathy: Political Power and Policy Design." In Merilee Grindle, ed., *Politics and Policy Implementation in the Third World*. Princeton: Princeton University Press.

Cleaves, Peter S., and Martin J. Scurrah. 1980. *Agriculture, Bureaucracy, and Military Government in Peru*. Ithaca: Cornell University Press.

Cloward, Richard, and Frances Fox Piven. 1974. *The Politics of Turmoil*. New York: Pantheon.

CNPI (Coordinadora Nacional de Pueblos Indígenas). 1982. "Documentos." *Textual* 3(10), December.

Coalición de Ejidos Colectivos de los Valles del Yaqui y Mayo. 1982. "En defensa del ejido." CEESTEM/SMP.

_____. 1985. "Ponencia [untitled]." Presented at the Jornada Nacional en Defensa del Ejido, Mexico City, August 5–8.

Cobo, Rosario, and Lorena Paz Paredes. 1991. "El sistema de abasto campesino en la Costa Grande de Guerrero." Instituto Maya.

Cockcroft, James. 1983. *Mexico*. New York: Monthly Review Press.

Cohen, Jean L. 1985. "Strategy or Identity: New Theoretical Paradigms and Contemporary Social Movements." *Social Research* 52(4), Winter.

Colburn, Forrest, D. 1988. "Statism, Rationality, and State Centrism." Review article, *Comparative Politics* 20(24), July.

———, ed. 1989. *Everyday Forms of Peasant Resistance*. Armonk: M. E. Sharpe.

Colegio de Posgraduados, Chapingo. 1985. "La efectividad de los elementos de la estrategia del Plan Puebla en el desarrollo, 1967–1985." Centro de Estudios del Desarrollo Rural/Centro de Enseñanza, Investigación y Capacitación para el Desarrollo Regional, Colegio de Posgraduados. Chapingo, draft, unpublished.

Coleman, Kenneth, and Charles Davis. 1983. "Preemptive Reform and the Mexican Working Class." *Latin American Research Review* 18(1).

Collier, David, ed. 1979. *The New Authoritarianism in Latin America*. Princeton: Princeton University Press.

Collier, David, and Ruth Berins Collier. 1977. "Who Does What, to Whom and How: Toward a Comparative Analysis of Latin American Corporatism." In James M. Malloy, ed., *Authoritarianism and Corporatism in Latin America*. Pittsburgh: University of Pittsburgh Press.

Collier, Ruth. 1982. "Popular Sector Incorporation and Political Supremacy: Regime Evolution in Brazil and Mexico." In Sylvia Ann Hewlett and Richard Weinert, eds., *Brazil and Mexico: Patterns in Late Development*. Philadelphia: ISHI.

Collier, Ruth, and David Collier. 1979. "Inducements versus Constraints: Disaggregating 'Corporatism.'" *American Political Science Review* 73, January.

CONASUPO. 1980. *Informe Anual*. Mexico City: CONASUPO.

———. 1982a. "Producción nacional, consumo nacional aparente y operaciónes CONASUPO en compras y ventas, 1965–1981." Gerencia de Planeación, May, unpublished.

———. 1982b. "Producción anual y comercialización por CONASUPO de granos y semillas de oleaginosas por entidad federativa, 1971–1981." Gerencia de Planeación, July, mimeographed.

———. 1982c. *La intervención del estado en el abasto y la regulación del mercado de los productos básicos*. Mexico: CONASUPO, Coordinación de Información, November.

———. 1983. "Los granos básicos en el mundo y en México, 1975–1982." Gerencia de Planeación, mimeographed.

Concha Malo, Miguel. 1988. "Las violaciones a los derechos humanos individuales en México (período: 1971–1986)." In Pablo González Casanova and Jorge Cadena Roa, eds., *Primer informe sobre la democracia: México 1988*. Mexico: Siglo XXI/UNAM.

Cook, Maria Lorena. 1990a. "Organizing Opposition in the Teachers' Movement in Oaxaca." In Joe Foweraker and Ann Craig, eds., *Popular Movements and Political Change in Mexico*. Boulder, Colo.: Lynne Reinner.

———. 1990b. "Organizing Dissent: The Politics of Opposition in the Mexican Teachers' Union." Ph.D. diss., University of California, Berkeley.

COPLAMAR. 1982. *Necesidades esenciales en México.* 5 vols. Mexico: Siglo XXI/COPLAMAR.

Cordera, Rolando, and Carlos Tello. 1982. *La disputa por la nación.* Mexico: Siglo XXI.

Córdova, Arnaldo. 1972. *La formación del poder político en México.* Mexico: Era.

———. 1974. *La política de masas del Cardenismo.* Mexico: Era.

———. 1980. "México: Revolución burguesa y política de masas." In Adolfo Gilly et al., *Interpretaciones de la revolución mexicana.* Mexico: Nueva Imagen.

———. 1983. "El poder del estado." *Economía Informa* 109, October.

———. 1989. *La revolución y el estado en México.* Mexico: Era.

Córdova, Arnaldo, Gerardo Unzueta, and Edmundo Jardón Arzate. 1984. *La revolución mexicana y la lucha actual por la democracia.* Mexico: Ediciones de Cultura Popular.

Cornelius, Wayne A. 1973a. "Nation Building, Participation, and Distribution: The Politics of Social Reform Under Cárdenas." In Gabriel Almond et al., eds., *Crisis, Choice and Change: Historical Studies of Political Development.* Boston: Little, Brown.

———. 1973b. "Contemporary Mexico: A Structural Analysis of Urban Caciquismo." In Robert Kern, ed., *The Caciques, Oligarchical Politics, and the System of Caciquismo in the Luso-Hispanic World.* Albuquerque: University of New Mexico Press.

———. 1975. *Politics and the Migrant Poor in Mexico City.* Stanford: Stanford University Press.

———. 1977. "Leaders, Followers and Official Patrons in Urban Mexico." In Steffen Schmidt et al., eds., *Friends, Followers, and Factions: A Reader in Political Clientelism.* Berkeley: University of California Press.

———. 1985. "The Political Economy of Mexico under De la Madrid: Austerity, Routinized Crisis and Nascent Recovery." *Mexican Studies/Estudios Mexicanos* 1(1), Winter.

Cornelius, Wayne A., Judith Gentleman, and Peter H. Smith, eds. 1989. *Mexico's Alternative Political Futures.* La Jolla: University of California, San Diego, Center for U.S.–Mexican Studies.

Correa, Guillermo. 1983. "Instalada en el PRI, la burguesía agraria domina economía y política." *Proceso* 329, February 21.

———. 1990. "El PRONASOL, que nació como esperanza, ha generado corrupción y protestas." *Proceso* no. 727, October 8.

Corro, Salvador. 1991. "Esperanza gubernamental: Solidaridad igual a votos." *Proceso,* no. 771, August 12.

Cox, Thomas E., and R. Christopher Whalen. 1990. "From the U.S. to Mexico: Friendly Advice on Ending the Farm Crisis." *Backgrounder* (Heritage Foundation), February 12.

Craig, Ann. 1983. *The First Agraristas.* Berkeley: University of California Press.

———. 1990. "Legal Constraints and Mobilization Strategies in the Countryside." In Joe Foweraker and Ann Craig, eds., *Popular Movements and Political Change in Mexico.* Boulder, Colo.: Lynne Reinner.

Cumings, Bruce. 1981. "Interest and Ideology in the Study of Agrarian Politics." *Politics and Society* 10(4).

Cummings, Ronald G., et al. 1989. "Waterworks: Improving Irrigation Management in Mexican Agriculture." World Resource Institute Paper no. 5, December.

Davis, Charles L. 1989. *Working-Class Mobilization and Political Control: Venezuela and Mexico*. Lexington: University of Kentucky Press.

De Grammont, Hubert, ed. 1986. *Asalariados agrícolas y sindicalismo en el campo mexicano*. Mexico: Juan Pablos.

――――. 1989a. "La Unión General de Obreros y Campesinos de México." In Julio Moguel, ed., *Historia de la cuestión agraria mexicana*. Vol. 8, *Política estatal y conflictos agrarios, 1950–1970*. Mexico: Siglo XXI/CEHAM.

――――. 1989b. "Jaramillo y las luchas campesinas en Morelos." In Julio Moguel, ed., *Historia de la cuestión agraria mexicana*. Vol. 8, *Política estatal y conflictos agrarios, 1950–1970*. Mexico: Siglo XXI/CEHAM.

De Janvry, Alain. 1981. *The Agrarian Question and Reformism in Latin America*. Baltimore: Johns Hopkins University Press.

De la Madrid, Miguel. 1987. "Introduction: The National Food Program, 1983–1988." In James E. Austin and Gustavo Esteva, eds., *Food Policy in Mexico: The Search for Self-Sufficiency*. Ithaca: Cornell University Press.

De la Mora Gómez, Jaime. 1990. "La banca de desarrollo en la modernización del campo." *Comercio Exterior* 40(10), October.

Del Carmen Prado, María. 1984. "La reforma administrativa para el desarrollo social en México." *Foro Internacional* 25(2), October.

De los Angeles Moreno, María. 1987. "Strategic Thrusts of the New Policy." In Austin and Esteva, eds., 1987.

Del Val, José. 1980. "El informe, la crisis y el presidente." *Nueva Antropología* 4(13–14), May.

――――. 1981. "A quien beneficia el SAM?" *Nueva Antropología* 5(17), May.

Dennis, Philip. 1973. "The Oaxacan Village President as Political Middleman." *Ethnology* 12(4), October.

――――. 1987. *Intervillage Conflict in Oaxaca*. New Brunswick, N.J.: Rutgers University Press.

DeWalt, Billie. 1985. "Mexico's Second Green Revolution." *Mexico Studies/Estudios Mexicanos* 1(1), Winter.

DGEA (Dirección General de Economía Agrícola/SARH). 1982. "Determinación de los precios de garantía para los productos del campo." *Econotécnia Agrícola*, November.

Díaz Gómez, Floriberto, 1988. "Principios comunitarios, derechos indios." *México Indígena*, no. 25.

Díaz Montes, Fausto, and José Luz Ornelas López. 1989. "Problemática municipal de Oaxaca." *Cuadernos de Investigación*. Instituto de Investigaciones Sociológicas, Universidad Autónoma Benito Juárez de Oaxaca.

Díaz Polanco, Héctor. 1981. "Productivismo y estrategia alimentaria." *Nueva Antropología* 5(17), May.

DICONSA. 1982a. "DICONSA y el programa CONASUPO-COPLAMAR en el contexto del SAM." Paper presented at COPIDER-Harvard Workshop, Mexico City, CIESS, October, mimeographed.

――――. 1982b. *Reglamento de operación del sistema CONASUPO-COPLAMAR*. Mexico: DICONSA.

———. 1983. *Reunión nacional de evaluación del sistema de Distribuidores CONASUPO*. Mexico: DICONSA.

———. 1985. *Primera reunión nacional de jefes de almacén de abasto comunitario*. Mexico: DICONSA.

———. 1986a. *Evolución del sistema de distribuidoras CONASUPO 1983–1985 y líneas centrales del programa 1986*. Mexico: DICONSA.

———. 1986b. *Distribuidora e impulsora comercial CONASUPO, S.A. (DICONSA)*. Serie de Cuadernos de Divulgación no. 6. Mexico: DICONSA.

Domhoff, G. William. 1979. *The Powers That Be*. New York: Vintage.

Domínguez, Marcelino. 1988. "Poder comunal: Instrumento de autodesarrollo: Caso de Cacalotepec Mixe, Oaxaca." *El Medio Milenio* no. 3, June.

Dresser, Denise. 1991. *Neopopulist Solutions to Neoliberal Problems: Mexico's National Solidarity Program*. Current Issues Brief no. 3. La Jolla: University of California, San Diego, Center for U.S.–Mexican Studies.

Dromundo, Baltazar. 1934. *Emiliano Zapata, biografía*. Mexico: Imprenta Mundial.

Durán, Evelyne, Ma. Teresa Fernández, Evelyne Sinquin, Javier Gil, and Pedro Magaña. 1986. *Los productores rurales y sus problemas en el occidente de México*. Mexico: Facultad de Economía, UNAM/DICONSA no. 3.

Durand Ponte, Victor Manuel, and Maria Angélica Cuéllar Vázquez. 1989. *Clases y sujetos sociales: Un enfoque crítico comparativo*. Mexico: Universidad Nacional Autónoma de México.

Durston, John. 1981. "El Sistema Alimentario Mexicano (SAM): Un nuevo estilo de desarrollo social rural?" CEPAL, In. 15, October 30, mimeographed.

———. 1982. "Class and Culture in the Changing Peasantry." *CEPAL Review* 16, April.

Echeverría Zuno, Rodolfo, ed. 1982. *Transnacionales, agricultura y alimentación*. Mexico: Nueva Imagen/CNE.

Eckstein, Susan. 1976. "The Irony of Organization: Resource and Regulatory." *British Journal of Sociology* 27(2), June.

———. 1977. (2nd ed., 1988) *The Poverty of Revolution*. Princeton: Princeton University Press.

Economía Informa. 1980. "Mesa redonda: El SAM y la Ley de Fomento Agropecuario." April.

Edelman, Marc. 1980. "Agricultural Modernization in Smallholding Areas of Mexico: A Case Study of the Sierra Norte de Puebla." *Latin American Perspectives* 12(4), Fall.

Ejea, Gabriela, and Luis Hernández, eds. 1991. "Cafetaleros, la construcción de la autonomía." *Cuadernos Desarrollo de Base*, no. 3.

Ejea Mendoza, Guillermo. 1989. "Haberes y deberes de la concertación." *El Cotidiano* 31, September–October.

Encinas R., Alejandro, and Fernando Rascón F. 1983. *Reporte y cronología del movimiento campesino e indígena: Julio–diciembre 1982*. 2 vols. Mexico: Universidad Autonóma de Chapingo.

Equipo Pueblo. 1987. "¿Por qué luchan los campesinos?" *Cuadernos Campesinos*, nos. 2, 3.

Equipo Pueblo/Instituto Maya. 1987. "Un paso más, producción, comercialización, abasto." Proceedings of grass-roots network conference, October.

Escobar, Saúl. 1987. "Rifts in the Mexican Power Elite, 1976–1986." In Sylvia Maxfield and Ricardo Ansaldúa Montoya, eds., *Government and Private Sector in Contemporary Mexico*. La Jolla: University of California, San Diego, Center for U.S.–Mexican Studies.

Esman, Milton, and Norman Uphoff. 1984. *Local Organizations: Intermediaries in Rural Development*. Ithaca: Cornell University Press.

Espinoza, Gisela, and Miguel Meza. 1991. "La organización para el abasto en el sureste de la Costa Chica." Instituto Maya.

Esteva, Gustavo. 1979. "La experiencia de la intervención estatal reguladora en la comercialización agropecuaria de 1970 a 1976." In Ursula Oswald, ed., *Mercado y dependencia*. Mexico: Nueva Imagen/CIS-INAH.

——. 1980. *La batalla en el México rural*. Mexico: Siglo XXI.

——. 1981. "El SAM y la geometría." *Nueva Antropología* 5(17), May.

——. 1982. "Las transnacionales y el taco." In Rodolfo Echeverría Zuno, ed., *Transnacionales, agricultura y alimentación*. Mexico: Nueva Imagen/CNE.

——. 1983a. "Políticas de comercio y coyuntura nacional." In Iván Menéndez, ed., *Inflación, devaluación y desarrollo rural en México: Un análisis de la coyuntura postdevaluatoria, 1982*. Mexico: Nueva Imagen/CEESTEM.

——. 1983b. *The Struggle for Rural Mexico*. South Hadley, Mass.: Bergin and Garvey.

——. 1987. "Food Needs and Capacities: Four Centuries of Conflict." In James Austin and Gustavo Esteva, eds., *Food Policy in Mexico: The Search for Self-Sufficiency*. Ithaca: Cornell University Press.

——. 1988. "El desastre agrícola: Adiós al México imaginario." *Comercio Exterior* 38(8), August.

Esteva, Gustavo, and David Barkin. 1981. "El papel del sector público en la comercialización de los productos agrícolas básicos en México." Mexico, CEPAL/1051, June 19, mimeographed.

Esteva, Gustavo, and Gustavo Gordillo. 1983. "Programa nacional de alimentación: Alternativa o demagogia?" *Textual* 4(14), December.

Evans, Peter. 1979. *Dependent Development: The Alliance of Multinational, State, and Local Capital in Brazil*. Princeton: Princeton University Press.

Evans, Peter, Dietrich Rueschemeyer, and Theda Skocpol, eds. 1985. *Bringing the State Back In*. Cambridge: Cambridge University Press.

Evans, Sara, and Harry Boyte. 1986. *Free Spaces: The Sources of Democratic Change in America*. New York: Harper and Row.

Falcón, Romana. 1977. *El agrarismo en Veracruz: La etapa radical (1928–1935)*. Mexico: Colegio de México.

——. 1984. *Revolución y caciquismo: San Luis Potosí, 1910–1938*. Mexico: Colegio de México.

Felstehausen, Herman, and Heliodoro Díaz-Cisneros. 1985. "The Strategy of Rural Development: The Puebla Initiative." *Human Organization* 44(4), April.

Fernández, Luis, and María Tarro García. 1983. *Ganadería y estructura agraria en Chiapas*. Mexico: UAM-Xochimilco.

Fernández, María Teresa, and Fernando Rello. 1984. *La organización de productores en México*. Mexico: DICONSA.

Fernández Christlieb, Paulina. 1979. "Reforma política: Viejos ensayos, nuevos fracasos." *Nexos* 20, August.

Fernández Villegas, Manuel. 1981. "Dos concepciones sobre la Alianza Estado/ Campesino (o no dejemos el SAM a la SARH)." August, mimeographed.

——. 1991. "No queremos que nos den, no más con que no nos quiten: La autonomía campesina en Mexico." *Cuadernos Desarrollo de Base*, no. 2.

FERTIMEX. 1980. *Memoría*. Mexico: FERTIMEX.

——. 1982a. "Apoyos al 'SAM.'" Paper presented at COPIDER-Harvard Workshop, Mexico, CIESS, October, mimeographed.

——. 1982b. *Testimonio de una administración, 1976–1982*. Mexico: FERTIMEX.

Finegold, Kenneth, and Theda Skocpol. 1984. "State, Party and Industry: From Business Recovery to the Wagner Act in America's New Deal." In Charles Bright and Susan Harding, eds., *Statemaking and Social Movements*. Ann Arbor: University of Michigan Press.

FIRA (Fideicomisos Instituidos en Relación con la Agricultura en el Banco de México). 1982. "Datos básicos." Paper presented at COPIDER-Harvard Workshop, Mexico City, CIESS, October, mimeographed.

——. 1983. *Informe anual 1982*. Mexico.

Fishlow, Albert. 1990. "The Latin American State." *Journal of Economic Perspectives* 4(3), Summer.

Fitzgerald, E. V. K. 1978. "The Fiscal Crisis of the Latin American State." In J. F. J. Toye, ed., *Taxation and Economic Development*. London: Frank Cass.

——. 1979. "The State and Capital Accumulation in Mexico." *Journal of Latin American Studies* 10(2).

——. 1985. "The Financial Constraint on Relative Autonomy: The State and Capital Accumulation in Mexico, 1940–1982." In Christian Anglade and Carlos Fortin, eds., *The State and Capital Accumulation in Latin America*. Pittsburgh: University of Pittsburgh Press.

Flanet, Véronique. 1979. *Viviré si Dios quiere: Un estudio de la violencia en la Mixteca de la Costa*. Mexico: INI.

Flores Lúa, Graciela, Luisa Paré, and Sergio Sarmiento. 1988. *Las voces del campo: Movimiento campesino y política agraria, 1976–1984*. Mexico: Siglo XXI/IIS, UNAM.

Fondo de Cultura Campesina (FCC). 1984. "Los precios de garantía." Mimeographed.

Foweraker, Joe. 1989. "Popular Movements and the Transformation of the System." In Wayne A. Cornelius, Judith Gentleman, and Peter H. Smith, eds., *Mexico's Alternative Political Futures*. La Jolla: University of California, San Diego, Center for U.S.–Mexican Studies.

Foweraker, Joe, and Ann L. Craig, eds. 1990. *Popular Movements and Political Change in Mexico*. Boulder, Colo.: Lynne Rienner.

Fowler Salamini, Heather. 1978. *Agrarian Radicalism in Veracruz, 1920–1938*. Lincoln: University of Nebraska Press.

——. 1988. "The Mexican Revolution: A Peasant Revolution?" *Peasant Studies* 15(3), Spring.

Fox, Jonathan. 1980. "Has Brazil Moved toward State Capitalism?" *Latin American Pespectives* 7(1), Winter.

——. 1985a. "Agrarian Reform and Populist Politics." *Latin American Perspectives* 12(3), Summer.

_____. 1985b. Review of Fernando Rello and Ruth Rama, "Estrategias de las agroindustrias transnacionales y política alimentaria en México." *Estudios Sociológicos* 3(8), May–August.

_____. 1986. "The Political Dynamics of Reform: The Case of the Mexican Food System." Ph.D. diss., Department of Political Science, Massachusetts Institute of Technology.

_____. 1989. "Towards Democracy in Mexico?" *Hemisphere* 1(2), Winter.

_____, ed. 1990a. *The Challenge of Rural Democratisation: Perspectives from Latin America and the Philippines.* London: Frank Cass. Also in *Journal of Development Studies* 26(4), July 1990.

_____. 1990b. "La dinámica del cambio en el Sistema Alimentario Mexicano, 1980–1982." In Julio Moguel, ed., *La historia de la cuestión agraria mexicana*, vol. 9. Mexico: Siglo XXI/CEHAM.

_____. 1991. "Popular Participation and Access to Food: Mexico's Community Food Councils." In Scott Whiteford and Ann Ferguson, eds., *Harvest of Want: Struggles for Food Security in Central America and Mexico.* Boulder, Colo.: Westview Press.

_____. 1992a. "Democratic Rural Development: Leadership Accountability in Regional Peasant Organizations." *Development and Change* 23(2), April.

_____. 1992b. "Targeting the Poorest: The Role of the National Indigenous Institute in Mexico's Solidarity Program." Paper presented to Mexico's National Solidarity Program (PRONASOL): A Preliminary Assessment, Center for U.S.–Mexican Studies, University of California, San Diego, February.

Fox, Jonathan, and Gustavo Gordillo. 1989. "Between State and Market: The Campesinos' Quest for Autonomy." In Wayne A. Cornelius, Judith Gentleman, and Peter H. Smith, eds., *Mexico's Alternative Political Futures.* La Jolla: University of California, San Diego, Center for U.S.–Mexican Studies.

Fox, Jonathan, and Luis Hernández. 1989. "Offsetting the Iron Law of Oligarchy: The Ebbs and Flows of Leadership Accountability in a Regional Peasant Organization." *Grassroots Development* 13(2).

_____. 1992. "Mexico's Difficult Democracy: Grassroots Movement, NGOs and Local Government." *Alternatives* 17(2), April.

Fox, Jonathan, and Robin Marsh. 1986. "Summary Report of the U.S.–Mexico Project Conference on Strengthening Linkages among Policymakers, Researchers and Small Farmers." Pátzcuaro, December 3–8, 1985. Working Paper, Stanford University Project on U.S.-Mexico Relations.

Frey, Frederick. 1985. "The Problem of Actor Designation in Political Analysis." *Comparative Politics* 17(2), January.

Friedland, Roger, Frances Fox Piven, and Robert Alford. 1977. "Political Conflict, Urban Structure and the Fiscal Crisis." *International Journal of Urban and Regional Research* 1(3). Also in Douglas Ashford, ed., *Comparing Public Policies.* Beverly Hills, Calif.: Sage, 1977.

Friedmann, Santiago, and Larissa Lomnitz. 1977. "El papel de las organizaciónes locales tradicionales en el desarrollo rural." *Narxhí-Nandhí* 4–5.

Friedrich, Paul. 1965. "A Mexican Cacicazgo." *Ethnology* 4(2).

_____. 1968. "The Legitimacy of a Cacique." In Marc Swartz, ed., *Local-Level Politics: Social and Cultural Perspectives.* Chicago: Aldine.

———. 1977. *Agrarian Revolt in a Mexican Village*. 2d ed. Chicago: University of Chicago Press.

Fritscher, Magda. 1985. *Estado y sector rural en México: 1976–1982*. Iztapalapa: Universidad Autónoma Metropolitana.

Fuentes, Jorge, and Esther Rossel. 1982. *La comunidad campesina, la organización política de los pueblos en la Meseta Tarasca*. Morelia: IMISAC.

Gamboa Rodríguez, Ricardo. 1984. "El selecto mundo de los FIRA." *Canícula* 1(4), March.

García, Arturo. 1989. "Organización autónoma de productores y lucha campesina en Guerrero." *Pueblo* 12(140), January.

———. 1990. "Propuestas para avanzar en el difícil camino de la unidad del movimiento campesino, sustentadas en la experiencia de la Coordinadora Nacional de Organizaciones Cafetaleras." *Hojas*, no. 1, March.

García, Emilio. 1989a. "El movimiento campesino, hoy." *Pueblo* 12(144–45), May–June.

———. 1989b. "La CNPA diez años después." *Pueblo* 12(147), September–October.

———. 1989c. "Encuentro Nacional Agrario en Cuautla." *Pueblo* 12(147), September–October.

———. 1990. "Triunfos, desaveniencias, retrocesos y lecciones de la Coordinadora Nacional Plan de Ayala." *Hojas*, no. 1, March.

García, Philip. 1978. "Market Linkages of Small Farms: A Study of the Maize Market in Northern Veracruz, Mexico." Ph.D. diss., Cornell University.

García de León, Antonio. 1989. "Encrucijada rural: El movimiento campesino ante las modernidades." *Cuadernos Políticos* 58, September–December.

García López, Luca. 1984. *Nahuatzen, agricultura y comercio en una comunidad serrana*. Mexico: Colegio de Michoacán/CONACYT.

García Mata, Roberto, ed. *La comercialización de productos agrícolas en México*. 2 vols. Chapingo: Colegio de Posgraduados.

Garduño, Francisco. 1978. "Problemas de la organización económica de los campesinos." *Narxhí-Nandhí* 8–10, September.

Garrido, Luis Javier. 1982. *El partido de la revolución institucionalizada*. 4th ed. Mexico: Siglo XXI.

Gereffi, Gary. 1983. *The Pharmaceutical Industry and Dependency in the Third World*. Princeton: Princeton University Press.

Gibson, William, Nora Lustig, and Lance Taylor. 1987. "SAM's Impact on Income Distribution." In James Austin and Gustavo Esteva, eds., *Food Policy in Mexico: The Search for Self-Sufficiency*. Ithaca: Cornell University Press.

Gilly, Adolfo. 1980. *The Interrupted Revolution*. London: Verso.

Gilly, Adolfo, et al. 1980. *Interpretaciones de la revolución mexicana*. Mexico: Nueva Imagen.

Gledhill, John. 1988. "Agrarian Social Movements and Forms of Consciousness." *Bulletin of Latin American Research* 7(2).

Goicoechea, Julio. 1990. "Agricultural Price Policy in Mexico: Explaining Guarantee Prices, 1959–88." Boston: Northeastern University Department of Economics, August, mimeographed.

Goldfield, Michael. 1989. "Worker Insurgency, Radical Organization, and New Deal Labor Legislation." *American Political Science Review* 83(4), December.

Gómez Leyva, Ciro, 1991. "Solidaridad gratuita en todas las pantallas." *Este País*, no. 7, October.

Gomezjara, Francisco. 1979. *Bonapartismo y lucha campesina en la Costa Grande de Guerrero.* Mexico: Ed. Posada.

Gómez Tagle, Silvia. 1974. "Organización de las sociedades de crédito ejidal de La Laguna." *Cuadernos del CES*, no. 8.

——. 1981. "El SAM: Intenciones ocultas o fuerzas reales." *Nueva Antropología* 5(17), May.

——. 1982. "La reforma política en México y el problema de la representación política de la clases sociales." In Jorge Alonso, ed., *El estado mexicano.* Mexico: Nueva Imagen/CIESAS.

——. 1984. "Estado y reforma política en México: Interpretaciones alternativas." *Nueva Antropología* 7(25), October.

González, Luis. 1981. *Historia de la revolución mexicana.* Vol. 15, *Los días del Presidente Cárdenas.* Mexico: Colegio de México.

González Casanova, Pablo. 1970. *Democracy in Mexico.* London: Oxford University Press.

——. 1979. "El partido del estado, II. Fundación, lucha electoral y crisis del sistema." *Nexos* 17, May.

——, ed. 1985. *Las elecciones en México: Evolución y perspectivas.* Mexico: Siglo XXI.

——, ed., 1990. *Segundo informe sobre la democracia: México el 6 de julio.* Mexico: Siglo XXI/CIIH/UNAM

González Graf, Jaime. 1989. *Las elecciones de 1988 y la crisis del sistema político.* Mexico: Instituto Mexicano de Estudios Políticos/Diana.

González Navarro, Moisés. 1985. *La CNC en la reforma agraria.* 3d ed. Mexico: El Día.

Goodman, Louis W., Steven E. Sanderson, Kenneth Shwedel, and Paul L. Haber. 1985. "Mexican Agriculture: Rural Crisis and Policy Response." Latin American Program Working Paper no. 168, Washington, D.C., Wilson Center, July.

Gordillo, Gustavo. 1979. "Estado y sistema ejidal." *Cuadernos Políticos* 21, July.

——. 1980. "Pasado y presente del movimiento campesino en México." *Cuadernos Políticos* 23, January.

——. 1982. "Programa de reformas para el sistema ejidal." *Cuadernos Políticos* 33, July.

——. 1985a. "La alianza del movimiento campesino con el estado." *El Día* 15, July 16–19.

——. 1985b. "Estado y movimiento campesino en la coyuntura actual." In Pablo González Casanova and Héctor Aguilar Camín, eds., *México ante la crisis.* Mexico: Siglo XXI.

——. 1986. "Movilización social como medio de producción." *Investigación Económica* 175, January–March.

——. 1987. "El movimiento campesino en la década de los ochentas." *Siempre* (Suplemento Cultural), no. 1296, February 4.

——. 1988a. *Unos campesinos al asalto del cielo: La experiencia de los Ejidos Colectivos en los Valles del Yaqui y Mayo.* Mexico: Siglo XXI.

———. 1988b. *Estado, mercados, y movimiento campesino.* Zacatecas: Plaza y Valdes/UAZ.

———. 1990. "La inserción de la comunidad rural en la socieded global: Hacia un nuevo model de desarrollo para el campo." *Comercio Exterior* 40(9), September.

Gordillo, Gustavo, and Sergio Block. 1988. "El camino hacia la autonomía campesina." In Armando Labra, ed., *El sector social de la economía: Una opción ante la crisis.* Mexico: Siglo XXI/CIIH/UNAM.

Gordillo, Gustavo, and Fernando Rello. 1980. "El campo mexicano a la hora de la sequía." *Nexos* 32, August.

Gramsci, Antonio. 1971. *Selections from the Prison Notebooks.* New York: International Publishers.

Granados, Otto. 1983. *Las organizaciones campesinas.* Mexico: Océano.

Granados, Vicente. 1977. "La economía rural en el período 1970–1976." *Narxhí-Nandhí*, April 2.

———. 1978. "La acción institucional como expresión de tendencias de los movimientos campesinos." *Narxhí-Nandhí*, September 8–10.

Greenberg, James. 1989. *Blood Ties.* Tucson: University of Arizona Press.

Greenberg, Martin Harry. 1972. *Bureaucracy and Development: A Mexican Case Study.* Lexington, Mass.: D. C. Heath.

Greenhouse, Carol J. 1989. "Law and Society in Rural Mexico." *Peasant Studies* 16(3), Spring.

Grindle, Merilee. 1977. *Bureaucrats, Politicians and Peasants in Mexico.* Berkeley: University of California Press.

———, ed. 1980. *Politics and Policy Implementation in the Third World.* Princeton: Princeton University Press.

———. 1981. "Official Interpretations of Rural Underdevelopment: Mexico in the 1970s." *Working Papers in U.S.–Mexican Studies* 20.

———. 1983. *Issues in U.S.–Mexican Agricultural Relations: A Binational Consultation.* Monograph Series 8. La Jolla: University of California, San Diego, Center for U.S.–Mexican Studies.

———. 1986. *State and Countryside: Development Policy and Agrarian Politics in Latin America.* Baltimore: Johns Hopkins University Press.

———. 1988. *Searching for Rural Development: Labor Migration and Employment in Mexico.* Ithaca: Cornell University Press.

———. 1991. "The New Political Economy: Positive Economics and Negative Politics." In Gerald M. Meier, ed., *Politics and Policy Making in Developing Countries.* San Francisco: ICS Press.

Grindle, Merilee S., and John W. Thomas. 1989. "Policy Makers, Policy Choices, and Policy Outcomes." *Policy Sciences* 22.

Guerrero, Francisco Javier. 1981. "El Sistema Alimentario Mexicano y la estrategia de ventajas comparativas." *Nueva Antropología* 5(17), May 1981.

Gutiérrez, Jorge. 1975. "Comunidad agraria y estructura de poder." In Roger Bartra et al., *Caciquismo y poder político en el México rural.* Mexico: Siglo XXI.

Haber, Paul. 1989. "Cárdenas, Salinas and Urban Popular Movements in Mexico: The Case of the CDP de Durango." Paper presented at the Fifteenth International Congress of the Latin American Studies Association.

Haber, Paul, and Mark Nechomod. 1985. "The Sistema Alimentario Mexicano: An Economic and Political Analysis of Mexican Food Policy, 1980–1982." *Occasional Paper 6*, Johns Hopkins School of Advanced International Studies, June.

Hall, Lana, and Turner Price. 1982. "Price Policies and the SAM: A Wheat-Maize Comparison." *Food Policy* 7(4), November.

Hall, Richard, and Robert Quinn, eds. 1983. *Organizational Theory and Public Policy*. Beverly Hills, Calif.: Sage.

Hamilton, Nora. 1982. *The Limits of State Autonomy: Post-Revolutionary Mexico*. Princeton: Princeton University Press.

Hansen, Roger. 1974. *The Politics of Mexican Development*. Baltimore: Johns Hopkins University Press.

Hardy, Clarisa. 1984. *El estado y los campesinos*. Mexico: Nueva Imagen/ CEESTEM.

Hart, Gillian. 1986. "Interlocking Transactions: Obstacles, Precursors or Instruments of Agrarian Capitalism?" *Journal of Development Economics* 23(1).

Harvey, Neil. 1988. "Personal Networks and Strategic Choices in the Formation of an Independent Peasant Organisation: The OCEZ of Chiapas, Mexico." *Bulletin of Latin American Research* 7(2).

———. 1989. "Corporatist Strategies and Popular Responses in Rural Mexico: State and Opposition in Chiapas, 1970–1988." Ph.D. diss., University of Essex.

———. 1990a. "Peasant Strategies and Corporatism in Chiapas." In Joe Foweraker and Ann Craig, eds., *Popular Movements and Political Change in Mexico*. Boulder, Colo.: Lynne Rienner.

———. 1990b. "The New Agrarian Movement in Mexico, 1979–1990." *Research Paper* 23, University of London, Institute of Latin American Affairs.

———. 1990c. "The Limits of Concertation in Rural Mexico, 1988–1990." Paper presented to research workshop, "Mexico in Transition," Institute of Latin American Studies, London, May 18–19.

Heath, John. 1985. "Contradictions in Current Mexican Food Policy." In George Philip, ed., *Politics in Mexico*. London: Croom Helm.

———. 1987. "Constraints on Peasant Maize Production: A Case Study from Michoacán." *Mexican Studies/Estudios Mexicanos* 3(2), Summer.

———. 1988. "El financiamiento del sector agropecuario en México." In Jorge Zepeda Patterson, ed., *Las sociedades rurales hoy*. Zamora: Colegio de Michoacán.

———. 1990. "Enhancing the Contribution of Land Reform to Mexican Agricultural Development." *Working Paper* no. 285, World Bank, Department of Agriculture and Rural Development, February.

Heaver, Richard. 1982. "Bureaucratic Politics and Incentives in the Management of Rural Development." World Bank Staff Working Paper no. 537.

Hector, Michael. 1987. *The Principles of Group Solidarity*. Berkeley: University of California Press.

Heimpel, Gretchen. 1981. *Mexico: Agricultural and Trade Policies*. Washington, D.C.: U.S. Department of Agriculture/FAS.

Hellman, Judith A. 1983. *Mexico in Crisis*. 2d ed. New York: Holmes and Meier.

Hernández, Franco Gabriel. 1979. "De la educación indígena tradicional a la educación indígena bilingue-bicultural." *Revista Mexicana de Ciencias Políticas y Sociales* 25(97), July.

Hernández, Luis. 1989a. "El fantasma del general: Notas sobre la cuestión electoral y el movimiento campesino." In Carlos Monsiváis et al., *Crónica del nuevo México*. Mexico: Equipo Pueblo.

——. 1989b. "Autonomía y desarrollo: La lucha en el campo." *Pueblo* 12(147), September–October.

——. 1990a. "Las convulsiones rurales." *El Cotidiano* 34(7), March–April.

——. 1990b. "Campesinos y poder: 1934–1940." In Everardo Escárcega López, ed., *Historia de la cuestión agraria Mexicana*, vol. 5, *El Cardenismo: Un parteaguas histórico en el proceso agrario nacional (1934–1940)*. Mexico: Siglo XXI/CEHAM.

——. 1990c. "La Unión de Ejidos 'Lázaro Cárdenas.'" *Cuadernos Desarrollo de Base*, no. 1.

——. 1991. "Nadando con los tiburones: La Coordinadora Nacional de Organizaciones Cafetaleras." In Gabriela Ejea and Luis Hernández, eds., "Cafetaleros: La construcción de la autonomía." *Cuadernos Desarrollo de Base*, no. 3.

——. 1992. "Maiceros: De la guerra por los precios al desarrollo rural integral." In Cynthia Hewitt de Alcántara, ed., *Reestructuración económico y subsistencia rural: El maíz y la crisis de los 80*. Geneva: UNRISD, forthcoming.

Hernández Xolocotzi, Efraím. 1988. "La agricultura traditional en México." *Comercio Exterior* 38(8), August.

Hewitt de Alcántara, Cynthia. 1976. *Modernizing Mexican Agriculture*. Geneva: UNRISD.

——. 1980. "Land Reform, Livelihood, and Power in Rural Mexico." In D. A. Preston, ed., *Environment, Society and Rural Change in Latin America*. London: John Wiley.

——. 1984. *Anthropological Perspectives on Rural Mexico*. London: Routledge and Kegan Paul.

——. 1987. "Feeding Mexico City." In James Austin and Gustavo Esteva, eds., *Food Policy in Mexico: The Search for Self-Sufficiency*. Ithaca: Cornell University Press.

——, ed. 1992. *Reestructuración económica y subsistencia rural: El maíz y la crisis de los 80*. Mexico: Colegio de México/Centro Tepoztlán/UNRISD.

Hill, Raymond. 1984. "State Enterprise and Income Distribution in Mexico." In Pedro Aspe and Paul Sigmund, eds., *The Political Economy of Income Distribution in Mexico*. New York: Holmes and Meier.

Hirschman, Albert. 1963. *Journeys toward Progress*. New York: Twentieth Century Fund.

——. 1981. *Essays in Trespassing*. Cambridge: Cambridge University Press.

——. 1984. *Getting Ahead Collectively*. New York: Pergamon Press.

Hoffman, Odile. 1989. "Márgenes de acción campesina y obras públicas: El caso de los caminos en pueblos de la sierra veracruzana." *Nueva Antropología* 10(35), June.

Holloway, John, and Sol Picciotto, eds. 1978. *State and Capital: A Marxist Debate.* London: Edward Arnold.

Hoyo, José Felix. 1980. "Acumulación capitalista, lucha de clases y movimientos guerrilleros en el estado de Guerrero." In *Sociología del desarrollo rural*, vol. 1. Memoria. Mexico: Universidad Autónoma de Chapingo.

Huacuja, Mario. 1980. "La lucha por el SAM." *Nexos* 30, June.

Huacuja, Mario, and José Woldenberg. 1983. *Estado y lucha política en el México actual.* 4th ed. Mexico: El Caballito.

Hughes, Steven, and Kenneth Mijelski. 1984. *Politics and Public Policy in Latin America.* Boulder, Colo.: Westview Press.

Huizer, Gerritt. 1972. *The Revolutionary Potential of Peasants in Latin America.* Lexington, Mass.: D. C. Heath.

Huntington, Samuel P. 1965. "Political Development and Political Decay." *World Politics* 17(3).

Ibarra Mendivil, Jorge Luis. 1989. *Propiedad agraria y sistema político en México.* Mexico: Colegio de Sonora/Miguel Angel Porrúa.

IMISAC (Instituto Michoacano de Investigaciones Sociales)/CEE/CAM. 1981. *¿Qué es el SAM?* Mexico: SEPAC.

IMSS. 1983. *Diagnóstico de salud en las zonas marginadas rurales de México.* Mexico: Instituto Mexicano de Seguridad Social.

INCA Rural. N.d. "El Sistema Alimentario Mexicano." In *Cuaderno de lectura para productores rurales.* Mexico: Instituto Nacional de Capacitación del Sector Agropecuario.

———. 1981. "Documentos de apoyo para la operación del Sistema Alimentario Mexicano." *Cuadernos de Capacitación* 4.

———. 1984a. *Impacto del crédito oficial en la producción y productividad del maíz.* Mexico: INCA Rural.

———. 1984b. "Dinámica de la organización campesina y sus determinantes económicos." *Boletín de Investigación* 3, October.

Jacobi, Pedro. 1989. *Movimentos sociais e políticas públicas.* São Paulo: Cortez Editora.

Jessop, Bob. 1983. *Theories of the State.* New York: New York University Press.

Jones, Leroy, et al., eds. 1982. *Public Enterprise in Less Developed Countries.* New York: Cambridge University Press.

Joseph, Paul. 1981. *Cracks in the Empire.* Boston: South End Press.

Jusidman, Clara. 1987. "Problems of Defining and Operating the New Food Policy in Mexico." In Austin and Esteva, eds., 1987.

Katz, Friedrich. 1981. *The Secret War in Mexico: Europe, the United States and the Mexican Revolution.* Chicago: University of Chicago Press.

———, ed. 1988. *Riot, Rebellion, and Revolution: Rural Social Conflict in Mexico.* Princeton: Princeton University Press.

Katzenstein, Peter, ed. 1978. *Between Power and Plenty.* Madison: University of Wisconsin Press.

Kerkvliet, Benedict J. T. 1990. *Everyday Politics in the Philippines: Class and Status Relations in a Central Luzon Village.* Berkeley: University of California Press.

Kern, Robert, ed. 1973. *The Caciques, Oligarchical Politics and the System of Caciquismo in the Luso-Hispanic World*. Albuquerque: University of New Mexico Press.

Knight, Alan. 1986. *The Mexican Revolution*. 2 vols. Cambridge: Cambridge University Press.

———. 1990. "Historical Continuities in Social Movements." In Joe Foweraker and Ann Craig, eds., *Popular Movements and Political Change in Mexico*. Boulder, Colo.: Lynne Rienner.

Kohli, Atul. 1987. *The State and Poverty in India: The Politics of Reform*. New York: Cambridge University Press, South Asian Studies.

Krasner, Stephen. 1984. "Approaches to the State: Alternative Conceptions and Historical Dynamics." *Comparative Politics* 16(2), January.

Labastida Martín del Campo, Julio. 1979. "La crisis y la tregua, crisis de confianza y sucesión presidencial." *Nexos* 21, September.

Labra, Armando, ed. 1988. *El sector social de la economía, una opción ante la crisis*. Mexico: Siglo XXI/CIIH/UNAM.

Lacroix, Richard L. J. 1985. "Integrated Rural Development in Latin America." *World Bank Staff Working Paper* no. 716.

Landsberger, Henry A., and Cynthia N. Hewitt. 1970. "Ten Sources of Weakness and Cleavage in Latin American Peasant Movements." In Rodolfo Stavenhagen, ed., *Agrarian Problems and Peasant Movements in Latin America*. Garden City, N.Y.: Anchor Books.

Lassen, Cheryl. 1982. "Political Strategies for Transforming Industrializing Economies: A Populist-Mobilizing Approach in Mexico." Ph.D. diss., Cornell University.

Leal, Juan Felipe. 1975a. "The Mexican State, 1915–1973: A Historical Interpretation." *Latin American Perspectives* 2(2), Summer.

———. 1975b. *México: Estado, burocracia y sindicatos*. Mexico: Caballito.

Leff, Gloria. 1982. "El partido de la revolución: Aparato de hegemonía del estado mexicano." In Jorge Alonso, ed., *El estado mexicano*. Mexico: Nueva Imagen/CIESAS.

León, Arturo. 1986. *El movimiento campesino en los Llanos de Victoria, Durango, 1970–1980*. Mexico: Universidad Autónoma Metropolitana, Xochimilco.

León, Arturo, and Cristina Steffen. 1986. *Estado y organizaciones en el altiplano central*. Mexico: DICONSA/UNAM, no. 2.

Leonard, David. 1982. "Analyzing the Organizational Requirements for Serving the Rural Poor." In David Leonard and Dale Rogers Marshall, eds., *Institutions of Rural Development for the Poor: Decentralization and Organizational Linkages*. Berkeley: University of California, Institute of International Studies.

Levy, Ignacio. 1977. "Los movimientos rurales en México y la reforma agraria: Estudio de cuatro ejidos." *Revista Mexicana de Sociología* 39(3), July.

LFA (Ley de Fomento Agropecuario). 1981. *Nueva Antropología* 5(17), May.

LICONSA. 1987. *Historia del abasto social de leche en México*. Mexico: Leche Industrializada CONASUPO.

Lieuwen, Edwin. 1968. *Mexican Militarism*. Albuquerque: University of New Mexico Press.

———. 1984. "Depoliticization of the Mexican Revolutionary Army, 1915–1940." In David Ronfeldt, ed., *The Modern Mexican Military: A Reassessment.* La Jolla: University of California, San Diego, Center for U.S.–Mexican Studies.

Lijphart, Arend. 1971. "Comparative Politics and the Comparative Method." *American Political Science Review* 65(3).

———. 1975. "The Comparable-Cases Strategy in Comparative Research." *Comparative Political Studies* 8(2), July.

Linck, Thierry. 1988. *El campesino desposeido.* Mexico: CEMCA/El Colegio de Michoacán.

Lindblom, Charles. 1977. *Politics and Markets.* New York: Basic Books.

Lindheim, Daniel Noah. 1986. "Regional Development and Deliberate Social Change: Integrated Rural Development in Mexico." Ph.D. diss., University of California, Berkeley.

Link, John. 1981. "Mexico Aims at Self-Sufficiency in Basic Foods, Reduced Imports." *Foreign Agriculture,* January.

Lipsky, Michael. 1980. *Street-Level Bureaucracy.* New York: Russell Sage Foundation.

Little, Daniel. 1989. "Marxism and Popular Politics: The Microfoundations of Class Conflict." *Canadian Journal of Philosophy,* supplementary vol. 15.

Loaeza, Soledad. 1981. "¿Pero hubo alguna vez autonomía sexenal?" *Nexos* 42, June.

———. 1985. "Las clases medias mexicanas y la coyuntura económica actual." In Pablo González Casanova and Héctor Aguilar Camín, eds., *México ante la crisis,* vol. 2. Mexico: Siglo XXI.

———. 1991. "La vía mexicana a la democracia." *Nexos* 166, October.

Loeffler, William. 1982. "Class, State and Hegemony: Theoretical Issues and Mexico." Ph.D. diss., Rutgers University.

Long, Norman. 1980. "Some Concluding Comments: Directive Change and the Question of Participation." In David A. Preston, ed., *Environment, Society, and Rural Change in Latin America: The Past, Present, and Future in the Countryside.* Chichester: John Wiley.

López, Arturo, et al. 1989. *Geografía de las elecciones presidenciales de México, 1988.* Mexico: Fundación Arturo Rosenblueth.

López Monjardin, Adriana. 1986. *La lucha por los ayuntamientos: Una utopía viable.* Mexico: Siglo XXI/IIS.

———. 1987. "Organización y luchas de los obreros agrícolas en México." Paper presented at the Workshop on Unions, Workers, and the State in Mexico, University of California, San Diego, Center for U.S.–Mexican Studies, May.

———. 1988. "1982–88: Un proyecto anticampesino y antinacional." *Cuadernos Políticos* 53, January–April.

———. 1991. "Organization and Struggle Among Agricultural Workers in Mexico." In Kevin Middlebrook, ed., *Unions, Workers and the State in Mexico.* La Jolla: University of California, San Diego, Center for U.S.–Mexican Studies.

López Portillo, Jorge. 1982. "Las perspectivas del crédito rural ante la nacionalización de la banca." *Economía Informa* 98, October.

López Portillo, José. 1977. *Pensamiento agrario del Presidente López Portillo.* Mexico: SRA.

Lowi, Theodore. 1964. "American Business, Public Policy, Case Studies and Political Theory." *World Politics* 16(4), July.

———. 1972. "Four Systems of Policy, Politics and Choice." *Public Administration Review*, July.

Lucas, Ann. 1982. "El debate sobre los campesinos y el capitalismo en México." *Comercio Exterior* 32(4), April.

———. 1985. *The Contemporary Peasantry in Mexico.* New York: Praeger.

Luiselli, Cassio. 1980a. "Agricultura y alimentación: Premisas para una nueva estrategia." In Nora Lustig, ed., *Panorama y perspectivas de la economía mexicana.* Mexico: Colegio de México.

———. 1980b. "¿Por qué el SAM?" *Nexos* 32, August.

———. 1982. *The Sistema Alimentario Mexicano (SAM): Elements of a Program of Accelerated Production of Basic Foodstuffs.* Research Report Series 22. La Jolla: University of California, San Diego, Center for U.S.–Mexican Studies.

———. 1985. *The Route to Food Self-Sufficiency in Mexico.* Monograph Series 17. La Jolla: University of California, San Diego, Center for U.S.–Mexican Studies.

Luiselli, Cassio, and Jaime Mariscal. 1981. "La crisis agrícola a partir de 1965." In Rolando Cordera, ed., *Desarrollo y crisis de la economía mexicana.* Mexico: Fondo de Cultura Económica.

Lukes, Stephen. 1974. *Power: A Radical View.* London: Macmillan.

Luna, Matilde. 1983. "Las transformaciones del régimen político mexicano en la década de 1970." *Revista Mexicana de Sociología* 45(2), April.

Luna, Matilde, Ricardo Tirado, and Francisco Valdés. 1987. "Businessmen and Politics in Mexico, 1982–1986." In Sylvia Maxfield and Ricardo Anzaldúa Montoya, eds., *Government and Private Sector in Contemporary Mexico.* La Jolla: University of California, San Diego, Center for U.S.–Mexican Studies.

Lustig, Nora. 1982. "Fighting Malnutrition in Mexico: The Fiscal Cost of Alternative Policy Options." *Food and Nutrition Bulletin* 4(4), October.

———. 1984a. "Distribution of Income, Food Consumption and Fiscal Cost of Alternative Policy Options." In Pedro Aspe and Paul Sigmund, eds., *The Political Economy of Income Distribution in Mexico.* New York: Holmes and Meier.

———. 1984b. "Fiscal Cost and Welfare Impacts of the Corn Subsidy Scheme in Mexico." Working Paper 298, Department of Agricultural and Resource Economics, University of California, Berkeley, May.

———. 1986. "Food Subsidy Programs in Mexico." International Food Policy Research Institute Working Paper no. 3, Washington, D.C.

Lustig, Nora, and Antonio Martín del Campo. 1985. "Descripción del funcionamiento del Sistema CONASUPO." *Investigación Económica* 44(173), July.

Lustig, Nora, and Rosario Pérez Espejo. 1982. "Sistema Alimentario Mexicano (SAM): Antecedentes, características, estrategias y efectos." *Problemas del Desarrollo* 51–52, August.

Malloy, James M., ed. 1977. *Authoritarianism and Corporatism in Latin America.* Pittsburgh: University of Pittsburgh Press.

———. 1979. *The Politics of Social Security in Brazil.* Pittsburgh: University of Pittsburgh Press.

Mann, Michael. 1988. *States, War and Capitalism.* Oxford: Basil Blackwell.

Mares, David. 1985. "Mexico's Strategies for Development." *International Organization* 39(4), Autumn.

———. 1987. *Penetrating International Markets: Theoretical Considerations on Mexican Agriculture.* New York: Columbia University Press.

Martin, Cathie Jo. 1989. "Business Influence and State Power: The Case of U.S. Corporate Tax Policy." *Politics and Society* 17(2).

Martín del Campo, Antonio. 1988. "La política económica reciente y la agricultura." In Jorge Zepeda Patterson, ed., *Las sociedades rurales hoy.* Zamora: Colegio de Michoacán.

Martínez, Marielle, et al. 1980. "Los caminos de mano de obra como factores de cambio socioeconómico." *Cuadernos del CES*, no. 27.

Martínez Assad, Carlos. 1979. *El laboratorio de la revolución: El Tabasco Garridista.* Mexico: Siglo XXI.

———, ed. 1985. *Municipios en conflicto.* Mexico: IIS/UNAM.

Martínez Assad, Carlos, and Alicia Ziccardi. 1987. "El municipio entre la sociedad y el estado." *Mexican Studies/Estudios Mexicanos* 3(2), Summer.

Martínez Borrego, Estela. 1991. *Organización de productores y movimiento campesino.* Mexico: Siglo XXI/UNAM.

Martínez Fernández, Braulio. 1990. "Los precios de garantía en México." *Comercio Exterior* 40(10), October.

Martínez Vásquez, Victor Raúl. 1975. "Despojo y manipulación campesina: Historia y estructura de dos cacicazgos del Valle del Mezquital." In Roger Bartra et al., *Caciquismo y poder político en el México rural.* Mexico: Siglo XXI.

———. 1990. *Movimiento popular y pólitica en Oaxaca: 1968–1986.* Mexico: Dirección General de Publicaciones, Consejo Nacional para la Cultura y las Artes.

Martínez Vásquez, Victor Raúl, and Anselmo Arellanes. 1985. "Negociación y conflicto en Oaxaca." In Carlos Martínez Assad, ed., *Municipios en conflicto.* Mexico: IIS/UNAM.

Marwell, Gerald, and Pamela Oliver. 1984. "Collective Action Theory and Social Movements." *Research in Social Movements, Conflict and Change*, vol. 7.

Masferrer Kan, Elio. 1986a. "Tosepan Titataniske (unidos venceremos)." *México Indígena*, no. 11, July–August.

———. 1986b. "Coyotes y coyotitos: Cambios en los sistemas de intermediación en la Sierra Norte de Puebla." *México Indígena*, no. 12, September–October.

Matus Gardea, Jaime A., and Roberto R. Cruz Aguilar. 1987. "Agricultural Policy and International Trade in Mexico, 1970–1982." In Bruce Johnston, Cassio Luiselli, Celso Cartas Contreras, and Roger D. Norton, eds., *U.S.–Mexico Relations: Agriculture and Rural Development.* Stanford: Stanford University Press.

Maxfield, Sylvia. 1990. *Governing Capital: International Finance and Mexican Politics.* Ithaca: Cornell University Press.

Maxfield, Sylvia, and Ricardo Anzaldúa Montoya, eds. 1987. *Government and Private Sector in Contemporary Mexico.* La Jolla: University of California, San Diego, Center for U.S.–Mexican Studies.

Maydón Garza, Marín. 1988. "El crédito agropecuario en tiempos de inflación." *Comercio Exterior* 38(7), July.

Mayer, Arno. 1970. *The Dynamics of Counterrevolution in Europe*. New York: Harper.

Mayo, Baloy. 1980. *La guerrilla de Genaro y Lucio: Análisis y resultados*. 2d ed. Mexico: Ed. Diógenes.

McClintock, Cynthia. 1980. "Reform Governments and Policy Implementation: Lessons from Peru." In Merilee S. Grindle, ed., *Politics and Policy Implementation in the Third World*. Princeton: Princeton University Press.

———. 1981. *Peasant Cooperatives and Political Change in Peru*. Princeton: Princeton University Press.

Mecatl, José Luis, Amarco Antonio Michel, and Alicia Ziccardi. 1987. *Casa a los damnificados*. Mexico: UNAM.

Meissner, Frank. 1981. "The Mexican Food System (SAM): A Strategy for Sowing Petroleum." *Food Policy* 6(4), November.

Mejía Piñeros, María Consuelo, and Sergio Sarmiento Silva. 1987. *La lucha indígena: Un reto a la ortodoxia*. Mexico: Siglo XXI/IIS.

Melucci, Alberto. 1988. "Getting Involved: Identity and Mobilization in Social Movements." In Bert Klandermans, H. Kreisi, and Sidney Tarrow, eds., *International Social Movement Research*, vol. 1. Greenwich, Conn.: JAI Press.

Merino Castrejón, José. 1982. "Almacenamiento de productos básicos para la alimentación." Paper presented at COPIDER-Harvard Workshop, Mexico City, CIESS, October.

Mesa Lago, Carmelo. 1989. *The Politics of Social Security in Latin America*. Pittsburgh: University of Pittsburgh Press.

Mestries, Francisco. 1981. "El SAM: ¿Una alternativa real?" *Teoría y Política* 1(3), January–March.

Meyer, Lorenzo. 1978. *Historia de la revolución mexicana, período 1928–1934*. Vol. 13. Mexico: Colegio de México.

———. 1982. "Andamios presidenciales: El todo y sus partes." *Nexos* 60, December.

Michaels, Albert. 1970. "The Crisis of Cardenismo." *Journal of Latin American Studies* 2(1).

Middlebrook, Kevin. 1981. "Political Change and Political Reform in an Authoritarian Regime: The Case of Mexico." *Latin American Program Working Paper* no. 103, Washington, D.C., Wilson Center.

———. 1986. "Political Liberalization in an Authoritarian Regime: The Case of Mexico." In Guillermo O'Donnell, Philippe Schmitter, and Laurence Whitehead, eds., *Transitions from Authoritarian Rule: Latin America*. Baltimore: Johns Hopkins University Press.

Migdal, Joel S. 1987. "Strong States, Weak States: Power and Accommodation." In Myron Weiner and Samuel P. Huntington, eds., *Understanding Political Development*. Boston: Little, Brown.

———. 1988. *Strong Societies and Weak States*. Princeton: Princeton University Press.

———. 1990. "The State in Society: Struggles and Accommodations in Multiple Arenas." *States and Social Structures Newsletter* 13, Spring.

Miliband, Ralph. 1969. *The State in Capitalist Society*. London: Winfield and Nicholson.

Moe, Terry. 1980. *The Organization of Interests.* Chicago: University of Chicago Press.

Mogab, John. 1984. "The Mexican Experience in Peasant Agricultural Credit." *Development and Change* 15.

Moguel, Julio. 1987. *Los caminos de la izquierda.* Mexico: Juan Pablos.

——, ed. 1988. *Historia de la cuestión agraria mexicana.* Vol. 7, *La época de oro y el principio de la crisis de la agricultura mexicana (1950–1970).* Mexico: Siglo XXI/CEHAM.

——. 1989. *Historia de la cuestión agraria mexicana.* Vol. 8, *Política estatal y conflictos agrarios (1950–1970).* Mexico: Siglo XXI/CEHAM.

——. 1990. *Historia de la cuestión agraria mexicana.* Vol. 9, *Los tiempos de la crisis (1970–1982).* Mexico: Siglo XXI/CEHAM.

——. 1991a. "El Programa Nacional de Solidaridad, ¿para quién?" *Cuadernos Desarrollo de Base,* no. 2.

——. 1991b. "La Coordinadora Estatal de Productores de Café de Oaxaca." In Gabriela Ejea and Luis Hernández, eds., "Cafetaleros: La construcción de la autonomía." *Cuadernos Desarrollo de Base,* no. 3.

Moguel, Julio, et al. 1981. *Ensayos sobre la cuestión agraria y el campesinado.* Mexico: Juan Pablos.

Moguel, Julio, Carlota Botey, and Luis Hernández, eds. 1992. *Autonomía y nuevos sujetos sociales en el desarrollo rural.* Mexico: Siglo XXI/CEHAM.

Molinar, Juan. 1991. *El tiempo de la legitimidad: Elecciones, autoritarismo y democracia en México.* Mexico: Cal y Arena.

Moncada, María. 1983. "Movimiento campesino y estructura de poder: Venustiano Carranza, Chiapas." *Textual* 4(13), September.

Monsiváis, Carlos. 1987. *Entrada libre: Crónicas de una sociedad que se organiza.* Mexico: Era.

Monsiváis, Carlos, et al. 1989. *Crónica del nuevo México.* Mexico: Equipo Pueblo.

Montalvo, Enrique, ed. 1988. *Historia de la cuestión agraria mexicana.* Vol. 4, *Modernización, lucha agraria y poder político (1920–1934).* Mexico: Siglo XXI/CEHAM.

Montanari, Mario. 1987. "The Conception of SAM." In James Austin and Gustavo Esteva, eds., *Food Policy in Mexico: The Search for Self-Sufficiency.* Ithaca: Cornell University Press.

Montañez, Carlos. 1988. "Los condicionantes de la política agropecuaria." *Comercio Exterior* 38(8), August.

Montañez, Carlos, et al. 1982. *El cultivo del maíz en México.* Mexico: CECODES.

Montañez, Carlos, and Horacio Aburto. 1979. *Maíz: Política institucional y crisis agrícola.* Mexico: Nueva Imagen/CIDER.

Montañez, Carlos, and Arturo Warman. 1985. *Los productores de maíz en México: Restricciones y alternativas.* Mexico: CECODES.

Montes, Margarito. 1982. "El movimiento campesino en el México actual." *Textual* 3(10), December.

Montes de Oca, Rosa Elena. 1977. "The State and the Peasants." In José Luis Reyna and Richard Weinert, eds., *Authoritarianism in Mexico.* Philadelphia: ISHI.

Montes de Oca, Rosa Elena, and Fernando Rello. 1981. "Hacia un proyecto alimentario alternativo." *Economía Informa* 84, August.
———. 1982. "Hacia un proyecto alimentario diferente." *Comercio Exterior* 32(2), February.
Mora Aguilar, Sergio. 1979. "La organización campesina en el desarrollo rural: Una experiencia de la Sierra Norte de Puebla." In *Sociología del desarrollo rural*, vol. 2. Chapingo: Universidad Autonóma de Chapingo.
Mújica Vélez, Rubén. 1980. "El Sistema Alimentario Mexicano, los problemas estructurales." *Comercio Exterior* 30(4), April.
———. 1983. "Autonomía alimentaria: Necesidad, opción, estrategia." *Economía Informa* 109, October.
———. 1984. "El sector agropecuario: Crónica de una muerte anunciada." *Economía Informa* 113, February.
Mummert, Gail, ed. 1987. *Almacenamiento de productos agropecuarios en México*. Mexico: Colegio de Michoacán/Almacenes Nacionales de Depósito.
Munck, Gerardo L. 1990. "Identity and Ambiguity in Democratic Struggles." In Joe Foweraker and Ann L. Craig, eds., *Popular Movements and Political Change in Mexico*. Boulder, Colo.: Lynne Rienner.
Myhre, David. 1989. "Agricultural Credit and the Changing Structure of Mexican Agriculture." Paper presented at the Fifteenth International Congress of the Latin American Studies Association (LASA), Miami.
Nagengast, Carole, and Michael Kearney. 1990. "Mixtec Ethnicity: Social Identity, Political Consciousness and Political Activism." *Latin American Research Review* 25(2).
Nauman, Talli. 1989. "La Laguna Unleashed." *Mexico Journal*, June 12.
Newell, Roberto, and Luis Rubio. 1984. *Mexico's Dilemma: The Political Origins of Economic Crisis*. Boulder, Colo.: Westview Press.
Niño, Edilberto. 1985. "Organización campesina: Presión desde la base." Paper presented at U.S.–Mexico Project Conference on Building Linkages between Policymakers, Researchers and Small Farmers, Pátzcuaro, December 3–8.
Nordlinger, Eric A. 1987. "Taking the State Seriously." In Myron Weiner and Samuel P. Huntington, eds., *Understanding Political Development*. Boston: Little, Brown.
North, Liisa, and David Raby. 1977. "The Dynamic of Revolution and Counterrevolution: Mexico under Cárdenas, 1934–1940." *LARU Studies* (Latin American Research Unit) 2(1), October.
Norton, Roger. 1987. "Policy Choices in Agricultural Trade between Mexico and the United States." In Bruce F. Johnston, Cassio Luiselli, Celso Cartas Contreras, and Roger D. Norton, eds., *U.S.–Mexico Relations: Agriculture and Rural Development*. Stanford: Stanford University Press.
O'Connor, James. 1973. *The Fiscal Crisis of the State*. New York: St. Martin's Press.
Odile, Marie, and Marion Singer. 1984. *El movimiento campesino en Chiapas, 1983*. Mexico: CEHAM.
O'Donnell, Guillermo. 1977a. "Corporatism and the Question of the State." In James Malloy, ed., *Authoritarianism and Corporatism in Latin America*. Pittsburgh: University of Pittsburgh Press.

———. 1977b. *Apuntes para una teoría del estado*. Buenos Aires: CEDES.

———. 1988. "Challenges to Democratization in Brazil." *World Policy Journal* 5(2).

O'Donnell, Guillermo, and Philippe C. Schmitter. 1986. *Transitions from Authoritarian Rule: Tentative Conclusions about Uncertain Democracies*. Baltimore: Johns Hopkins University Press.

Offe, Claus. 1974. "Structural Problems of the Capitalist State." *German Political Studies*. Vol. 1. London: Sage Publications.

———. 1975. "The Theory of the Capitalist State and the Problem of Policy Formation." In Leon Lindberg et al., eds., *Stress and Contradiction in Modern Capitalism: Public Policy and the Theory of the State*. Lexington, Mass.: D.C. Heath.

———. 1981. "The Attribution of Public Status to Interest Groups: Observations on the West German Case." In Suzanne Berger, ed., *Organizing Interests in Western Europe*. Cambridge: Cambridge University Press.

Offe, Claus, and Helmut Wiesenthal. 1980. "Two Logics of Collective Action: Theoretical Notes on Social Class and Organizational Form." In Maurice Zeitin, ed., *Political Power and Social Theory*. Vol. 1. Greenwich, Conn.: JAI Press.

Oliver, Pamela, Gerald Marwell, and Ruy Texeira. 1985. "A Theory of the Critical Mass. I., Interdependence, Group Heterogeneity, and the Production of Collective Action." *American Journal of Sociology* 91(3), November.

Olmstead, Alan, Bruce Johnston, and Brian Sims. 1985. "Forward to the Past: The Diffusion of Animal-Powered Tillage Equipment on Small Farms in Mexico." *Working Paper in Agricultural History*, University of California, Davis, October.

Olson, Mancur. 1986. "Space, Agriculture and Organization." *American Journal of Agricultural Economics* 67(5).

O'Malley, Ilene. 1986. *The Myth of Revolution: Hero Cults and the Institutionalization of the Mexican State, 1920–1940*. Westport, Conn.: Greenwood.

Ornelas López, José Luz. 1989. "Los municipios indígenas." *Cuadernos de Investigación*. Oaxaca: Universidad Autónoma "Benito Juárez."

Ortiz Pinchetti, Francisco. 1981a. "Al rechazo indígena se unen las deficiencias de las clínicas IMSS-COPLAMAR." *Proceso* 236, May 11.

———. 1981b. "DICONSA frena la organización campesina y traiciona al programa en cuatro estados." *Proceso* 241, June 15.

Otero, Gerardo. 1986. "Political Class Formation in Rural Mexico: Class, State and Culture." Ph.D. diss., Department of Sociology, University of Wisconsin.

———. 1989. "The New Agrarian Movement: Self-Managed, Democratic Production." *Latin American Perspectives* 16(4), Fall.

Ovalle, Ignacio. 1980. "Responsabilidad de COPLAMAR en el SAM." *México Indígena*, August.

Page, Benjamin I. 1983. *Who Gets What from Government*. Berkeley: University of California Press.

Page, Stephen. 1989. "The Politics of Rural Development Administration: Mexico and the World Bank in the PIDER Program." Master's thesis, Department of Political Science, Massachusetts Institute of Technology.

Palacios, Enrique. 1981. "La política hidroagrícola en México." CEPAL/MEX/ SAC/70, January 13, mimeographed.

Paoli, Francisco José. 1985. *Estado y sociedad en México, 1917–1984.* Mexico: Océano.

Paoli, Francisco José, and Enrique Montalvo. 1987. *El socialismo olvidado de Yucatán.* 3d ed. Mexico: Siglo XXI.

Paoli, J. Antonio. 1984. "Caciquismo y control del PRI." In V. Amalia Muñoz Rocha, ed., *Jornada el campo y el campesino: Producción y hambre.* Mexico: UAM-Xochimilco.

Paré, Luisa. 1975. "Caciquismo y estructura de poder en la Sierra Norte de Puebla." In Roger Bartra, ed., *Caciquismo y poder político en el México rural.* Mexico: Siglo XXI.

———. 1977. *El proletariado agrícola en México.* Mexico: Siglo XXI.

———. 1980a. "Virajes en la política agraria actual." In *Sociología y desarrollo rural,* vol. 1. Memoria. Mexico: Universidad Autónoma de Chapingo.

———. 1980b. "El culto a SAM hambrosio." *El Machete* 4, August.

———. 1982. "La política agropecuaria, 1976–1982." *Cuadernos Políticos* 33, July.

———. 1990. "The Challenge of Rural Democratisation in Mexico." In Jonathan Fox, ed., *The Challenge of Rural Democratisation in Developing Countries: Perspectives from Latin America and the Philippines.* London: Frank Cass. Also in *Journal of Development Studies* 26(4), July 1990.

Parnell, Philip C. 1988. *Escalating Disputes: Social Participation and Change in the Oaxacan Highlands.* Tucson: University of Arizona Press.

Patron Guerra, Fernando, and Jess Fuentes Navarro. 1982. "Acciones y coordinación FIRA en relación con el Sistema Alimentario Mexicano." Paper presented at COPIDER-Harvard Workshop, Mexico City, CIESS, October, mimeographed.

Paz Paredes, Lorena, and Julio Moguel. 1979. *Santa Gertrudis: Lucha campesina.* Mexico: Era.

Peón Escalante, Fernando. 1988. "El papel del estado en el abasto popular (1910–1986)." In Armando Labra, ed., *El sector social de la economía: Una opción ante la crisis.* Mexico: Siglo XXI/CIIH/UNAM.

Pereyra, Carlos. 1979. "¿Quien mató al comendador? Notas sobre estado y sociedad en México." *Nexos* 13, January.

———. 1980. "El SAM, respuesta a la urgente necesidad de cambiar, en serio, la estructura agraria." *Proceso* 179, April 7.

———. 1981. "México: Los límites del reformismo." In Rolando Cordera, ed., *Desarrollo y crisis de la economía mexicana.* Mexico: Fondo de Cultura Económica.

———. 1982. "Los dados del juego." *Nexos* 60, December.

———. 1985. "La agenda de la democracia." *La Jornada Semanal,* July 30.

Pérez Correa, Fernando. 1982. "Elites, Masses and Parties." In Tommie Sue Montgomery, ed., *Mexico Today.* Philadelphia: ISHI.

Pérez Espejo, Rosario. 1987. *Agricultura y ganadería: Competencia por el uso de la tierra.* Mexico: Ediciones de Cultura Popular/UNAM.

Pérez Haro, Eduardo. 1990. "La modernización del sistema CONASUPO." *El Cotidiano* 34(7), March–April.

Pessah, Raúl. 1987. "Channeling Credit to the Countryside." In James Austin and Gustavo Esteva, eds., *Food Policy in Mexico: The Search for Self-Sufficiency.* Ithaca: Cornell University Press.

Piven, Frances Fox, and Richard Cloward. 1977. *Poor People's Movements: How They Succeed and Why They Fail.* New York: Pantheon.

Pizzorno, Alessandro. 1985. "On the Rationality of Democratic Choice." *Telos* 63, Spring.

Poitras, Guy. 1973. "Welfare Bureaucracy and Clientele Politics in Mexico." *Administrative Science Quarterly* 18(1).

Poulantzas, Nicos. 1974. *Political Power and Social Classes.* London: New Left Books.

———. 1980. *State, Power and Socialism.* London: New Left Books, Verso.

PRONASE. 1982. *Origen, desarrollo y producción de la Productora Nacional de Semillas.* Mexico: SARH/Pronase.

PRONASOL. 1991a. *El combate a la pobreza: Lineamientos programáticos.* Mexico: Nacional.

———. 1991b. *Solidaridad a debate.* Mexico: Nacional.

PRONDAAT. 1976. *Un enfoque para el desarrollo agrícola en áreas de temporal.* Mexico: Secretaría de Agricultura y Ganadería, November.

Przeworski, Adam. 1985. *Capitalism and Social Democracy.* Cambridge: Cambridge University Press.

———. 1990. *The State and the Economy under Capitalism.* Fundamentals of Basic and Applied Economics. Paris: Harwood Academic Publishers.

———. 1991. *Democracy and the Market: Political and Economic Reforms in Eastern Europe and Latin America.* Cambridge: Cambridge University Press.

Pueblo/Información Obrera, ed. 1990. *De las aulas a las calles.* Mexico: Equipo Pueblo/Información Obrera.

Purcell, John, and Susan Kaufman Purcell. 1977. "Mexican Business and Public Policy." In James Malloy, ed., *Authoritarianism and Corporatism in Latin America.* Pittsburgh: University of Pittsburgh Press.

Purcell, Susan Kaufman. 1973. "Decision Making in an Authoritarian Regime: Theoretical Implications from a Mexican Case Study." *World Politics* 25(3), April.

———. 1975. *The Mexican Profit-Sharing Decision: Politics in an Authoritarian Regime.* Berkeley: University of California Press.

———. 1981. "Business-Government Relations in Mexico: The Case of the Sugar Industry." *Comparative Politics* 13(2), January.

Purcell, Susan Kaufman, and John Purcell. 1980. "State and Society in Mexico: Must a Stable Polity Be Institutionalized?" *World Politics* 32(2). Also in Spanish in *Foro Internacional* 20, January 1980.

Purnell, Jennie. 1989. "Organizing Peasants: Rural Politics under the Military in Peru." Unpublished paper, Department of Political Science, Massachusetts Institute of Technology.

Rama, Ruth. 1985. "Some Effects of the Internationalization of Agriculture on the Mexican Agricultural Crisis." In Steven Sanderson, ed., *The Americas in the New International Division of Labor.* New York: Holmes and Meier.

Rama, Ruth, and Fernando Rello. 1980. "La internacionalización de la agricultura mexicana." In Nora Lustig, ed., *Panorama y perspectivas de la economía mexicana*. Mexico: Colegio de México.

Ramos, Ignacio. 1985. "Concertación social en DICONSA." *Sistema C*, no. 36, August.

Ramos García, Héctor, et al. 1984. *El movimiento campesino en Veracruz, Puebla y Tlaxcala*. Mexico: Eds. Nueva Sociología.

Ramos Saenz Pardo, Jeronimo. 1984. "An Economic Evaluation of Government Intervention in the Mexican Agricultural Sector: The Corn and Wheat Sectors." Ph.D diss., Department of Economics, University of Minnesota.

Redclift, Michael. 1980. "Agrarian Populism in Mexico: The 'Via Campesina.'" *Journal of Peasant Studies* 7(4), July.

———. 1981a. "The New Sources of Environmental Conflicts in Rural Mexico." Department of Environmental Studies and Countryside Planning, Occasional Papers no. 4. University of London, Wye College, April.

———. 1981b. "The Mexican Food System (SAM): Sowing Subsidies, Reaping Apathy." *Food Policy* 6(4), November.

———. 1981c. "Development Policymaking in Mexico: The Sistema Alimentario Mexicano." *Working Papers in U.S.–Mexican Studies* 24.

———. 1983. "Production Programs for Small Farmers: Plan Puebla as Myth and Reality." *Economic Development and Cultural Change* 31(3), April.

Reig, Nicolás. 1985. "Las tendencias alimentarias a largo plazo en México: 1950–1984." *Problemas del Desarrollo* 16(61), February.

Rello, Fernando. 1980. "Los enemigos del SAM." *Economía Informa* 71–72, May.

———. 1981a. "Los apoyos del SAM." *Economía Informa*, 67 January.

———. 1981b. "Política agrícola y lucha de clases." *Nueva Antropología* 5(17), May.

———. 1982. "La política del estado y la lucha campesina." In Jorge Alonso, ed., *El estado mexicano*. Mexico: Nueva Imagen/CIESAS.

———. 1986a. *Bourgeoisie, Peasants and the State in Mexico: The Agrarian Conflict of 1976*. Geneva: United Nations Research Institute for Social Development (UNRISD).

———. 1986b. *El campo en la encrucijada nacional*. Mexico: Colección Foro 2000, Secretaría de Educación Pública.

———. 1987. *State and Peasantry in Mexico: A Case Study of Rural Credit in La Laguna*. Geneva: UNRISD.

———. 1988. "El significado de la democratización rural." In Rolando Cordera Campos, Raúl Trejo Delarbre, and Juan Enrique Vega, eds., *México, el reclamo democrático: Homenaje a Carlos Pereyra*. Mexico: Siglo XXI.

Rello, Fernando, and Ruth Rama. 1980. "Estrategias de las agroindustrias transnacionales y política alimentaria en México." Facultad de Economía, UNAM, Mexico, mimeographed.

Rello, Fernando, and Demetrio Sodi. 1989. *Abasto y distribución de alimentos en las grandes metrópolis: El caso de la ciudad de México*. Mexico: Nueva Imagen.

Renard, Marie-Christine. 1981. "La política de precios de garantía y el SAM." *Textual* 2(7), April.

Restrepo, Iván, and Salomón Eckstein. 1979. *La agricultura colectiva en México: La experiencia de La Laguna.* 2d. ed. Mexico: Siglo XXI.

Reyes, Antonio. 1982. "La estructura y dinámica crediticia oficial en el marco del Sistema Alimentario Mexicano." Paper presented at COPIDER-Harvard Workshop, Mexico City, CIESS, October.

Reyes Osorio, Sergio. 1977. "Organización campesina." *Narxhí-Nandhí* 2, April.

Reyna, José Luis, and Richard Weiniert, eds. 1977. *Authoritarianism in Mexico.* Philadelphia: ISHI.

Robles, Rosario. 1981. "Las organizaciones campesinas independientes en México." In Julio Moguel et al., *Ensayos sobre la cuestión agraria y el campesinado.* Mexico: Juan Pablos.

Robles, Rosario, and Julio Moguel. 1990. "Agricultura y proyecto neoliberal." *El Cotidiano* 34(7), March–April.

Rodríguez, Jorge. 1980. "27 tractores, perdidos; 81, casi inutiles, 44 ni siquiera se usaron." *Proceso* 203, October 22.

Rodríguez Araujo, Octavio. 1981. "Reforma política: Recuento y obituario." *Nexos* 42, June.

Rodríguez Chaurnet, Dinah. 1980. "El Sistema Alimentario Mexicano." *Problemas del Desarrollo* 41, January–April.

Rodríguez Sosa, Candelaria. 1985. "El INEA en Chiapas, un programa ambicioso: La alfabetización global." *Perfil de La Jornada*, May 24.

Rogers, Beatrice Lorge, Catherine Overholt, et al. 1981. "Consumer Food Price Subsidies." Study 5. In James Austin, ed., *Nutrition Intervention in Developing Countries.* Cambridge: Oelgeschlager, Gunn and Hain.

Romero Maura, Joaquín. 1977. "Caciquism as a Political System." In Ernst Gellner and John Waterbury, eds., *Patrons and Clients in Mediterranean Societies.* London: Duckworth.

Ronfeldt, David. 1973. *Atencingo: The Politics of Agrarian Struggle in a Mexican Ejido.* Stanford: Stanford University.

———, ed. 1984. *The Modern Mexican Military: A Reassessment.* Monograph 15. La Jolla: University of San Diego, Center for U.S.–Mexican Studies.

Roniger, Luis. 1987. "Caciquismo and Coronelismo: Contextual Dimensions of Patron Brokerage in Mexico and Brazil." *Latin American Research Review* 22(2).

Ros, Jaime, and Gonzalo Rodríguez. 1987. "Mexico: Study on the Financial Crisis, the Adjustment Policies and Agricultural Development." *CEPAL Review* 33, December.

Roxborough, Ian. 1984a. "Unity and Diversity in Latin American History." *Journal of Latin American Studies* 16(1), May.

———. 1984b. *Unions and Politics in Mexico: The Case of the Automobile Industry.* Cambridge: Cambridge University Press.

Rubin, Jeffrey. 1987. "State Policies, Leftist Oppositions and Municipal Elections: The Case of the COCEI in Juchitán." In Arturo Alvarado, ed., *Electoral Patterns and Perspectives in Mexico.* Monograph 22. La Jolla: Center for U.S.–Mexican Studies, University of California, San Diego.

——. 1990. "Popular Mobilization and the Myth of Corporatism." In Joe Foweraker and Ann Craig, eds., *Popular Movements and Political Change in Mexico*. Boulder, Colo.: Lynne Rienner.

Rubio, Andrés, and Eric Villanueva M. 1980. "La respuesta de los trabajadores henequeneros a la nueva política de BANRURAL." *Cuadernos Agrarios* 5(10–11), December.

Rubio, Blanca. 1987. *Resistencia campesina y explotación rural en México*. Mexico: Ediciones Era.

Rubio Canales, Abraham. 1982. "La participación del Programa de Apoyo a la Comercialización Rural (PACE) dentro de la estrategia SAM." Paper presented at COPIDER-Harvard Workshop, Mexico City, CIESS, October, mimeographed.

Rubio Vega, Blanca. 1983. "La nueva modalidad del desarrollo capitalista en la agricultura mexicana, 1965–1980." *Teoría y Política* 10, April.

Rueschemeyer, Dietrich, and Peter B. Evans. 1985. "The State and Economic Transformation: Toward an Analysis of the Conditions Underlying Effective Intervention." In Peter B. Evans, Dietrich Rueschemeyer, and Theda Skocpol, eds., *Bringing the State Back In*. Cambridge: Cambridge University Press.

Rutsch, Mechtild. 1981. "El Sistema Alimentario Mexicano y la ganadería bovina de carne." *Nueva Antropología* 5(17), May.

——. 1984. *La ganadería capitalista en México*. Mexico: Editorial Linea/CIIS.

Sabel, Charles. 1981. "The Internal Politics of Trade Unions." In Suzanne Berger, ed., *Organizing Interests in Western Europe*. Cambridge: Cambridge University Press.

Saldívar, Américo. 1981. *Ideología y política del estado mexicano (1970–1976)*. Mexico: Siglo XXI.

Salinas de Gortari, Carlos. 1982. *Political Participation, Public Investment, and Support for the System: A Comparative Study of Rural Communities in Mexico*. Research Report Series 35, University of California, San Diego, Center for U.S–Mexican Studies.

——. 1984. "Production and Participation in Rural Areas: Some Political Considerations." In Pedro Aspe and Paul Sigmund, eds., *The Political Economy of Income Distribution in Mexico*. New York: Holmes and Meier.

——. 1988. "Inaugural Address." Mexico: Office of the Presidency.

Salinas de Gortari, Raúl. 1990. "El campo mexicano ante el reto de la modernización." *Comercio Exterior* 40(9), September.

Salmerón Castro, Fernando. 1984. "Caciques: Una revisión teórica sobre el control político local." *Revista Mexicana de Ciencias Políticas y Sociales* 30(117–118), July.

——. 1988. "Crisis y actualización del intermediarismo político." In Jorge Zepeda Patterson, ed., *Las sociedades rurales hoy*. Zamora: Colegio de Michoacán.

SAM (Sistema Alimentario Mexicano). 1979. *Notas analíticas y lineamientos metodológicos para el proyecto Sistema Alimentario Mexicano*. Mexico: SAM.

——. 1980a. "Esquema del uso de los instrumentos de política económica para el sector agrícola." January, mimeographed.

——. 1980b. *Primer planteamiento de metas de consumo y estrategia de produc-*

ción de alimentos básicos. Mexico: SAM. Also in *Nueva Antropología* 5(17), May 1981.

———. 1980c. *Medidas operativas agropecuarias y pesquera, estrategia de comercialización, transformación, distribución y consumo de los productos de la canasta básica recomendable.* Mexico: SAM.

———. 1980d. *Estrategia de comercialización y distribución de alimentos básicos e insumos productivos.* Mexico: SAM.

———. 1981a. "Política de subsidios." Discussion paper, Dirección General de Análisis Macroeconómico, mimeographed.

———. 1981b. "Evaluación de las medidas operativas: Reporte de resultados." Mimeographed.

———. 1981c. "Propuesta de una nueva política de subsidios." Mimeographed.

———. 1981d. "Propuesta para la integración agroindustrial del sistema maíz." Dirección General de Estudios y Estrategias.

———. 1981e. "Estrategia y política alimentaria actual en México." May, mimeographed.

———. 1981f. "Política de precios de garantía del Sistema Alimentario Mexicano." Discussion paper, July, mimeographed.

———. 1981g. "Estrategia y políticas de organización y capacitación campesina." Discussion paper, July, mimeographed.

———. 1981h. "Proyecto: Relaciones económicas y sociales en la cadena alimentaria." July, mimeographed.

———. 1981i. "Sistema global de alimentos para ganado." Dirección General de Estudios y Proyectos. September, mimeographed.

———. 1981j. "Estrategia productiva agropecuaria, resultado de la evaluación Sistema Alimentario Mexicano." December, mimeographed.

———. 1982a. "Presupuesto de egresos de la Federación 1981, participación sectorial y programática del Sistema Alimentario Mexicano." Mimeographed.

———. 1982b. "Plan alimentario: Ideas fuerza del diagnóstico y propostivas." April, mimeographed.

———. 1982c. "Críticas al SAM." May, mimeographed.

———. 1982d. "Impacto de la publicidad del SAM." Dirección General de Comunicación Social, June, mimeographed.

———. 1982e. "Cultura alimentaria y publicidad comercial televisada." Dirección General de Comunicación Social, September, mimeographed.

SAM-SARH. 1981–82. *Informe de resultados del sector agropecuario y forestal.* Mexico: SARH.

SAM-STGA. 1981. "Programa de apoyos y estímulos del Sistema Alimentario Mexicano a la producción de alimentos básicos." April, mimeographed.

Sánchez Daza, Alfredo, and Sergio Vargas Velázquez. 1986. "Debilidad y fortaleza de CONASUPO." *El Cotidiano* 13(3):40–46, September–October.

Sánchez Hernández, Miguel. 1987. "Local Organization in Rural Development Programs: The Case of the Puebla Project." Ph.D. diss., Development Studies, University of Wisconsin–Madison.

Sánchez Oñate. 1983. "Problemática de los acreditados indígenas y comportamiento de las instituciones del sector en su atención y apoyos." BANRURAL, June, mimeographed.

Sanders, Thomas. 1979. "The Plight of Mexican Agriculture." In Barbara Huddleston and Jon McLin, eds., *Political Investments in Food Production*. Bloomington: Indiana University Press.

Sanderson, Steven. 1981. *Agrarian Populism and the Mexican State*. Berkeley: University of California Press.

———. 1983. "Presidential Succession and Political Rationality in Mexico." *World Politics* 35(3), April.

———. 1986. *The Transformation of Mexican Agriculture*. Princeton: Princeton University Press.

Sanderson, Susan Walsh. 1984. *Land Reform in Mexico: 1910–1980*. Orlando, Fla.: Academic Press.

San Juan, Carlos. 1984. "El dilema de la historia obrera reciente: Revolución pasiva y acumulación de fuerzas en 1970–1982." *Historias* 5, January.

Santoyo Meza, Enrique, and José Urquiaga. 1982. "Sistema LICONSA-Cider." Paper presented at COPIDER-Harvard Workshop, Mexico City, CIESS, October, mimeographed.

SARH (Secretaría de Agricultura y Recursos Hidráulicos). 1980. "Programa de participación inmediata del sector agropecuario en el Sistema Alimentario Mexicano." April, mimeographed.

———. 1981. *Informe de labores*. Mexico: SARH.

———. 1982a. *Memoria, 1976–1982*. Mexico: SARH.

———. 1982b. *El desarrollo agropecuario de México*. 12 vols. Mexico: SARH/ Dirección General de Planeación.

———. 1990. "Programa nacional de modernización del campo, 1990–1994." *Comercio Exterior* 40(10), October.

Sarmiento Silva, Sergio. 1981. "El Consejo Nacional de Pueblos Indígenas ante el control del estado y la organización política independiente de los indios de México." Undergraduate thesis in sociology, Universidad Nacional Autónoma de México.

———. 1989. "El movimiento campesino y el Congreso Agrario Permanente." *Pueblo* 12(144–45), May–June.

Schatan, Jacobo. 1986. "SAM's Influence on Food Consumption and Nutrition." In James Austin and Gustavo Esteva, eds., *Food Policy in Mexico: In Search of Self-Sufficiency*. Ithaca: Cornell University Press.

Schattschneider, Elmer Eric. 1960. *The Semisovereign People: A Realist's View of Democracy in America*. New York: Holt Reinhart and Winston.

Scherer García, Julio. 1990. *El poder: Historias e familia*. Mexico: Grijalbo.

Schmidt, Steffen W., James C. Scott, Carl Landé, and Laura Guasti, eds. 1977. *Friends, Followers, and Factions: A Reader in Political Clientelism*. Berkeley: University of California Press.

Schneider, Ben Ross. 1992. *Politics within the State: Elite Bureaucrats and Industrial Policy in Authoritarian Brazil*. Pittsburgh: University of Pittsburgh Press.

Schryer, Frans. 1980. *The Rancheros of Pisaflores*. Toronto: University of Toronto Press.

———. 1990. *Ethnicity and Class Conflict in Rural Mexico*. Princeton: Princeton University Press.

Schumacher, August. 1981a. "Mexican Rural Development: SAM and PIDER." Harvard Business School, World Food Systems Seminar, mimeographed.

———. 1981b. "Agricultural Development and Rural Development: A Mexican Dilemma." *Working Papers in U.S.–Mexican Studies* 21.

Schurmann, Franz. 1974. *The Logic of World Power*. New York: Pantheon.

Scott, James. 1969. "Corruption, Machine Politics and Political Change." *American Political Science Review* 63(4), December.

———. 1985. *Weapons of the Weak*. New Haven: Yale University Press.

Segura F., Jesús Jaime. 1980. "El sistema de cargos en Teotitlán del Valle, Oaxaca." In Raúl Benítez Zenteno, ed., *Sociedad y política en Oaxaca 1980: 15 estudios de caso*. Oaxaca: Universidad Autónoma Benito Juárez.

Shapira, Yoram. 1977. "Mexico: The Impact of the 1968 Student Protest on Echeverría's Reformism." *Journal of Interamerican Studies and World Affairs* 19(4), November.

Sherraden, Margaret. 1989a. "Influences on Health Policy Development in Mexico: The Case of IMSS-COPLAMAR." Paper presented at the Fifteenth International Congress of the Latin American Studies Association, Miami.

———. 1989b. "Social Policy Reform in Mexico: Rural Primary Health Services." Ph.D. diss., Washington University.

Silos Alvarado, José. 1988. "Nuevas estructuras de producción y de financiamiento rural." *Comercio Exterior* 38(8), August.

Simpson, Eyler. 1937. *The Ejido: Mexico's Way Out*. Chapel Hill: University of North Carolina Press.

Singelmann, Peter. 1978. "Rural Collectivization and Dependent Capitalism: The Mexican Collective Ejido." *Latin American Perspectives* 5(3), Summer.

Skocpol, Theda. 1979. *States and Social Revolutions*. Cambridge: Cambridge University Press.

———. 1985. "Bringing the State Back In: Strategies of Analysis in Current Research." In Peter Evans, Dietrich Rueschemeyer, and Theda Skocpol, eds., *Bringing the State Back In*. Cambridge: Cambridge University Press.

Sloan, John W. 1984. *Public Policy in Latin America: A Comparative Survey*. Pittsburgh: University of Pittsburgh Press.

Smith, Peter. 1977. "The Making of the Mexican Constitution." In William Aydelotte, ed., *The History of Parliamentary Behavior*. Princeton: Princeton University Press.

———. 1979. *Labyrinths of Power: Political Recruitment in Twentieth-Century Mexico*. Princeton: Princeton University Press.

Sodi de la Tijera, Demetrio. 1988. "El sector social en la comercialización: Factor de justicia y eficiencia." In Armando Labra, ed., *El sector social de la economía*. Mexico: Siglo XXI.

Solís, Leopoldo. 1984. "Food Marketing and Income Distribution." In Pedro Aspe and Paul Sigmund, eds., *The Political Economy of Income Distribution*. New York: Holmes and Meier.

Solís, Samuel Aguilar, and Hugo Andrés Araujo. 1984. "Estado y campesinado en La Laguna: La lucha campesina por la tierra y el excedente." *Folleto de Divulgación* (Universidad Autónoma Agraria Antonio Narro) 1(5).

Sosa, José Luis. 1990. "Dependencia alimentaria en México." *El Cotidiano* 7(34), March–April.

Spalding, Rose. 1981. "State Power and Its Limits: Corporatism in Mexico." *Comparative Political Studies* 14(2), July.

——. 1984. *The Mexican Food Crisis: An Analysis of the SAM.* Research Report Series 33. University of California, San Diego, Center for U.S.–Mexican Studies.

——. 1985. "Structural Barriers to Food Programming: An Analysis of the 'Mexican Food System.'" *World Development* 13(12): 1249–62.

SPP (Secretaría de Programación y Presupuesto). 1981. *El sector alimentario en México.* Mexico: SPP.

——. 1982. *El papel del sector público en la economía Mexicana.* Mexico: SPP.

——. 1984. *Anuario de estadísticas estatales.* Mexico: SPP.

Stanley, William D. 1991. "The Elite Politics of State Terrorism in El Salvador." Ph.D. diss., Dept. of Political Science, Massachusetts Institute of Technology.

Stavenhagen, Rodolfo. 1975. "Collective Agriculture and Capitalism in Mexico: A Way out or a Dead End?" *Latin American Perspectives* 2(2), Summer.

Stepan, Alfred. 1978. *The State and Society: Peru in Comparative Perspective.* Princeton: Princeton University Press.

——. 1985. "State Power and the Strength of Civil Society in the Southern Cone of Latin America." In Peter Evans, Dietrich Rueschemeyer, and Theda Skocpol, eds., *Bringing the State Back In.* Cambridge: Cambridge University Press.

——. 1988. *Rethinking Military Politics.* Princeton: Princeton University Press.

——, ed. 1989. *Democratizing Brazil.* New York: Oxford University Press.

Stephen, Lynn. 1991. *Zapotec Women.* Austin: University of Texas Press.

Stevens, Evelyn. 1974. *Protest and Response in Mexico.* Cambridge: MIT Press.

——. 1975. "Protest Movements in an Authoritarian Regime: The Mexican Case." *Comparative Politics* 7(3), April.

Story, Dale. 1982. "The Mexican GATT Decision." *International Organization* 36(4), Autumn.

——. 1985. "Policy Cycles in Mexico Presidential Politics." *Latin American Research Review* 20(3).

——. 1986. *Industry, the State, and Public Policy in Mexico.* Austin: University of Texas Press.

Street, Susan Linda. 1988. "Organized Teachers as Policymakers: Domination and Opposition in Mexican Public Education." Thesis, Graduate School of Education, Harvard University.

Strickon, Arnold, and Sidney Greenfield, eds. *Structure and Process in Latin America: Patronage, Clientage, and Power Systems.* Albuquerque: University of New Mexico Press.

Swaminathan, Madhura. 1991. "The Changing Role of Formal and Informal Credit in Rural Mexico." Center for International Studies, Massachusetts Institute of Technology, Cambridge, May, mimeographed.

Székely, Gabriel. 1983. *La economía política del petróleo en México, 1976–1982.* Mexico: Colegio de México.

Székely, Miguel. 1977. "La organización colectiva para la producción rural, la acción promotora oficial y las reacciones e iniciativas de los campesinos." *Comercio Exterior* 27(12), December.

Tannenbaum, Frank. 1950. *The Struggle for Peace and Bread*. New York: Alfred A. Knopf.

Tarrow, Sidney. 1983. "Struggling to Reform: Social Movements and Policy Change during Cycles of Protest." *Western Societies Program Occasional Papers* no. 15, Center for International Studies, Cornell University.

———. 1989. "Struggle, Politics, and Reform: Collective Action, Social Movements, and Cycles of Protest." *Western Societies Program Occasional Papers* no. 21, Center for International Studies, Cornell University.

Taylor, William. 1972. *Landlord and Peasant in Colonial Oaxaca*. Stanford: Stanford University Press.

———. 1979. *Drinking, Homicide and Rebellion in Colonial Mexican Villages*. Stanford: Stanford University Press.

Teichman, Judith A. 1988. *Policymaking in Mexico*. Boston: Allen and Unwin.

Tejera Gaona, Héctor. 1981. "La concepción del campesino y la estructura crediticia en el Sistema Alimentario Mexicano." *Nueva Antropología* 5(17), May.

Tello, Carlos. 1984. *La nacionalización de la Banca en México*. Mexico: Siglo XXI.

Tendler, Judith. 1982. "Rural Projects through Urban Eyes: An Interpretation of the World Bank's New-Style Rural Development Projects." *Working Paper* no. 532. Washington, D.C.: World Bank.

Tharp Hilger, Marye. 1980. "Decision-Making in a Public Marketing Enterprise: CONASUPO in Mexico." *Journal of Interamerican Studies and World Affairs* 22(4), November.

Thelen, Kathleen, and Sven Steinmo. 1992. "Historical Institutionalism in Comparative Politics." In Sven Steinmo, Kathleen Thelen, and Frank Longstreth, eds., *Structuring Politics: Historical Institutionalism in Comparative Analysis*. New York: Cambridge University Press, forthcoming.

Tilly, C. 1978. *From Mobilization to Revolution in Mexico: Social Bases of Agrarian Violence, 1750–1940*. Princeton: Princeton University Press.

Timmer, C. Peter, Walter P. Falcon, and Scott R. Pearson. 1983. *Food Policy Analysis*. Baltimore: Johns Hopkins University Press/World Bank.

Tobler, Hans Werner. 1988. "Peasants and the Shaping of the Revolutionary State, 1910–40." In Friedrich Katz, ed., *Riot, Rebellion and Revolution: Rural Social Conflict in Mexico*. Princeton: Princeton University Press.

Toledo, Carlos, Julia Carrabias, and Enrique Provencio. 1992. "El manejo integrado de los recursos naturales y los precios del maíz: Un estudio de caso en Alcozauca, Guerrero." In Cynthia Hewitt de Alcántara, ed., *Reestructuración económico y subsistencia rural: El maíz y la crisis de los 80*. Geneva: UNRISD.

Toledo, Víctor Manuel, Julia Carabias, Cristina Mapes, and Carlos Toledo. 1985. *Ecología y autosuficiencia alimentaria*. Mexico: Siglo XXI.

Toledo, Víctor Manuel, Julia Carabias, Carlos Toledo, and Cuauhtémoc González-Pácheco. 1989. *La producción rural en México: Alternativas ecológicas*. Mexico: Fundación Universo Veintiuno.

Torres, Guillermo. 1981. "El SAM, ¿via terrateniente?" *Economía Informa* 80, August.

Trimberger, Ellen Kay. 1978. *Revolution from Above*. New Brunswick, N.J.: Transaction.

Tucker, Robert C. ed. 1978. *The Marx-Engels Reader.* 2d ed. New York: W. W. Norton.
Tuohy, William, and David Ronfeldt. 1969. "Political Control and the Recruitment of Middle-Level Elites in Mexico: An Example from Agrarian Politics." *Western Political Quarterly* 22(2), June.
Turrent Fernández, Antonio. 1987. "Research and Technology for Mexico's Small Farmers." In Bruce F. Johnston, Cassio Luiselli, Celso Cartas Contreras, and Roger D. Norton, eds., *U.S.–Mexico Relations: Agriculture and Rural Development.* Stanford: Stanford University Press.
Tutino, John. 1988. *From Insurrection to Revolution in Mexico: Social Bases of Agrarian Violence.* Princeton: Princeton University Press.
Ugalde, Antonio. 1973. "Contemporary Mexico: From Hacienda to PRI, Political Leadership in a Zapotec Village." In R. Kern, ed., *The Caciques: Oligarchical Politics and the System of Caciquismo in the Luso-Hispanic World.* Albuquerque: University of New Mexico Press.
Uphoff, Norman. 1984. "Rural Development Strategy: The Central Role of Local Organizations and Changing 'Supply-Side' Bureaucracy." In M. R. El Ghonemy et al., *Studies on Agrarian Reform and Rural Poverty.* Rome: FAO.
Uvince Rojas, Pedro Pablo. 1982. "Descripción y análisis del programa CONASUPO-COPLAMAR de abasto a grupos marginados." Undergraduate thesis in social anthropology, Escuela Nacional de Antropología e Historia, Mexico.
Varela, Gonzalo, and Carlos Arcos, with Clarisa Hardy. 1982. "Las organizaciones gremiales de los empresarios agrícolas." CEPAL, May 25, mimeographed.
Vera, Ramón. 1990. "Expulsados por el paraíso." *México Indígena,* no. 7, April.
Vera Ferrer, Oscar. 1980. "An Appraisal of Price Policy for Selected Agricultural Commodities in Mexico." M. Phil. thesis, University of York, September.
_____. 1987. *El caso CONASUPO, un evaluación: Un estudio comparativo de los objetivos y los logros de la paraestatal.* Mexico: Centro de Estudios en Economía y Educación, A.C.
Villanueva Mukul, Eric. 1983. "En torno de la política agraria y la Ley Agropecuaria." *Cuadernos Agrarios* 7(12), May.
Villegas Montiel, Francisco Gil. 1984. "La crisis de legitimidad en la última etapa del sexenio de José López Portillo." *Foro Internacional* 25(2), October.
Ward, Peter. 1986. *Welfare Politics in Mexico: Papering over the Cracks.* London: Allen and Unwin.
Warman, Arturo. 1979. "Andamos arando, el problema agrario y campesino." *Nexos* 13, January.
_____. 1980a. *"We Come to Object": The Peasants of Morelos and the National State.* Baltimore: Johns Hopkins University Press.
_____. 1980b. *Ensayos sobre el campesinado.* Mexico: Nueva Imagen.
_____. 1980c. "Desarrollo capitalista o campesino en el campo mexicano." In Nora Lustig, ed., *Panorama y perspectivas de la economía mexicana.* Mexico: Colegio de México.
_____. 1981. "El futuro de una crisis." *Nexos* 43, June.
_____. 1988. "The Political Project of Zapatismo." In Friedrich Katz, ed., *Riot,*

Rebellion, and Revolution: Rural Social Conflict in Mexico. Princeton: Princeton University Press.

Wasserstrom, Robert. 1983. *Class and Society in Central Chiapas.* Berkeley: University of California Press.

Waterbury, Ronald. 1975. "Non-revolutionary Peasants: Oaxaca Compared to Morelos in the Mexican Revolution." *Comparative Studies on Society and History* 17(4), October.

Wells, Miriam, and Jacob Climo. 1984. "Parallel Process in the World System: Intermediate Agencies and Local Factionalism in the United States and Mexico." *Journal of Development Studies* 20(2), January.

Weyl, Nathaniel, and Sylvia Weyl. 1939. *The Reconquest of Mexico: The Years of Lázaro Cárdenas.* New York: Oxford University Press.

Whitehead, Laurence. 1980. "Mexico from Boom to Bust: A Political Evaluation of the 1976–1979 Stabilization Programme." *World Development* 8.

———. 1981. "On 'Governability' in Mexico." *Bulletin of Latin American Research* 1(1).

Whiting, Van. 1987. "State Strength, Regime Resilience: Sources of Mexico's Endurance." *Occasional Papers in Latin American Studies,* University of Connecticut/Brown University.

Wilson, James Q. 1973. *Political Organizations.* New York: Basic Books.

Wionczek, Miguel. 1982. "La aportación de la política hidráulica entre 1952 y 1970 y la actual crisis agrícola mexicana." *Comercio Exterior* 32(4), April.

Wolf, Eric. 1969. *Peasant Wars of the Twentieth Century.* New York: Harper and Row.

Womack, John. 1969. *Zapata and the Mexican Revolution.* New York: Alfred A. Knopf.

Woodgate, Graham. 1988. "The Search for Self-Sufficiency in Rural Mexico." *Bulletin of Latin American Research* 7(2).

World Bank. 1983. *Mexico: Incentive Policies in Agriculture,* 3 vols. Washington, D.C.: World Bank, Agriculture Division.

Wright, Angus. 1990. *The Death of Ramón Gonzales.* Austin: University of Texas Press.

Yates, Paul Lamartine. 1981. *Mexico's Agricultural Dilemma.* Tucson: University of Arizona Press.

Yescas Martínez, Isidoro. 1982. "La coalición obrero-campesino-estudiantil de Oaxaca, 1972–1974." In Raúl Benitez Zenteno, ed., *Sociedad y política en Oaxaca, 1980.* Mexico: IIS/UABJO.

Zafra, Gloria. 1982. "La problemática agraria en Oaxaca, 1971–1975." In Raúl Benitez Zenteno, *Sociedad y política en Oaxaca, 1980.* Mexico: IIS/UABJO.

Zaid, Gabriel. 1985. "Escenarios sobre el fin del PRI." *Vuelta* 9(103), June.

Zepeda Patterson, Jorge, ed. 1988. *Las sociedades rurales hoy.* Zamora: Colegio de Michoacán.

Zermeño, Sergio. 1978. *México, una democracia utópica: El movimiento estudiantil del 68.* Mexico: Siglo XXI.

Index

Food Systems and Agrarian Change

Edited by Frederick H. Buttel, Billie R. DeWalt,
and Per Pinstrup-Andersen